WARWICKSHIRE GRAZIER AND LONDON SKINNER 1532-1555

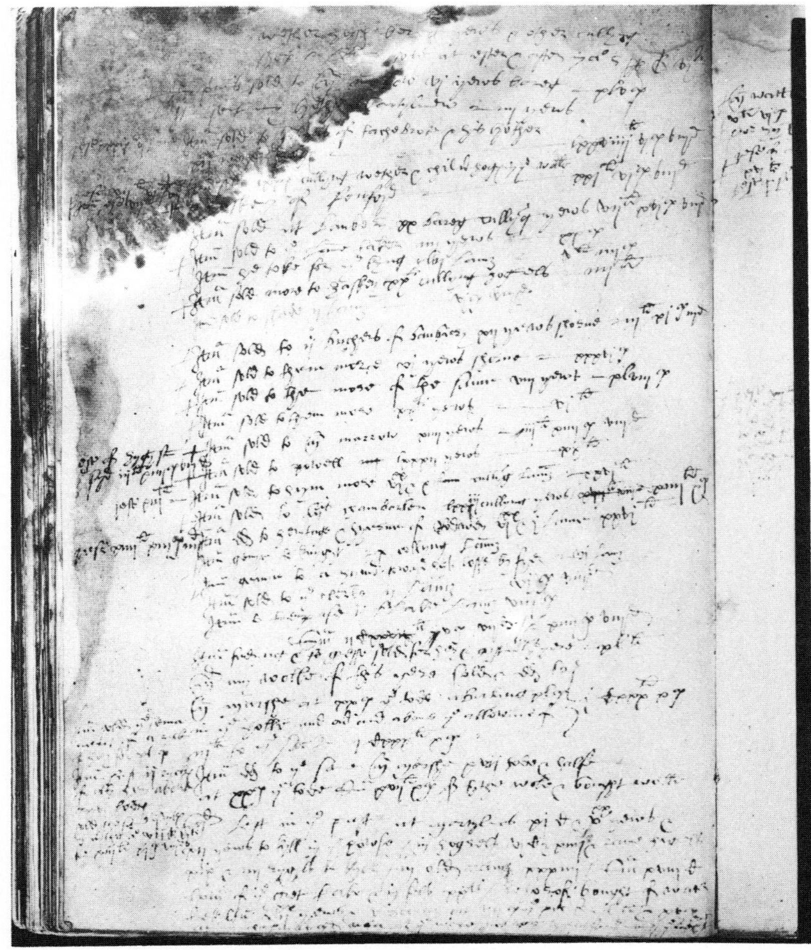

Peter Temple's account for sheep sales in 1551. The foot of the page carries the receipts for pasture letting and for sales of wool, followed by the flock count for the year. Huntington Library, Stowe MS. 36, f. 62 v (item 71).

[Photograph: Huntington Library]

RECORDS OF SOCIAL AND ECONOMIC HISTORY
NEW SERIES · IV

WARWICKSHIRE GRAZIER AND LONDON SKINNER 1532-1555

The account book of Peter Temple and Thomas Heritage

N.W. ALCOCK

LONDON · *Published for* THE BRITISH ACADEMY
by THE OXFORD UNIVERSITY PRESS

Oxford University Press, Walton Street, Oxford OX2 6DP
OXFORD LONDON GLASGOW
NEW YORK TORONTO MELBOURNE AUCKLAND
KUALA LUMPUR SINGAPORE HONG KONG TOKYO
DELHI BOMBAY CALCUTTA MADRAS KARACHI
NAIROBI DAR ES SALAAM CAPE TOWN

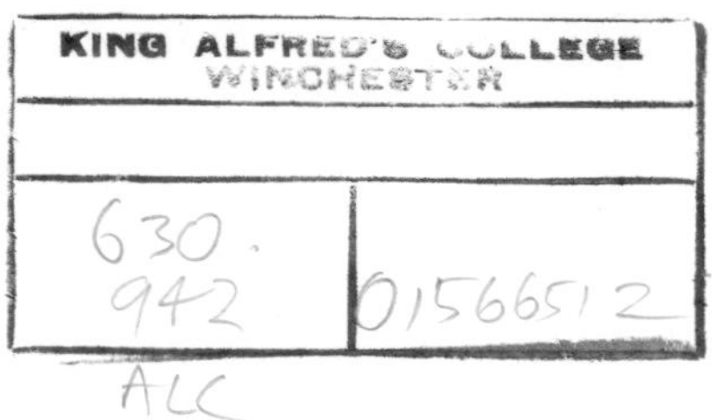

British Library Cataloguing in Publication Data

Temple, Peter
Warwickshire Grazier and London Skinner, 1532–1555
—(Records of social and economic history. New series; 4)
1. Temple, Peter—Archives
2. Heritage, Thomas—Archives
3. Agriculture—England—Burton Dassett—Accounting—Early works to 1800
4. Wool trade and industry—England—London—Accounting—Early works to 1800
I. Title II. Heritage, Thomas III. Alcock, N. W. IV. Series
332.024′636 S567

ISBN 0-19-726008-X

Printed by Whitstable Litho Ltd, Whitstable, Kent.

TO ELLEN

INTRODUCTORY NOTE TO THE NEW SERIES

DR. ALCOCK'S edition of the accounts kept by the sixteenth-century Warwickshire grazier, Peter Temple (founder of the well-known landed family, the Temples of Stowe) and by his cousin, Thomas Heritage, constitutes the fourth volume in the New Series of 'Records of Social and Economic History' published under the auspices of the British Academy. The original series, launched in 1914, lapsed in 1935 and most of its nine volumes were until recently out of print. Arrangements for their photographic reprinting have been made and all nine are now available from Kraus (for details, see p. 282). The New Series was inaugurated in 1972 with Greenway's *Charters of the Honour of Mowbray* and continued with Glasscock's *The Lay Subsidy of 1334* (1975) and MacFarlane's *Diary of Ralph Josselin* in 1976. The appearance of further volumes since then has been delayed till now by a combination of circumstances unhappily including the death of Professor Carus-Wilson, the former Chairman of the Committee, in February 1977. The present Committee has sought to recover and maintain the momentum of the New Series, which she did so much to stimulate, and currently has nine further volumes in course of preparation. Of these four are of medieval records and five, of which this work is one, are concerned with records of social and economic history in the sixteenth and seventeenth centuries. Two of the medieval volumes will, it is hoped, be ready for publication in the near future. They comprise an edition by Dr. Marjorie Chibnall of the Surveys of the English Estates of the Abbey of Holy Trinity, Caen, and Dr. Michael Gervers' edition of the Cartulary of the Knights of St. John of Jerusalem relating to the Order's holding in Essex. Amongst the sixteenth and seventeenth century volumes to follow later are editions of the Diary of Bulstrode Whitelocke and of the correspondence of Sir John Lowther of Whitehaven.

D. C. COLEMAN

Chairman
Records of Social and Economic History Committee

PREFACE

WHEN E. F. Gay wrote the first of his three studies of the Temple family, based on the Stowe archives at the Huntington Library, he picked out the rise of Peter Temple from obscurity to the possession of a considerable landed estate as a paradigm of Tudor success.[1] However, the evidence he could produce was largely indirect, showing the framework and results of success, but leaving the mechanism to be inferred. He commented regretfully that 'account books were kept by Peter Temple ... but they have disappeared'.[2] The Stowe MSS. contain an almost continuous series of estate account books from the time of Thomas Temple in the early seventeenth century onwards, which have been drawn on by historians.[3] However, the most remarkable of all went undiscovered by Gay and unnoticed by later students. Huntington manuscript ST 36 was kept by Peter Temple from 1541 to 1555,[4] and gives precisely the detailed evidence that Gay could not find. In it, Peter recorded every detail of his farming and personal income and expenditure during the very period that saw his metamorphosis from insignificance to wealth, and from it far more can be discovered about his life and activity than is possible for any other Tudor grazier. In addition, the book contains an interesting though select set of accounts recorded from 1532 to 1540 by his cousin, Thomas Heritage, a London skinner.

It is the remarkable character of this manuscript as historical evidence for the rise of a sixteenth-century gentry family, and for many individual facets of Tudor life, that has led to its unusual treatment in the present volume. This attempts firstly a historical commentary, framed around the biography of Peter Temple. Secondly, it provides a complete text of the manuscript, because its potential as a source for sixteenth-century studies does not begin to be exhausted by the main study. For example, there appear to be no other documents which give detailed year-by-year accounts

[1] Gay, 1938. The study of the family through the seventeenth century is continued in E. F. Gay, 'The Temples of Stowe and their Debts', *Huntington Library Quarterly*, 2 (1939), pp. 399–438, and 'Sir Richard Temple: The Debt Settlement and Estate Litigation: 1653–1675', ibid, 6 (1943), pp. 255–91.

[2] Gay, 1938, p. 369.

[3] *Ag. Hist.*, p. 640.

[4] The greatest detail covers the period 1544 to 1551.

of either cattle or sheep farming at this period (frontispiece), or any which summarize the running of a Tudor gentleman's household (Plate V).

The manuscript poses some particular problems which have controlled the detailed treatment. Physically it is in good condition, although two or three pages have been cut out. It has been heavily stained by water, but virtually every word can still be read. A few portions form coherent sections, such as ff.51 to 59, containing the bailiff's accounts for 1548 to 1551. However, most of it is extraordinarily disordered, with related material often separated by many pages, and with up to half a dozen separate topics on one page (Plate IV). A continuous text would have left this confusion for the reader to unravel. Therefore the entries are collected by subject, in chronological order.[5] One benefit of this has been that virtually every item can be dated, even though only about half directly incorporate dates.

Only one small group of accounts survives from after the main series of entries. These were written on loose sheets of paper, each devoted to a different subject, and this is probably the form that Peter Temple's later accounts took. This particular group exists because when Peter Temple was in prison in 1562–4, no doubt very short of paper, he used the backs for drafting his legal defence; they were then filed with the rest of the law papers. These accounts are included at appropriate places, together with one or two other strays.

The main part of the book is preceded by a review of the background to the compilation of the accounts. It concentrates particularly on the family background and early life of Peter Temple, and on the history and topography of Burton Dassett in Warwickshire, where he farmed. The concluding section brings together the more scattered information about his later life, and aims in particular to show how his grazing profits were put to use.

In seeking out material related to the accounts and the life of Peter Temple, one naturally turns to the Stowe archive at the Huntington Library. This collection has lost almost all its organic structure, and work on sorting and listing is still in progress. Thus, although all the likely, and some unlikely, boxes have been examined, there may still be a few relevant documents that have not come to light. The archive contains some 500,000 pieces, but even so it does not

[5] The Appendix provides a full collation between the items as printed and the original manuscript. Bold numbers give the cross references to individual items in the transcribed text.

exhaust the former muniments of Stowe House. Large groups are found in the Buckinghamshire, Greater London, Middlesex and Northamptonshire Record Offices, of which the last is of major importance to this study; there are strays at the Folger Shakespeare Library and in one or two other repositories. At least two groups are in private hands: a small collection including a mid-seventeenth century account book,[6] and a substantial series of genealogical papers, brought together in the early seventeenth century.[7] There are also, of course, records independent of the Stowe estate in both the Public Record Office and local repositories; in particular, the Warwick Record Office contains many documents relating to Burton Dassett.

In working with this material, I have received much kindness, assistance and advice from the staff of the various Record Offices and other organizations. They are too numerous to mention individually, but I would like to offer them my thanks in general. To Mary Robertson, however, as curator of manuscripts at the Huntington Library, with special responsibility for the English historical archives, I owe the greatest debt of all for having provided invaluable assistance to this study in very many ways. I would also like to thank the other staff of the Library who always succeed in making a research visit there a most pleasant experience. The library has kindly given its permission for reproduction of the text of MS. ST 36, of the other documents printed here, and of the photographs. Baroness Kinloss and Anthony Temple generously allowed me access to the documents in their possession. I am also grateful to Dr Joan Thirsk who read the entire text, and made many suggestions for its improvement.

[6] In the hands of Anthony Temple of Sandbach, Cheshire. The account book is commented on by E. C. Westmancott, 'Some Account of the Parish of Burton Dasset, Warwickshire, from November 1660 to January 1665', *Trans. Birmingham Archaeol. Soc.*, 60 (1936), pp. 96–111.

[7] In the hands of Baroness Kinloss of Sheriff Hutton, Yorkshire.

CONTENTS

ILLUSTRATIONS

PLATES

FIGURES

ABBREVIATED REFERENCES

Ag. Hist.	Joan Thirsk (ed.), *The Agrarian History of England and Wales, Vol. IV: 1500–1640.* Cambridge: Cambridge University Press, 1967.
Bowden, 1962	P. J. Bowden, *The Wool Trade in Tudor and Stuart England,* London: Macmillan, 1962.
Peerage	G.E.C. *Complete Peerage.*
Dugdale	W. Dugdale (revised W. Thomas), *The Antiquities of Warwickshire,* 1730.
E.D.D.	J. Wright, *English Dialect Dictionary.*
Finch, 1956	M. E. Finch, *Five Northamptonshire Families,* Northamptonshire Record Society, *19,* 1956.
Gay, 1938	E. F. Gay, 'The Rise of an English Country Family: Peter and John Temple to 1603', *Huntington Library Quarterly, 4* (1938), 367.
Kinloss	MSS. in the ownership of Baroness Kinloss, Sheriff Hutton, Yorkshire (numbered from a typescript list).
L. &P. Henry VIII	J. S. Brewer, J. Gairdner and R. H. Brodie (eds.), *Letters and Papers Foreign and Domestic of the Reign of Henry VIII,* London: H.M.S.O., 1862–1932.
N.R.O.	Northamptonshire Record Office, Northampton.
O.E.D.	Oxford English Dictionary.
P.R.O.	Public Record Office, London.
S.B.T.	Shakespeare Birthplace Trust Record Office, Stratford-upon-Avon.
ST	Stowe Mss. at Huntington Library, San Marino, California.
V.C.H.	*Victoria History of the Counties of England,* London: Oxford University Press. For Warwickshire, unless another county is specified.
Visitation	W. H. Rylands (ed.), *Visitation of the County of Buckingham,* Harleian Society, *58* (1909).
Winchester, 1955	B. Winchester, *Tudor Family Portrait,* London: Jonathan Cape, 1955.
Wood-Jones, 1963	R. B. Wood-Jones, *Traditional Domestic Architecture in the Banbury Region,* Manchester: Manchester University Press, 1963.
W.R.O.	Warwickshire Record Office, Warwick.

Plate I. John Temple (detail). The inscriptions read: [*left*] 1587/AE^{te} 46; [*right*] John Temple Esq. of Stowe/Father to Sir Thomas Temple.

[*Collection of Lord Saye and Sele. Photograph: N. W. Alcock*]

Plate II. Vertical air photograph centred on Burton Dassett church (north-west to top). Church Farm is west of the church, and The Grove to its north-west. The boundary of Heritage Field runs down the left-hand side, with ridge-and-furrow within it. Further ridge-and-furrow appears within the medieval enclosures to the east, and what may be the medieval village street appears below The Grove.

[A historic air-photograph from the Crawford Collection (National Monuments Record), taken in December 1929. *Crown Copyright reserved.*]

Plate III. Northend Manor, Burton Dassett, a typical Banbury Region house (Wood-Jones, 1963, pp. 207–9). Despite its name, it was a farmhouse within Burton manor, in the part assigned to Anthony Cooke in 1576, when it was probably the home of Giles Spencer. The central section is the late medieval or sixteenth-century hall. In 1664, the north (left-hand) wing was added by Sir Richard Temple, providing a parlour, kitchen and chambers (no doubt replacing part of the earlier building). The south wing is modern.

[*Photograph: N. W. Alcock*]

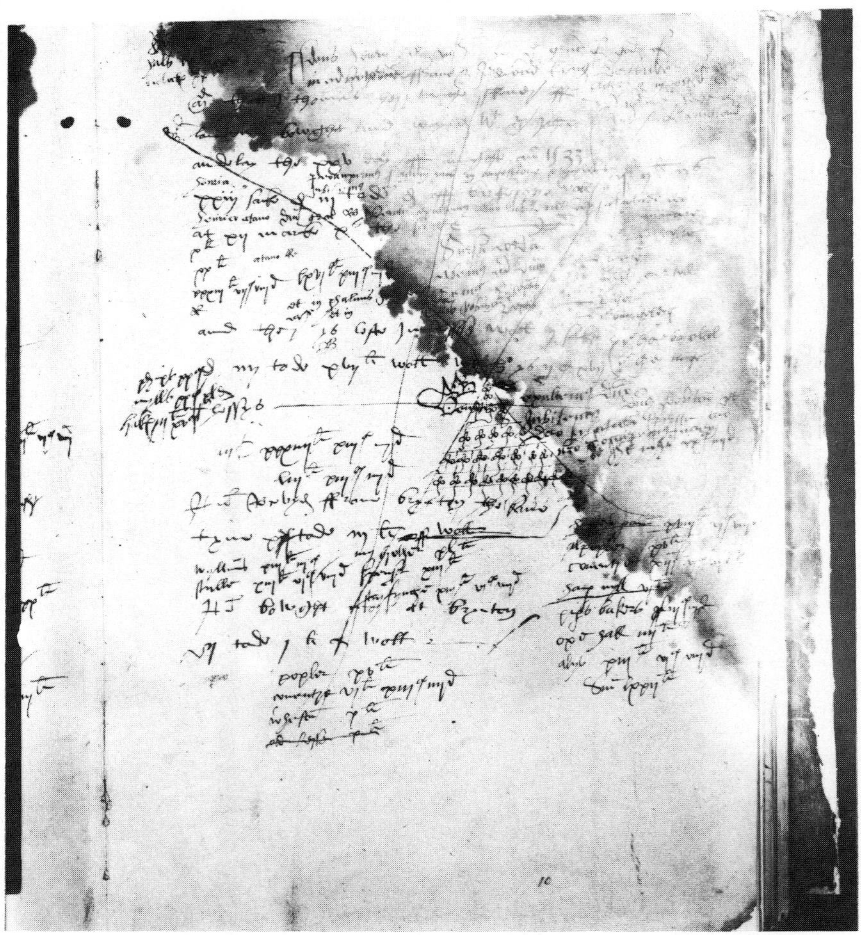

Plate IV. ST 36, f. 10, comprising Thomas Heritage's account for wool bought in 1533 (**99**), a draft financial summary by Peter Temple for 1543, in several sections (**209**), and jottings by Peter Temple (**244**). The diagonal markings here and on the other plates result from photographic reprocessing of the water-darkened corners of the pages.

[*Photograph: Huntingdon Library*]

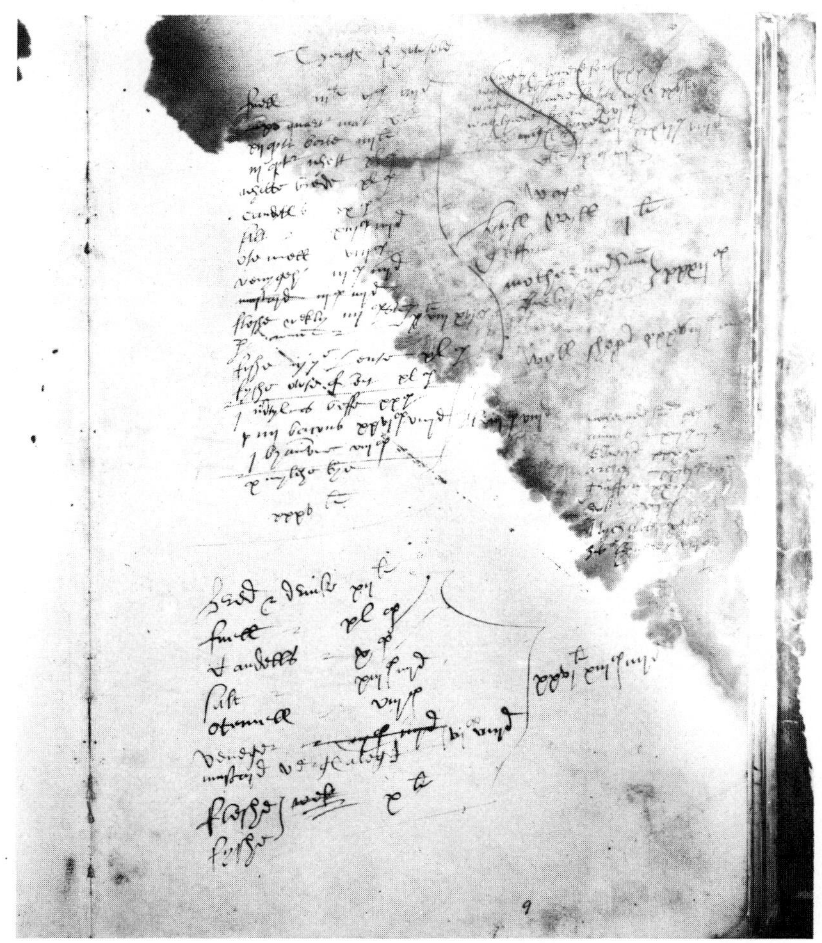

Plate V. Peter Temple's account for household expenses and servants' wages for three years, probably 1543–5. ST 36, f. 9 (182).

[Photograph: Huntington Library]

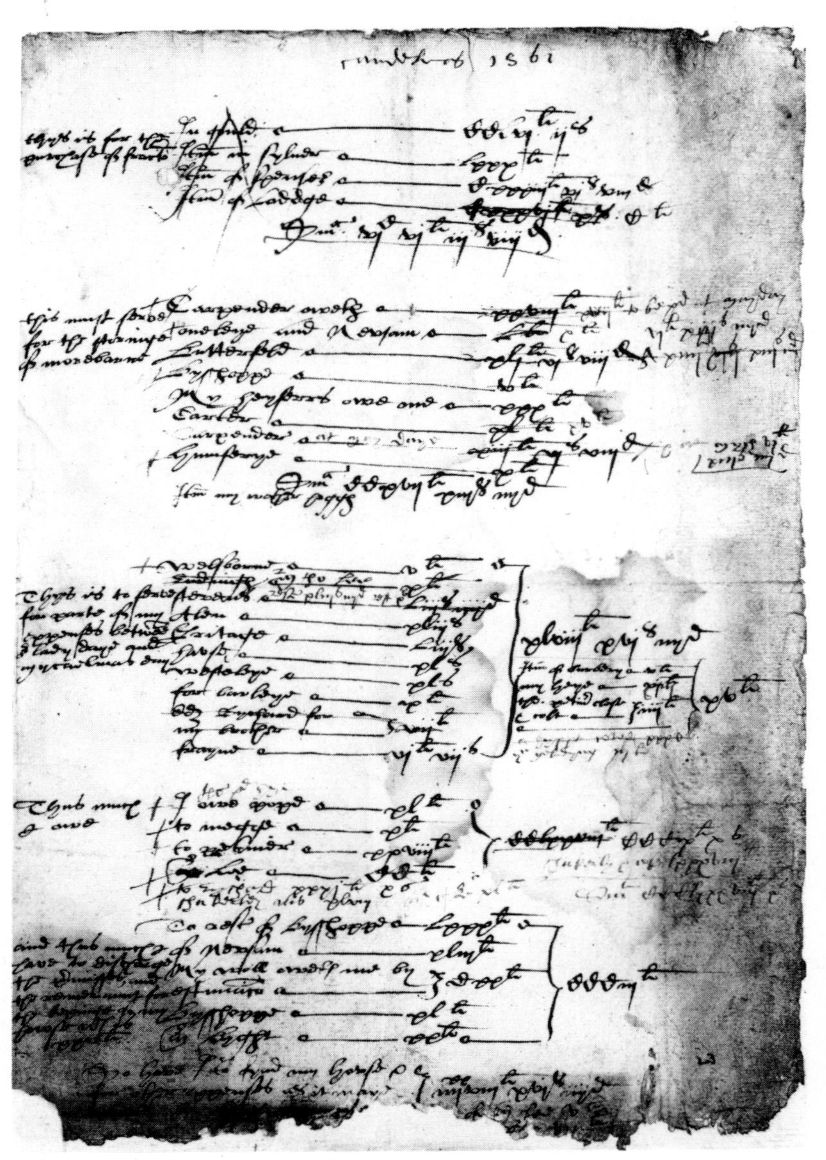

Plate VI. Peter Temple's financial summary for 1562, ST Temple Law case 211, f. 23 (236).

[*Photograph: Huntington Library*]

PETER TEMPLE AND THOMAS HERITAGE

In 1541, Peter Temple married Millicent, the widow of his cousin, Thomas Heritage, and received through her two endowments. The first was a lease of pasture land in the parish of Burton Dassett. This led to a redirection of his career, and to his becoming a successful grazier. The second was a modest account book, which Thomas had begun and which Peter continued. Over the next years, as his large-scale pasture farming developed, he recorded in it every aspect of his finances. The book covers cattle, sheep, wool, hay, wood, bailiff's accounts, building accounts, personal debts and credits, and more besides. He was an indefatigable note-taker and jotter, with a magpie-like habit of collecting snippets of information. The trait was common to his descendants,[1] and merits our gratitude for the opportunity it gives to reconstruct his life in detail.

Peter Temple's profits as a tenant sheep-farmer enabled him to buy the land he farmed at Burton Dassett in Warwickshire, and to invest in much other property. This success, followed by that of his son John, established one of the great families of English landed gentry, Temple of Stowe. Ultimately, the Stowe estate was broken up in the twentieth century, and its archives moved to the H. E. Huntington Library in California. Peter Temple's account book became MS. ST 36. Since then, it has been surprisingly overlooked.

The accounts cover in detail the critical period in Peter Temple's life. They start soon after he began farming at Burton Dassett, and record some seven years of his career as a large-scale grazier. Before we can understand the advantage which he took of his opportunity, we must look backwards. How much assistance did he have from his family? from his education? from his wife? These aspects of his background are intertwined through social and family links in a way that was typical of Tudor society, whether on a national scale among the nobility, on a county scale among the gentry, or a village scale among yeomen and peasants.[2] Peter Temple's own strand lay somewhere between the gentry and the yeomen at the beginning of his

[1] As well as his account books, Sir Thomas Temple has left several fascinating, though thoroughly confused, memoranda books in the Stowe muniments.

[2] Almost any study of the period, if it looks beyond the general to the personal, reveals these links. Among many examples can be cited the Northamptonshire gentry families studied by Finch (1956), the merchant family of the Johnson brothers (Winchester, 1955) and the unique view of interrelationships at lower levels of society, provided by Richard Gough in *The Antiquities and Memoryes of the Parish of Myddle* (Shrewsbury: Shropshire Records Committee, *c.* 1960, reprinting the 1875 edition).

career. His own family was undistinguished, even less notable in reality than the line of gentry provided by the Heralds College as ancestors. His father was an Oxfordshire merchant, certainly wealthy, but Peter was a younger son, orphaned when a boy, and can have received very little for his start in life. It was with his mother's family, the Heritages, that he was most closely connected. His uncle assisted in his education. His cousin was possibly his mentor and associate in business, and certainly by his death provided Peter with a wife, the lease at Burton Dassett and an account book. His wife, in her own right, or rather as a widow from a previous marriage, brought him useful income from property near London (Stepney) and in Coventry. Although this was only hers for life, a complex accommodation was reached with her daughters, the ultimate owners, leaving the Temple family in secure possession of part of the property.

All these influences were brought together when Peter Temple came to Burton Dassett. However, it was above all the place itself that provided the opportunity. The profits of grazing could only be taken where the medieval farming pattern of the open fields had been replaced, where the intensive arable husbandry of the strip fields had given way to extensive pasture land. Typically, though paradoxically, for the few people studied in detail, it was not the encloser himself who reaped the financial harvest of the pasture, but a successor, twenty, forty or fifty years later. So it was at Burton Dassett. By following the history of the farms back from the well-recorded situation at the beginning of the nineteenth century, we can see how this enclosure was carried out, and the nature of the pasture that Peter Temple farmed. Records of his actual leases survive, so that we can pick out his own fields on the map and on the ground.

In the accounts, the largest sections deal with his farming, and undoubtedly these are the most significant. He built up his stock of cattle and sheep in parallel, and it was perhaps not clear at first which was the most profitable. The accounts for cattle farming are the more unusual, and are also particularly detailed and clearly recorded. They show him buying lean Welsh stock, fattening them and selling them on for the London market. There is virtually no other detailed evidence for the cattle trade at this period,[3] and so these accounts illuminate one of its major branches for the first time.

[3] W. G. Hoskins, *The Age of Plunder* (London: Longmans, 1976), p. 81.

Tudor sheep farming is rather better documented, and after some initial variation, we find Peter Temple following a recognized pattern, with a breeding flock of ewes, whose offspring were sold at different ages, depending on their sex. Again, many of them seem to have been destined for the London table. The second side of sheep farming, the wool, was particularly profitable, with very low direct costs. For a couple of years, Peter Temple also traded in wool, buying up the clip from the local villages. His role here was that of the wool brogger, the notorious middlemen of the Tudor wool trade.[4] He can hardly have been a typical example, and was not very successful, but these accounts do give an idea of how their activities may have been carried out.

Smaller sections in the accounts round off the view of Peter Temple's farming. They deal with his occasional hay sales, when he had some to spare in the spring, and with the more regular letting of pasture. One account is even for arable farming though this refers to Hertfordshire, in the year before Peter moved to Burton Dassett. Surprisingly, he seems to have had no interest at all in either horse trading or horse breeding.

In 1548, Peter Temple became bailiff and receiver for the joint owners of Burton Dassett, and the account book contains a series of reckonings of his receipts and expenditure on their behalf. Their income was principally rents from Burton and a number of less important properties in Warwickshire. These accounts therefore show the landowner's receipts, in contrast to the direct farming profits of the tenants, such as Peter Temple himself. As bailiff, he also had to administer sales of wood, not from Burton Dassett itself but from another property ten miles to the north. These accounts are particularly interesting for the wide distribution of the people who bought the timber.

Much of Peter Temple's expenditure was directly connected with his farming, but his household also had to be supported. For two years the account book gives short but informative summaries of how much this would cost. We also have a couple of unusual trifles: shopping lists of special things to be bought, probably on visits to London. Servants' wages are recorded, and show his establishment growing during the 1540s. This must have been part of the reason for building a new house in 1548–9. The accounts for this are informative on the cost, but unfortunately less so on its character. Most

[4] P. J. Bowden, *The Wool Trade in Tudor and Stuart England* (London: Macmillan, 1962), p. 79.

personal of all are the jottings and scribblings with which he adorned many pages of the account book.

A series of entries relating directly to his finances include statements of his overall assets and lists of debts due to him. These are the least clearly recorded sections of the account book, and it is not easy to derive useful evidence from them. We can, however, get some information on his annual income and expenditure, and rather less on his general financial situation.

Peter Temple gradually gave up his account book during the early 1550s, even though it was by no means full. His rent receipts from Coventry were continued longest (until 1555), probably because he wanted a permanent record that could be agreed with his bailiff. He probably still kept accounts, but on sheets of paper, like the one or two that survive. However, the accounts that we do have are more than enough to show us the pattern of his success, and to explain the wealth he displayed in the 1550s. It was deployed on the purchase of land. For several years this took the form of speculation, principally in Crown lands. Then, from the later 1550s his investments were for permanent retention, building up a landed estate. His most important purchases were a third share in the manor of Burton Dassett, bought between 1557 and 1560, and two leases of land at Stowe, Buckinghamshire; their freehold was bought by his son John in 1590, and they became the main home of the Temple family.

Peter Temple added to his possessions year by year, but the 1560s brought an interruption. By his purchase at Burton Dassett, he incurred the bitter enmity of Sir Anthony Cooke, owner of another third of the manor. This opposition was that of the old established country gentleman for the *nouveau riche* upstart, and it was pursued vindictively through most of the courts of the land, and with the aid of the Privy Council, who imprisoned Peter Temple for two years. In the eventual outcome, Peter was confirmed in his position, and the last decade of his life was passed in quiet prosperity. At his death in 1578, he had laid the foundation of a great landed estate, and had achieved a corresponding social status.

The life of Peter Temple provides a classic example of that particularly Tudor phenomenon, the rise of the gentry. There were many routes to fortune, and their relative importance has been the subject of much controversy.[5] Individual cases cannot prove general theories,

[5] See G. E. Mingay, *The Gentry* (London: Longmans, 1976) for a concise summary of the discussion.

but the evidence is at least clear for Peter Temple. His circumstances provided the opportunity, but it was his farming, and particularly his sheep, that gave him the income of a member of the gentry, and enabled him over a space of twenty years to add the estates that converted the prospect into the reality.

Thomas Heritage, the skinner, must not be forgotten in introducing the account book, as its original owner. His accounts are a trifle compared to those of Peter Temple, but in their own right are of considerable interest. He called himself a skinner, and was indeed a member of the Skinners' Company as well as a citizen of London. However, his items in the account book from 1532 to 1540 show that his business had nothing to do with fur. Instead, his main concern was wool, and in a most satisfactory way his accounts dovetail with those of Peter Temple. He bought wool in bulk from producers or dealers in the South Midlands, and brought it to London for resale; in one transaction, he shipped it to Calais for a Scottish merchant. The second half of his trade was in the opposite direction, supplying specialist groceries, spices, dried fruit and wine to the people who sold him wool.

Some of the later entries show him branching out, as did many successful merchants. He obtained a lease of land in Hertfordshire, conveniently near to London, no doubt with a view to making it the centre of a landed estate. This intention, though, was terminated by his death.

Thomas Heritage's accounts are fragmentary, but they show us some of the activities of a Tudor merchant in a detail that is not seen in the few larger scale account books that survive.

PART I: THE BACKGROUND

1. *The Families*

FROM his own family, Peter Temple's start in life was by no means substantial; however, he received much more help from the relatives of his mother, Alice Heritage, with whom his life became very closely linked. They, in their turn, were connected to the Northamptonshire gentry family of Spencer (of Everton) who provided a wife for Peter's son, John. As well as the bare outlines of life and death, for a few members of these families we can construct brief biographies, to illuminate their connections with Peter Temple.

TEMPLE

For Peter Temple's parentage and ancestry, we have a detailed pedigree recorded in the Heralds' Visitations,[1] linking him to the well-known family of Temple of Temple Hall, Whalesborough (in West Leicestershire) by a cadet branch settled at Witney, Oxfordshire (Pedigree 1a). The main family had a well-documented pedigree back to the thirteenth century,[2] so this gave the Temples of Stowe a most respectable ancestry. In the seventeenth century, a truly splendid descent was provided for Henry de Temple, deriving him at three generations from Leofric, Earl of Mercia, with a sable eagle on gold for the arms of Mercia. This exercise of imagination was exploded in the nineteenth century, and now takes its right place as an example of the historical thought and social pretensions of its period.[3]

As far as the principal pedigree is concerned, the strange descent from Nicholas de Temple to Roger Temple is well documented and there is no doubt that the line from Henry de Temple to Nicholas is

[1] W. H. Rylands (ed.), *Visitation of the County of Buckingham* (Harleian Soc., 1909), 58, pp. 211-5. Two versions are given, of which that compiled by Le Neve (p. 213) provides a skeleton of dates and an indication of their sources.

[2] There are too few generations, even for a long-lived family, but the general correctness is not in doubt.

[3] E. A. Freeman, 'Pedigrees and Pedigree-Makers', *Contemporary Review*, 30 (1877), 11-41.

PEDIGREE 1. *The Temple Family*

1a. Outline Pedigree as published (with additional dates)

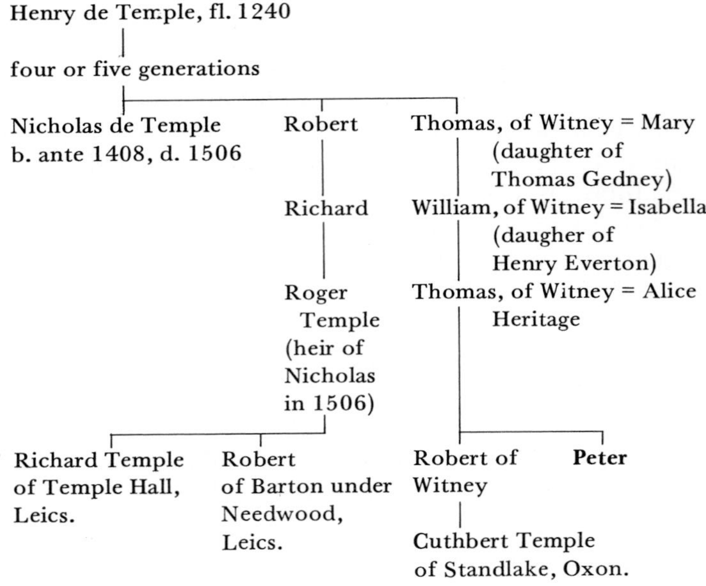

1b. The Temple family, according to present evidence

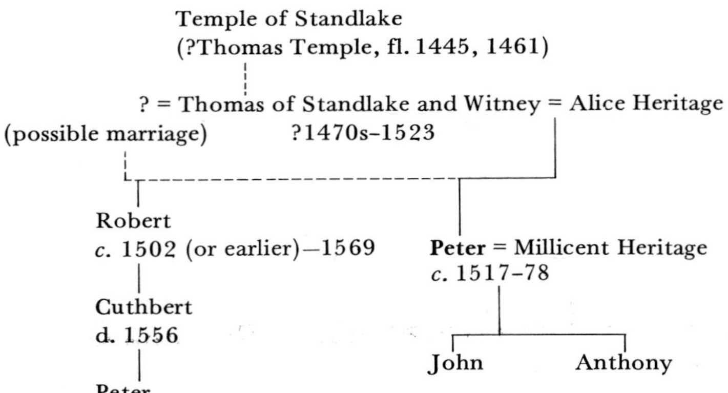

correct, even if the precise stages are unclear.[4] However, the Witney line is another matter. The published pedigrees give circumstantial detail, including the names of the wives in each generation, but not dates or supporting evidence. Further, in one draft pedigree compiled in the early seventeenth century, two alternatives for Peter Temple's father are shown by dotted lines, (a) Thomas Temple of Witney and (b) Robert, brother of Roger Temple of Temple Hall; thus there was no certain family tradition.[5] The remark of J. H. Round about another family seems relevant. 'Alleged descent from a cadet should be viewed with suspicion ... In the old days of pedigree-making, it was a favourite device ... but the expert knows the extreme difficulty of finding any proof. In this case, the alleged cadet is found in another county'.[6]

Robert Temple (c. *1502 or 1495–1569*)[7]

The elder brother of Peter Temple provides a sound start for a re-examination of the Temple family. For much of his life he lived at Witney, and we shall see him later, buying cattle with and wool from Peter Temple, and buying iron from Thomas Heritage (no doubt for re-sale), Witney, 12 miles west of Oxford, was at this time one of the centres of the Cotswold wool trade, and by the late fifteenth century was the home of several wealthy cloth merchants.[8] That Robert was one of these is shown by the subsidy return of 1523.[9] For Witney, sixty-seven men are listed, including Robert Temple

[4] *Inquisition Post Mortem* of Nicholas; the original no longer survives, though it was seen by Le Neve (op. cit. in note 1) and a copy was made by Sir Peter Temple (baronet) in 1635 (ST L9 D4, Temple Inquisitions Post Mortem). Nicholas' birth date is inferred here from his being of full age in a deed of 1428–9 (op. cit. in note 1, p. 214), though it is possible that this refers to another member of the family. However, he was clearly of great age in 1506.

[5] Kinloss 56, annotated by Sir Peter Temple (1592–1653). This Sir Peter Temple was very interested in the family history and collected pedigree information in the 1630–40s. (He is here titled *baronet* to distinguish him from contemporaries of the same name.) The original Visitation pedigrees pre-date this example, indicating that Sir Peter was not satisfied by their claims.

[6] J. H. Round, *Family Origins and other Studies* (London: Woburn Books, 1930), p. 15.

[7] His birth date is not recorded, but can be estimated. He was presumably of age when he inherited his father's holding in 1523–4 (see p. 12), and was recorded as a prominent Witney man in that year. An earlier limit is possibly set by the mention in 1501 of his presumed mother, Alice Heritage, under her maiden name (see p. 21). It is perhaps more reasonable that he was the son of an earlier marriage (though there is no independent evidence for this), and was born around 1495. This would be consistent with the age of his son Cuthbert, who was trading independently with Peter Temple as early as 1544. It would also explain why Peter alone benefited from Thomas Heritage's assistance.

[8] Patricia Hyde, 'The Winchester Manors at Witney and Adderbury, Oxfordshire, in the later Middle Ages'. Thesis, B. Litt. (Oxon.), 1954, p. 215 ff. (Copy at Bodleian Library.)

[9] P.R.O. E179/161/172.

who was assessed on £16 in goods; this was exceeded by only three others. He also held the chief post in the Borough, that of bailiff, in 1542-4.[10] In 1545 he was described as a clothier,[11] and in 1548 he was still in Witney.[12] However, a striking change is recorded ten years later when he was appointed by the Earl of Shrewsbury to be Constable of Goodrich Castle, Herefordshire, and Receiver for the Earl's estates in Herefordshire and Gloucestershire.[13] How he came to obtain this post is unclear,[14] but he held it until his death in 1569.[15] His will shows that he still held land in Witney, in Northmoor[16] and in Standlake, Oxfordshire. The last is described as 'one piece of land called Brighthampton, which came unto me from my ancestors, lying in Staynlake', a most significant clue to the authentic ancestry of the Temple family.

The Temple Ancestry

Following the Temples back in Witney is more difficult than might be expected, as the records of the town only belatedly reflect its rising prosperity.[17]

The parish of Witney belonged to the Bishopric of Winchester, and was divided administratively into two parts: the Borough itself, the close-packed area of houses held by burgage right, and the Bailiwick, the outlying hamlets and surrounding agricultural land, mostly in copyhold tenure. This area also included the 'assart' lands, cleared later than the original fields, which were usually held by borough tenants.[18] For either section, the vital records for identifying individuals would be a series of rentals, and unfortunately these

[10] Bodleian Library, MS. DD. Par. Witney, d.1, Witney Borough court books, vol. 1, ff. 11 v, 16 r, Bodleian Library. I thank Marjorie Maslen for this reference.

[11] In the will of William Ablye, Bodleian MS. Wills, Oxon., 179, f. 128 r.

[12] Op. cit. in note 10, f. 23 v; he entered a plea of debt against one Randall Margeis.

[13] N. R. O. Temple Stowe, Box 7/3A contains the grant of this office.

[14] A Robert Temple was servant to Thomas Hastings, brother of Francis, Earl of Huntingdon, in 1549 and apparently in 1558. (M. Bateman (ed.), *Records of the Borough of Leicester* (Cambridge, 1905), vol. III, pp. 59, 92). The Earl of Shrewsbury is mentioned very frequently in the Borough accounts, in close connection with the Earl of Huntingdon. However, this Robert Temple is more likely to be the son of Robert of Barton-under-Needwood than to be Robert of Witney.

[15] Will, P.R.O. PROB 11/51, f. 27 v (4 Sheffield), dated 2 September 1568, proved 8 February 1568/9; also in ST. L9 D3, Temple Family Wills, Box 1.

[16] His Northmoor land was lost in a law suit late in 1568 to St. John's College, Oxford (Muniments, Group XV). Their deeds name an otherwise unknown second wife of Robert Temple: Katherine, widow of Christopher Assheton.

[17] The parish registers only exist from 1578, and the large number of deeds for borough property that we might expect have not survived in any obvious collections.

[18] Hyde, op. cit. in note 8.

are entirely lacking for both the fifteenth and sixteenth centuries. The first surviving individual documents are for the manor courts, for the Bailiwick from 1505 (with gaps),[19] and for the Borough from 1535.[20] These give the names of people who happened to be involved with the court for some chance reason, and also, more systematically, they list entry fines, paid on taking up land or succeeding to holdings. There is one other series of records which covers the fifteenth and early sixteenth centuries in almost unbroken sequence. These are the annual pipe rolls, containing transcripts of the accounts for each of the bishop's manors. For the Borough, these accounts hardly vary from year to year, and apart from the names of the two bailiffs, they say nothing about individuals. The Bailiwick accounts are more helpful. The rents are in summary form apart from a few tenancies in the hamlets, but the rolls include full lists of the entry fines, for both copyhold and assart lands; thus they name a considerable number of Witney men, many living in the borough. Happily, they contain a conclusive identification of Thomas Temple as father of Robert (1523–4; references summarized in Table 1), and show him from 1506 to 1514 as one of the chief men of the Borough: bailiff four times within fifteen years, and also tenant of a quantity of land in the Bailiwick. Before this, a thorough check from 1480,[21] with sampling earlier in the century, showed no other Temple references. It is implausible that Thomas Temple, let alone his family before him, had been living for many years in the town. We can, instead, confidently include him with other wealthy newcomers to Witney, attracted like the Fermor and Wenman families[22] by the flourishing wool trade.

It was certainly from Standlake, 5 miles south of Witney, that he came. Apart from the evidence of Robert Temple's will, Temples are mentioned in the Standlake records[23] throughout the fifteenth and sixteenth centuries (Table 2), and indeed the family continued there into the seventeenth century. Curiously, in the mid-sixteenth century, Robert Temple and his family began to establish themselves as

[19] Hampshire Records Office, Eccles 1, Boxes 73 and 85.

[20] Bodleian Library, MS. DD. Par. Witney, d.1.

[21] There are, however, an unusual number of gaps between 1480 and 1506 (totalling thirteen years); no doubt one of the missing rolls contained the original admittance of Thomas Temple to a holding.

[22] Hyde, p. 215. Richard Wenman was the wealthiest man in the town in 1523 (see note 9).

[23] At Magdalen College, Oxford. Court rolls and books survive from 1445 (Oxon. Court Rolls, Bundle 1) but have many gaps until a more continuous series starts in 1548 (Court books, vol. 6). There are also a few rentals and deeds.

Table 1: *Thomas Temple in Witney*

Date		*Reference*[a]
20 October 1506	Thomas Temple for 3 acres assart land in Hailey.	85/1
20 September 1507	Thomas Temple for 1 acre assart land in Hailey, fine 2s.	73/2
Michaelmas a/c for 1507–8	Thomas Temple, bailiff of the Borough; for 3 acres assart land, fine 6s.; for 1 acre assart land, fine 2s.; for ½ acre assart land, fine 1s., all in Hailey. Pledge for Robert Godard, smith.	155855
Michaelmas a/c for 1508–9	Thomas Temple, bailiff of the Borough, for 1 acre assart land in Hailey, fine 2d.	155856
Michaelmas a/c for 1515–6	Thomas Temple, bailiff of the Borough.	155862
10 October 1517	Thomas Temple for 4 acres assart land, fine ?8s.	73/4
Michaelmas a/c for 1518–9	Thomas Temple, bailiff of the Borough.	155865
Michaelmas a/c for 1523–4	Robert Tempull, son and heir of Thomas Tempull, for 1 toft and 1 cotland in Hailey, in hand after the death of Thomas, the previous tenant, fine, 5s. 4d.; for 18 acres, 1 rod land in 3 closes in Hailey, fine 36s. 6d.	155869
6 October 1540	Robert Temple, customary tenant of one cotland in Hailey, cut down timber without license.	85/3

[a] Hampshire Record Office, Eccles.

landed proprietors in Standlake. Robert obtained a lease of Gaunt's house there, in which Cuthbert also lived.[24] In 1555, the latter bought a portion of the manor, but he soon sold it to Magdalen College.[25] Unfortunately the surviving documents are not complete enough to provide continuous links between all the members of the family until after 1500. However, there were in the mid-sixteenth century two Temples with freeholdings, John of Standlake and Robert of Goodrich. There were again two Temple freeholders in 1445 and 1461, and it is *prima facie* likely that it was from one of them that Robert Temple inherited his holding. We can therefore identify Peter Temple's true ancestors as minor freeholders in this

[24] Will of Robert Temple (see note 15).
[25] Magdalen College, deeds.

Table 2: *Temples in Standlake before 1500 (principal references)*

Date		*Reference*[a]
4 August 1385	List of tenants includes no Temples.	Oxon. Court Rolls, Bundle 1
c. 1430	John Temple born (see under 1494).	
22 January 1433	John Temple receives land in Standlake (either on his own behalf or as a trustee)	P.R.O. Ancient Deeds C.146/2680
27 June 1445	In a list of free tenants: John Temple of Brightyngton; Thomas Temple. Probable customary tenant: John Temple of Standlake who received a house, land and a quarter part of a water mill on lease for thirty years.	Oxon. Court Rolls Bundle 1
2 June 1461	Rental of free tenants: Thomas Temple, 2s. 6d. John Temple, 7d. Tenant at will: William Temple, for a mill (description as for John Temple in 1445).	Oxon. Court Rolls Bundle 1
2 March 1464	William Temple, tenant at will of 10 acres arable land.	Oxon. Court Rolls Bundle 1
1 May 1486	John Temple of Brighthampton named.	Oxon. Court Rolls Bundle 1
7 October 1486	John Temple. tenant; Thomas Temple fined 2d. for failing to attend manor court (and again on 31 March 1487).	P.R.O. SC2/209/57
12 April 1494	Evidence by tenants, including John Temple of Standlake, aged 64.	Standlake deed 14
8 March 1558	John Temple had died, possessed of a freeholding.	Court Books, vol. 6

[a] At Magdalen College, Oxford, apart from the two from P.R.O.

Oxfordshire village, perhaps a touch above their neighbours in status but no more.

What then of the Visitation pedigree? Could the Heralds have seen documents that no longer survive, substantiating their accounts?[26] On the contrary, it is most unlikely that documents ever existed recording such information as the wives of the fifteenth-century

[26] Even transcripts of documents would have to be considered critically as there are some pedigrees for which support was drawn from seventeenth-century forgeries; see J. H. Round, *Peerage and Family History* (London, 1901), Chapter V.

Standlake villagers, let alone the pedigree of one of them.[27] What is relevant, though, is that Temple is not a very uncommon name. Apart from the Leicestershire family, there was, for example, a Thomas Temple of Leamington Priors, Warwickshire, who died in 1457,[28] and a William Temple of Banbury in 1437.[29] Most prominent was Thomas Temple who was escheator for Bedfordshire and Buckinghamshire, and died in 1487, owning the manor of Aspley, Buckinghamshire and leaving as heir his son William, aged eight.[30] What the Heralds seem to have done is to stitch together the pedigree from recorded Temples, irrespective of any true relationship, or of their dates. The last mentioned Thomas and William may perhaps be recognized in the resulting pedigree, grafted on to Thomas Temple of Witney, and it may well be this Buckinghamshire Thomas whose wife was Mary Gedney. There was possibly a distant relationship between these people which is no longer to be established, because the Christian names Thomas and William are surprisingly frequent. A later William Temple was the King's fletcher (arrow-maker), and in his will in 1546 he left a ring to Peter Temple of Lincoln's Inn, the subject of our study.[31] Was this because of a blood relationship or merely the concurrence of names?

One shred of evidence which might suggest, despite all the above, that Peter Temple's family was connected with the Leicestershire Temples, is the presence in the Stowe archive of six original medieval deeds from Leicestershire, relating to this family.[32] On a closer look, though, they too seem suspicious. For two, Henry de Temple is mentioned only as a witness, while one is a lease of 1462 by Nicholas de Temple; this should not have passed to any cadet branch. These

[27] As there is for the Gedney family in British Library Add. MSS. 5524, a collection dating from about 1600.

[28] F. R. H. du Boulay (ed.). *Registrum Thome Bourgchier* [Archbishop of Canterbury], Canterbury and York Society, 54 (1957); P.R.O. Ancient Deeds, E210/995.

[29] Oxford Records Office, DIL VII/a/3, deed.

[30] *Cal. Fine Rolls, 1485–1509*, under 6 February 1486. *Cal. Inq. Post Mortem, Henry VII*, vol. 1, no. 306. Aspley (modern Apsley) is in Ellesborough parish, where several other Temples are recorded in the sixteenth century (e.g. P.R.O. Cl/1273/16–18). William and his son Francis appear in a deed of 1527 (Philadelphia Free Library, Carvalho Coll., 1575 folder).

[31] Will, P.R.O. PROB 11/31, f. 294 (37 Alen). He is also mentioned frequently in *L. &P. Henry VIII*. Another William Temple was yeoman of the King's Ordnance in 1474 (*Cal. Patent Rolls, 1467–77*, p. 473).

[32] ST Deeds List 1, Box 14 and Box 22 (Polesworth). The latter is particularly interesting in its own right, a gift (dated between 1237 and 1269) by Henry de Temple to Lady Margaret, Abbess of Polesworth, of his villein (nativus) John, son of John Toki (cf. S. Lysons, *Magna Britannia*; Buckinghamshire (1813), p. 640).

deeds, however, are very similar to a group in the Public Record Office which also include references to the Temple family; they are part of a large series from South Leicestershire.[33] What is most likely, therefore, is that the Stowe deeds strayed, because of their family interest, from the Public Record Office group (or another similar collection).

HERITAGE

In contrast to Temple, the name of Heritage was extremely uncommon, being virtually restricted to a small area of South Warwickshire, where the family still remains. A number of members of the family are mentioned in Peter Temple's account book, in particular two John Heritages, one of Kineton and one of Radway. How they were all related is not obvious, but the most important group is clear, stemming from Roger Heritage of Burton Dassett. Our information comes particularly from a sixteenth-century pedigree, most of which can be independently confirmed (Pedigree 2).[34]

At some date in the mid-fifteenth century, Roger Heritage bought a land-holding in Burton Dassett,[35] and prospered there, to become a wealthy yeoman, principally involved with sheep-farming (see p. 35). His status was sufficient for three of his daughters to marry members of the local landowning gentry, and the fourth a prosperous provincial merchant, while his second son, Thomas, could make a career in the church. The eldest son, John, left Burton and went to London (see p. 18), where we find his son, Thomas, by the 1520s. It was with the two Thomas Heritages, that Peter Temple was vitally involved.

[33] In the Ancient Deeds, C146 series.

[34] The original, probably of about 1585, is Kinloss 62; it is directed to Thomas Temple *at Mr. Thorneton's Chamber in Lincoln's Inn.* A copy made by Sir Peter Temple, Baronet, is Kinloss 45. Thomas Temple was admitted to Lincoln's Inn in 1584 (*Records of the Honourable Society of Lincoln's Inn, Admissions 1420–1799*, Vol. 1 (London: Lincoln's Inn, 1896)). In the account book, John Heritage is described as of *Kyngston* (e.g. p. 106), rather than *Kyngton* (apart from pp. 90, 218), implying Kingston in Chesterton parish and not Kineton. However, the survival of the earliest volumes of both parish registers disproves this. That for Chesterton (W.R.O. DR31/1) contains no Heritage entries from 1538 to 1600, while that for Kineton (W.R.O. DR212/1) contains no less than eight, despite a gap in the 1550s and 1560s. John himself is not mentioned, though baptisms, probably of his children, appear (1547–50); the parents' names are omitted.

[35] ST Temple Law, 83, is the answer by John Heritage to a case brought by Marion Ma ... n (*defective*) claiming wrongful occupation of his land at Burton Dassett, in which he gives the history of the family. The complaint is missing from this file, and it has not been possible to find the originals, nor identify in which court the case was prosecuted.

PEDIGREE 2: The Heritage Family

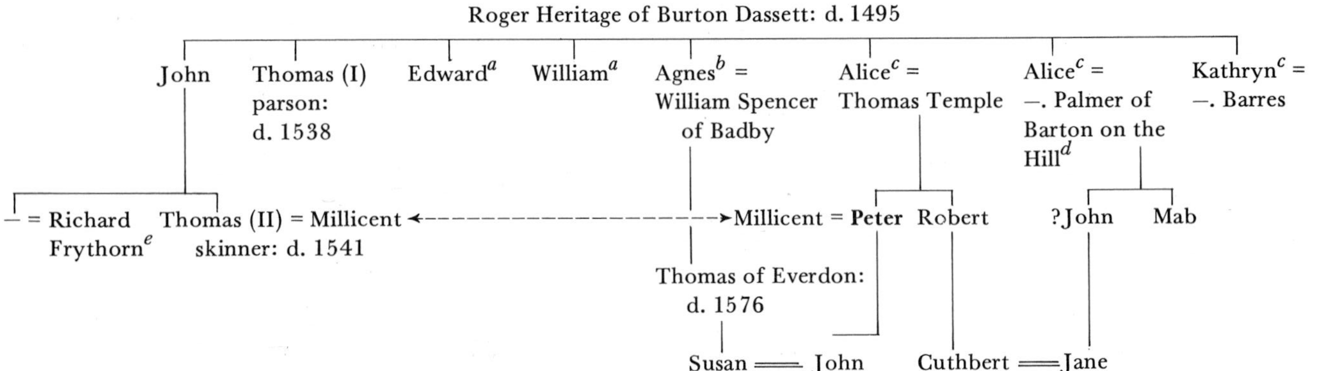

[a] Named only in Roger Heritage's will; P.R.O. PROB 11/10 f. 231 v.

[b] George Baker, *History and Antiquities of the County of Northampton* (London, 1822–1830), vol. 1, p. 364, gives her name.

[c] Roger's daughters are not named in the family pedigrees; Roger Heritage's will (an office copy) names his four daughters as Kathryn, Agnes, Alys and Alys (*sic*). Thomas (II) refers to his aunt Alice Palmer (**102** below) and cousin Mab Palmer (**100**). For Alice Temple, see p. 21. J. Fetherston (ed.), *The Visitation of Warwickshire*, Harleian Society, 1877, p. 150, gives Agnes, d. of John Heritage = Robert Palmer, with sons Robert and Richard. Other visitation pedigrees also give John Heritage as the father of Alice and Agnes, but the overall evidence makes it clear that this is wrong.

[d] In Bidford on Avon, Warwickshire (J. E. B. Gover, A. Mawer, F. M. Stenton, and F. T. S. Houghton, *The Place-Names of Warwickshire* (Cambridge: University Press, 1936)). The will of Agnes Palmer of Bidford was proved at Worcester in 1546 (Worcs. R.O. probate records vol. V, no. 431), but shows no recognizable Heritage links.

[e] Thomas (II) probably had a sister, as 'brother Richard Frythorn' is named in **109**.

Thomas Heritage, parson (c. *1480–1537*)[36]

The elder Thomas achieved an unusual but strikingly successful career[37] despite an apparent lack of family influence. He started at Oxford, presumably as an undergraduate, and then from 1500 to 1513 was a fellow of Oriel. In 1505 he took holy orders, and obtained his first living in 1513 at Great Brington, Northamptonshire. This was the result of a family connection; the presentation was in the hands of Sir John Spencer, his brother-in-law's cousin.[38] The Spencer family may also have sponsored his next move, into the royal service, through Thomas Spencer who was a member of Thomas Cromwell's entourage.[39] Heritage was appointed Chaplain to the King in 1530, and also Surveyor to the King's Works at the Palace of Whitehall. How he acquired the architectural expertise that he displayed in the latter post remains a mystery. He was consulted later by Oriel College for their new dining hall, and was also involved with a building at Lincoln's Inn (see p. 22). He is mentioned once in his nephew's accounts, in relation to a purchase of iron (p. 114). Clerical promotions came fast, with at least seven new livings and a deanery acquired before 1536, when he became Rector of Hackney. This was a most fashionable parish, rural, but conveniently near the capital, and was a favoured retreat for prominent families.[40]

Thomas Heritage died in 1537 and in his will appointed his two nephews, Thomas the younger and Peter Temple, as his executors, to pay his debts and distribute his goods charitably.[41] His probate inventory is preserved in the Stowe records, and shows that his rectory was of considerable luxury, with at least eighteen rooms, including a gatehouse and a chapel.[42]

[36] He was under 21 in 1495, but was the first-named and so presumably the eldest of the three younger sons in his father's will. His own will, dated 10 October 1537, was proved on 10 July 1538, and his inventory was taken on 27 December 1537 (see notes 41, 42).

[37] A. Emden, *Biographical Register of the University of Oxford to A.D. 1500* (Oxford: Clarendon Press, 1957), Vol. II, p. 917 gives a thorough outline. *L. &P. Henry VIII*, from 1531, provides many references; some of these and others from unpublished sources are collected in H. M. Colvin, D. R. Ransome and J. Summerson, *History of the King's Works* (London: H.M.S.O., 1975), Vol. III (i).

[38] J. Bridges, *History of Northamptonshire* (Northampton, 1791), Vol. I, p. 474.

[39] Suggested by Colvin *et al.*, op. cit., p. 15 n; *L. &P. Henry VIII*, 5, 1461, also shows Heritage in charge of the building of a house for Cromwell.

[40] cf. Leslie Hotson, *Mr. W. H.* (London: Hart-Davis, 1964), p. 289.

[41] P.R.O. PROB 11/27, f. 150 (19 Dyngeley). The payment of his debts was apparently not easy, as Peter Temple still owed £30 on behalf of his uncle to the executors of one Dawling, a bricklayer, when he made his own will in 1571.

[42] N.R.O. Temple Stowe, Box 40; this lacks the foot of the inventory, which is in ST L9 B4, Temple, unsorted a/c's, Box 56; there may still be a membrane missing, as the totals do not tally.

Thomas Heritage, skinner (c. 1500–41)

As the originator of the account book that Peter Temple used, the younger Thomas Heritage has a particularly important place in this study. Unfortunately, apart from his accounts, our knowledge of him is limited. His birth date can be estimated from the date of his apprenticeship, and from a guess of 1470–5 for his father's birth (probably over 21 in 1495, but not by much). By 1500 his father was probably established in London as he had left Burton Dassett by 1497 (see p. 33); later he was living outside Cripplegate, probably in the parish of St. Giles.

Thomas was apprenticed as a skinner just after 1516, probably for seven years, and in 1525–6 paid his four shillings entry money as a freeman of the Skinners' Company.[43] By 1534–5, he was sufficiently well established to pay a further twenty-two shillings to have his name inscribed in the magnificent illuminated volume of the Brethren of Corpus Christi, an association emphasizing the social rather than trade aspects of the Company. For his business activities as a skinner, we can only turn to his accounts, which are very selective (see pp. 112–4). They reveal that though he did many things, these did not include the expected dealing in skins and furs. In the 1530s he was also farming, both in Burton Dassett and in Hertfordshire (pp. 124–33).

Between 1532 and about 1536, Thomas Heritage married Millicent Jekyll, then the widow of Hugh Radcliff (see p. 24) and they had two children, Margaret and Millicent. Thomas died early in 1541.[44] His inventory survives and, like his uncle's, shows that he was living comfortably, in a house of seven rooms, with a total wealth of £131.[45]

[43] The records of the Skinners' Company are at Skinners' Hall, and I thank Mr. J. W. Cross for permission to study them. Their first Register of Apprentices and Freemen runs from 1496 to 1602, but has a series of blank pages from 1517 to 1546. However, the Company's Account Book, Vol. II, 1510–35, includes the payment in 1525–6 of entry money for Thomas Eritage. As the minimum apprenticeship period was seven years, he must have been apprenticed between 1517 and 1519. The gap in the apprentice register is unfortunate, as it deprives us of information on his master, parentage and home. 'The Book of the Fraternity of Corpus Christi' gives the names of brethren from 1485 onwards.

[44] Probate Inventory taken 16 February 1540–1 (N.R.O. Temple Stowe, Box 40). The endorsed grant of probate on 28 May 1541, to Millicent Heritage, shows that he died intestate. The Court is not stated, but the grant is recorded in the Prerogative Court in P.R.O. PROB 29/12, f. 118.

[45] He also left debts, which remained unpaid until Peter Temple made bequests to the creditors (cf. note 41).

SPENCER

Next to the two Thomas Heritages, members of the Spencer family were most closely involved with Peter Temple. Happily, this family was of considerable wealth and status, and has been the subject of more than one study.[46] Pedigree 3 shows the two major branches.

The senior line was settled in Badby, Northants, and its members were of gentry status; Thomas (II), for example, was high sheriff of Northamptonshire in 1562. The first link to the Heritage and Temple families came with William's marriage to Agnes Heritage. She ('Aunt Spencer') and their son, 'Cousin Thomas' Spencer (II), are mentioned frequently in Thomas Heritage's and Peter Temple's accounts, mainly owing small sums of money. The family connection became much closer in 1561, when Peter Temple's son, John, married Susan Spencer, and they were linked again by the marriage of her sister Dorothy to Gabriel Pultney, related to the husband of John's half-sister Millicent Heritage.[47]

The Spencers owned land in Burton Dassett parish which eventually came to the Temple family.[48] This passed in the first place to Thomas Spencer (III) who left it to his relative Thomas (II).[49] The main block was in Northend, a hamlet of Burton Dassett. Thomas (II) transferred this to his brother Giles in 1559,[50] and Giles lived there until his death in 1609.[51] Giles also leased a large block of the Burton pastures (see p. 166). His holding was sold to Thomas Temple by Giles' grandson, Spencer Horley in 1613.[52] Thomas Spencer (II) also owned land in Burton Dassett itself. This he gave to John Temple in 1567, certainly as a marriage portion for his daughter, Susan. It is not then described, but it consisted of 6 acres of meadow, 30 acres of pasture and 20*s*. of rent in 1594.[53]

[46] See particularly Finch, 1956.

[47] The Temple-Spencer marriage is recorded in the parish register of Little Everdon, cited by Baker, op. cit. in Pedigree 3. There is some uncertainty about the connection between Gabriel Pultney of Misterton, Leicestershire, and Millicent's husband John and son Gabriel Pultney of Exhall, Warwickshire.

[48] Inquisition Post Mortem of John Spencer of Hodnell, d. 4 January 1496–7, *Cal. Inq. Post Mortem Henry VII*, vol. II, 245.

[49] His widow Margaret was disputing their ownership in 1532–3; P.R.O. Cl/709/4.

[50] ST Deeds List 1, Box 22.

[51] ST L9 D5, Temple Inventories, 1609, Giles Spencer of Northend.

[52] N.R.O. Temple Stowe, Box 5/4.

[53] No marriage settlement survives; ST Deeds List 1, Box 36 is the enfeoffment of 1594. Thomas Spencer's land in Burton was the virgate owned by John Spencer of Hodnell in 1497 (op. cit. in n. 48). By 1580, this land had been absorbed into the demesnes of the manor (and was probably included silently when the manor was partitioned in 1576; see p. 29). John Temple then received 20s. rent for it, in his wife's right; Estate Account of Sir Thomas Wotton, Bodleian Library, Broxbourne 84.15/R267. I am most grateful to Paul Morgan for drawing my attention to this important document, the only item of estate administration to survive for the Wotton family.

PEDIGREE 3: The Spencer family (outline pedigree)[a]

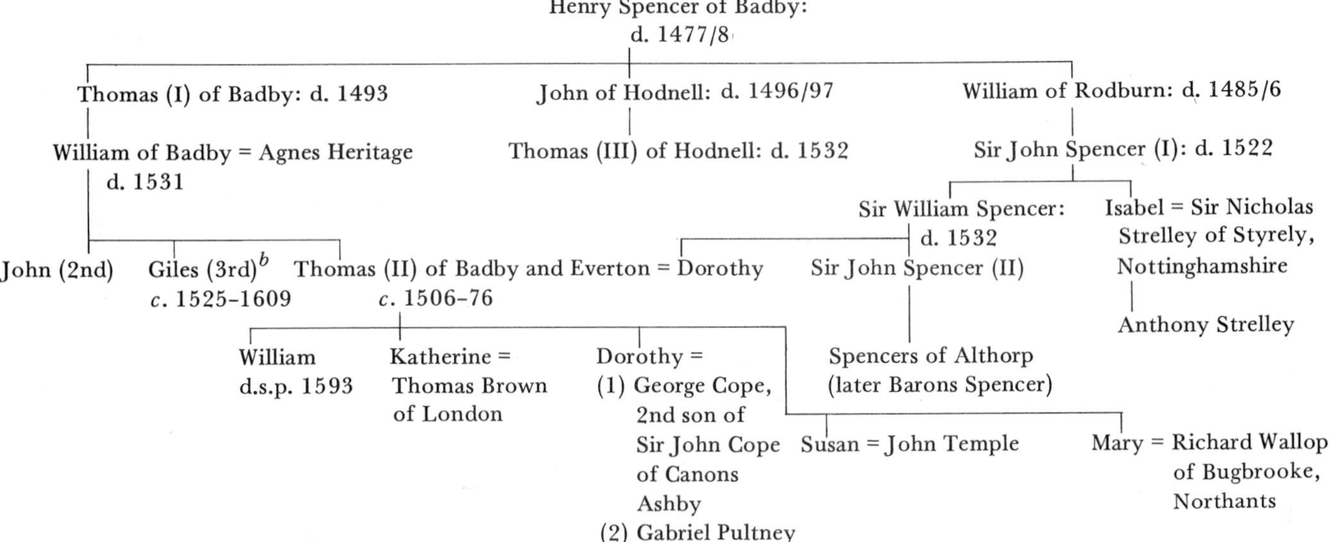

[a] From Finch, 1956, and George Baker, *History and Antiquities of Northamptonshire* (London, 1822–30), vol. 1, pp. 109–364. The date of death for William Spencer of Badby has not hitherto been recorded, but can be added from a recently discovered inquisition post mortem, P.R.O. E150/696/1; that for Thomas (III) has been corrected from his inquisition, E150/1136/12.

[b] Giles was over 80 in 1606—N.R.O. Temple Stowe Box 4/17.

The junior branch of the Spencer family took a very different path from the even course of the senior members. The career of Sir John Spencer (I) in particular parallels quite closely that of Peter Temple some fifty years later.[54] He began as a tenant of land in Snitterfield, Warwickshire, in the late fifteenth century; from the profits of sheep farming and cattle breeding he extended his leaseholds, and then from 1506 was able to start buying the land he farmed.[55] There is also an indication that John Spencer acted as receiver of rents for a local family, as did Peter Temple.[56] During the century, the family prospered yet further, until by 1600 Sir Robert Spencer (created Baron Spencer) was reputed to be the most wealthy man in the kingdom. He made his home at Wormleighton (three miles east of Burton Dassett), though later the Northamptonshire manor of Althorp was preferred.

The link between Peter Temple and this branch of the Spencer family was not direct, but through their close connection to the senior Spencer line (evident in the marriage of Thomas Spencer (II) to Dorothy, grand-daughter of Sir John Spencer (I)). A business relationship with Peter Temple also appears, seen in sheep purchases by Sir John Spencer (II) (51) and dealings with Lady Spencer (widow of Sir William) on behalf of Cuthbert Temple (221, 232).

2. *Young Peter Temple* (born *c.* 1517; died 1578)

By family tradition, Peter Temple was born on 4 or 28 November 1509 or 1510.[57] However, his career suggests that this is five or ten years too early. As we have seen, he was the second son of a prominent Witney merchant, Thomas Temple, while his mother was the daughter of a Warwickshire yeoman. By a surprising chance, we can identify her as well as his father in Witney, for she is mentioned in 1501 in the will of Dame Emote Wenman, widow of the wealthiest man of the town[58]—'to my servant Alice Heritage, twenty shillings,

[54] Finch, 1956; H. Thorpe, 'The Lord and the Landscape', *Trans Birmingham Archaeol. Soc.*, 80 (1965), pp. 38–77.

[55] Finch, 1956, p. 38.

[56] Spencer MSS. 1858 (list at N.R.O.) is a rental of 1519 of the lands of Walter Smith (in Burton Dassett and elsewhere in Warwickshire), delivered by Master John Spencer.

[57] Kinloss 2 gives 25 November, 1 Henry VIII (1509); Kinloss 50 gives 4 November, 2 Henry VIII (1510). Both are in the hand of Sir Peter Temple (baronet).

[58] P.R.O. PROB 11, 22 Moone, abstracted in J. R. H. Weaver, *Some Oxfordshire Wills, 1393–1510*, Oxford Record Society, 39 (1958).

a brass pot and a tod of myddullwolle'. She may also be the Goodwife Temple in the will of Dame Emote's daughter-in-law, Anne Wenman (1536).[59] Her place in 1501 can easily be understood as the consequence of a business relationship between her father, the Warwickshire sheep farmer, and Wenman, the Witney wool merchant, leading to a more personal connection, and through this to the marriage of Thomas and Alice.

In the earliest direct evidence of Peter Temple's upbringing, we see him as the protégé of his influential uncle, Thomas Heritage. On 8 December 1533, the Provost of Oriel agreed that 'a certain person called Temple, kinsman of Master Erytage', should have the vacant place of the Exhibition of Doctor Dudley, if he had sufficient grammar, and could play the organ a little (*aliquantulum pulsare organa*). This must refer to Peter Temple, as Robert had already been established in Witney for ten years. Heritage was no longer a fellow of Oriel, but a month later was consulted by the Provost about building a new hall.[60]

Next summer, on 26 August 1534, Peter Temple was admitted to Lincoln's Inn.[61] This is consistent with his going to Oriel, as it was not uncommon for young lawyers to be admitted and gain a few years seniority while at University.[62] However, he cannot have held the Dudley exhibition long, because by October 1534, there was a full quota of six exhibitioners, not including him.[63] We can, in any event, infer that he had already had a good education in grammar (and perhaps music), and that he was almost certainly between fifteen and twenty years old (thus born between 1514 and 1519).[64]

Peter Temple may have taken up residence at Lincoln's Inn in 1536, for in November 1535, Thomas Heritage and the Benchers of the Inn agreed that in consideration of Heritage finishing one of the

[59] P.R.O. PROB 11/27, f. 116 (15 Dyngeley).

[60] G. E. Richards and H. E. Salter (eds.), *Dean's Register of Oriel, 1446–1661*, Oxford Hist. Soc., 84 (1926), pp. 96, 99. No other Oriel or Oxford records exist that might mention him.

[61] Joseph Forster (ed.), *Records of the Honourable Society of Lincoln's Inn, Admissions, 1420–1799*, Vol. 1 (London: Lincoln's Inn, 1896).

[62] W. R. Prest, *The Inns of Court under Elizabeth I and the Early Stuarts; 1590–1640* (London: Longman, 1972). p. 9.

[63] The exhibitioners can be identified in the Dean's Register (op. cit. in note 60); Lewys and Thompson were elected before Temple, Ward, Ferwood, Taylor and Webster between April and October 1534.

[64] H. Rashdall (ed. F. M. Powike and A. B. Emden), *The Universities of Europe in the Middle Ages* (Oxford: Oxford University Press, 1936), Vol. III, p. 352f. The normal age for entry to University was 13 to 16 and was 16 to 20 to the Inns of Court (Prest, op. cit., p. 9). Peter Temple can hardly have been more than twenty years old in 1534.

chambers in the new building and paying £10, two of his kin, 'and especially Peter Temple' could occupy the said chamber for their lives.[65] This was not an unusual arrangement,[66] though of course it suited Heritage's special skill. He was also involved in supplying building materials for the new building.[67]

This substantial investment in Peter Temple's education may also have extended to paying his expenses at Lincoln's Inn.[68] Heritage certainly made what could have been a profitable bargain for him in 1536, when he agreed with Sir Nicholas Strelley (or Styrley), of Styrely, Nottinghamshire, to have the wardship of his son, Anthony. Anthony's mother was Isabel Spencer (see Pedigree 3), daughter of Sir John Spencer (I), and so related by marriage, though distantly, to the Heritage family. On 12 November 1537, Thomas Heritage granted the right to this wardship to Peter Temple (of Lincoln's Inn) and John Palmer of London, whose money had been used to buy the wardship;[69] John Palmer may have been another nephew of Thomas Heritage (see Pedigree 2). Unfortunately, this bargain came to nothing as Sir Nicholas Strelley did not die until 1561, when Anthony was 32 years old and his wardship valueless.[70]

In November 1538, Peter Temple was named as steward,[71] a post of responsibility among the juniors at Lincoln's Inn. He seemed set for a legal career, and one which with his uncle's influence could have been very successful, but it was broken off short. The obvious cause is his uncle's death (1537–8), removing both present financial support and future hopes of advancement. In any event, he and his cousin, Thomas Heritage the skinner, were executors to his uncle,[72] and it was this new association which was to set the future pattern.

He did not sever his relationship with Lincoln's Inn, however, and was named as 'of Lincoln's Inn' in 1546 and 1552.[73] In 1568 he paid £8 to become an Associate of the Inn, a post of considerable seniority, ranked only below the benchers.[74] The family connection

[65] W. P. Baddon (ed.), *Records of the Honourable Society of Lincoln's Inn. The Black Books* (London: Lincoln's Inn, 1897), p. 244. The original agreement (incomplete) is in ST L9 F3, Stowe Accounts.

[66] Prest, op. cit., p. 18.

[67] *Black Book*, p. 259.

[68] Cf. Prest, op. cit., p. 27.

[69] ST L9 T1, Temple Business and Legal, Box 1, 1537–1626.

[70] Inquisition Post Mortem, P.R.O. C142/133/82.

[71] *Black Book*, p. 253.

[72] P.R.O. PROB 4/27, f. 150; 19 Dyngeley.

[73] Will of William Temple, P.R.O. PROB 11/31, f. 294; (37 Alen); purchase of the manor of Popham, Hampshire; P.R.O. C54/482, m. 6. When this was resold in the next year, he was 'of Burton Dassett'; P.R.O. C54/488, m. 39.

[74] *Black Book*, p. 360.

continued, when his son John Temple was admitted on 14 February 1559–60 and his grandson, Thomas, on 13 October 1584; both occupied Peter's own corner chamber.[75]

We have no records of Peter Temple's association with Thomas Heritage the skinner, but it may well have involved more than the administration of their uncle's estate. It was perhaps from him that Peter obtained his facility with accounts.

Three years later, Thomas died. Peter married his widow and the pattern of his life changed again, as he began to farm the land she had inherited.

Wife and Family[76]

When Millicent Heritage married Peter Temple, she brought with her not only the leases that Thomas Heritage held, but also property in Coventry and Stepney which had belonged to her first husband, as well as two daughters by each husband. Her daughters also made a habit of remarrying, and the pedigree (4) for only three generations is remarkably complicated. The various relatives also make occasional appearances in Peter Temple's account books and the family papers.

Millicent was probably born some years before 1510, the daughter of William and Margaret Jekyll. They were members of a prosperous family living in Stoke Newington, a village 4 miles east of London.[77] Her first husband was Hugh Radcliff of the Middle Temple of whom nothing is known directly, apart from his will. He owned property in Stepney and in Coventry (see pp. 138–41) and in 1531 left this to 'Mylisen my wife . . . for life and after to her children of my body'.

These unnamed children were his daughters, Alice and Margaret, and their descendants did eventually obtain part of Hugh's property, but not for more than fifty years. Millicent's next husband was Thomas Heritage, the skinner, and she bore him two further daughters, Millicent and another Margaret. When he died intestate, they would automatically have been his heirs, subject to their mother's rights and her control until their marriage. His possessions, apart from some cash, household goods and farm stock (p. 125) consisted of valuable leases of land in Hertfordshire and at Burton Dassett, Warwickshire. These had all expired, or been surrendered by the mid-1540s, and Millicent Heritage had only a modest dower of

[75] Op. cit. in note 61. *Black Book*, p. 409.

[76] For detailed references, see the notes to Pedigree 4.

[77] The prosperity is demonstrated by their Prerogative Court wills, and by Margaret's will, which mentions a wealth of silver.

PEDIGREE 4: Millicent Jekyll and her family[a]

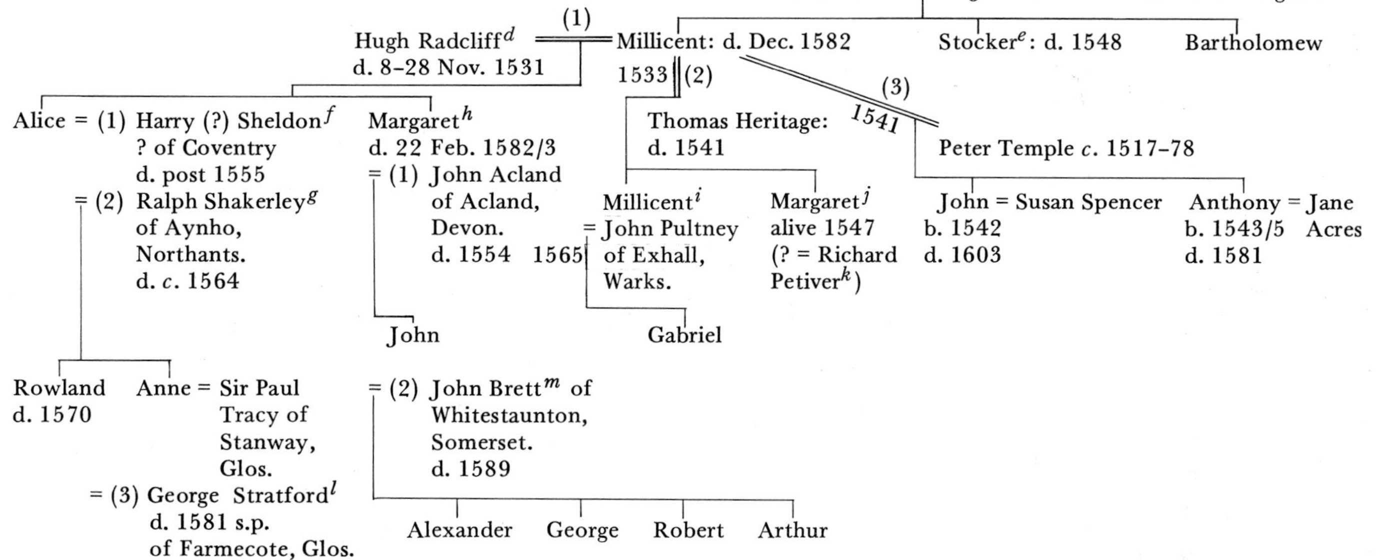

[a] Mainly based on a pedigree in ST L9 D8, Temple Land O/S, confirmed and supplemented by original sources.
[b] Will, P.R.O. PROB 11/27, f. 265; 33 Dyngeley.
[c] Will, P.R.O. PROB 11/32, f. 196; 26 Populwell: dated 20 December 1545; proved 23 February 1548.
[d] Will, P.R.O. PROB 11/24, f. 81 v; 11 Thower.
[e] Will, P.R.O. PROB 11/32, f. 195 v; 26 Populwell.
[f] Possibly the Harry Sheldon, died 1558 (and then of Stoulton, Worcs.), with a wife, Alice; Worcs. R.O. probate records.
[g] See A. P. Green, *Shakerley Marmion, Caroline Dramatist and Poet*, Ph.D. thesis, Rutgers University, 1974.
[h] Information from Archivist, Somerset Record Office.
[i] Mentioned in her mother's will, P.R.O. PROB 11/65, f. 41; 5 Rowe. Marriage settlement, 18 December 1565, Lincs. R.O. Jarvis 1/C/6.
[j] Mentioned in will of Margaret Jekyll, 20 December 1545, and in P.R.O. E326/12003, 14 March 1547, surrender by Peter Temple.
[k] Millicent Temple's will (as note i) mentions her son-in-law Richard Petiver. He is unidentified, but could be the husband of Margaret Heritage.
[l] Will, P.R.O. PROB 11/63, f. 321 v; 40 Darcy.
[m] Will, P.R.O. PROB 11/73, f. 310; 41 Leicester.

£70 when she married John Pultney, member of a respectable Midlands gentry family.[78] Of Margaret we hear nothing after 1547, and she may have died young.[79]

Millicent Jekyll's third marriage probably took place in the summer of 1541, when Peter Temple had perhaps been involved with her in the administration of his cousin's estate.[80] Their first son, John, was probably born early in 1542, and their second child, Anthony, before 1546.[81]

John's upbringing seems to have been fairly similar to that of his father. He went to Lincoln's Inn in 1560, occupying Peter's chambers. Before this, he had a grounding in business, for in 1556 he was apprenticed to a wool merchant, Christopher Lyght of Horley, Oxfordshire, a member of the Calais Staple.[82] Considerably earlier, he seems to have been brought up for a time in the home of a local yeoman, James Clarke, who received money for his board (see p. 216). He was married in 1561[83] to his second cousin, Susan Spencer, and they seem to have set up house in due course at Stowe, Buckinghamshire; after Peter's death, this became and remained the main home of the Temple family.

It is through John that we come closest to seeing Peter in the flesh. A portrait named as Peter Temple and dated 1560 hung at Stowe in the eighteenth century, but disappeared after 1832.[84] However, John had his portrait painted in 1587 at the high point of his career, when he was High Sheriff for Buckinghamshire, and this picture now hangs in the Long Gallery at Broughton Castle (Plate I).

Perhaps we can guess a little more about Peter's personality from the knowledge that Millicent, a widow with considerable property, chose to marry him when he was a young man whose only assets

[78] The family died out or sold up in the seventeenth century, and only one relevant document has been located (Pedigree 4, note i).

[79] See Pedigree 4, note j.

[80] She was still Millicent Heritage on 28 May 1541, when she was granted the administration of Thomas' estate.

[81] John was aged 46 in 1587 according to his portrait (plate I), and was 'of 61 years' at his death on 9 May 1603 (on his memorial in Burton Dassett church). For Anthony, see pp. 238–9.

[82] Two copies of this indenture are in ST L9 D1, Temple Business and Legal, Box 1.

[83] See note 47 on p. 19.

[84] Exhaustive searching has yielded no trace of this picture. A portrait of 'Peter Temple' was sold in 1922 (Sothebys, sale catalogue, no. 1681), but this was attributed either to Verelst or to Lely (Inventory of goods of Fifth Earl Temple, 1940, in custody of Farrar and Co., 66 Lincoln's Inn Fields, London, examined with the kind permission of Earl Temple). It was destroyed in 1940, but from these attributions and a description provided by Anthony Temple, it was of the late seventeenth century.

were his education and his character. It is worth remembering too that their second son, Anthony, also married a wealthy widow.

Peter Temple died at Stowe on 28 May 1578, and was buried at Burton Dassett, while Millicent survived him until December 1582.[85] She was also buried at Burton, though she died at Stowe, and a large tomb with an inlaid brass was erected as their memorial.[86]

3. *Burton Dassett: the place*

Standing on the hill at Burton Dassett, beside the fifteenth-century Beacon tower, one looks out over two very different landscapes. To the north stretches the flat Warwickshire plain, the claylands laid out in the geometric pattern of Parliamentary enclosure. These were the open fields of the hamlets of Northend and Knightcote, in intensive arable cultivation until 1772. Southward, among the hummocks of little quarries[87] on the hill and over the undulating southern end of the parish (Fig. 1) the sheep have grazed since 1500. Even here, under their feet, are the ridges and furrows of medieval arable fields, which covered all but the steepest slopes (Plate II).

It was in this southern end of the parish that the Heritage family had been established, and it was here that Peter Temple came in 1543 to take over his cousin's lease of Heritage Field. To understand how he could develop this into the centre of a landed estate, the topography and history of the parish must be explored.

The first necessity is to reconstruct the landscape in 1540 and then to consider how it reached this pattern. Before the fields themselves, the overall ownership must be examined.[88] In 1500 there were three manors in the parish. The smallest was Hardwick or Temple Hardwick in the south-west of the parish, which had been the property of the Knights Templar and then the Knights Hospitaller.[89] After the order was dissolved by King Henry VIII (1538), it passed in 1553 to the owners of the main manor and was absorbed into it.

[85] Burton Dassett Parish Register, W.R.O. DR 98/1.

[86] Dugdale records some of the inscription, though it was already damaged in his day.

[87] In this area, the stone is a sandy ferruginous limestone (the Middle Lias) known as marlstone, of a most attractive red-brown colour. (Wood-Jones, 1963, pp. 2–3.) The hill is part of the Jurassic escarpment, which runs north-eastward from Gloucestershire to Northamptonshire. For the position of Burton Dassett in relation to neighbouring towns, see Fig. 3, p. 42.

[88] *V.C.H.* vol. V, p. 71 (1949) is used as a general source for the manorial history.

[89] It was administered by them in a group of scattered small properties, from their preceptory at Temple Balsall, near Warwick; a few court rolls survive. The name is also spelt Hurdwick.

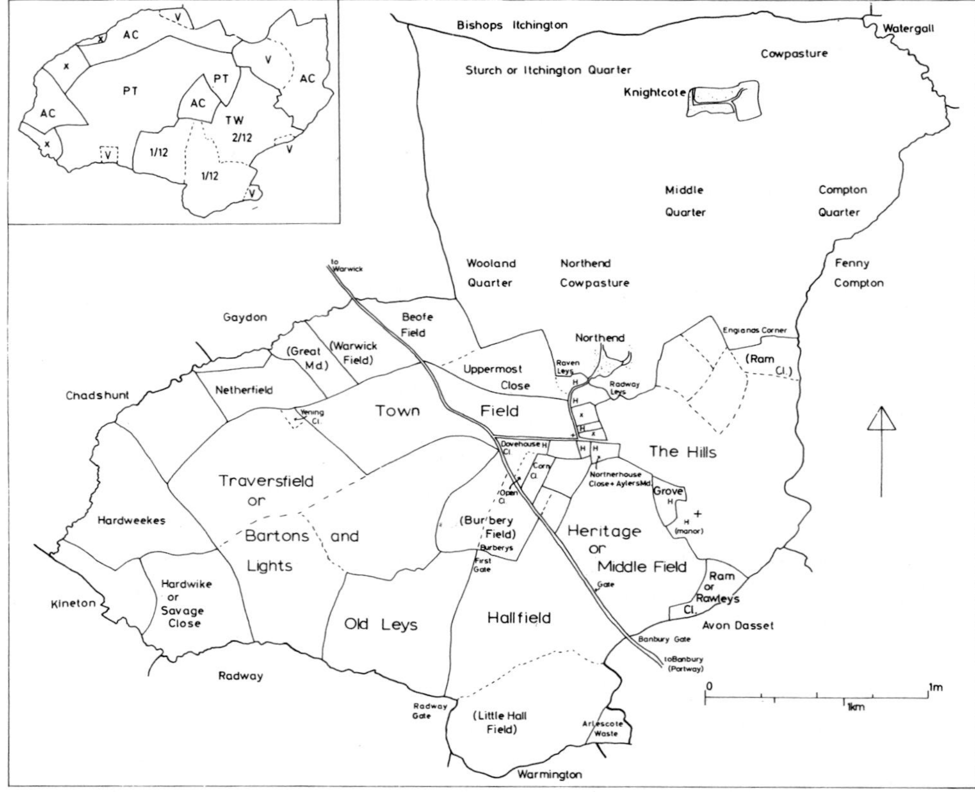

Fig. 1. A reconstructed map of Burton Dassett in 1567, when the partition of the manor was proposed. This is based on the map of 1826, transcribed to fit the first edition 6 in. Ordnance Survey map (1883). The field names are those given in 1567 or earlier, apart from those in ( ), which are from later sources. The thin field boundaries are those directly recorded in 1567, while dotted lines show uncertain boundaries and internal divisions that seem to be major, original hedge lines. The names of the major sections of the open fields of Knightcote and Northend are from the Enclosure Award and earlier deeds. H = house, + = church (*large*) and chapel of Chipping Dassett (*small*). Inset: Partitioning of the manor in 1576 and 1702; PT = Peter Temple, AC = Anthony Cooke, TW = Thomas Wotton, V = vicar, X = freeholding.

Although it had contained a hamlet with a number of houses, by 1553 it consisted of one farm, held on lease by Anthony Cooke.[90]

The northern part of the parish contains two hamlets, about a mile apart, called Knightcote and Northend. The manor of Knightcote, which covered this area, came into the ownership of John Smith, a successful Coventry lawyer, in about 1500. His family held it until the mid-seventeenth century, when all their estates were sold and the manorial rights were apparently abandoned.[91] Knightcote and Northend, in contrast to Hardwick, contained about twenty-five separate

[90] A copy of the Augmentation Office particulars are in ST L8 B4, Temple Land, Berks.-Leics., attached to a 1579–80 rental of John Temple's property.

[91] No allotment in lieu of manorial rights was made in the 1772 Enclosure award, W.R.O. QS 75/43.

holdings, and all were held freehold. Thus the most the lord of the manor could expect would be some quit rents and perhaps small profits from manor courts.[92] It is not surprising therefore that these were simply given up.

The main manor was that of Burton Dassett itself, which by 1540 consisted almost entirely of very profitable leaseholds. In 1498 it belonged to Sir Edward Belknap; he died in 1521, leaving it by will to three of his four sisters as co-heirs (Pedigree 5), though his widow, Alice, retained extensive rights until her death, probably in 1547.[93] Peter Temple bought one-third in 1557–60 and his son John obtained a second in 1595 (see Part III), but the remainder stayed with the Wootton family, descendants of Sir Robert Wotton (husband of Anne Belknap) until 1631. It was then further divided between the four daughters of Thomas Lord Wotton, each holding one-twelfth. The three co-owners held the manor in common until 1576, sharing all the rents, but in that year it was divided between them by private agreement, formalized by exchange of deeds. Similarly the Wootton third remained undivided until 1702 when it was partitioned by Act of Parliament. Curiously, the 1576 partition assigned all the land in Peter Temple's tenure not to him but to Wootton, and it was therefore described in 1702.

The foundation of any topographical reconstruction has to be a large scale map showing the fields, coupled with a survey to name them and indicate their ownership. For Burton Dassett, finding these proved unexpectedly hard. The most obvious source, a tithe map and apportionment (made for most parishes in the 1840s) fails because the tithes were entirely in the landowners' hands, with the tithe payment already included in the tenants' rents; thus no redemption of tithe was needed. For most great landed estates, periodic maps and surveys were made, often of very high quality, approaching works of art. One does exist for Burton Dassett but it covers only four fields in a corner of the parish.[94] For the Stowe estate as a

[92] The only evidence for a manor court is from 1384 (S.B.T. DR 10/2368) and in the seventeenth century, the tenants had to appear at the main Burton court (N.R.O. Temple Stowe, Box 6).

[93] She was left the right to lands worth £84 a year by Sir Edward, which was chosen as large parts of Burton Dassett. In due course, she leased the lands for considerably more than £84, and the Belknap heirs started a suit in Chancery, settled in 1543 largely in their favour; P.R.O. C78/3/24; copy (damaged) in N.R.O. Temple Stowe, Box 4/1a/5. The date of Dame Alice's death is not directly recorded. Two leases to follow her death were made on 25 June 1545 and 8 July 1546 (ST L9 E1 Temple Land, Bucks., book of leases), and the first is endorsed '28 Day of August', presumably the day of her death. The year could have been 1546, but item 172 in the account book shows that she must have died not long before this was written, apparently in 1548; thus 1547 is most likely.

[94] S.B.T. DR98/1825.

PEDIGREE 5: Sir Edward Belknap and the manor of Burton Dassett[a]

Sir Edward (1) = Alice (2) = John
Belknap d. 1521 (*whole*) — Alice d. 1547 — John Brugge

Alice = Sir William Shelley
(*none*)

Anne = Sir Robert Wotton
(*1/3*)
Sir Edward Wotton (d. 1566)
Thomas Wotton (d. 1580)
Edward, Lord Wotton (d. 1628)
Thomas, Lord Wotton (d. 1631)

Elizabeth = Sir Philip Cooke
(*1/3*)
Sir Anthony Cooke (d. 1576)
Richard Cooke
Anthony Cooke (sold *1/3* to John Temple in 1595)

Mary = Gerald Dannett
(*1/3*)
John Dannet
Leonard Dannet (sold *1/3* to Peter Temple in 1557–60)

Sold by Earl Temple to Lord Willoughby de Broke, 1828[b]

Children of Thomas, Lord Wotton:

Catherine = Henry Stanhope
(*1/12*)
Philip, Earl of Chesterfield (*1/12*)

Hester = Viscount Campden
(*1/12*)
Edward, Earl of Gainsborough (sold *1/12* to Sir Richard Temple in 1686)

Margaret = Sir John Tufton
(*1/12*)

Anne = Sir Edward Hales
(*1/12*)

(both sold to Thomas Woodward before 1683)

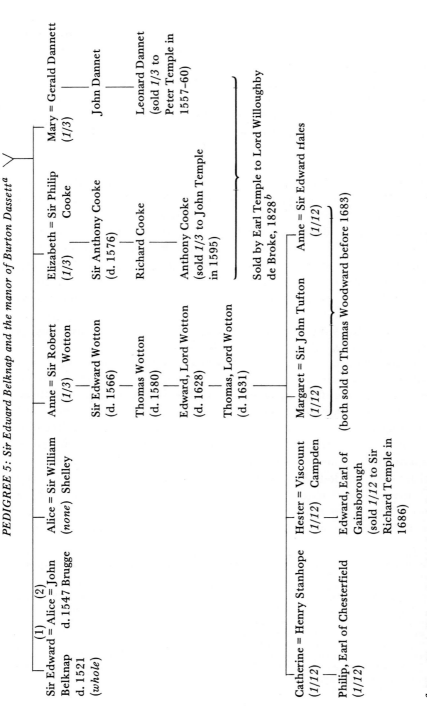

[a] Quantities in italics refer to fractions of the manor.
[b] The Temple family were in the eighteenth century dealing with 5/9th of the manor. It is not clear why this was 1/9th short of the 2/3rd part they apparently held.

whole, no such surveys were made, or what is less likely, they have not survived. For the northern half of the parish, the 1772 enclosure award[95] is effectively a survey, but the accompanying map is lost. Eventually, in the Willoughby de Broke muniments, a survey came to light, describing only ten farms in the south of the parish, but accompanied by a 'Sketch Map' of the whole parish, dated 1826 and mapping and numbering every field.[96] Then, quite independently, a 'Valuation' was discovered[97] that provides the key to this map with the field names and areas. The reason that the map was made is by no means clear. It could have been in preparation for the sale by Earl Temple to Willoughby de Broke of his part of the parish, but if so it need not have covered other property.[98] It is more likely therefore that it was intended to value the land, perhaps to revise a parish rate assessment. The surviving copy may well have been kept by Earl Temple, the largest landowner, and handed over to Willoughby de Broke in 1828. Although the map is detailed, it is clearly not based on an instrumental survey but is, as it states, a sketch. Individual field shapes are recognizable, but the whole parish is squashed in the east–west direction. The two other documents particularly useful for the reconstruction are the 1702 and 1576 partitions.[99] Both of these name and give the area of the different parcels, and note some of the fields that they adjoined.

The reconstruction (Fig. 1) proved comparatively easy, establishing a pattern of large fields bounded by the very well-marked major hedgerows. Those around the Wotton third of the manor could be directly identified as sixteenth-century field boundaries from the later records, and it is logical that the the others were similar.[1] The only difficulties concern the land not owned by Cooke, Temple and Wotton and not mentioned in the partition. The evidence indicates

[95] W.R.O. QS75/43.

[96] S.B.T. DR98 (Willoughby de Broke)/1807.

[97] S.B.T. ER (Early accessions) 17/8/1.

[98] It was, however, used as the map to accompany this sale; although the sale deed has not been found, one abstract of title that starts with it is accompanied by a map which reproduces exactly a small part of the 1826 'Sketch Map'; Treasury Solicitor Deeds Registry, Deeds for C. A. D. Kineton, 2241/60.

[99] (a) 1576: ST L8 B4, Warwickshire Land, Box 2, contains the partition as agreed, dated 26 November 1567. It did not take effect until 1576, though the details were precisely the same; ST L8 B4 Warwickshire Land, Box 2, July 1576, is a draft deed. (b) 1702: House of Lords Record Office, Private Acts 1 Anne, stat. 2, cap. 17.

[1] The acreages given are only of limited use; though those in 1567 are stated to the nearest perch, the actual statute acreages do not correspond very closely. No doubt the problems of surveying large uneven fields with curved hedges were responsible for the discrepancies.

that a few small freeholdings in Burton Manor adjoined Northend,[2] and two larger ones lay near Hardwick.

Of later changes, the most important has been the steady dissection of the big fields. This had started in a few places even in 1567, and is intermittently recorded in early deeds, though most of the subdivision must have taken place during the eighteenth century.[3] Only two significant changes in ownership occurred, apart from those affecting the manor as a whole. In 1595, Anthony Cooke sold his third of the manorial rights to John Temple, but he divided the bulk of the land between Henry Clarke and John Temple, while he sold his field in Hardwick to the Millett family.[4] Twenty years later, Sir Thomas Temple was able to buy both Clarke's and Millett's parts, but after only another decade the latter was sold, at a time when the family was suffering financial problems.[5]

The second change concerns the vicarage. In 1567 no glebelands were recorded, and in 1542 the vicar had renounced his claim to the vicarage lands in exchange for pasture for eight kine on Burton Hills, until he was assigned 'a certain close' (unspecified).[6] Glebe terriers[7] and the 1826 map show the later position. The most interesting features are the four small pieces on the extreme edges of the manor (V in Fig. 1). These lie in the separate thirds of the manor and they were probably assigned between 1576, when the partition took effect, and 1595. They must have been extraordinarily inconvenient to farm. Much later, probably as a fresh endowment by the Grenville family, the vicar also received the 90 acres of Burton Hill.[8]

In Knightcote and Northend the Temple family never extended their ownership very fully. By 1772 Earl Temple held $3\frac{1}{2}$ yardlands[9] for which he was allotted at enclosure 145 acres (out of a total of 1,792 acres), but this was not the largest single holding, being second to the $4\frac{7}{8}$ yardlands of Sir Robert Ladbroke. The Temple property

[2] ST L9 D8 Temple Land O/S is a deed of 1581–2, selling a house and two closes there.

[3] For example, in the Wotton third very few divisions were present in 1702, but the 1826 map shows a mass of smaller fields. At the same time new farmhouses appeared, scattered over the big fields.

[4] Enrolled copies: P.R.O. C54/1493, 21 January 1595 to Clarke and Temple; P.R.O. C54/1494, m. 3–4, 15 February 1595, to Millett.

[5] ST Deeds List I, Box 22, 1608, license to alienate, Clarke to Temple; W.R.O. CR607, deeds (1611–1716) relating to Hardwick; see E. F. Gay, 'The Temples of Stowe and their Debts', *Huntington Library Quarterly,* 2 (1939), pp. 399–438.

[6] ST Deeds, list 2, Box 36.

[7] W.R.O. Glebe Terriers, Burton Dassett.

[8] This has not been closely dated but must be after 1677 when 'The Hills' was listed in a Temple settlement (S.B.T. DR98/1357a).

[9] The yardland was a measure of the size of an open field holding. Although formally it corresponded to 32 acres, this varied very much from place to place.

was only bought in the seventeenth century and they were again obliged to sell part of it soon afterwards.[10]

How and when had Burton Dassett been laid out in the great closes, that were so well adapted to Peter Temple's sheep farming? In the medieval period the whole of the manor had been under the plough, and the ridge and furrow rolls over the landscape up to the steepest slopes of The Hills. Furthermore, as well as the settlements Burton itself and Hardwick, an entire small market town of Chipping Dassett with a chapel, lay in what was later Town Field (Fig. 1).[11] All three had their own open field systems.[12] In 1517 Sir Edward Belknap was indicted by the Inquisition on Enclosures for converting 360 acres of arable to pasture, and allowing twelve houses to decay.[13] By contrast, a lease of 1488 by Richard Verney mentions land in the fields of Chipyng Dorset[14] and must precede the enclosure. On 1 May 1497, Edward Belknap bought for £60 from John Erytage, late of Byrton, a messuage (house) with a close and grove lying thereto, 1¾ yardlands and some meadow.[15] Two days later, Belknap leased to Heritage, for forty-one years at an annual rent of £21, 'all the closes of the township of Burton with a field adjoyning to the said closis, called the Medull Feld ... reserving ... the courte plasse with all other howsyng of the said town, [*to be demolished and removed*] and all such closes as be above the partission, now in the holdyng of John Spencer'.[16] These deeds record the very moment of enclosure.[17]

Its causes must be sought much earlier, in the problems of arable farming on the heavy lands of South Warwickshire, and following on from this, in the readiness of the peasants to dispose of their land,

[10] N.R.O. Temple Stowe, Box 5/4, 1613, for land that had previously belonged to Thomas Spencer. Another holding passed through Temple hands in the seventeenth century, leaving deeds in the Stowe collection, ST Deeds, List 1, Box 22; List 2, Box 36.

[11] Chipping Dassett was a seignorial borough with a fair and a Friday market. *V.C.H.*, vol. V, p. 70. It may earlier have been called South End, in parallel to the adjoining Northend. The two together made up Dassett, while Burton was the name of the settlement near the parish church.

[12] S.B.T. DR98/188, 28 February 1435, an inquisition on the lands of Richard Verney, describes his 15 acre holding in Chipping Dassett, consisting of twenty-eight strips in as many furlongs, lying in East Field and North Field. ST Temple Law 83 makes clear the distinction between the Burton and Dassett field systems.

[13] In reality a much larger area was enclosed, but even as presented, this was the largest enclosure recorded in Warwickshire. I. S. Leadam, *The Domesday of Enclosures* (London: Royal Historical Society, 1897), p. 424.

[14] S.B.T. DR98/190.

[15] N.R.O. Temple Stowe, Box 4, 1a/1.

[16] ST Deeds, List 2, Box 36. This was John Spencer (d. 1497; Pedigree 4) who was already a large scale grazier at Hodnell a couple of miles to the north.

[17] The Inquisition gives the date 23 October 1498.

leading to the consolidation of holdings and decrease in population.[18] Superimposed on this, however, were circumstances which varied from lordship to lordship: enclosure became particularly easy when one, or a very few, owners were in possession of the land.[19] Although a number of medieval deeds survive for Burton Dassett,[20] these do not throw any light on the consolidation of ownership in the parish. However, by the 1490s, Sir Edward Belknap must have owned at least 80 per cent of the land, while of the three or four other proprietors, two were local gentry themselves involved in enclosure and not likely to raise objections.[21] Evidence of declining population at Hardwick in the beginning of the fifteenth century comes from a court roll for 1415-6.[22] Several tenants were in possession of more than one holding, and one was excused from the obligation to repair the buildings on his holding. Similarly, the inquisition on Richard Verney in 1438 speaks of a toft, *i.e.* a plot without a house, although in 1488 it was a messuage (with a house). Edward Belknap prepared a defence for the Inquisition on Depopulation[23] in which he stated that the houses had fallen into ruin in the time of William Belknap (1473-84) and his own minority (1488-90). He also claimed that Roger Heritage had at that time leased the manor and had converted much of it to pasture.[24] This is, however, not the full story. In 1482 there was still a 'Bothehall' (a market hall for booths) with a shop beside it,[25] and these were certainly destroyed in the enclosure and not rebuilt. The 1497 deed shows that the same was true of the houses of Burton itself, by the church. We can believe that decreasing

[18] They are examined in detail for the neighbouring village of Wormleighton by H. Thorpe, 'The Lord and the Landscape', *Trans. Birmingham. Arch. Soc.*, 80 (1965), 38.

[19] The paradoxical situation at Burton, where the lands on the hill were enclosed while the clays of Northend and Knightcote remained open clearly follows from the accidents of ownership.

[20] Especially in P.R.O. Ancient Deeds, class E.40 and in S.B.T. DR98.

[21] Sir Edward Raleigh of Farnborough who was enclosing at Wormleighton (Dugdale, 1656, p. 405) held about 20 acres. Richard Verney, who had 15 acres (see note 12) had enclosed Compton Verney (then called Compton Murdak) in the fifteenth century.

[22] W.R.O. CR 1122/1. This is the only surviving roll with appreciable details of the manor. It is very possible that Hardwick was enclosed before Burton.

[23] Existing in a seventeenth-century copy in ST L8 B9 Temple Land, Warwickshire, printed in N. W. Alcock 'Enclosure and Depopulation in Burton Dassett: a 16th Century View', *Warwickshire History,* III (5), 1977, 180-4. It is also commented on by Gay, 1938, who gives details of the proceedings against Belknap and his successors, which failed ultimately to enforce any re-conversion to tillage.

[24] The only manorial account (for 1482) shows that Heritage was indeed the lessee, but of the demesnes only, with the warren and the mill, paying £20 a year. N.R.O. Temple Stowe, Box 6/2.

[25] Ibid. Warwick had a very large 'Bothehall' in the sixteenth century (information from M. W. Farr; W.R.O. CR 1618/WA 12/1). In Gloucester, in 1455, the Guildhall was called 'Bothall', J. Langton 'Late Medieval Gloucester: some data from a rental of 1455', *Trans. Inst. Brit. Geographers, NS*2 (1977), 259.

population had led to the abandonment of some houses, while in 1495, Heritage must have had grazing land for his 860 sheep and forty cattle. However, he also had sixteen plough oxen and just before his death had harvested corn crops worth £7 (including some of the previous year's wheat and peas). The tilth of his fallow land was also valued at £3.[26]

Roger Heritage was conveniently dead and could be blamed, but in fact his death in 1495 looks like one of the immediate stimuli for the enclosure; John, no longer living in Burton, may well have been more cooperative than his father. On 11 May 1496 the actual opportunity came when Edward Belknap obtained clear possession of the manor, after he and Sir John Norbury divided their inheritance from Lord Sudeley.[27]

From the map we can deduce that the procedure for enclosure was very simple. Each of the arable open fields, for example Middle Field at Burton, was taken as an individual enclosure; they must already have had hedges to keep stock in the fallow field off growing crops. Part of Burbery Field seems to have been cut out of the north end of Halls Field, which was probably another of the Burton fields (with The Hills as the third). The rest of Burbery Field and Old Leys belonged to Burton rather than to Dassett[28] and were apparently pastures fringing the main manor fields. The name 'Old Leys', certainly recorded as early as 1540, indicates that this was a pasture close before the enclosure, although both it and Burbery Field show ridge and furrow.[29] Thus they must represent a first step towards the conversion from arable to pasture, having been cut off from the open fields in an earlier rearrangement, and presumably used as common grazing by the Burton tenants. Similarly, by 1772 there were some small leys by Northend village, and also two larger areas called Northend and Knightcote Cowpastures.[30]

[26] Listed in his inventory, P.R.O. PROB 2/457; his will was proved in November, 1495. The survival of this inventory is perhaps the most fortunate chance in the whole saga of the Temple family documents. It is one of only 750 inventories which survive in the probate records of the Prerogative Court of Canterbury for the whole of southern England from the fifteenth century to 1660.

[27] British Library. Add. Ch. 5684.

[28] So recorded in a rental of Sir Edward Belknap's lands (ST 37). This is dated 1540, though internal evidence suggests that it may be a copy of a rental from as early as 1522; an annuity from the manor given in the rental under the name of Odyngseles was in that year transferred to Makepeace (see p. 148, note 15).

[29] Plotted from air photographs by David Pannett, to whom I am most grateful for this information.

[30] Several leys (pasture strips) are mentioned in the seventeenth century Stowe deeds referred to in note 10. Evidence for the creation of pasture from arable has been found for other Warwickshire villages, though this usually took the form of ley strips rather than whole closes (information from C. C. Dyer).

The fields in Dassett clearly suffered more rearrangement. Travers Field, for instance, seems to have covered three separate portions of the earlier system. The boundary with the Northend fields is irregular both east and west of Northend village, and this suggests that the different field systems were originally closely connected. In the re-allocation, the few free-holdings seem to have been pushed off to the fringes. Ram Close (S.E. boundary) was assigned to Anthony Rawleigh,[31] and the fields along the Gaydon boundary probably held the other freeholders' allotments, including those of Richard Verney and Sir Davy Owen. For the latter, a significant comment is recorded that he was to have the first crop of hay off another close, because his own meadow lay 'in amongst our [Belknap's] enclosures'.[32]

One person's rights seem to have been ignored in the enclosure—the vicar, who, as we have seen, received no allotment. This explains why the Bishop of Lichfield in 1501 reaffirmed the vicar's right to his former house and glebe[33] (with a pension of £12 a year as well). Apparently as a consequence, a most curious deed was drawn up in 1503, conveying to sixteen respected local people[34] three cottages in Dassett and sixteen acres of land divided in the fields of Dassett and Hardwick. Its endorsement, 'the Church dede', shows that it was

[31] In ST 37, it is 'a close in Byrtun which Sir Edward Belknappe bought [before his death in 1521] of Anthony Rawleigh' (brother of Edward Raleigh, according to J. Fetherstone (ed.), *The Visitation of the County of Warwickshire, 1619* (Harleian Society, 1877). In 1546, Rawlyns, or the Ram Close, adjoined Heritage Close (copy lease in L9 E1, Temple Bucks); in 1567 Ram or Rawleys Close was reserved unassigned; its area was given as 21 acres. A Ram Close adjoining The Hills appears in Anthony Cooke's part of the manor by 1594 (P.R.O. C66/1432, m. 8). This may be the later Ram Close to the north-east of The Hills (22 acres in 1826), in which case it cannot be the one described as adjoining Heritage Field. A better alternative is the area due south of that field. Part of this was later assigned to the vicar, and is called Ram Close and Meadow in the glebe terriers, while another part belonging to Wotton's third in 1702 was also called Ram Close; the map suggests that the adjoining small field in the Cooke third also formed part of the original field. The sub-division may well have taken place when the vicarage lands were assigned.

[32] ST 37. The Verney holding was bought by Dannett and Wotton in 1547 (Birmingham Reference Library, 437926; ST Deeds List 2, Box 36). The Owen holding must have passed into Temple hands at some date, as a deed of 1568 transferring it to one John Wilkyns is in a Stowe group (Folger Shakespeare Library, MS. Z.c.659). The free holding at the south-west corner of the manor (Fig. 1) can be traced continuously from 1570, when it was the property of William Underhill of Idlicote (P.R.O. I.P.M., C142/154/117), described as 40 acres of pasture and a barn, called Hardwyke Closes. It eventually passed to the Willoughby de Broke family in 1811; W.R.O. CR556/722A–B; S.B.T. ER6/48/1, DR98/1825, 1830. The 1567 partition indicates that the remaining large freeholding, east of Hardwick, belonged to John Woodwarde (see p. 148).

[33] Cited in Dugdale, p. 523.

[34] Including John Spencer of Hodnell, his son William, and John Eritage.

stating a claim to the glebe land, even though this no longer had any separate existence.[35]

Peter Temple's own interest in Burton Dassett started with his inheritance from his cousin, Thomas Heritage, of the lease of Middle Field (which by 1533 was called Heritage Field (120)).[36] Peter also obtained a lease of Halls Field and Old Leys, probably by assignment from the original lessee.[37] Both leases were only valid until Dame Alice Belknap's death, and in 1545–6 he safeguarded his position by obtaining new leases, paying £26 rent for Heritage Field, and £60 for the other two;[38] he also had to pay £3 10s. and £6 in lieu of tithe.[39] Together these fields cover 655 acres.[40] As a whole, this was the biggest individual holding in the manor, but there were three other substantial blocks, Town Field (210 acres), The Hills (380 acres, held in 1567 with 131 acres at Hardwick), and Traversfield (506 acres, held in 1567 with the 95 acre Savage Close).[41]

Peter's fields formed a compact block in the centre of the manor (Fig. 1), running down from the flank of Burton Hill by the church, to the level ground of Old Leys. They were watered by two streams, one running through Halls Field to Old Leys, and the other north through the centre of Heritage Field; beside them were small meadow closes that could be cut for hay. Altogether, they must have been excellently suited to large-scale pasture farming. The scene is set for us by Peter Temple himself. In 1545, he paced the boundaries of the fields, and recorded what he measured.

[35] S.B.T. ER1/6, f. 22 and f. 69 (two copies), in a collection compiled *c.* 1850 by James Saunders. The location of the original is not known.

[36] The original lease had been renewed by Thomas Heritage, at an increased rent of £26 (121).

[37] This had been leased by Dame Alice Belknap in 1528, though in 1543 the land was assigned by the Court of Chancery to Wotton, Dannet and Cooke (ref. cited in note 93, p. 29).

[38] The Heritage Field lease (dated 8 July 1546) was for twenty-one years, starting after Dame Alice's death (ST L9 E1, Temple Land, Bucks, f. 30). The other lease has not survived, but Kinloss 18 gives its date, 14 March 1545, with that of the first one. The rent is recorded in several places in the account book (e.g. 77, 208). On at least one occasion (226), Peter Temple sub-let part of the land on a regular basis, rather than just for short-term pasturing.

[39] Also recorded frequently in the account book (e.g. 76–7).

[40] As he estimated in about 1545 (76–7). In the 1567 partition, the corresponding area was given as 885 acres, while in the 1702 Act of Parliament (see note 99, p. 31), it was 855 acres.

[41] Areas from the 1567 partition.

FIELD PERAMBULATION, [PROBABLY 1545][42]

1 f. 14 v. B

Halles Feld	The cyrcuytt theroff (ys)^{er} by the hedge from Banbery gatte unto Rodwey gatte ys xxv^{c} pace of the gret talle[43] and from Rodweye gate to Burberyes fyrst gat xj^{c} and from thence Herytage Feld gate xiiij^{c} pace and from thens to Banbery gate iiij^{c} pace. Sum of the holle cyrcuyt of the sayd Hallsfeld alonge by the hedges ys liiij^{c} pace.
The Old Lesse	The cyrcyitt therof ys xxxviij^{c} pace Wherof the hedge that parteth the Old Lesse and Hals Feld ys in lenght xj^{c} pace, the which being mette on both sydes takyth xxij^{c} pace, with xxij^{c} pace being deducte and the Old Lesse and Halles Felde being mete al under one, the circuyt of the holl (the seyd partyng hedge being put outt and not metted) ys as before apperyth lxx^{c} paces of the gret talle.
Herytage Feld	The cyrcuyt therof with the hyg' close alone ys xxxvij^{c} and lx pace, but the Grove and the sheperdes being putte and mette all under one makyth hit about iij^{c} pace more

'The Grove', which he noted, can be identified under that name in 1826 as a house and small field to the east of Heritage Field, and this in its turn in the 1576 partition as 'a messuage, orchard and garden', with The Hills to the east and the manor house to the south, and in the 1546 lease as 'a certain house that Peter Temple dwells in' (see p. 197).

It is ironic that the full reward from the enclosure and final depopulation of Burton and Dassett went not to the successors of Sir Edward Belknap, the depopulator, but to the nephew of the man whose sale to Belknap made the enclosure possible. The delay between the enclosure and the realization of its profits can be seen as part of a general pattern, however. The wave of enclosure that came to an end with the Inquisition on Depopulation of 1517 had as its driving force the reduction of labour costs, and indeed the people to undertake the onerous tasks of arable farming often could not be found at all. However, the profits of pasture farming really became impressive with the rising prices of the mid-sixteenth century inflation. Peter Temple's account book reveals just how much more valuable was the occupation of pasture land than its ownership.

[42] The date of all the adjacent items in the account book. For details of the editing procedure, see the Appendix.

[43] i.e. counting 120 paces to every hundred.

PART II: THE ACCOUNTS

SECTION A: FARMING

1. *Introduction*

PETER TEMPLE's first farming account was for his cousin's arable land in Hertfordshire in the 1541–2 season (134; see section 7). However, in the next winter he moved to Warwickshire, and in 1543 began to record his very different farming there. For the first year, only scraps survive (208), but 1544 has the first full cattle account (2), and the sheep are covered in detail in the next year (50). By its nature, it is for the cattle fattening that there is most information, because each year the herd was built up and then sold. This was only moderately profitable, but the accounts are in some ways more significant than those for the financially more important sheep. This is partly because of their bulk, the largest single section in the account book,[1] and partly because extremely little is known of the sixteenth-century cattle trade.[2] They also show the development of Peter Temple's methods with experience and in response to market forces.

The balance between sheep and cattle cannot be precisely established, but cattle certainly made up a substantial proportion, and may have been dominant at first. This is surprising in view of the image of the Midland enclosures as bearing sheep and shepherd alone. However, incidental references show that cattle were also significant. Thus, Sir John Spencer in his petition against the order of the Enclosure Commissioners to return his land to tillage (probably in 1519) stated 'his lyvyng ys . . . by the brede of cattell in his pastures'.[3] Similarly, the author of the *Discourse of the Common*

[1] They are also in comparatively good order, with ff. 13 v–37 in continuous sequence for 1545 to 1554.

[2] W. G. Hoskins, *The Age of Plunder* (London: Longmans, 1976), p. 81. Work by Dr. P. Edwards has thrown light on the traffic between Wales and England ('The Cattle Trade of Shropshire in the late sixteenth and seventeenth centuries, *Midland History*, forthcoming). He demonstrates in particular that there were many other aspects to this trade than just the traffic in store cattle, with which Peter Temple was involved.

[3] I. S. Leadam (ed.), *The Domesday of Enclosures* (London: Longman Green, 1897), II, p. 486.

Weale (*c.* 1549), had his Knight say 'Inclosures is the thing that nourisethe [cattle] most of anie other'.[4]

The sheep entries are more complex than those for cattle, with purchases, sales and payments, and stock counts of various sorts. They are also less thorough for the first years, but by the later 1540s, their evidence is probably complete. By 1550, it is clear that sheep were much more profitable than cattle, and the pattern of Peter Temple's farming was changing to match this. His wool also made a handsome contribution to his income, particularly because he was breeding the long-fleeced Cotswold sheep. The producer's side of the wool trade is complemented by Peter Temple's own purchases in the local villages, and also by the activities a few years earlier of his cousin, Thomas Heritage. The latter was buying wool for sale in London, and on one occasion for strictly illegal export to Calais. Further vignettes of the inland trade come from Heritage's return to his customers, in the form of fine groceries and sundries. These are so closely mingled with the wool accounts proper, that the two cannot usefully be separated.

Thomas Heritage had some direct involvement with grazing on his land in Warwickshire, in partnership with a local man. He was also concerned in the minor farming activities that complete this section of the accounts. These included occasional sales of surplus hay, and the letting of pasture by the week, for which Heritage used his Hertfordshire property. Finally, in complete contrast, the arable farming of the same land is recorded, in the successive accounts of Thomas and Peter.

2. *Peter Temple: Cattle*

Peter Temple used his pasture for cattle in one way only. He bought 'lean besse' in the spring principally from Wales, fattened them and sold them off from midsummer to December, keeping only a few till the next year. The accounts run from 1544 to 1554, though they are incomplete for the first year,[5] and scrappy after 1550 when cattle farming became unimportant. In the first couple of years, each beast is lovingly described ('the old whit face blake cow'), but

[4] E. Lamond (ed.), *A Discourse of the Common Weale of this Realm of England* (Cambridge: University Press, 1893), p. 17. It should be said, however, that cattle, in contemporary parlance, could embrace sheep, and the author also noted (p. 48) 'Nowe is there nothinge but only shepe'. The *Discourse* is attributed to Sir Thomas Smith, but Dr. Joan Thirsk suggests that it may rather be by John Hales of Coventry.

[5] For this year, the sale of the Welsh oxen is absent; this may well have been on a leaf of the account book that is known to be missing after f. 3. Some purchases may also be lost. An incidental reference (**208**) shows some activity in 1543.

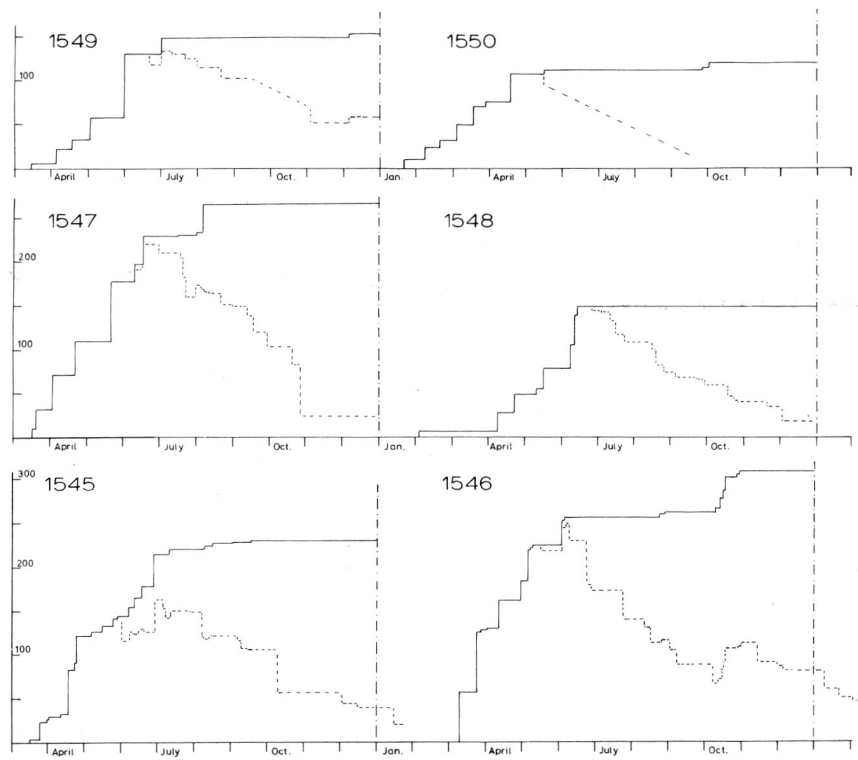

Fig. 2. Cattle fattening: stock numbers. The solid line shows the purchases, and the broken line the net number remaining in the pasture after sales.

thereafter the accounts are more prosaic. However, from 1545 to 1550 they give unique evidence: the exact date and place where each beast was bought and sold. The pattern of these years is shown in Figs. 2 and 3. The build-up of the herd usually started in March, though in 1550 cattle were bought in Tamworth as early as 20 January. Stocking was essentially complete by the end of June, and sales started just before this. The largest herd on the pasture at any time was about 220 in 1546 and 1547; in every year cows were the most important with a substantial minority of oxen (Table 2.1). Other types of cattle were much rarer, and in particular cows in calf or with calves were hardly ever bought.[6] However, at the end of each

[6] The types of cattle that were only bought occasionally are as follows (*O.E.D.*)

Bulchin	bull calf
Stirk (sturke)	young beast, 1–2 years old
Heifer	young cow which has had no calf
Steer	young ox
Runt	ox or cow of small breed (especially 'Welsh runts')
Shott	poor quality beast, usually sheep or pig, but also cattle (*E.D.D.*)

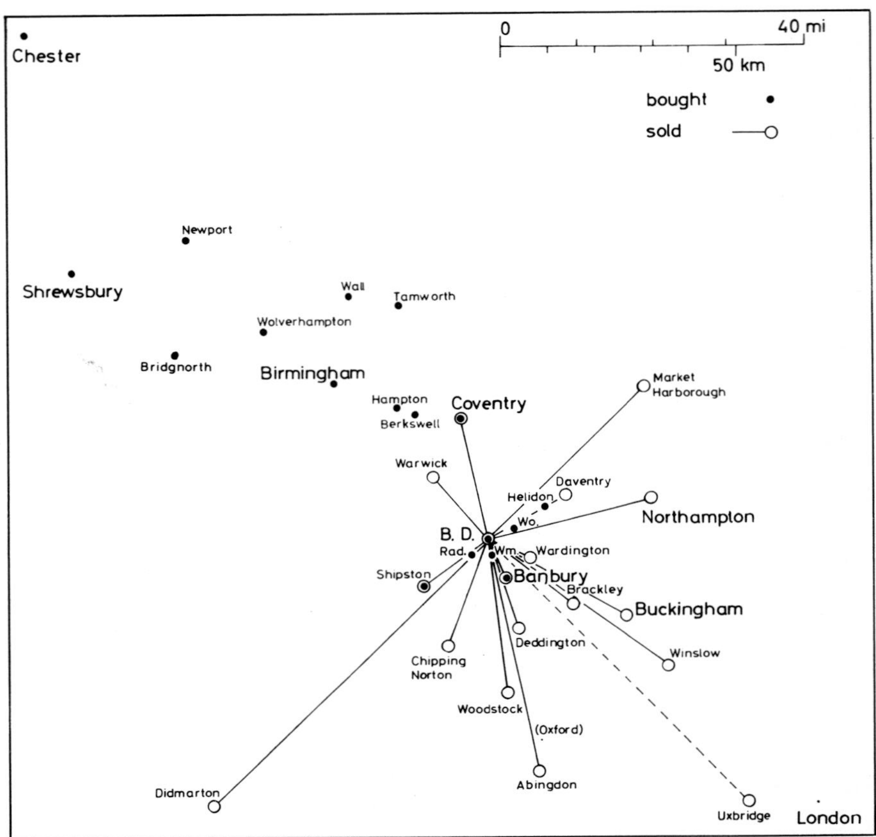

Fig. 3. Cattle dealing, 1544–51: location of purchases and sales. Cattle were also bought at Northend, Avon Dassett and Fenny Compton, very close to Burton Dassett. The butchers from Uxbridge and Daventry (or Newnham, a couple of miles south) came to Burton to buy. Rad. = Radway; Wo. = Wormleighton; Wm. = Warmington.

year when the cattle had been sold, a few milking cows (13; f. 15 v) and weaning calves (10) were kept, with oxen for the wain and a bull or two (37). The bulls were particularly useful as meat for the household at Christmas, and also as gifts to friends and relatives (13; f. 15 v). The major departure from this policy was in 1546 when forty-five cattle were bought in October and sixty were overwintered, and only sold in June 1547. This year, as well as showing the largest purchases, also returned the highest profit, about £80 on an outlay of £233 (Table 2.2).

The five years from 1545 all achieved respectable profits of about 40 per cent of the purchase money, but 1550 was a disaster. Almost as much money was laid out as in 1549, but it bought thirty-eight fewer head, and the total return was a meagre £14. The next year,

Table 2.1: *Cattle dealings and prices*

The 'number bought' is the total of that type for the year. If not all the buying or selling prices are known, then the number in brackets after the price gives the number used for calculating the average price.

Year		*Cow*	*Cow & Calf*	*Heifer*	*Bull*	*Bullock*	*Bulchon*	*Steer*	*Ox*	*Runt*	*Sturke*
1554	No.	12	1	2	1	4		4	47[a]		
Bought	Price	14s. 10d. (2)	17s. 4d.	11s. 3d.		14s. 0d.		10s. 8d. (1)	16s. 2d.		
Sold	Price	17s. 10d. (6)	19s. 8d. (2)	15s. 7d. (5)		13s. 4d. (1)	21s. 8d. (1)		23s. 0d. (3)		
1545	No.	139		2	1			13	71	4	
Bought	Price	12s. 10d. (128)		11s. 6d.	13s. 2d.			13s. 3d. (12)	17s. 8d.	17s. 0d.	
Sold	Price	17s. 4d. (115)	16s. 9d. (4)	15s. 3d. (11)	15s. 0d. (1)			16s. 5d. (14)	25s. 10d. (53)	21s. 2d. (25)	
1546[b]	No.	194	3	8	4			23	64		1
Bought	Price	12s. 11d. (185)	15s. 10d.	13s. 8d. (7)	13s. 6d. (3)			16s. 0d. (21)	20s. 9d. (62)		7s. 8d.
Sold	Price	19s. 4d. (160)	20s. 8d. (9)	15s. 6d. (14)				20s. 4d. (8)	28s. 0d. (59)		
1547	No.	204		3	1			2	53	1	
Bought	Price	14s. 11d.		12s. 4d.	13s. 6d.			10s. 0d. (1)	20s. 5d.		
Sold	Price	21s. 0d. (182)		16s. 0d. (4)				16s. 8d. (1)	30s. 4d. (56)		
1548	No.	101		4					25	2	1
Bought	Price	15s. 10d.		15s. 4d. (1)					21s. 10d.	17s. 2d.	
Sold	Price	19s. 8d. (110)		18s. 7d. (5)				18s. 0d. (2)	26s. 10d. (30)	20s. 0d. (1)	
1549	No.	112		3	2			24	18	13	
Bought	Price	15s. 7d.		12s. 1d.	15s. 0d. (1)			14s. 6d. (23)	26s. 3d. (17)	19s. 5d.	
Sold	Price	21s. 6d. (94)						23s. 0d. (23)	37s. 8d. (17)	26s. 7d. (10)	
1550	No.	85	4	2	1				21		
Bought	Price	16s. 10d.	32s. 9d.	14s. 6d.					28s. 8d.		
Sold	Price	22s. 5d. (76)[c]						74s. 0d. (2)	51s. 6d. (9)		
1561											
Sold	Price	33s. 4d. (2)				13s. 4d. (3)			47s. 8d. (34)	48s. 4d. (20)	

[a] Composed of 8 English oxen at 16s. 7d. and 39 Welsh oxen at 16s. 1d.
[b] In 1546, 1 shott was bought at 9s. 4d.
[c] Including 2 runts. Undated item **72** gives the sale price for 4 bullocks of 18s. 5d.

Table 2.2: *Cattle receipts and payments*

Year	*Gross cost*	*Total head*	*Gross*[a] *receipts*	*Net*[b] *cash profit*	*Beasts unsold* *Died*	*Lost/ stolen*	*Killed/ gifts*	*Corrected*[c] *net profit*
1544	£31 18s. 0d.	46	£23 13s. 7d.	–[d]	1	1	–	
	+£31 8s. 9d.	39	unknown					
1545	£202 2s. 5d.	230	£229 3s. 1d.	£27	1	1	5	£32
1546	£233 8s. 11d.	309	£302 0s. 2d.	£69	10	3	10	£79
1547	£214 12s. 4d.	266	£280 18s. 10d.	£66	7	3	1	£67
1548	£122 1s. 9d.	149	£157 2s. 8d.	£35	2	4?	15[e]	£50
1549	£132 7s. 8d.	155	£173 9s. 0d.	£40	2	1	6	£46
1550	£116 3s. 3d.	117	£128 9s. 6d.	£11	1	2	3	£14
1554–4	No proper figures for purchases or sales							

[a] Receipts for all beasts bought in the year, even if sold the following year.
[b] Allowing for all recorded costs, except the possible (but small) sale costs.
[c] Corrected by adding £1 for each beast killed or given away.
[d] Sales of twenty-eight only.
[e] Includes eight beasts sold, whose price is unknown.

and in 1553, some of the money earmarked for buying cattle even had to be returned unspent (**41, 45**). The cause of these problems must have been a lack of store cattle, and there are indications that this was not merely local, but was reflected in national circumstances that required government attention. In 1548, John Hales proposed that all men keeping more than 120 sheep should also have to keep two kine and one calf for each 100 sheep.[7] The purpose of this was to increase the supply of cattle, and so ensure the provision of milk, butter and cheese, for the diet of the poor. The immediate effect of the difficulties with store cattle was that fattening became an insignificant part of Peter Temple's farming.[8] Probably as a consequence, he sold significant amounts of his pasture for grazing in 1550 and 1551 (**70, 71**). In contrast, by 1561 conditions had changed, as a loose sheet (**46**) shows that some seventy head were bought and sold. As the purchase price is not given, the profit, if any, is unknown.

Low profit was not the only hazard. A few cattle always died, ten in the worst year (1546), six of them almost as soon as they had been bought. There were also strays, cattle that 'came not out of Shropshire' (**18**), and outright theft. In 1548 (**28**) Peter Temple sold twenty cattle to 'a knave that ran away' who, we know from a financial jotting (**30**), passed himself off as a butcher from Steeple Aston (a North Oxfordshire village). He paid 10s. as an earnest, and went off with the first ten cattle, never to reappear.

The cattle came from two quite different sources (Fig. 3). Some were bought locally by Peter Temple himself, or occasionally by his servants (e.g. **33**) and usually in small numbers; after 1546 these local cattle were unimportant. The main supply came from the north-west, Welsh cattle brought into England for sale. The major markets were Chester, Shrewsbury,[9] Bridgnorth and Newport in the far west, and a ring of towns in north Warwickshire and Staffordshire: Birmingham, Wolverhampton, Coventry, Tamworth, Berkswell, Hampton and Wall.[10] The last three are surprising, as none are now more than villages, but it is quite clear that they were major centres of the cattle trade. Hampton, in particular, provided large numbers every

[7] E. Lamond, op. cit. (n. 4, p. 40), pp. lxii–lxiii; *Ag. Hist.* p. 226. Although the bill failed on its first proposal in Edward VI's reign, it was passed in 1556, under Mary.

[8] With his decreasing financial interest, he also stopped keeping such detailed records.

[9] The only cattle toll book known to survive from this early date is that for Shrewsbury (Shropshire R.O. 3365/2645, from 1542). Though it covers the two annual fairs fully (apparently on 22 June and 1 August), unfortunately it only has rare references to the weekly markets that Peter Temple must have used.

[10] Hampton is Hampton-in-Arden, Warwickshire, as Wolverhampton is mentioned explicitly in 1550. Wall (or Walls) is the hamlet of that name in Lichfield parish, lying on Watling Street.

year. Peter Temple did not tour the western markets himself, but used an agent, Thomas Hygynson (or Hygins).[11] He probably lived in Coventry, where he served as bailiff for the Temple family (see p. 140), and he spent much of the spring buying cattle, for which he was suitably rewarded at the year's end (17). At intervals he received sums of money (probably on visits to Dasset) and acknowledged their receipt in the account book, in a very fine formal hand; he was sometimes sent money by servants, and he also used the money he had collected in Coventry. While buying, he sometimes travelled fast, apparently visiting Birmingham, Hampton, Coventry and Berkswell all on the 20 March 1546 (17; f. 19), but he took with him the Dasset wain (41) which was no doubt useful during the slow journeys home, driving the cattle. Some of this was done by hired men, and with their wages, toll charges and pasture along the way had to be paid for; the cattle would probably cover 15 to 20 miles a day.[12]

The marketing, like the purchasing, developed rapidly. In 1545 and 1546, cattle were sold at dozens of markets and fairs[13] around Dasset (Fig. 3), but thereafter only the major markets were visited: Banbury, Coventry and Warwick (with Deddington, Northampton and Woodstock once each). More important were the sales made at Dasset itself. In particular, three men were major purchasers: Mr. William Gyfford,[14] who bought 120 head in 1545, William Raynor of Uxbridge (1547 and 1549) and Randall of Newnham, near Daventry, Northants (1548);[15] the last two were both butchers, probably supplying the London market. Peter Temple's brother, Robert, also bought a few head, and they may have been jointly concerned in buying cattle (28). In 1551, thirteen oxen were taken all the way to Essex to Sir Anthony Cooke at Romford, but were then brought back again. Perhaps the price asked was too high, or too many other cattle were available; it is a further indication of the difficulties of the cattle trade at this period.

[11] His role is first made clear in 1546 (16), but the mentions in 1545 (7, 8) suggest that he may have been employed then. The reference to Cousin Hygyns (8) implies that he was a relative of Peter.

[12] R. J. Colyer, *The Welsh Cattle Drovers* (Aberystwyth: University of Wales Press, 1976). p. 60.

[13] The dates for some of the fairs are uncertain, but as far as possible they have been provided from *V.C.H.*

[14] Probably the same man who was an agent for the Johnson brothers (Winchester, 1955, p. 218); *L. & P. Henry VIII*, several references in vols. XVII–XX. He worked through his bailiff Benet (214).

[15] Randoll of Newnham, Randoll of Daventry and 'The Bocher of Newnham' probably refer to the same person.

CATTLE ACCOUNTS

2 f.1v.A Oxen and kyne bought into Herytage Feld
anno xxxvj^{to} H viij^{o} [1544]

First of my owne iij kyne	
Of Spenser j bryndyd cow	xix s.
Item bowght of Spenser viij kyne and j bull	viij li. iij s.
Item of Heritage j cowe and calfe	xvij s. iiij d.
Item at Banbery Faire ij red bullockes	xxxiij s.
Item ij heifers, j pied browne and j red	xxij s. vj d.
Item j browne stere	x s. viij d.
Item j cattyd[16] fallow cow	x s. viij d.
Item j blod red ox	x s. vj d.
Item x sters and heyfers markyd with piche	vj li. xiij s. iiij d.
Item j red cow and j browne stere	xxvj s. viij d.
Item j gret oxe with a whit face	xxj s.
Item j bulock with a whit face	xvj s.
Item of Higins j red oxe chyok hornd and j black with a whit bely	xxxviiij s. iiij d.
Item j lytyl bryndyd bullock	vij s.
Of Stonle iiij oxen, j browne and j blak with a stere in in the forehed	xxxix s.
and j black with whit horns	xix s.
and j black	xv s.
Of my brother ij steres, j cow	xxxvj s.

3 f.2[17] Besse Sold

1	One dyed	
1	Sold to Peni j hore[18] cowe that I bought of Spenser	xix s.
1	Sold Peni j cow bowght of my brother	xviij s.
1	Sold to Phips j black blowid cow and calf bought of Spenser	xxj s.
5	Sold to Peny ij red hefers, j black blowed heifer and one red stere and j old red cow at xv s. iiij d. the pece	iij li. xvj s. viij d.
1	Sold at Banbery j red heifer	xvj s.
1	Item agayne j red heifer	xvj s.
3	Item ij blake sters and j browne	xliiij s.
1	(Item)[er] and one lytyll brown	xij s. vij d.
1	Item at Banbery sold j bryndyd stere	xvj s. iiij d.
1	Item one lytyll rede stere	xiij s.
1	Sold the lame oxe	xxiij s. iiij d.
1	Sold the old whit face blake cow	xvij s.

[16] Perhaps *cut-tailed*; cf. *cutayl* in 3.

[17] From here, the left margin gives the number of cattle in arabic numerals, and from 12, also the place concerned.

[18] For *horned?*

1	Sold the red bulchon whitface	xxj s. viij d.
2	Sold the cutayl cow and on blak cow	xxxviij s.
2	Sold the pyed cow and cutayl bullok	xliij s. iiij d.
1	Sold the crok holpe[18] red cow	xv s. viij d.
	her calf	ij s. viij d.
1	Sold the bryndyd bullok	xiij s. iiij d.
1	Sold the gret blake oxe	xxiiij s.
1	Sold the blake whitface oxe	xxij s.
1	Kyld in my house one bulle	
1	Kyld in my house one oxe red	
	(Item one dyed)[er]	

4 f. 2 v. A [*Cattle Bought, probably 1544*]
[?Shropshire] and Chester

[iij oxe]n	xlviij s. viij d.
j oxe	xvj s. viij d.
ij oxen	xxxv s. iiij d.
ij oxen	xxxiiij s. iiij d.
ij oxen	xxxiiij s. iiij d.
j ox	xix s.
j ox	xvj s. iiij d.
ij oxen	xxxv s. iiij d.
j ox	xvj s. vj d.
j ox	xv s.
ij oxen	xxxiiij s. viij d.
ij oxen	xxx s.
ij oxen	xxxiiij s. x d.
j ox	xviij s.
j ox	xv s. iiij d.
j ox	xvij s. iiij d.
ij oxen	xxj s. vj d.
ij oxen	xliij s. iiij d.
ij oxen	xxix s.
j ox	xvj s.
ij oxen	xxix s. viij d.
ij oxen	xxxiij s. vij d.
j ox	xvj s.
spent	xij s.
ij oxen	
(ij oxen prec')[er]	

5 f. 3. B [*Probably 1544*]

[*top margin*]	xxxj li. xiiij s. iij d.
j browne cow	xiij s. viij d.
ij oxen	xxviij s. j d.
j blake cow	xiiij s.
ij oxen, j blake and [j pale?]	[*blank*]

6 f. 11. C [*Miscellaneous entries, possibly 1544*][19]

Gryffin bought for my wyffe the xijth of Maye	
Of Gybins j red cow and j pyed	xxvij s.
Item of Thomas Gryffyn j blake cow	xiiij s.
Item of Lysterle[20] j brown pyed	xiij s.

7 f. 11 v. B

xxvj li. xxv d.		
x li.	v li.	
xx li.	iiij li.	
x li.	iij li.	
xviij li.	Hygins ij bulls, ij buls, j stere	
	j bull	
Sold at St. James[?] fayre j red cow		xvj s. viij d.
Sold to Mr Gyffords baly[21] iij kyne		lv s.

8 f. 7 v. B The 14 of July

Remayneth in my cosyn Hygyns handes	vij li. xij s. j d.

9 f. 12. B

j stere	xvj s.	
x bath[?]	xj li. v s. vj d.	xxx li. x s. vj d.
xxx kyne	xxvij li. x s.	

10 f. 13. E [*Probably early 1545*][22]

Memorandum I had in my pastur the xix day of Marche xj besse and j bullocke and iij weyners the which I kept in my pasture all the wynter
Item I weyned ij calves the xixth of Marche
Lost j blak taggyd kow

[11 f. 13. F] Sold j bulloke that I kept all wynter	xxij s. viij d.
Sold old Herytage	xvij s.
Item lost j taggyd cow	
Sold the wenelyng bulchin	xij s.

[19] Dated by their position between the 1544 and 1545 items.
[20] Preceded by a blank space.
[21] Called Benet (214).
[22] It precedes the 1545 account (12), and does not fit any other year.

[*Cattle in 1545*]

12 f. 13 v. Emtes anno (xxxvj H)^{er} 1545

Coventre market 3	Bought the xx day of Marche iij blake	
	kyne at xij s. viij d. the pece. Sum	xxxviij s.
	Spent at the same tyme ij s. j d.	ij s. j d.
Coventre 20	Bought (at Cov)^{er} the xxvijth daye	
	of Marche xx Welshe kyne and	
	heyfers at xij s. iiij d. the pece.	
	Sum	xij li. vj s. viij d.
(Wormlyton 4	Bought the fyrst daye of Aprill at	
	Wormeleyton ij oxen	xxxviij s. viij d.
	and j stere	xiiij s. ij d)^{er}
Drayton[23]	Bought the ij of Aprill j cow price	xij s. iij d.
2	and j cow	xj s. ij d.
	Spent	vj d.
Nowrthend 1	Bought the iiijth of Aprill j bull pric	xiij s. ij d.
Warmyngton 1	Bought the xth of Aprill j brusyd cow	
	pric	vj s. viij d.
Walls[24] 2	Bought the xvijth of Aprill ij oxen	
	prec'	xliiij s.
Walls 11	Bought the xvijth of Aprill xj oxen	
	at xv s. viij d. the pec	viij li. xij s. iiij d.
Walls 38	Bought the xvijth of Aprill xxxviij	
	kyne at xiij li. the schore	xxiiij li. xiiij s.
Tomworth 8	Bowght the xxiijth of Aprill j blake	
	cow xiij s. iiij d. and j broune cow	
	xij s. viij d. and j bryndyd cow	
	xiij s. viij d. and ij blake heyvers	} v. li. vj s. vj d.
	xxiij s. and j blake dunnyshe cow	
	xij s. viij d. and j blake cow	
	xij s. vj d.	
	Item spent in charges ther (ij s.	
	viij d.)^{er}	ij s. viij d.
Barkeswell 1	Bought the xxiiijth of Aprill one	
	grett blake cowe	xiiij s.
Coventre	Bought the xxiiijth of Aprill ij sters	xxij s. iiij d.
Market	Item xx^{ti} kyne	xiij li. iij s. iiij d.
30	Item iiij oxen	iij li. iiij d.
	Item ij oxen	xxxvj s. iiij d.
	Item j blake oxe	xviij s. viij d.
	Item one cowe	xij s. x d.
	Item ij sters	xxij s. iiij d.
	Spent the same tyme	iiij s. vj d.
		80 li. 6 s. j d.

[23] Not identified; from the context, Market Drayton, Shropshire, is unlikely.

[24] Wall, Staffordshire.

[f. 14. B]

Barkeswell 1	Bought the viijth of May j blake cow	xij s. viij d.
Avone Dasset 1	Bought the viijth of May j red bulchyn	viij s. viij d.
Compton[25] 1	Bought of Gryffyn the viijth of May	
	j blake stere	xiiij s.
Coventre 5	Bought the xvth of Maye ij kyne	xxv s.
	Item iij sters	xlij s.
	For dryvyng	x d.
Bremycham	Bought the xxijth of Maye x kyne	
	and j bull at merkes.[26] Sum	viij li. vj s. viij d.
13	Item for a cow and a stere	xxj s. x d.
	For toll and costes	xij d.
	For dryvyng	xij d.
Coventre	Bought the xxviijth of Maye ij kyne	xxvij s.
2	Spent and dryvyng	xiij d.
2	Spencers ij kyne	xxvj s. iiij d.
Coventre	Bought the vjth of June viij sters at	
	xiij s. ij d. the pec. Sum	v li. v s. iiij d.
10	Item ij runtes at xvj s. the pec. Sum	xxxij s.
	Spent ther	ij s.
Coventre	Bought the xijth of June (viij)^{er} iiij	
	oxen at xxj s. viij d. the pece	iiij li. vj s. viij d.
10	Item iij oxen at xxj s. the pec	iij li. iij s. iiij d. [*sic*]
	Item ij oxen	xxxviij s.
	Item j brynded oxe	xviij s. j d.
	Spent there	xiiij d.
Coventre	Bought the xixth of June iij kyne	xxxiiij s. iiij d.
13	Item iij kyne	xxxix s. vj d.
	Item vij kyne	iiij li. xiiij s.
	Spent	ij s. viij d.
		41 li. 1 s. 11 d.[27]

[f. 14 v. A]

Salop and	Bought the xxixth of June xxxvij	
Chester 37	oxen	xxxj li. xiij s. iiij d.
Coventre	Bought the xth of July j blake and	
	j browne cow	xxvij s. viij d.
4	Item j ster	xxviij s.
	(Item ij kyne	xxvij s. viij d.
		35 li. 16 s. 8 d.)[28]

34 li. 9 s.

[25] Probably Fenny Compton, Warwickshire.
[26] For *market*?
[27] Altered to *41 li. 19 s. 5 d.*
[28] Inserted and then erased.

Avene[29] 2	Bought the xth of July of Jhon Hygyns ij oxen prec'	xliiij s.
Barkeswell 3	Bought the ix of August ij kyne	xxvij s. vj d.
	Item j ster	xvij s.
Compton 2	Bought the xvjth of August ij runtes	xxxvj s.
Coventre 3	Bought the iiijth of September iij kyne at	xxxvj s. j d.
Dassett 2	Bought the xviijth of Septembre of Gryffyn ij kyne	xxx s.
	Summa	xliij li. xix s. viij d.

13 f. 15. Besse Sold Anno 1545 [*margin*][30]

Dassett 1	Lost j cow		
Banbery 4	Sold the ijth of June j cowe and calfe	xviij s.	
	Sold at Banbery the vth of June ij kyne and calvs	xxxj s. viij d.	xx d.
	and one old bruseld cow	ix s.	
Coventre 20	Sold at Coventre the vjth of June xx kyne	xvj li. iij s. iiij d.	ij s. iiij d.
Shipston Faire 6	Sold the xjth of June v kyne	iiij li. iij s. iiij d.	xij d.
	Item to Tharward j stere	xx s.	
Banbery 6	Sold the xviijth of June vj kyne	iiij li. xiiij s. ij d.	xij d.
Bokyngham 14	Sold the xxvijth x gret kyne at xvij s. viij d. the cow. Summa	ix li. vj s. viij d.	iiij s.
	Item iiij hefers at xvj s. the cow. Summa	iij li. iiij s.	
Ward[31] 9	Sold the vjth of July vj oxen	vij li.	
	Item ij lene oxen	xl s.	
	Item j cow and calf	xvij s.	
Cheping Norton 2	Sold the vijth of July ij heyfers	xxxij s.	xx d.
Banbery 4	Sold the ixth of July ij heyfers	xxvij s.	
	Item j bryndyd stere	xiiij s.	viij d.
	Item j fallowed cowe	xvj s. viij d.	
Dasset 3	Kyld j heyfer		
	Item sold to Mr. Gyffords bayly j stere	xvj s.	
(Northampton)^{er}	Item sold to Brybs j blake heyfer	xvij s.	
Northampton 4	Sold the xxvth of July j cow	xix s. viij d.	
	Item j (cow)^{er} haukyd old cow	xvij s. viij d.	xviij d.

[29] Presumably Avon Dassett, the next village south of Burton Dassett.

[30] This column of marginal figures is unheaded, but probably gives the costs for each sale, as there are no figures against the places nearest to Burton Dassett.

[31] Probably Wardington, Oxfordshire.

	Item j heyfer	xvj s.	
	Item j blake stere	xvj s iiij d.	
Dassett 1	Sold to Brybs the xxixth of July a blake heyfer	xj s. vj d.	
Dasset 38(41)^{er}	Sold the vijth of August to Mr. Wylliam Gyfford xxvij kyne at xviij s. iiij d. the pece	xxiiij li. xv s.	
	Item sold to hym xj runtes at xx s. vj d. the pec	xj li. v s. vj d.	
Dedmarton 3	Sold ij sters the xth of August	xxix s.	xij d.
	Item lost j blake heyfer calfe, and skyne	iiij s.	
(Banbery)^{er} Dassett 4	Sold the xviijth of August j stere	xv s.	
	Item j cow	xvj s.	
	Item ij steres	xxxvij s.	
Dassett 1	Sold the vijth of Septembre j cow to Mr. Wylliam Gyffordes bayle	xvij s.	
Northampton	Sold the viijth of Septembre iij runtes	iij li. vij s.	
14	Item vij kyne and iij steres at xvij s. viij d. the pece. Summa	ix li. xiiij s. iiij d.	
Banbery 1	Sold the xjth of September j stere	xij s.	
	Summa	119 li. 18 s. 1 d.	

[f. 15 v.]

Banbery 2	Sold the xvjth of Septembre j cutayl and j blake cowe	xxvj s. iiij d.	iiij d.
Banbery 1	Sold the viijth of October j pyed cow	xv s.	ij d.
Dassett 50	Sold the ix of October to Mr. Wylliam Gyfford xx^{ti} oxen at xxiiij s. the pec	xxiiij li.	
	Item to hym the same tyme x runtes at xxij s. the pec	xj li.	
	Item to hym the same tyme xix kyne, j runt at xviij s. iiij d. the pece. Summa	xviij li. vj s. viij d.	
Dassett 12	Sold the iiijth of Decembre to Mr. Wylliam Gyfford xij oxen at xxx s. the pec	xviiij li.	
(Dassett	Sold the viijth of (Octobre)^{er} Decembre to Edlow ij kyne at xviij s. the pec	xxxvj s.)^{er}	

Dassett 3	Sent to my wyffes mother j haukyd bull and j blake stere and to my brother sent j blake bull	xv s.
Dassett 1	Kyld for my house j blake bull	
Dassett 18	Sold the xiiijth of Januarye to Mr. Wylliam Gyfford xiij oxen	xvj li. xij s. viij d.
	Item to hym the same tyme v kyne at xviij s. the pece. Summa	iiij li. x s.
Banbery	Sold the iiijth of Maye j blake cow	xxij s.
2	Item j browne cow	xx s.
Banbery	Sold the xxvjth of August j cow	xviij s.
2	Sold the [*blank*] j cow	xviij s. viij d.
	Item reservyd for my owne store ij mylche kyne	
	Summa 99 li. 4 s.	

14 f. 18. B [*item erased*] Venditis anno (xxv)^{er} 1545[32]

Stonlie 3	Sold the xxijth daie of Aprill j stere and ij bullockes price lvj s.	lvj s.

15 f. 18. C

	xx^{o} die marcii anno 1546[33] in Halls Feld the cattell that I kept all the wynter	
j	Of the smyth of Avne Dassett j hefer	j Spensers cow
3	Of Hygins iij sters	j Higins cow
(..)[34]	Of the last yers kyne bought iiij kyne	
	Of my owne j bulchin and ij younge heyfers	
	Delyvered to Gryffyn of Comton vj heyfers to breke wheroff j ys dede	

[*right margin*] Delyverd to Staner[?] iij steres. 1[?] dyed.

Heritage Feld

xj	Of mylche kyne x and j wenelyng	
	Sold j blake cow	xxj s. iiij d.
	Sold j rede cow	xxij s. viij d.
	(Delyvered to Gryffyn to somer. wenlyng)^{er}	
	Item there dyed j red mylche cowe	

[32] i.e. from the 1545 purchases, though this is presumably April 1546. Stonlie is probably a person (as 2), rather than the village three miles south of Coventry.

[33] From the sequence, this must be the spring of 1546, not 1546/7.

[34] Marginal numbers erased.

Sold the xiij[th] of January j blake cow	xxvj s.
Sold the last of January j mylche cow	xxx s.
Item the same tyme j browne mylche cow	xxv s.
(Bought the last of Septembre of Thomas Burbery iij sters and j heyfer	xxx s. viij d.)[er]

77 [*at foot of page; head of cattle*]

Cattle in 1546

16 f. 18. D [*Probably for cattle purchases*]

Delyvered to Higyns 30 li.; 60 li.; [?2 li.]; 8 li.; 3 li.; . .; 14 li.; 20 li.; 6 li.

17 f. 18 v. Emptis anno 1546

Salop, Chester and Walls	Bought the vij[th] of Marche ij oxen	xxxiij s.
	Item ij sters	xxvj s. viij d.
	Item ij kyne	xxvj s. j d.
55	Item j cow	xiiij s. v d.
	Item j cow	xj s. viij d.
	Item j cow	xiiij s. viij d.
	Item j cow	xvj s.
	Item j cow	xiij s.
	Item j cow	xiij s. viij d.
	Item j cow	xiij s. viij d.
	Item j cow	xiiij s.
	Item j cow	xv s.
	Item j shott	ix s. iiij d.
	Item j cow	xvj s.
	Item j bull	xv s. iiij d.
	Item ij kyne	xxix s. iiij d.
	Item j cow the xx day of Marche[35]	xiiij s.
	Item j cow	xiij s.
	Item j cow	xiiij s. viij d.
	Item j cow	xiij s.
	Item j cow	xj s. x d.
	Item ij kyne	xxij s. viij d.
	Item j cow	xiiij s. xj d.
	Item j cow	xv s.
	Item j cow	xvj s.
	Item j cow	xiij s. iiij d.
	Item j cow	xij s.
	Item j cow	xiiij s.
	Item j cow	xiij s. iiij d.
	Item iiij kyne	liij s. viij d.
	Item iij kyne	xxxvj s.
	Item j cow	xiij viij d.

[35] Perhaps for *10 March*.

	Item j cow	xij s. viij d.
	Item j cow	xiij s. ij d.
	Item j cow	xij s. viij d.
	Item ij kyne	xxvj s.
	Item ij kyne	xxvij s. viij d.
	Item j cow	xiij s. vj d.
	Item iij kyne	xlvj s. vj d.
	Item j cow	xiiij s. viij d.
	Spent at Salope, Chester and Wall pro toll	xxiij s. j d.
		Summa paginis 28 li. 14 s. 6d.

f. 19 Emptis anno 1546

Hampton[36]	Bought the xx day of Marche iiij kyne	iij li.
16	Item ij kyne	xxxiiij s.
	Item x kyne	vj li. xviij s. iiij d.
Bremicham	Bought (at Bremycham)^{er} the xxth of Marche j cow	xj s. j d.
2	Item j stere	xiiij s.
Coventre	Bought the xxth daye of Marche j bull	xiij s.
47	Item ij kyne and calves	xxix s. vj d.
	Item j cow	xvj s. ij d.
	Item j cow	xiij s.
	Item vj kyne	iiij li. xj s. vj d.
	Item xx kyne	xiiij li.
	Item xij kyne	viij li. xvj s.
	Item iij kyne	xxxiij s. iiij d.
	Item j cow	x s. vj d. [?]
Barkeswell	Bought the xxth of Marche j lost cowe	x s.
5	Item ij oxen	xl s.
	Item ij oxen	xxxiij s. iiij d.
	Spent at Coventre the xxth of Marche	iij s. iiij d.
Coventre 3	Bought the xxviijth of Marche iij kyne	xxxix s. iiij d.
Rodwey 1	Bought the ij day of Aprill j cow and her calfe	xviij s.
(Hampton and Shropshire)^{er}	Bought the xth of Aprill (xxxxij)^{er} j cow	xv s. iiij d.
Coventre 2	Item j cowe	xiiij s.
	Spent at Coventre	v s.
Hampton and	Bought the xth of Aprill vij kyne	v li. ij s. j d.
Shropshire	Item ij kyne	xxvj s. iij d.
30	Item j cow	xv s. viij d.

[36] Probably Hampton-in-Arden, Warwickshire.

	Item j cow	xv s. iiij d.
	Item j cow	xiij s. viij d.
	Item j cow	xij s. viij d.
	Item j cow	xiiij s. iiij d.
	Item j cow	xj s. xj d.
	Item iij kyne	xxvj s. v d.
	Item vj kyne	iiij li. xvij s.
	Item iij kyne	xlj s. vj d.
	Item ij kyne	xxvj s. ij d.
	Item ij kyne	xxvj s.
	Spent at Hampton and Wuyghorne[37]	viij s. vj d.
		Summa paginis 77 li. 14 d.
[f. 19 v.]		
Warwyke	Bought the first of Maye j bryndyd oxe	xxj s.
Dassett 2	Bought the vj^th^ of Maye ij blake oxen	xxxix s.
	Spent at Warwyke the fyrst of Maye	xiiij d.
Tomworthe	Bought the xxix^th^ of Aprill j cow	xvij s.
21	Item j cow	xvj s.
	Item j cow	xv s. iiij d.
	Item j cow	xiiij s.
	Item j cow	xiij s. iiij d.
	Item ij kyne	xxviij s.
	Item j kow	xiij s. iiij d.
	Item j cow	xiij s.
	Item ij kyne	xxx s. vj d.
	Item j cow	xvj s.
	Item iiij oxen	iij li. xviij s.
	Item ij oxen	xxxvj s.
	Item ij oxen	xl s.
	Item j oxe	xviij s. iiij d.
	Item spent at Tomworth	iij s. vj d.
(Shropshire)^er^		
Hampton 18	Bought the vth of May vj kyne and j bull	v li. v s.
	Item v kyne and ij oxen	v li. vij s. iiij d.
	Item iiij oxen	iij li. xiiij s. vj d.
Shropshire	Bought the vth of Maye xiij kyne	viij li. xix s.
19	Item ij kyne	xxviij s. ij d.
	Item iij oxen	iij li. xvj s. ix d.
Coventre[38]	Bought the vij^th^ of Maye j cow	xv s. iiij d.
3	Item j bull	xij s. j d.
	Item j sturke	vij s. viij d.
	Expenses at Hampton and Shropshire	ix s.
		(Summa xlviij li. vj s. ij d.)^er^
64 [*total head*]		Summa lj li. vij s. iiij d.

[37] Probably *Wigorn*, for Worcester.

[38] The next three lines were entered twice, and erased once.

[f. 20. A]

Bremychame Fayre 28	Bought the iij^{d} of June [*Ascension Day Fair*] ij kyne	xxx s.
	Item j cow	xv s.
	Item j cow	xv s.
	Item j cow	xv s. vj d.
	Item j cow	xvj s.
	Item j cow	xiiij s.
	Item x oxen	ix li. vj s. viij d.
	Item j oxe	xviij s. viij d.
	Item x oxen	xj li. xj s. viij d.
Coventre 4	Bought the iijth of June ij kyne	xxx s. viij d.
	Item ij sters	xxiij s. vj d.
	Exspenses at Bremycham	ij s.
	To the bocher of Kynton for an exchange of ij kyne for ij oxen and ij s. to boote	ij s.
Bramley[39] 4	Bought the xxiiijth of August ij oxen	1 s.
	Item ij oxen	xlij s. iiij d.
	Spent	iij s. iiij d.
Coventre 2	Bought the xxviijth of August ij oxen	xxxvj s.
	(6 li. 11 s. 8 d.)^{er}	xxxvj li. xiiij s.
Heliden 2	Bought the xjth of October ij sters	xxxj s. iiij d.
Dassett 3	Bought the xjth of October ij sters and j heyfer	xxxj s.
Tomworth 11	Bought (of Tho)^{er} the xiijth of Octobre j oxe	xxxj s. viij d.
	Item iiij sters	lvij s.
	Item ij oxen	xxxvij s.
	Item ij oxen	xlvj s. viij d.
	Item ij oxen	xlviij s. viij d.
	Item spent there and comyng home	iij s. iiij d.
Dassett and Northend 9	Bought the xvth of October of Thomas Makepes ij sters	xxxvj s.
	Item of Wylliam Makepese vij sters	vj li. xj s.
	63 [*head*]	Summa paginis lix li. ix s.
		[*in corner*] 22 li. 14 s. 8d.

[f. 20 v.]

Brigenorth 16	Bought the xviijth of October v heyfers	iij li. x s.
	Item ix sters and heyfers	vj li. vj s.
	Item ij heyfers	xxvj s. ij d.
	Spent there and in brynging them home	iiij s. j d.
Helyden 1	Bought the xxvjth of October j cow bryndyd	xvij s.
		(11 li. 6 s. 3 d.)^{er}

[39] Unidentified.

Northende 1	Bought the xxvijth of October j blake stere	xvj s.	
Warwyke 3	Bought the xxviijth of October ij oxen	xlvj s.	
	Item j oxe	xxiiij s.	
	Item spent there	xij d.	
Dassett	Item gevyn the xxviijth of Novembre pro pace in domine	vj s. viij d.	

Summa totalis animali 309. Summa paginis xvj li. xvj s. xj d.
Summa totalis ijcxliij li. ix. s.[40]

	Item gevyn to Hygyns for part of his labor and travayll	xxvj s. viij d.	

18 f. 21. Besse sold anno 1546

Barkeswell 3	Lost at Barkeswell iij kyne that dyed		
Dassett 3	Item lost at Dasset by deth iij kyne that dyed		
Banbery 1	Sold the xiijth of Maye one cowe	xxiiij s.	
Abyngton 20	Sold the ixth of June xxti kyne	xx li. x s.	v s.
	(Item j cow	xx s.)er	
Dassett 1	Kyld in to my howse 1 shott		
Coventre 39	Sold the xxvth of June vj oxen	viij li.	5 s.
	Item iiij kyne and calves	iiij li. iiij s.	
	Item xx kyne	xix li.	
	Item viij kyne	vij li. vj s.	
Dassett 5	Sold the xxijth of July to my brother v kyne and calfes	v li. ij s.	
Dassett 1	Lost at Dassett j cow that dyed		
Woodstocke 46	Sold the xxijth of Julye xxti kyne	xx li.	5 s.
	Item there other xxti kyne	xix li. iiij s.	
	Item more sold there vj oxen	viij li xij d.	
Wynslow 9	Sold the xth of August vj oxen	vij li. xix s. vj d.	vj s.
	Item sold iij kyne	iij li. iiij s.	
Banberye 2	Sold the xijth of August j cow	xvij s. x d.	
	Item one heyfer	xvj s.	
Northampton 14	Sold the xvth of August ij oxen	liij s. iiij d.	xij d.
	Item sold the same tyme xij kyne	xj li.	
Banberye (4)er 3	Sold the xxvjth of August j stere	xviij s. ij d.	
	Item j cow	xix s. vj d.	
	Item j heyfer	xvij s.	
Dassett 1	Kyld in to my house and savyd j cow		

[40] The correct sum of the recorded page totals is £233 8s. 11d.

Banberye 10	Sold the ij of Septembre viij kyne at xix s. the pece and ij heyfers at xv s. vj d. the pece. Summa	ix li. iij s.	iiij d.
Dassett 2	Ther was stolen at Dassett j cow and j cow that was not brought owt of Shropshere		
160 [*head*]		150 li. 19 s. 2 d.	

[f. 21 v.]

Northampton 17	Sold the viijth of September xv kyne at xix s. the pece. Summa	xiiij li. v s.	iij s.
	Item ij oxen	xlix s. viij d.	
Compton 1	Lost at Compton j stere		
Dassett 1	Lost at Dassett j cuttayll cowe that dyed		
Harborow[41] 20	Sold the ix of October xx^{ti} kyne	xix li. xiij s. iiij d.	iij s. iiij d.
Dassett 1	Kyld into my house the xxiijth of October j bull		
Dedyngton 19	Sold the xjth of Novembre vij kyne	vij li. xj s. viij d.	
	Item xij oxen at xxvj s. the pece	xv li. xij s.	
Dassett 2	Sold the [*blank*] of Novembre ij oxen	iij li. ij s.	ij s. iiij d.
Brakley 7	Sold the xxxth of Novembre vij sters	vij li. v s.	xx d.
Dasset 1	Kyld and savyd into my house j cow the iiijth of Decembre		
Northampton 2	Sold the viijth of Decembre j oxe and j stere	lvij s.	xvj d.
Dassett 1	Lost at Dassett j browne cowe that dyed		
Dassett 1	Kyld into my house the xxiijth of December j bull		
(Dassett)[42]	Sold the xiijth of Januari ij oxen	lix s.	
Banbery 12	Item ij oxen	lix s.	
	Item j cow	xviij s.	
	Item (ij kyne)^{er} j cow	xxiiij s. (1 s.; xxiiij s.)^{er}	20 d.
	Item v oxen	viij li.	
	Item j cow	xx s. viij d.	

[41] Probably Market Harborough, Leicestershire.
[42] Erased, with pointing hand to previous entry.

Dassett 1	(sold)^{er} Kyld into my howse j bull	
Dassett 10	Sold the xxj of January x oxen at xxviij s. the pec	xiiij li.
Dassett 2	Sold the xxviijth of January ij oxen	lj s. viij d.
Dassett 1	(Sold the last of January j blake oxe	xxvj s.)^{er}
	Kyld and savyd into my house the xxjth of Marche i kow	
Summa animalum 99		Summa paginis j^{c} vj li. viij s.

[f. 22]

Coventre	Sold the xth of June xx sters and iij oxen	xxiij li xiij s. iiij d.
40	Item x heyfers at xviij s. vj d. the pec	vij li. viij d.
	Item ij oxen at liiij s.	liiij s.
	Item ij oxen	iij li. xiij s. iiij d.
	Item ij sters and j heyfer	lvij s.
	Item ther dyed j gret dunne old cow the xxxth of Septembre	
	(Gevyn to Als j blake heyfer)[43]	
	(Item geven to Cutbard j red heyfer)^{er}	
	Item kyld into my house j blacke cow	
	Item kyld into my house the xxvjth of December j blak bull	
	Item sold the xijth of January j cortall cow	xiij s. viij d.
	Item sold to Byker ij oxen at	liiij s.
		Summa xliiij li. xiij s.

19 f. 83 v. C [*Cattle Summary and Valuation, 1546-7*][44]

Remayneth 21 die januari in the pastur (x)^{er} lxij besse, wherof xxxij heyfers and .. sters and ix oxen and iiij kyne and a cow with her calfe ar to be sold, and [ij?] oxen for my brother, ij bulls for myself and j yerling for Alys and j morkyn and viij kyne for the payll.
Sold iij oxen for lj s. viij d. (Item j oxe xxvj s.)^{er}

20 f. 83 v. D[45]

[*Top margin*] For my brother ij oxen	
Rem. [?] xxxij steres and heyfers at	xxxij li.
and ix oxen at xxxiij s. iiij d. the pece	xj li.
a cow and her calfe	xviij s.

[43] Erased, but marked *stet* in margin.

[44] Dated by comparison with **18**, and from the numbers given. Morkyn: a beast that dies by disease or mischance [*O.E.D.*].

[45] The right margin has the values: *xx^{xx}; xiij^{xx}; iiij^{xx}; ij^{xx}; ix^{xx}*.

and iiij kyne at	iiij li.
In the canvas bage	xl li.
In gold	xiij li.
Mr Grey oweth	xx li.
In drybletes	xxvj li.

[j^{c}l] xiiij li. [*£164 by addition*]

21 f. 25 [*Money for Cattle Purchase, 1547*]

Money delyvered to Thomas Hygynson to bye lean besse and by hym received in the first yere of the raygne of Kynge Edward the vjth [*1547*] as followeth:

Delyvered to Thomas Hygynson the xvijth of February in the yere aforesaid	xx li.
By me Thomas Hyginson[46]	
Delyvered to Thomas Higinson the xijth of Marche by thandes of my wyffe	xvij li.
By me Thomas Hyginson	
Delyvered to Thomas Higynson the xxixth of Marche	xxx li.
By me Thomas Hygynson	
Delyvered to Thomas Higynson the vijth of Aprill	xxvj li.
By me Thomas Hygynson	
Delyvered to Thomas Hygynson the xvjth of Maye	xxvj li.
By me Thomas Hygynson	
Delyvered to Thomas Hygynson the xxijth of Maye	iij li.
By me Thomas Hygynson	
Delyvered to Thomas Hygynson the xth of June	xlij li. xvij s. iiij d.
By me Thomas Hygynson	
Delyvered to Thomas Higynson the xxiijth of July	xx li.
By me Thomas Hygynson	
Sent to Thomas Hygynson the last of July by hys servant and delyvered hym myself the vth of August	vij li.
By me Thomas Hygynson	

22 f. 25 v. [*Miscellaneous Cattle Entries, 1547*][47]

Bought of Ryly of Compton by Gryffyn j cow	xvj s.
Item Gylles Spenser hath a bryndyd heyfer for me	
For my brother [tuke?] ij oxen sold the iiij of August for	lv s.
Of Higyns ij kyne	
Bought of Thomas Gryffyn of Compton j cow	xv s.

23 f. 26. Besse bought by Thomas Hyginson in anno primo regni regis Edwardi sexti [*1547*] as here after apperyth

Thamworth 4	Imprimis bought the xvth of Marche iiij oxen	v li. ij s.

[46] All countersigned in Hygynson's hand, in a formal style.

[47] Dated by comparison with the base of f. 27 v. (23). This item is retained in its order in the volume, though it may have been written after 23.

Hamtun	Item ij oxen	xlvij s. iiij d.
6	Item j oxe	xxv s. iiij d.
	Item j oxe	xx s.
	Item j oxe	xx s.
	Item j cow	xv s. x d.
Hampton	Bought the xviiijth of Marche iiij kyne	iij li. iiij s.
22	Item ij kyne	xxx s. ij d.
	Item j cow	xiiij s. iiij d.
	Item vj kyne at xv s. viij d.	iiij li. viij s.
	Item ij kyne	xxviij s. viij d.
	Item iiij kyne	iij li. iiij s.
	Item j kowe	xij s. viij d.
	Item ij oxen	xlj s. (xxxix s.)^{er}
	Spent at Tamworth for tolle etc.	v d.
	At Hampton for tolle and exspenses	xvj d.
	At Hampton for toll and exspenses	iij s. j d.
Hampton	Bought the ijth of Aprill xx kyne	xv li. x s.
39	Item vj kyne and j bull at xiij s. vj d.	v li. xviij d.
	Item vj kyne at xv s. iiij d. the pec	iiij li. xij s.
	Item ij heyfers	xxvj s.
	Item j kowe	xvj s. ij d.
	Item ij kyne	xxx s. viij d.
	Item j stere	x s.
	Item for toll	xiij d.
	Spentt	xij d.
	Costes and dryvyng home	xxiij d.
	Item for dyvers necessaryes	v s. ij d.
Summa animali 71		Summa paginis xlviij li. xiij s. viij d.

[f. 26 v.] The xxth of Aprill

Hampton	Item j cow	xv s. iiij d.
38	Item j cow	xv s.
	Item j cow	xv s. vj d.
	Item j cow	xv s. iiij d.
	Item j cow	xiiij s.
	Item j cow	xiij s. vj d.
	Item j cow	xiiij s.
	Item j cow	xv s. x d.
	Item j cow	xiij s. x d.
	Item j cow	xij s. vj d.
	Item j cow	xvj s.
	Item j cow	xv s. viij d.
	Item j cow	xiiij s. vj d.
	Item iiij kyne	iij li. iiij s.
	Item vij kyne at xvj s. j d.	v li. xij s. vij d.
	Item ij kyne	xxx s. j d.
	Item iij kyne at xv s. viij d.	xlvij s.
	Item ij kyne	xxviij s. iiij d.

	Item ij kyne	xxviij s. viij d.
	Item j cow	xiiij s. viij d.
	Item ij kyne	xxix s.
	Item j kow	xvj s.
	Item j cow	xiiij s.
	Item for tolle, costes and charges	xj s.
	Summa paginis	xxix li. x s. iiij d.

[f. 27.] The xix^th of Maye

Bremycham [42]	For viij oxen	vij li. xij s.
	Item vij kyne at xv s. viij d.	v li. ix s. viij d.
	Item xij kyne at xv s. and j d. the pec	ix li. xij d.
	Item vij kyne at xiiij s. the pec	iiij li. xviij s.
	Item j cow	xv s.
	Item j cow	xiij s. iiij d.
	Item ij kyne	xxviij s. x d.
	Item j oxe	xv s.
	Item j oxe	xviij s. viij d.
	Item j runt and j stere	xxvij s.
	Spent	xij d.
	Item for gresse	xiiij d.
	For chatern	iiij d.
	Bought the same tyme of Jhon and Jhon Hygynson xxiij kyne at xiij s. vj d. the pec	xvj li. xiij s. vj d.
	Item iiij oxen at xviij s. iiij d. the pec	iij li. xvij s. iiij d.
Coventre 19	Bought the xth of June ix oxen	ix li. xv s.
	Item iij oxen	iiij li. xij d.
	Item ij oxen	xxxj s.
	Item j oxe	xvj s. viij d.
	Item ij kyne	xxx s.
	Item j cow	xv s. iiij d.
	Item j cow	xiiij s. iiij d.
Coventre 33	Bought the xvj^th of June ij oxen	xliiij s.
	Item ij oxen	xxxviij s.
	Item iij oxen	lv s.
	Item iij oxen	iij li. iij s.
	Item j oxe	xix s.
	Item j oxe	xvj s.
	Item xxj kyne at xv s. the pec	xvj li. v s. vj d.
	Spent for grasse and dryvyng	iiij s.
Summa animali 121	Summa paginis	99 li. 15 s. 8 d.

[f. 27 v.]

Coventre 1	Bought the xv^th of July j cow	xiiij s.
Coventre 3	Bought the xxix^th of July iij kyne	xlvi s.

Hampton 30	Bought the vjth of August x kyne at xiiij s. vj d. the pece	vij li. v s.
	Item iij kyne at xiij s. viij d. the pec	xlj s.
	Item iij kyne at xv s. the pec and iiij d. farder	xlv s. iiij d.
	Item iij kyne at xiij s. viij d. and iiij d. farder	xlj s. iiij d.
	Item v kyne at xiiij s. iiij d. the pec	iiij li. xj s. viij d.
	Item j cow at xiij s. iiij d.	xiij s. iiij d.
	Item ij kyne at	xxvij s. iiij d.
	Item j cow at	xv s. iiij d.
	Item j cow at	xv s.
	Item j red pied heyfer at	xij s.
	Item for gres costes and xx easers [?]	iiij s. iiij d.
	Summa	xxiiij li. xj s. viij d.
	Item I bought myself of Ryle j cow	xvj s.
	and of Thomas Gryffyn j cow	xv s.
Summa totalis animali ij^{c}lxvj.	Summa totalis huius anni emptis	ij^{c}xiij li. xvij s. ij d.[48]

24 f. 28 [*Cattle Sales, 1547*]

Coventre 6	Sold the xth of June v kyne	v li. iij s. iiij d.
	Item j kow	xviij s. viij d.
Dassett 8	Sold the xxxth of June viij kyne	viij li. viij s.
	Sold the xviijth of July vij kine	vij li. xij d.
8	Item ther dyed j cow	
Dassett 1	Item ther dyed j cow	
Dassett 20	Sold the xxth of July xx^{ti} kyne	xxij li. vj s. viij d.
Woodstocke 29	Sold the xxijth of July xx^{ti} kyne	xxij li.
	Item j kow	xx s. ij d.
	Item iij kyne	lix s.
	(Item ij sters	xxxvij s.)^{er}
	Item j(ij)^{er} heyfer	xix s. (xxxviij s.)^{er}
	Item ij heyfers	xxxviij s.
	Item ij kyne	xl s.
Dassett 80	Sold the xxixth of July to Wylliam Rayner of Uxbryge lxxx kyne at xxj li. the schore, wherof delivered xv in hand and xv more he must fetche the xixth of August and xv more the ixth of September and xv more the xxviijth of September and xx more the xxth of Octobre. Sum	lxxxviij li.
Dassett 5	Sold the iiijth of August j stere	xvj s. viij d.
	Item iiij oxen	v li. vj s. viij d.

[48] The correct sum of the recorded page totals is £214 12s. 4d.

Dassett 2	Ther j cow (the)^er dyed the xij of August	
	Item j cow dyed the xvj^th of August	
Banbery 2	Sold the xviij^th of August ij kyne	xxxv s.
Dassett 1	Ther dyed j oxe the 4 of Septembre	
Dassett 20	Sold the xvj^th of Septembre to Wylliam Rayner of Uxbridge xx^ti oxen at xxxiiij s. the pec	xxxiiij li.
Summa animali 182		Summa ij^c iij li. xij s. ij d.[49]

[f. 28 v.]

Dassett 18[50]	Sold the xviij^th of October xx^ti oxen	xxix li.
	[*Margin*] Rebat lvj s. for ij of them	
Dassett 39[52]	Sold the xx^th of October xxix kyne	xxvij li. x s.[51]
	Item x oxen	xiij li. x s.
Dassett 2	Sold the iiij^th of August[53] ij oxen	lv s.
(Dasset 1	Kyld and saved in to my house j blake (rede)^er cow)[54]	
Banbery [4]	Sold the xij^th of January j brynded cow	xviij s. viij d.
	Item j brynded heyfer	xvij s. iiij d.
	Item j blake cow	xvj s. iiij d.
	Item j blake cow	xvj s. iiij d.
Dassett 3	Memorandum that ther was j cow that came not here and j cow sent back agayne and j cow was stolen or lost	
		Summa lxxiij li. viij s. viij d.
Banbery 1	Sold the fyrst of January j cow	xv s.
Dassett 3	Item ther dyed the xx^th of February j blake cow	
	Item kyld into my house the [*blank*] of January j bull	
	Item ther dyd the iiij^th of Maye j old blake cow	
	Item sold the xj^th of June ij oxen	iij li. iij s.

25 f. 29. A Besse by me Peter Temple in anno ij^do Edwardi vj^th [*1548*] bought as folowes

Inprimis of the carpenter at Kynston j red cow	xiiij s.

[49] Changed from *ij^c lxxiij li. xij s. ij d.*
[50] Altered from *20.*
[51] Altered from *xxviij li. x s.* and the *i* in *xxix* inserted.
[52] Altered from *40.*
[53] Perhaps in error for *November.*
[54] Erased, but marked *stet.*

	Item at Warwyke j rede heyfer	xv s. iiij d.
	Item at Warwyke fayer[55] j oxe	xxj s. iiij d.
Shipston	Bought the xjth of June x kyne	vij li. x s.
30	Item then of Wylliam Palmer viij oxen	vij li. iiij s.
	Item then of Perkyne at markes[56] xij kyne at xiij s. x d. [?]	vij li. xvij s. iiij d.
Banbery	Bought the xiiijth of June iij oxen	iij li. xiij s. iiij d.
10	Item j old cow	xiij s. iiij d.
	Item iij heyfers and j strurke	lvij s. viij d.
	Item then of Wylkyns ij oxen	lviij s. viij d.
		xxxv li. v s. iiij d.

26 f. 29. B Money delyvered to Thomas Hygynson for to bye besse for Peter Temple gentleman anno ij^{do} regni regis Edwardi vjth [*1548*] as followeth

Delyvered to Thomas Hygynson the xxvijth of January	viij li. x s.
By me Thomas Hyggynson[57]	
Item delyvered to hym the xxvth of Marche	xlviijj li. x s.
By me Thomas Hyggynson	
Item delyvered to hym the vijth of Maye	xij li.
By me Thomas Hyggynson	
Item delyvered to hym the viijth of June	xviij li.
By me Thomas Hyggynson	
	Summa lxxxviij li.

27 f. 29 v. Besse bought by Thomas Hygynson in anno ij Edwardi vj^{ti} [*1548*] for Peter Temple as followeth

Coventre 7	Bought the vth of February iiij oxen	iiij li. xiij s. iiij d.
	Item ij oxen	xlj s. j d.
	Item j oxe	xix s. iiij d.
	For dryvyng	iiij d.
[Hampton ?]	Bought the xjth of Aprill ij runtes	xxxiiij s. iiij d.
[21]	Item j cow	xvij s. ij d.
	Item j cow	xiiij s. iiij d.
	Item j cow	xiiij s. ij d.
	Item j cow	xiiij s. viij d.
	Item j cow	xviij s.
	Item j cow	xiij s. iiij d.
	Item j cow	xv s.
	Item j cow	xiij s. iiij d.
	Item ij kyne	xxvj s. ij d.
	Item ix kyne	vij li. x s.

[55] Probably the Ascension Fair, 10 May in 1548.

[56] For *market*?

[57] All countersigned, as in 21.

	Item for costes and toll	iiij s.
Coventre	Bought xxvjth of Aprill j cow	xv s. vj d.
21	Item xx^{ti} kyne	xvj li x s.
	Item for gresse and dryvyng	xij d.
Bremycham	Bought the xth of Maye ij oxen	l s. viij d.
6	Item ij oxen	xliij s. vj d.
	Item j cow	xv s. ij d.
	Item j cow	xiij s. iiij d.
		xlvij li. xvij s. vij d.

[f. 30]

Hampton	Bought the xvth of Maye (of)^{er} xv kyne	xij li.
23	Item viij kyne	vj li. iij s.
	Item for toll and costes	iij s. viij d.
Coventre	(Item)^{er} Bought the vijth of June	
4	j cow	xvij s. ij d.
	Item j cow	xv s. viij d.
	Item j cow	xiiij s. x d.
	Item j cow	xiiij s. viij d.
Hampton	Bought x kyne at (x)^{er}	viij li. x s.
21	Item j cow	xiiij s.
	Item vj kyne	v li. ij s. viij d.
	Item ij kyne	xxvj s. viij d.
	Item j cow	xvj s. iiij d.
	Item j cow	xv s. vj d.
	Item for gress and toll	iiij s. vj d.
	Item for dryvyng	iiij d.
		xxxviij li. xviij s. x d.

28 f. 30 v. Besse of Thomas Hyginsons bying sold anno ij^{do} Edwardi vjth [*1548*] as followeth

Dassett[58]	Inprimis sold the xxvijth of June	
10	j heyfer	xxj s.
	Item to Petyver Jhon the xxixth of June ij kyne	liij s. iiij d.
	Item at Banbery the vth of Julye j cow	xxiij s. iiij d.
	Item at Banbery the xijth of July vj kyne	vj li. xvj s. viij d.
Northampton	Sold the xvth of July xix kyne	xx li. xviij s.
30[59]	Item then sold j runt	xxix s.
	Sold the xvjth of August (to Newnham)^{er} to the Bocher of Newnham x kyne	ix li. iiij s. viij d.

[58] *Banbery* erased.

[59] Altered from *29*, when the second line of this group was inserted.

Dassett 11	Sold the xxviijth of August xj kyne to Randoll of Newnham	x li. ix s.
Warwyke 10	Sold apon Bartylmew Fayre [*24 August*] at Warwyke x kyne	x li.
Dassett	Sold the xxjth of Septembre to a knave that ran a waye (xx^{ti})^{er} x kyne	(xxj li.)^{er} x s.
(21)^{er} 11	Sold to Jamys Clerke j browne lame heyfer waster	xviij s.
Banbery	Sold the xviijth of October ij oxen	lvij s. iiij d.
12	Item iiij kyne	iiij li. iiij s.
	Item j cow	xix s.
	Item iij kyne	lvj s. viij d.
	Item ij kyne	xxxvj s.
Dasset	Sold the xixth of October to Jamz Clarke j hyppyd oxe (and j blake)^{er}	xix s.
(3)^{er} 4	Item ther dyed in the pastur j oxe and j cow	
	Sold to my brother j cow that was dryven home with hys cow	xxiij s.
Banbery	Sold the xxvjth of October ij kyne	xlij s.
3	Item j cowe	xxij s.
Dedyngton 6	Item at Martynmas Fayre [*11 Nov.*] ther vj oxen	x li. xviij s. viij d.
Dassett 16[60]	Item to Randoll the 3^{d} of Decembre xvij kyne	xviij li.
	Summa	j^{c}xj li. xv s. viij d.

29 f. 31 v. A Besse of my owne bying sold in anno ij^{do} Edwardi vj^{ti} [*1548*] as followeth

Dassett	Inprimis sold the viijth of June j rede	
11	heyfer	xxv s.
	Sold the xxijth of July to James Clarke of Feny Compton then viij oxen that I bought of Wylliam Palmer	viij li. iiij s.
	Sold at Northampton the xxvth of [July] j cow	xxij s.
	Sold to Clerke of Compton the xviijth of August j cow	xix s.
Dassett 12	Sold to Jams Clerke xij kyne Welshe bought at Shipston Fayre[61]	ix li. xvij s. viij d.
(Dassett 20	Sold the xxjth of Septembre xx^{ti} kyne	xxj li.)^{er}
Banbery	Sold the xxvijth of Septembre	
3	j heyfer	xiiij s. ij d.

60 Marginal number altered from *17*, but the main number unchanged.

61 11 June. See 25.

	Item to Jamys Clerke j brynded stere	xvj s.
	Item to Benege j redde pyed heyfer	xv s.
Banbery 1	Item at Banbery the xjth of January j red stere	xx s.
	Item at Coventre Fayre[62] xiiij oxen	xvij li. vj s. viij d. (xiiij li. xij s. j d.)^{er}
	Item j old blake cow	xv s.
		xlij li. xiij s. viij d.

30 f. 82 v. C [*Money due for Cattle, 1548*][63]

Memorandum Jams Clerke oweth me for xij kyne	x li. xvij s. viij d.
Item Randoll Bocher of Daventre oweth for xj kyne	x li. ix s.
Item the bocher of Newnham oweth for (vj)^{er} ij kyne	(xvj li. xvj s.)^{er} xxxvj s.
Jamys Clerke oweth ageyne for (ij kyne)^{er} (and j stere xlviij s.)^{er}	(xvj s.)^{er}
The bocher of Asheton Stepall oweth for xx^{ti} kyne	xxj li.
Item Hygynson oweth	(xl s.)^{er} xxj s.
Thomas Makepese	l s.
Summa l li.	
Jamz oweth for ij blacke pyed kyne	(xxxviij s.)^{er} xix s.

31 f. 82 v. D [*Fitted in beside* 30]

Resceyved of James Clarke in part of payment of hys kyne xl s. and for a saddell iiij s.
Item resceyved for Jhon bord vj s. viij d.

32 f 31 v. B Remayneth in my pasture the iiijth of Marche anno iiij^{tio} regni regis Edwardi vjth [*1549*] of the last yeres besse xviij. That ys to saye viij oxen, viij mylche kyne, j gret old blacke cow and her calfe, j bare browne old cowe

Sold to Jamz Clarke in Estheringe [?] j old blake cowe	xv s.
Sold at Coventre viij oxen	[*blank*]
Sold the old browne bare cow to Rayner	[*blank*]
Sold j gret brynded cow mylche that was my aunt Spensers	xxxviij s. iiij d.

33 f. 32. A Besse bought by me Peter Temple in anno iij^{tio} regni regis Edwardi vj^{ti} etc. [*1549*] the xiijth daye of Marche and afterwards as followeth

Inprimis bowght of Jamz Clarke v kyne	iiij li.
Item bought of Rychard Griffin ij small heyfers	xxiij s.
Item of Chantrnerll j heyfer	xiij s. iiij d.

62 A date between January and March seems to be indicated, but the main Coventry Fair was at Corpus Christi, 20 June in 1549.

63 This clearly corresponds to entries in items **28** and **29**, and must have been written on about 1 October.

Item bought of Hunt of Rodwey ij runtes	xlvij s. viiij d.
Item bought by Edward ij kyne	xxvij s.
Item of Rychard Gryfyne j browne cowe del'	xiij s. iiij d.
Item of Jamz Clarke j blake pyld oxe	xxiiij s. iiij d.
Item of Bocher of Compton ij kyne	xxix s.
Item of Jamz Clarke j fallow pyed oxe	xxv s.
Summa	xiiij li. iiij s. iiij d.
Memorandum that Edward bought at Dedyngton Fayre [*11 Nov.*?] iiij sters	liij s. vj d.
Memorandum that Hygyns resceyved of Byshell iiij sters at	iij li. vj s. viij d.

34 f. 32. B Money delyvered to Thomas Hygynson to by besse for me the viij^th^ of Marche in anno iij^do^ Edwardi vj^th^ (as followeth)^er^ and afterward as followeth

Inprimis delyvered then to Thomas Hygynson	v li. v s.
Item delyvered more to hym the xxij^th^ of Marche	xvij li.
Item Wast delyvered hym for me	xx li.
Item sent hym by Thomas	xv li.
Item delyvered hym more at Daventre Fayre	xvj li.
Item delyvered hym more for viij oxen	xvij li. vj s. viij d.
Item delyvered hym more for x kyne	x li. xvj s. viij d.
Item delyvered hym more for ix kyne	ix li. xv s.
Item he resceyved more for a heyfer	xix s. vij d.
Item he resceyved more for x kyne	ix li. xj s. iiij d.
Item he resceyved of Ansty for shep	iiij li. viij s. iiij d.; item ix s. iiij d.
Sum	j^c^xxij li. iij s.

35 f. 32 v. Besse bought by Thomas Hygynson anno ij regni regis Edwardi vj^ti^ [*1549*]

Tomworth	Bought there the xij^th^ of Marche iiij oxen	v li. xj s. viij d.
(Hampton	Item the vj^th^ of Aprill xvj kyne	x li. vj s.)^er^
(7	Item j oxe)^er^	
	Item for toll and costes	ix d.
Tomworth 10	Item the xvj^th^ of Aprill iiij oxen	iiij li. xv s. iiij d.
(Hampton)^er^	Item then vj kyne	iiij li. xj s. vj d.[64]
	Costes and tolles	xviij d.
Hampton	Item ther the vj^th^ of Aprill vj kyne at xvij s. vij d.	v li. vj s.
	Item iij kyne at xviij s. ij d.	liiij s. vj d.
	Item ij kyne	xxx s.
	Item j cow	xij s.
	Item ij kyne	xxx s.

[64] Another sum erased.

	Item j cow	xvij s. iiij d.
	Item j cow	xv s. viij d.
	Item j oxe	xxj s.
	Item the tolle	vj d.
	For costes	iij s. viij d.
Hampton 26	Bought ther the vj[th] of Maye j bull xv s. Item x kyne at xvij s. the pec xij d. bate	viij li. ix s.
	Item x kyne at xvj s. the pec and x d. further	viij li. iiij s. ij d.
	Item iij kyne	xlv s. vj d.
	Item ij runtes	xxxiij s. iiij d.
	Toll and costes	iij s. viij d.
Bremycham 48	Bought ther the [*blank*] of May ix runtes	viij li. xj s.
	Item xxxix kyne	xxxj li. ij s.
	Item toll costes and grasse	iiij s.
	Summa	lxxxx li. xvij s. viij d.[65]
Newport Faire 8	Bowght there ij oxen	iij li. ij s. viij d.
	Item ij oxen	lv s.
	Item ij oxen	lj s. iiij d.
	Item j bull, j ster	xxxij s.
Bremycham 10	Bought ther viij sters	v li. iiij s.
	Item ij kyne	xxx s.
	Toll and costes	xiiij d.
[*Against the items since the last sum*]	Summa	xvj li. xvj s. ij d.
	Item resceyved of hym[66]	xx li.
	Item he delyvered Byshell	xiij s. iiij d.
	Item he paid for tolles and for repares of the wayne	xiij s.
Coventre 7	Item[67] resceyved the [*blank*] of Decembre (xj)[er] vij steres from Hygyns	v li. ix s. iiij d.

36 f. 65 v. C [*Note of Purchase, 1549*][68]

Resceyved of Byshell	xlvij s. viij d.
Item resceyved of Byshell iiij sters at xvj s. viij d. the pece, wherof delyvered hym xiij s. iiij d., so that I resceyved there v li. and so he oweth me	iij s. iiij d.

[65] Altered from *lxxxx li. iij s. ij d.* (?).

[66] This and the next two entries written on the right hand side, opposite the last group. *Him* presumably refers to Hygynson.

[67] Entry added across the bottom of the page.

[68] Cf. the last entry of 33 and the last but three of 35.

37 f. 33.	Besse sold at Coventre Fayre and afterward in anno tercio regni regis Edwardi vj^{ti} [*1549*] as followeth	
Coventre 10	Inprimis sold the xxijth of June xj kyne	x li. xiiij s.
Coventre 10	Item sold the xiijth of July vj kyne	vj li. xiiij s.
	Item the xxth of July sold iij kyne	iij li. xij s.
	Item j cow	xix s. viij d.
Dasset 1	Item ther died in the pastur j cow	
Coventre 10	Item sold at Coventre the [*blank*] of August x kyne	x li.
Dasset 3	Item kyld into my howse j cow	
	Item j cow stolen and j runt died	
Warwyke 12	Item sold the xxiij of August xij kyne	xij li. vj s. viij d.
Dassett (50)^{er} 49	Item sold to Wylliam Rayner of Uxbridge the iiijth of Septembre xl^{ti} kyne at xxij s. iiij d. the pece and x kyne at xviij s. vj d. the pece to be delyvered at Mychelmas and Allhollowtyd. Rebat ther for a cow of the last yeres bying	liij li. viij s. viij d.
Dasset 15	Item sold the ij^{d} of Novembre to hym x runtes	xiij li. vj s. viij d.
	Item sold to hym v oxen	ix li.
Banbery 1	Item sold the xth of January j cow	xxij s.
Dasset 3	Item kyld in to my house j oxe and j stere	
	Item sold j cow	xxvij s. iiij d.
Dasset 7	Item sold the xxjth of January vij oxen	xiiij li. xiij s. iiij d.
Dasset 1	Item kyld in to my house at Ester j blake heyfer	
Dasset 29	Item sold the last of Maye xxiiij^{ti} sters	xxvij li. xij s.
	Item sold then v oxen	ix li. vj s. viij d.
	Summa	j^{c}lxxij li. vj s.

Remayneth in the pastur the last of May anno iiij^{to} Edwardi vj^{ti} [*1550*] of the last yers bying
ij oxen for the wayne, j cow mylche and ij buls. Item ther ys vij mylche more of the old store besydes al the mylche besse and other besse of this present yeres bying of anno iiij^{o} to be wrytten as hit aperyth yn the next leafe, wherof sold the cow with the strype about the neke — xxiij s.
Item kyld into my house j bull

38 f. 33 v — Money delyvered to Thomas Hyginson the iij^{d} and fowrth yere of Kyng Edward the vjth [*1550*] as followeth

Delyvered to Thomas Hygynson the xvjth January	vj li. viij d.
Item sent to Thomas Hygynson the xxth of January by George Harryson my servant	xx li.
Item delyvered hym myself the xxth of February	vj li.
Item delyvered to hym the xxiiijth of Februarye	xx li.
Item sent hym by Wase	xx li.
Item sent hym by Chatockes opon Good Frydaye	xl li.
Item he resceyved for me of Mr Hawse	liij s. iiij d.
Item sent hym by Mr Marrow	xlvj s. [v]iij d.
Summa	cxvij li. viij s., wherof
He hath layd owt[for] me for besse as appereth	j^{c}vij li. ij s. x d.
and he hath layd owt for me for dycers, a cart wayne and lockes, coles, lath and other thinges	vj li. xv s. iiij d.

Item he delyvered me ij s. vj d. Item he delyvered me iij li.

39 f. 34. Besse of Thomas Hygingsons buying in anno iij^{tio} et quarto regni regis Edwardi sexti [*1550*] as followeth

Tamworthe 8	Inprimis bought ther the xxth of January viij oxen	x li. xiij s.
	Item for tolle and costes	xiiij d.
Wolverhampton 15	Item the vjth of Februarye bought x besse	vij li. xx d.
	Item j oxe	xxiiij s.
	Item j cow	xvij s.
	Item j cow	xvj s. vj d.
	Item j heyfer	xiiij s.
	Item j heyfer	xvj s.
	Item for tolle and costes	iij s. x d.
Hampton 8	Item bought the xviijth of February v kyne	iiij li. x s.
	Item j cow	xviij s.
	Item j cow	xvij s.
	Item j cow	xvij s.
	Item for costes and tolles	ij s. xj d.
Hampton 18	Item bought ther the iij^{d} of Marche x kyne	vij li. xiij s. viij d.
	Item viij kyne at	vj li. ix s.
	Item for costes and toll and dryvyng	iiij s.
Hampton 21	Item bought ther the xvjth of Marche v kyne	iiij li. xiij s. iiij d.
	Item v kyne	iiij li. v s. iiij d.
	Item ij kyne	xxxij s.
	Item v kyne	iiij li. xj s.
	Item iiij kyne at	lvij s. viij d.
	Item paid for costes and tolles and dryvyng	iiij s. iiij d.
Coventre 5	Item bought ther the xxvjth of Marche iij kyne and calfes	v li.

	Item ij oxen	lj s. viij d.
	Item for dryvyng	vj d.
Hampton 32	Bought ther the xvjth of Aprill xiiij kyne	xij li. xiij s.
	Item xj kyne j bull	x li. xvj s.
	Item iiij kyne	iij li. xiiij s.
	Item ij kyne	xxxj s.
	Item for tolle, costes and dryvyng	vj s. v d.
	Summa lxxxxviij li. xvj s. vij d.	

[f. 34 v.]

Coventre 7	Item bought ther the xvth of Maye j cow and calf	xxxj s.
	Item ij oxen bought of Mr Hawse	iij li. vj s. viij d.
	Item[69] ij oxen bought the ij^{d} of August	iij li. viij s. viij d.
Banbery 4	Item Edward bowght ij oxen the xxiijth of September of Burbery of Geydon	iij li. x s. viij d.
	[Item] Edward bought ij oxen at Banbery in Octobre	iij li. ij s.
2	Item Edward bought ij oxen at Compton	ij li. vj s. viij d.
	Summa xviij li. vj s. viij d.	

40 f. 35 Besse sold after Ester in anno quarto regni regis Edwardi vjth [*1550*]

Dasset 16	Inprimis lost one before he came into the pastur	
	Item lost one that dyed in the pasture	
	Sold the last of May xiij kyne and sters and j oxe	xiiij li. (vj s.)^{er} ij d.
Dasset 73	Sold and delyvered at dyvers tyms before the fyrst daye of Septembre lxx kyne and ij runtes	lxxx li. x s. viij d.
	Lost on grett browne cowe that went astrey	
Dasset and Banbery 10	Sold to Rodwey j pied cowe	xxv s. iiij d.
	Sold j blacke cow to Banbery	xxxj s.
	Item sold at Banbery vj oxen xij li.	
	Item kyld into my house 1 gret oxe	
	Item saved into my house j blake cowe	
	Summa j^{c}ix li. ix s. ij d.	
	Sold ij grett oxen to Howe of Warwyke	viij li. iiij s. iiij d.
	Sold to Randoll 1 rede ster	iij li. viij s.
	Item sold to Randoll j blake oxe	iij li.

69 *xx d.* in the margin against the line.

Item sold into my house ther at xij[th] tyde anno regni regis Edwardi vj[th] quinto[70] 1 blacke oxe

Item sold to a strange bocher 1 rede stere — iiij li.

41 f. 35 v. Money delyvered to Thomas Hyginsyn to bye besse for me the xxij[th] of Aprill in the vth yere of Kynge Edward the vj[th] [*1551*]

Inprimis delyvered hym then	x li. v s.
Item delyvered hym then	xxx li.
Item he resceved of Mr. Croker for me	xvij li. x s.
Item delyvered hym by Henry Petyver	vj li. xiij s. iiij d.
Item sent hym by Wast	xv li.
Summa lxxx li. viij s. iiij d.	
Memorandum I sent Hygyns by Wast xviij li. and he sent me ageyne xx li., so have I resceved more ageyne of hym	xl s.
The seyd Thomas Hygynson hath leyd owt for besse as appereth	lix li. xiij s. x d.
Item he paid Thornall for a horse	v li.
So ther dyd remayne in his handes	xv li. xiiij s. vj d.
Which by the ij falls was but	vij li. xvij s. iij d.
Wherof he paid for me to Mistress Forster	iij li. vj s. viij d.
Item I resceved of hym as aperyth above	xl s.
So doth he owe me the Fryday after xij[th] tyde	l s. viij d.
Wherof he layd owt for me for fyndyng a cow	iij s. iiij d.
and to the parke keper at Kenelworth iiij s., to Chatow viij d., the kepers ij d., and for a cow and calfe l s., and a cow and calfe xlij s. iiij d., and paid to Balsall for May rent iij li. vj s. viij d. and for a bill xxj s. The dryvyng viij d. and for ij oxen iiij li. iij s. iiij d., for dryvyng vj d., for axeltreyng the wayne vj d., for ij cockes xij d., and paid to Susan for me v s. vij d.	
Summa xiiij li. ix d.	
Wherof owetthe me as aperyth above	l s. vij d.
Item allowed hym my rent at Coventre dew at the Annunciation	vj li. vj s. vj d.
Item paid hym at my house the xij of August	v li. iij s. viij d.
and so wee wil recon the sayd xij of August anno regni regis Edwardi vjth v[to] [*1551*], omnibus allocatis, et exceptis xx s. that I must have in Aprill delyvered me in hande	

42 f. 36. A Besse bought the vth yere of Kyng Edward the vj[th] [*1551*] as followeth

[70] This must be 1551, though Twelfth Night was in fact still 4 Edward VI (ending on 27 January).

Bremyngham	Besse bought ther the xijth of Maye xxij	xxiij li. x s. iiij d.
	Item ij kyne	xliij s. iiij d.
	Item tolle and dryvyng and other costes	iij s.
	Item paid for j cow	xxvj s. viij d.
	Item paid for j cow	xxiiij s.
	Item j cow and calfe	xl s.
	Item the charges of fyndyng my cow	xxij s. x d.
	Bought xiiij oxen prised at	xxix li. xx d.
	Item ther charges	ij s.
	Summa lix li. xiij s. x d.	
	Item ther charges proper to Essex[71] and bake ageyne	xxvj s. viij d.
	Item for the grasse of them	iiij li.

43 f. 36. B Besse solde the vth yere of Kyng Edward vjth [*1551*] et sequitur

Sold to Randoll of Davyntre xx^{ti} kyne	xl li., wherof lost iiij li.
Of one cow that died in the pasture, sold the hyde	iij s. viij d.
Sold at Banbery a blacke cow that was a strey	xlvj s. viij d.
Sold at Banbery viij oxen	xxv li.

44 f. 36. C

Memorandum that I bought at Coventre at Saynt Lukes Fayre [*18 Oct.*] in anno [*Edwardi*] vj^{to} vj^{ti} [*1552*] x sters and ij kyne	xij li.
Item bought then vij runtys oxen	vij li. xv d.

45 f. 36. D

Delyvered Hygyns the last of June anno regni regis Edwardi vj^{ti} vij^{o} [*1553*]	xxxij li.
Wherof resceyved at Our Lady the Assumption [*15 Aug.*]	x li.
and at Hallowtyde [*1 Nov.*]	xviij li. x s.
and he sent me in ij oxen	liij s. iiij d.
and a bull	xvij s.

46 f. 36 v. Besse bought at Maye and after in anno 1554

Rychard Petyver bought at Coventre Fayre for me ij oxen	lv s. iiij d.
Jhon Adwares bowght for me ther ij oxen	iiij li. iiij d.
Rychard bowght ij oxen more ther then for me	liij s. vj d.
Rychard and Harry bowght for me at Tamworth Fayre iiij oxen	v li. xvj s. viij d.

[71] See **160**, which shows that they were sent to Anthony Cooke.

Item Rychard bought ther then for me iiij kyne	iiij li. xviij s. viij d.
Item Edwardes the bocher sent me for gresse 1 cow	
Thomas Hygynson sent ij kyne for his gresse and Mr. Marrow	

47 S6. E Besse bought in anno 156[1?] of Oxon

Videlicet lxiiij, j runt, kyne v	
Wherof sold at Northampton oxen viij	xviij li. xviij s. iiij d.
Item sold to Rayner xx oxen	lvj li. xiij s. iiij d.
Item xx runtes	xlviij li. vj s. viij d.
Item xx runtes	xlviij li. vj s. viij d.
Item j bullocke	xvj s.
Item vj wayne oxen	xv li. x s.
Item ij kyne	iij li. vj s. viij d.
Item sold at Lyterworth ij lytyl buloks	xxiiij s.

48 f. 1. C[72] [*Miscellaneous Cattle items, undated*]

[j] oxe	xx s.
[ij] cow	xxj s.
. . cow	. . .
. . pyed cow	xx s.
ij lams	. .

49 f. 60. C

[*Top margin*] ij bulockes, j cow		xxxix s.
[*Centre*][73]	xxxix li. xv s. iiij d.; vij s. xj d.	

3. *Peter Temple: Sheep* (frontispiece)

The sheep accounts are rather less clear than those for cattle farming, and they are complicated by the specialized terms and the unique method of counting, by 'great tale' (Table 3.1). However, they demonstrate clearly the financial rewards of sheep farming in the sixteenth century.[74] The accounts extend from 1543 to 1551, but for the first two years give only incidental references.[75] The most

[72] Badly rubbed; written around f. 1. A (132).

[73] It is uncertain if this jotting refers to cattle.

[74] For the great sheep farms of Sir John Spencer, the earliest accounts are for 1576–80 (Finch, 1956, p. 40 ff.), when he was farming at Wormleighton and Althorp, not far from Burton Dassett. These seem to be the only other records for the Midland pastures, though for Norfolk several extensive series of documents have been examined by K. J. Allison, 'Flock Management in the Sixteenth and Seventeenth Centuries', *Econ. Hist. Rev.*, 2nd Ser. 11, 1958, 98–112.

[75] For 1543 (208), the financial summary gives sales of sheep, £45 and wool, £43, against purchases of sheep, £37 and wool, £6; for 1544 the field account gives the best evidence (74).

Table 3.1: *Naming and numbering of sheep*

The names of different sorts of sheep were very complicated, and usage differed from one area to another; the table shows the terms used by Peter Temple, with their probable meanings.

Age	*Name*	*Meaning*
First year	Lamb	
	Cade Lamb	Foundling lamb, reared by hand
Second year	Hog or Hogrell	One-year old sheep
	Chilver Hog	Ewe yearling
	Wether Hog	Gelded ram yearling
	Ram Hog	
	Teg	Apparently the same as hog
Third year	Shere Hoge	Gelded two-year old
	Thevy	Ewe two-year old (not having borne a lamb)
Full grown	Ewe	
	Ram	
	Wether	Gelded ram
Miscellaneous	Cople	Ewe and lamb
	Rygyll	'Half-castrated ram', or one not needing castrating (E.D.D.)
	Stew (73)	Uncertain, but the price suggests some type of sheep
	Fell	Sheepskin, from dead sheep

Counting was done by the *Great Tale*. Six score made a 'hundred' (= 120), and ten 'hundreds' a 'thousand' (= 1,200). However, Peter Temple did not always use the *Great Tale*, as can be established by comparing sub-totals in scores with totals in hundreds (e.g. sheep delivered in 1546).

important development was in 1548; until then, sheep were both bought and sold (Table 3.2), but thereafter the breeding flock was large enough to be self-sustaining. In the early years, when the flock was being built up, the main purchases were of lambs or couples (ewe and lamb), and relatively few lambs were sold, except for 332 couples which were bought and sold as a lot in 1546; a moderate number of ewes were disposed of, with other old stock. In 1545, Peter Temple also sold a number of his Welsh sheep for slaughter, pricing the carcases and the fells separately (51); he seems to have had the same in mind in his 1544 estimates (74) which included 928 fells.

Table 3.2: *Numbers of sheep bought and sold; receipts and costs*
R = ram; W = wether; E = ewe; X = unspecified.

Date		*Lambs*	*Couples*	*2nd year*			*3rd year*			*Full grown*				*Cost*	*Receipts*	*Wool sales*[a]
				W	E	X	W	E	X	R	W	E	X			
1545	bt.		249			18					60	321		£94 8s. 2d.		
	sold	2	1	400[b]		34					50	83			£62 10s. 2d.	£36?
	died	50									7	3				
1546	bt.	200	452		20							4		£163 15s. 8d.		
	sold		230									103			£102 18s. 0d.	£116?
1547	bt.	928[c]														
	sold	223					160					193			£75 1s. 8d.	£181
1548	sold	140					247	20	280			268			£138 0s. 0d.	£246
	killed											51				
1549	sold	175										302			£54 19s. 0d.	£291
	sold later[d]			250							240		65		£122 0s. 0d.	
1550	sold	360		280	122						157	204			£212 8s. 2d.	£180
1551	bt.									5		140		£50 15s. 0d.		
	sold	309		240		100						255			£228 0s. 3d.	£130
Predicted figures for sales																
1550s	I	480		480								420			£295	£200
	II	960		600								540			£430	£327
	III	660		—								200			£143[e]	£115[e]

[a] From Table 4.1. [b] From 213. [c] Possibly not bought, as cost unstated. [d] Possibly another year. [e] Probably incomplete.

From 1547 the classic pattern of sixteenth-century sheep rearing appears.[76] This can best be seen from the detailed autumn counts of the flock (Table 3.3). These are recorded for three known years (1548, 1550, 1551), and two others, later in the 1550s. Despite some inconsistencies (perhaps because of counting by 'great tale'), the pattern is well defined. More than half the flock were breeding ewes. By the autumn, the spring lambs had either been sold or renamed as *hogs*, about the same number of each sex being retained. However, in the next year all the wethers were sold, leaving the *thevys* to be promoted to breeding ewes a year later. Finally the old ewes were culled, selling barren ones (about one fifth of the total, implying a breeding life of five seasons). A few lambs were left ungelded and reared as replacement rams. For the flock before 1548, we have to rely on the numbers bought and sold each year (Table 3.2), and the sheep pastured on outside fields (Table 3.3). Fewer sales of ewes took place, as would be expected; also, a number of wethers were kept on and sold either as shere hogs or full-grown wethers.

We have little evidence for the most important statistic of a breeding flock, the number of lambs produced by each ewe. An approximate 1:1 ratio is suggested by the purchase of 'coples', and this was

Table 3.3: *Sheep numbers*
R = ram; W = wether; E = ewe; X = unspecified.

Date	*Lambs*	*2nd year*			*3rd year*			*Full grown*			*Total*
		R	W	E	X	W	E	R	W	E	
(i) Formal stocktaking											
1548, 1 Nov.	23(R)				632	233	240	37	254	1034	2453[a]
1550, 11 Nov.		10			684			32		1337	2063
1551, 11 Nov.		53			734			34		1432	2253[b]
1550s I			540	540			240	60		1920	3300
II			660	780			360	80		2940	4820
1562, 29 Sept.		28			261	645		69	27	1031	2061
(ii) Sheep in or delivered into named fields											
1546	349						225	47		449	1070
1547, March		50	260	240	195						745
Sept.	518					299	240			611	1668
1548[c]			80	200		779	178				1238
				(240)		*(859)*					*(1358)*
1550s I	540						240	60		1440	1980

[a] Text 2493. [b] Text 2223. [c] Possibly by *Great Tale*, the figures in italics.

[76] As in both Norfolk and Northamptonshire.

the standard medieval lambing expectation (never attained).[77] Only for the 1,337 ewes in 1550 can we be more precise, with 1,287 lambs produced (500 sold, with 53 ram and 734 other hogs in 1551).[78] By Norfolk standards,[79] this ratio of 0·96, clear of losses, was high, and if typical must have contributed significantly to the profits of the flock. Only one specific factor appears that might have contributed to the lambing rate. The thirty to sixty rams that Peter Temple kept is many more than the two or three per thousand ewes found in Norfolk.[80] When not with the ewes, the rams had their own field, 'Ram Close' (78); the name is recorded in 1546[81] and remained in use permanently.

The 1550–1 lamb figures show the position after any deaths during the year. Losses were only clearly recorded in 1545, when the lambs were most susceptible, particularly in the geld; three were also taken 'giddy'.[82] In later years, there is only incidental evidence, from the number of fells sold. Deaths seem to have been few, which is surprising, as murrain was very prevalent in these years.[83]

The marketing of the sheep was simpler than for cattle. The core of the flock in early years was Welsh sheep, but they came from no further away than Coventry. For English sheep, two breeds are named, Berkshires and Cotswolds; both were from hill or downland areas, and were noted for their wool yield.[84] Again, most of the English sheep were bought near at hand (Fig. 4). The neighbourhood also provided the purchasers. Normally, they bought direct from Peter Temple at Burton Dassett, and very few sheep were sent to market in Banbury or Coventry. Every year, one or two buyers took large numbers. They included John Spencer of Wormleighton, the great sheep farmer,[85] who bought 230 couples in 1546. William

[77] Stated in many medieval account rolls, e.g. P. D. A. Harvey, *Manorial Records of Cuxham, Oxon., c.* 1200–1359 (London: H.M.S.O., 1976), p. 347.

[78] These figures are not completely consistent with the flock counts. As an example, following the 1551 sales of 340 second-year sheep from a total of 614 (November 1550), 270 third-year sheep should have been left at the year's end in 1551, which are not recorded. They were presumably ewes, and might have been included with them, but the figures still fail to tally.

[79] Allison, op. cit. in note 74, p. 103, Tables 8–9; Finch, 1956, p. 42 gives a doubtful estimate of 0·81 for the Spencer flocks.

[80] Allison, Table 7.

[81] See note 31 on p. 36.

[82] The result of an infection with *Coenurias cerebralus*, a tape-worm that forms a cyst in the brain.

[83] *Ag. Hist.*, p. 625; Winchester, 1955, p. 175.

[84] M. L. Ryder, 'The History of Sheep Breeds in Britain', *Agricultural Hist. Rev.*, 12, 1964, pp. 1, 63; see also M. L. Ryder, *Sheep and Man* (London: Duckworth, forthcoming), and P. L. Armitage & J. A. Goodall, 'Medieval Horned and Polled Sheep', *Antiquaries J.* 57, 1977, 73–89.

[85] See Finch, 1956 and p. 21.

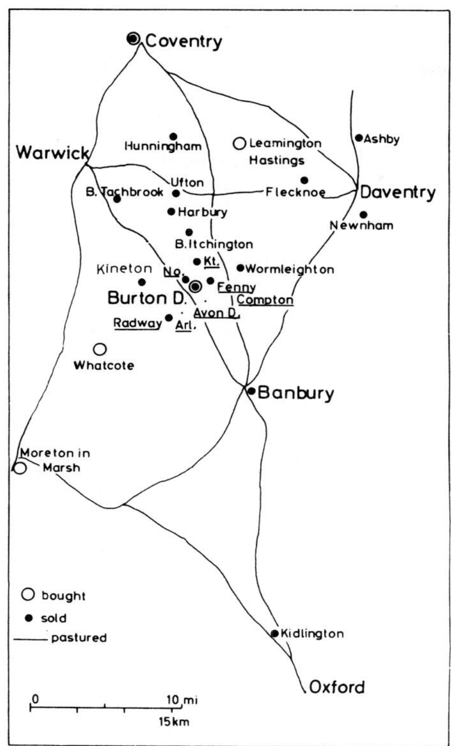

Fig. 4. Sheep farming: location of purchases, sales and pastures. Major roads and some large towns are also shown. D. = Dassett; Arl. = Arlescote; B. Itchington = Bishops Itchington; B. Tachbrook = Bishops Tachbrook; Kt. = Knightcote; No. = Northend.

Gyfford (1545) and Randall of Newnham (1548), two of the butchers whose main trade was cattle, also bought sheep. Relatives appear, including Cuthbert Temple (1548), and the two John Heritages, while in 1549, Thomas Hygynson, Peter Temple's cousin, cattle agent and bailiff in Coventry, with his mother, his two brothers and his servant, bought 85 lambs and ewes. A striking number of local people bought a few sheep each. In particular, in 1548 James Clarke bought 280 sheep, as agent in a joint transaction by twelve villagers. Finally, Peter Temple was visited once by the King's 'lamb-taker', i.e. the Crown Purveyor (1551); he took fifty-two lambs, but also bought four ewes on his own behalf. The purveyor could take lambs at the penal price of 1s. per lamb,[86] but in fact he paid 2s., close to the market rate. Perhaps the four private ewes were part of a convenient accommodation with Temple.

[86] A. Woodward, 'Purveyance for the Royal Household in the Reign of Queen Elizabeth', *Trans. Amer. Phil. Soc.*, NS, 35, 1945, 3 (see p. 31).

The prices for the different sheep (Table 3.4) show, of course, great variations depending on conditions we cannot know, but some trends emerge. Wethers were always more valuable than ewes; the worn-out culling ewes were cheaper than the second or third year sheep. Most significant of all is the doubling in price between 1544 and the later 1550s. This increase reflects the inflation of the period, though the prices show a rather larger increase than the national average (1544: 198 to 1559: 303).[87] With fixed costs, Peter Temple was ideally placed to profit from rising prices, even though the increase in his income was less in real terms than its money value.

The receipts from sheep sales only reached substantial levels clear of purchase costs in 1548, and they varied from year to year. The most informative figures are the predictions made in the 1550s (Table 3.4), showing an income of £300 to £400 from the largest flocks recorded. The wool profits were also estimated, and these are considered in the next section. Ten years earlier, when Peter Temple started farming, he put down some similar estimates for a flock totalling 2,200 (76, perhaps for 1546). The proportion of culling ewes was smaller as the flock was younger, and the account values all the lambs, but it makes no mention of selling any wethers, which the flock must have included. Most important though, the accounts itemized the costs for the fields. In this year the out-goings totalled £36 and £73 12s. 6d. respectively for the two fields. The major component was rent and tithe; the latter had been fixed advantageously by an ancient composition at 8d. for every 6s. 8d. (80d.) of rent.[88] Each field had a shepherd and he needed hurdles, while the sheep were daubed with tar against scab, washed and sheared, and the wool wound. Hay was cut on parts of the fields, which must have been fenced off.

These accounts are accompanied by a unique comment on management, 'Memorandum now I have provyd that this pound will not kepe 1000 shepe' (presumably because the feed was exhausted). More generally, one aspect of the flock handling is prominent in the flock counts, that the different types of sheep were segregated. This was standard sixteenth-century practice.[89] Evidence from the 1560s also shows that Peter Temple took care that his breeding stock was

[87] *Ag. Hist.*, p. 825.

[88] This was a matter of much dispute later in the century, reflected in many papers in the Stowe collection. For an unknown reason, since at least 1538 (121), Heritage Field paid £3 10s. as its tithe composition, not £2 12s.

[89] Allison, op. cit., p. 101.

Table 3.4: *Sheep prices*

R = ram; W = wether; E = ewe; X = unspecified.

The figures in brackets give the numbers on which the averages are based. Sheep not priced separately are omitted.

Date		*Lambs*	*Couples*	*2nd year*			*3rd year*			*Full grown*			
				W	E	X	W	E	X	R	W	E	X
(i) Actual figures													
1545	bought		3s. 4d. (249)			2s. 4d. (18)					2s. 9d. (60)	2s. 7d. (321)	
1545	sold	1s. 4d. (2)	4s. 8d. (1)	2s. 0d. (400)		3s. 2d. (34)					2s. 10d. (50)	1s. 6d. (83)	
1546	bought	2s. 4d. (200)	5s. 6d. (452)										
	sold		8s. 0d. (230)									2s. 0d. (101)	
1547	sold	2s. 4d. (223)					3s. 4d. (160)					2s. 5d. (193)	
1548	sold	1s. 9d. (140)					4s. 3d. (247)	3s. 0d. (20)	2s. 8d. (280)			2s. 5d. (268)	
1549	sold	1s. 7d. (171)										2s. 9d. (302)	
	sold later		4s. 3d. (250)								5s. 0d. (240)		2s. 8d. (65)
1550	sold	2s. 5d. (360)		5s. 3d. (280)	4s. 2d. (122)						5s. 4d. (157)	3s. 2d. (202)	
1551	bought									7s. 0d. (7)		7s. 0d. (140)	
1551	sold	3s. 9d. (309)		6s. 7d. (240)		5s. 1d. (100)						4s. 11d. (255)	
(ii) Predicted figures													
1544				3s. 9d.									
1540s	I	1s. 6d.											
	II	1s. 5d.										1s. 5d.	
1550s	I–III	3s. 4d.		6s. 0d.								3s. 4d.	

kept pure (see p. 244). However, in one way Peter Temple's methods are surprising. From 1546 to 1548 the flocks were sent to pasture in all the near-by villages;[90] eight are named, including Knightcote and Northend, the hamlets in Burton Dassett parish. All these were still common field villages, and the sheep were being grazed on the fallow fields. They were entrusted to prominent villagers whose names recur through the accounts, including the two John Heritages. Cattle fattening was at its height in these years, which must have taken up much of the pasture of the home fields. The use of these village pastures is puzzling in two ways. Pasturing of 'foreign' sheep—not the property of tenants of the manor—was always one of the most serious offences condemned in the manor court; for example, at Elmley Castle, Worcestershire, in 1473: 'they shall not keep any sheep except they be the owners or their relations', with a large penalty of 20s.[91] However, one order from Stoneleigh, Warwickshire, gives a rather more favourable view: 'no tenant shall take in any beastes of eny straungers . . . except it be oxen to ploughe, kyne to the peale (*pail*) or sheep to folde'.[92] Given that Peter's sheep must have been accepted on the neighbouring fields, there remains the problem of how the villagers who took them were rewarded. There are no specific payments for this, and it may be that their recompense was the dunging of their fields.

SHEEP ACCOUNTS

50 f. 16. B Emptis Anno 1545 Welshe Coples and other Welshe [?sheep][93]

Coventre lviij coples	Bought the viijth of Maye xl coples at (iij li.)^{er} lviij s. the schore. Summa	v li. xvj s.
	Item xviij coples at ij s. viij d. the pec.	xlvj s. iiij d.
Coventre v^{xx} ix coples	Bought the xv of May v schore coples at iij s. the pece. Sum	xv li.
	Item ix coples at ij s. ij d. the pec	xxj s.
	For the dryvyng and expences	xij d.
Coventre 22(23)^{er} coples	Bought the xxijth of Maye xxij coples at ij s. viij d. the pec, lackyng in the holl xvj d.	lvij s. iiij d.

[90] Probably also in 1545, when the sales mention Northend and 'Kyngston' (?Kineton; see p. 15).

[91] W. O. Ault, *Open Field Farming in Medieval England* (London: Allen and Unwin, 1972), no. 162, p. 133.

[92] S.B.T., DR18, Stoneleigh Manorial, 176; Easter, 1573.

[93] A word is lost at the end. The head of this page, above f. 16.A carries the heading *Emtes Anno 1545*, no doubt referring to this item.

1	Item j bareg[94] owe	ij s. j d.
Coventre	Bought the xxijth of Maye lx wethers	
60 wethers	at ij s. ix d. the pece. Summa	viij li v s.
	For dryvyng	xij d.
	Spent	ij s. viij d.
	Bought the xxvijth of May xviij teges	
	at ij s. iiij d. the pec. Summa	xlij s.
	Paid for dryvyng	v d.

51 f. 16 v. Welshe shepe sold anno 1545

	Sold to Wylliam Brokes j cople	iiij s. viij d.
	Item to hym ij lamz	ij s. viij d.
5	Item kyld iiij lams and j dyed	
4	Item there dyed in Northe Feld iij lamz. Item j ram lame	
40	Sold the vijth of Septembre to Mr. Wylliam Gyfford	
	by Benet his servant xl wethers	v li. xviij s. iiij d.
7	Lost in the geld vij lamz, the karkes and fels	vj s. viij d.
3	Item iij gedy lamz	
1	Lost j lambe. j lams fell	ij d.
2	Kyld ij wethers	
5	Lost v wethers. viij yews fels	ij s.
10	Gult bought x yews at xviij d. the pec	xv s.
3(4)^{er}	Ther dyed in the pastar (iij)^{er} ij yews and j in	
	Northen Feld	
30	Lost in the geld xxx^{ti}. For the skyns and karkes	xxxv s.
15	For xv fells Welshe	x s.
	viij fels kyld in my howse	v s. iiij d.
	For ij carkesses	xvj d.
	[*margin*] Sold to Mr Jhon Spenser xx^{ti} hogges	iiij li.
	Sold to Gardner lxxiij ews at xviiij d.	v li. ix s. vj d.
	[*margin*] Sold at Banbery xiiij hoges	xxvj s. viij d.

[*Carcases and Fells?*][95]

Sent to Badbye xxxj^{ti} at vj d. and the fells viij d.	xxvj s. ij d.
Sold to Geff vj at vj d. and ij fels viij d.	vij s.
Sold to West ij at vj d. and the fels viij d.	ij s. iiij d.
Sold to Gryffyn xv (xxiiij)^{er} at xvj d.	xx s.[96]
Sold to Colman vj at viij d. and the fell viij d.	viij s.
Sold to Blakwell iiij for xx d., the fels ij s. viij d.	iiij s. iiij d.
Sold to Carter iij for xij d., the fels ij s.	iij s.
From Kyngston vij fells remayth	vj s.
Sold to Heirs[97] j for	xv d.
Sold to Gerdner j	xv d.
Sold to Carter x Welshe wethers at ij s. iij d.	xxij s. viij d.

[94] This is written *bareg* here and elsewhere, with no bar for an omitted *n*, though it must mean *barren*.

[95] In the following items, the first figure is probably the unit price for the carcase, the second that for the skin.

[96] Other figures erased.

[97] Perhaps *Hierns*, as in 1551 (71).

52 f. 17. A — Englysche Shepe bought anno 1545

Barkshier	Bought iij schore coples	xv li.
Cotsold	Bought the viijth of October by (of)^{er} Heritage iiij^{xx} yews at iij s. ij d. the pec. Summa	xij li. xiij s. iiij d.
Barkshier	Bowght xth of October by Thurwod x^{xx} yews	xxiiij li.
	Bought the xxth of October of Robart Palmer xl yews. Sum	v li.

53 f. 24. A — Englishe sheepe bought in anno xxxviij Henrici viij^{ti} et anno grace 1546

Dassett 230 coples 2 yews	Bought the xxviijth of Aprill of Anthoni Ashefeld, gentleman, xij^{xx} and x coples and ij yews, prec' at vij s. the pec	lxxix li. ix s.
Lemyngton 200 lams	Bought the vjth of Maye of Jhon Palmer of Lemyngton, esquier x^{xx} wether lams, to be delyvered at Mychelmas next	xxiiij li.
	(Bought the vijth of Aprill vj^{xx} coples)^{er}	
Morton the Marshe 20	Bought the xijth of Maye of Rychard Palmer xx^{ti} chilver hoges, price iiij s. viij d. the pec. Sum	iiij li. xiij s. iiij d.
Whatcott 102 coples	Bought the xxth of Aprell of Wynchester v^{xx} and ij coples	xxv li. xiij s. iiij d.

54 f. 24. B — Englishe Sheepe sold anno supradicto [*1546*]

Wormleighton 232 coples	Wheroff sold to Mr Jhon Spenser 230 coples and ij yews at viij s. the cople. Sum	lxxxxij li. xvj s.

55 f. 24v. A — Bought Welshe shepe anno 1546

Bought the vj of Maye vj^{xx} coples and ij yews. Summa	xx li.
Whereof sold the xxixth of Septembre to Thomas Phelps v^{xx} and j yews at ij s. the pec	x li. ij s.
and for the woll of them	lij s. iiij d.[98]

56 f. 77. B — [*Fells sold, perhaps 1546*][99]

For iiij dosen and v felles	xxxv s. iiij d.
for xj dossen and viij fells	v li. vj s. viij d.

[98] Apparently erased and replaced by *l s.*

[99] The evidence of date is that the following item on the same page (57) is certainly of 1546.

57 f. 77. C [*1546*]

Memorandum payd to Mr Anthonye Ashefeld the vij of August anno xxxviij^{to} Henrici viijth [*1546*] xlvj li. xj s. viij d. for shepe of hym bought and so remayneth dew to hym more[1] xxxiij li.

58 f. 73. A [*Sheep deliveries, 1546 and 1547*]
Anno xxxviij^{o} Henrici viijth [*1546*]

Knyghtcote Feld

Delyvered to Lodbroke iiij^{xx} yews and liiij lamz.
Summa totalis j^{c}xxxiij
Delyvered to Profytt xliij yews and xxxviij lamz.
Summa totalis lxxi[2]
Delyvered to Swayne xlvij rames xlvij

Compton Feld

Delyvered to Edward his brother lxj yows and lxj lams.
Summa j^{c}xxij
Delyvered to Wylliam Robyns in (thevys)^{er} yows baren lx
Delyvered to Wylliam Palmer xl yows and xl lamz lxxx
Delyvered to my man Gryffyn xxxij yows and xxix lamz lxj[3]
Delyvered to Jhon Herytage vj^{xx} and ix thevys j^{c}xxix
Item to the sayd Jhon iiij^{xx} and xvj thevys
Delyvered to Gryffyn vj^{xx} and xiij yews and vj^{xx} and xvij lamz ij^{c}lxx

Anno primo Edwardi vj [*1547*]

Delyvered the vth of Marche in to Avne Dassett Feld in chilver hoges xij^{xx}
Delyvered the vij of Marche into Compton Feld in wetherhoges xiij^{xx}
Delyvered the ix of Marche to Lodbroke of Knyghtcott in ramz and ramehoges 1
Delyvered the xiiij of Marche to Thomas Makepese of Northend in wetherhoges, sherhoges and chilverhoges ix^{xx}xv

59 f. 77 v. A [*Sheep sales, 1547*]

Mense Septembris anno primo Edwardi vj^{ti} [*1547*]

Resceyved from Sylworth[4] xxv^{xx} and xj lamz and xx^{xx} and xvij lamz. Item vj lamz

[1] In the margin *soll'* for *soluto*, paid.
[2] Figures altered from *xliiij*, *xxxviiij* and *lxxiij*.
[3] Cf. 22 for the purchase of some of these.
[4] Sylworth cannot be recognized as a place, so it might be the shepherd's name, with the two groups of lambs coming from two flocks.

Sold to Wylliam Palmer the last of August vj^{xx} and j yews at — xiiij li.
Item sold the iiij of Septembre to Thomas Parkyns and Baldewyn Ward iij^{xx} and xij yews at — ix li. xij s.
Item to them the same tyme viij^{xx} sherhoges at — xxvj li. x s.
Sold to James Clarke of Compton the iij^{d} of September v^{xx} lamz, [one] half to be payd within one fortnyght at after Our Lady Daye [*25 March*] and the rest within a fortnyght after Maye Daye — xj li. vj s. viij d.
Sold the iijth of Septembre to Thomas Makepec and Thomas Swayne vj^{xx} and iij lamz at — xiiij li. xiij s.

60 f. 78. A [*Sheep delivered, 1547*]

10 die Septembris anno primo Edwardi vj^{ti} [*1547*]

Delyvered into Northend Feld xiij^{xx} lamz
Item xviij yews
Delyvered to Profeyt xx^{ti} yews
Item xviij lamz
Delyvered to Harry Basse xviiij sherehoges
Delyvered in Compton Feld to Gryffyn xiiij^{xx} sherhoges
Delyvered to Whitthed xij^{xx} and xv yews
Delyvered in Avne Dassett Feld to Jhon Petifer xij^{xx} thevys
Delyvered in Arleskot Feld to Palmer xij^{xx} lamz
Delyvered in Rodwey Feld to Herytage viij^{xx} yews
Delyvered to Herytage of Kyngton vij^{xx} and xviij yews

61 f. 65 v. A Cullyng shepe sold at Bartylmewtyde [*24 Aug.*] in Anno secundo regni regis Edwardi sexti [*1548*] ut sequitur

Imprimis sold to Mr. Thomas Hawse and and Jhon Byssell vj schore lamz and 2 yows — x li. vj s. viij d.
[*Margin*] Item received of Mr Haws liij s. iiij d.
Item James Clerke xlj yews — v li. vj s. viij d. (ij s. iiij d.)[5]
Item to Cutbert Temple and his man iiij^{xx} and xj yows — (xij li.; xl s.)^{er} xx s.
[*Margin*] viij d.; xl s. xx s.
Item to Mr. Vincent of Kydlyngton xx^{ti} thevys — iij li.
Item to Thomas Phelps xliij yews — v li. xiij s. iiij d.
Item Randall Bocher of Newnam xxj yews — xlvj s. viij d.
Item to Thomas Hygynson xxj yews — xl s. (xx.. viij d.)[6]
Item sold to Jamys Clerke xiiij^{xx} sherhoges and thevys — xxxvij li. vj s. viij d.
[*Margin*] There ys to resceyve of this sum v li. ix s. iij d. ut patet inferioris
Item sold to Herytage of Rodwey xx yews — xl s.
Item sold to Kytchyn xj yews — xxj s. iiij d.

[5] Right margin.
[6] Right margin, partly illegible.

Item sold to Dove vij sherhoges at ij s. viij d. the pec. Summa	xviij s. viij d.
Item Jamz Clarke xx^ti cullyng yews at ij s. the pec. Summa	xl s.
Item to Robyns of Tachebroke xij^xx sherehoges	l li.
Item I kyld in my house betwext the shertyme and Martylmas [*11 Nov.*] in cullyng yews about lj	
Item sold to Old Quiny of Flekno xx^ti lamz	xl s.

62 f. 65. B [*Money due for sheep, probably 1548*][7]

xxx	Henry Smyth of Feny Compton oweth for shep	iiij li. ij s. iiij d.	
lxxxx	Thomas Gryffyth of Feny Compton oweth	xij li. viij s. iiij d.	
xxxij	Item Thomas Perkyns of Honyngham oweth	iiij li. xx d. (xiij s. vij d.; vj s.)^er	
xx	Item Rychard Hacocke of Lemyngton[8] oweth	l s.	
xx	Item Wylliam Clarke of Feny Compton (iiij merkes iiij s. iiij d.)[9]	lvij s. viij d.	
viij	Item Wylliam Wylkyns of Feny Compton and his brother	xv s. iiij d.	
xxiij	Item Rychard Mylls of Harbery (iiij merkes x s. viij d.)	iij li. iiij s.	
x	Item Jhon Knybe of Feny Compton	xxiij s. iiij d.	
xxiij	Item Jhon Hygyns of Knyghtcott (iiij merkes xj s. iiij d.)	iij li. iiij s. viij d.	
x	Item Worall of Ufton	xxvj s. viij d.	
vj	Item Raynold Messenger, smyth of Harbery	xvij s.	
(j)^er	Item Wylliam that was sheperd in Harbery	ij s. viij d.	
j	Item Jamz Clarke	ij s. viij d.	
	. . .[10] the holl summa dew ys xxxvj li. xvj s., whereof resceyved	xxv li. xix s.	
	and there ys in thes mens handes:		
	Memorandum that Perkyns ys to paye	iiij li. xx d.	viij li. (bracketing these five sums)
	and Hawke of Lemyngton	xxx s.	
	and Myls wyffe of Harbery	xxxiij s.	
	and Wylkyns	v s. iiij d.	
	and Hygyns of Knyghtcot	x s.	
	And so remayneth in Jamz Clarkes handes to pay of this bargayne	liiij s. iiij d.	

[7] This and the next item probably relate to James Clarke's purchase in **61**, as noted *ut patet inferioris*. The leading numbers presumably give the number of sheep each buyer had, and their total (274) is almost the 280 in **61** and **63**; however, the sums cannot be exactly matched. The date cannot be earlier than 1548 (that of f. 65. A, **64**).

[8] Interlined, replacing *Harbery* [?]; *Hacocke* probably stands for *Hancocke*.

[9] The interlined sums in marks correspond to the main values (1 mark = 13s. 4d.).

[10] Erased word, *wthe*? The sum is given as £36 here and £37 in **61**.

63 f. 65 v. B [*Money received for sheep, probably 1548*][11]

Resceyved of Jamz Clarke in part of payment of xiiij^{xx} sherhoges the last of Maye	iiij li.
Item resceyved for the same of Thomas Gryffyn	iij li.
Item resceyved for the same of Henry Smyth	xl s.
Item the rest of Wylliam Lucas	xxvj s. viij d.
Item resceyved of Thomas Gryffyn	xj li. x s.
(Item resceyved of Mylls of Harbery	xx s.)^{er}
Item resceyved by Jamz Haukes senior	xxviij s.
Item[12] resceyved of Myls wyffe j tode wolle	xxij s.
Item of her more then x s.; item resceyved more xxxij s.; summa totalis	iij li. iiij s.
Item resceyved of Henry Smythe	xliij s. iiij d.
Item resceyved of Hancox of Lemyngton j tode woll	xx s.
Item resceyved of Parkyns xl s.; of hym more resceyved xxxiiij s. viij d.	

Summa xxxj li. vj s. viij d. (Summa receptis xxv li. xix s.)^{er}

64 f. 65. A [*Sheep deliveries, 1548*][13]

Delyvered ynto Harbery Feld to Mylls, Chebse and[14] that ys to saye ix thevys, iiij^{xx} and xij chylverhoges, iiij^{xx}xvij wether hogges	viiij^{xx}xviij (shepe)^{er} hoges and thevys
Delyvered to Lucas in sherehoges xiij^{xx} and xviij, whereof sold j fell	
Delyvered ynto Compton Feld to Archer and Robyns and Petifer wherof (iij dede)^{er} resceyved iij fells	iiij^{c}iij wetherhoges
Delyvered in to Avne Dassett Feld to Harry Petyfer	ij^{c} chilverhoges
Delyvered to Kynston Feld to Herytag	iiij^{xx} wetherhoges

65 f. 66. A Shepe remayning in my pastur and elswher at the fest of All Sayntes in anno ij^{do} regni regis Edwardi vjth [*1 Nov. 1548*] as followeth

Inprimis in Herytage Feld in wether and chylver hoggrells	xxxj^{xx} and xij
Item rame lamz	xxiij^{ti}
and old ramz	xxxviij^{ti}
Item in Hawls Feld and the Old Leesse in yews	lj^{xx} and xiiij
Item Avne Dassett Feld in thevys	xij^{xx}
Item in Harbery Feld in wethers	xij^{xx}[15] and xiiij
Item in Compton Feld in Sherhoges	xj^{xx} and xiij

Summa ij^{m}lxxxxiij [= *2493*],[16] wherof

[11] This is clearly the same transaction as the last item, at a slightly earlier stage.

[12] Line erased, but marked *stet* in the margin.

[13] Dated by comparison with the next item, and from f. 65. B (62), also 1548.

[14] Followed by a gap.

[15] Apparently altered from 13 score.

[16] For totals in *great tale*, see Table 1. The decimal total is in brackets. The correct total for this item is 2453.

Sold iij fells, xvij sherling fels, vij sherlyng fels, staple fels lxvj, iij pyld fels, viij sherlyns

66 f. 63 v. Cullyng shep and lamz sold abowt Mychelmas in anno iij[rd] regni regis Edwardi vj[th] [*29 Sept. 1549*] ut sequitur

Inprimis sold to Thomas Hygynson xxj lamz	xxxiij s. iiij d.
Item to the same Thomas xxj yews	xl s.
Item to his mother xxj lamz	xxxiij s. iiij d.
Item to hys brother (Richard)[er] Gregory ix lamz	xvj s. viij d.
Item to hys brother Byshop x yews	xviij s. iiij d.
Item to Jhon Rodford, Hygynsons man, iij lamz	iij s. iiij d.
[*margin*][17] I must have iij quarter ottes	
Item sold to Heritage of Rodwey xx[ti] lamz	xxxiij s. iiij d.
Item sold to Thomas Gryffyn of Compton xxxj yews	iij li. vj s. viij d.
Item to hym more lvj lamz	iij li. xiiij s. viij d.
Item to hym more iiij lamz for a lode of straw	
Item sold to Tomkyns of Ichington xij[xx] yews	xxxv li.
[*margin*][17] resceyved xx li.; item v li.	
Item sold to Thomas Hygynson xlj lamz	iiij li.

67 f. 66. B [*Sheep sales, 1549*][18]

Sold to Lapworth and other xij[xx] wethers	lx li.
Sold to Scrivener and Robyns (x)[er] x[xx] and x wetherhoges	xlvj li. xiij s. iiij d.
Item sold at Coventre xx[ti] sherlynges	iij li. xiij s. iiij d.
Item sold at Coventre xl[ti] sherlyng yews	v li.
Summa	j[c]xxij li.

68 f. 24 v. C

Nota that over and besydes all this aforesayd I have sold to Lapworth of Sow and other this present yere xij[xx] wethers lx li.; resceyved xxx li.

Item sold lykweys to Robyns of Tachebroke and Scryvener of Ashebye tene schore wetherhoges and x	xlvj li. xiij s. iiij d.
[*margin*] resceyved xxxvj li. xiiij s. iiij d.	
Item sold unto Edward Petyver xl wetherhoges	vj li. xiij s. iiij d.
Item xx[ti] baren yewes and wethers shorne	iij li. xiij s. iiij d.
Item sold xlv sherlynges yews and wethers	v li.

69 f. 66. C. [*Sheep sales, 1550*][19]

[*margin*] He hath made me a byll of hys hand for all this, wherfore I have crossed this owt.

[17] Marginal note referring to the preceding entry.

[18] This lies between items for late 1548 and early 1550 on f. 66; **68** gives a second note of the same facts, with a few additions; it follows a list of debts for 1549 (**231**), apparently the *aforesayd* item. The disagreement between the final entries of **67** and **68** should be noted.

[19] The whole item is crossed through.

Sold to Jamz Clarke the xjth of Aperill anno regni regis Edwardi vjth iiij^{tio} [*1550*] vij^{xx} and xvij wethers at v s. iiij d. the [pec]	xxxvj li. x s. viij d.
Wherof resceyved at Whittsuntyde [*25 May*]	xxvj li. xiij s. iiij d.
Item resceyved mor of hym for the same on Lamas daye [*1 Aug.*]	v li.
Memorandum there ys to resceyve of this bargayne	iiij li. xvij s. iiij d.
Item he dothe owe me apon ij old rekenynges	ix li. iiij s. viij d.
Item he dothe owe me for the rent of [?Mylne] Close dew at Lammas in anno 4to regni regis Edwardi vjth [*1550*]	xxvj s. viij d.
Wherof he hath paid for me (to Makepes)^{er} to Holbage[20]	xxxiij s. iiij d.

70 f. 63 Cullyng shepe and other shepe sold at May Daye and after in anno iiij^{to} regni regis Edwardi vjth [*1550*] ut sequitur

In primis sold to Mr. Wattes, Wylliam Horby and Rychard Wryght xiiij^{xx} wether hogges at v s. iiij d. the pece. Summa	lxxiiij li. xj s. iiij d.
[*margin*] Mr. Wattes oweth v li. vj s. viij d. I owe hym l s.	
Item sold to Dode, Smyth and Basse of Feny Compton vj schore and ij chilver hoges at iiij s. ij d. the pece, savyng iij s. iiij d. to be abatyd in the holle	xxv li. v s.
[*margin*] Resceyved of Dode and Basse xvj li. xvj s. viij d. Resceyved of Smyth iiij li. viij s.	
Item sold at Banbery xx^{ty} barege yews	vj li.
Item sold ij barege yews	xviij s.
Item gevyn my cosyn Spenser ij barege yews	
Item sold to William Harbyd and Rychard Wryght viij^{xx} cullyng lamz at xx d. the pece. Sum	xiij li. vj s. viij d.
Item sold to them vij^{xx} cullyng yews at ij s. viij d. the pec. Summa	xviij li. xiij s. iiij d.
Item sold to Hygyns v^{xx} cullyng lamz at ij s. x d. the pec	xiiij li. iij s. ij d.
[*margin*] Resceyved (viij li.)^{er} xxiij s. ij d., in the which he ys allowyd [? x s.] that he paid for me to Mistris Foster, and he oweth me yet v li. Item he hath paid [yt].	
Item sold to Herytage of Rodwey xx^{ti} lamz	iij li.
Item sold to Thomas Gryffyne xx^{ti} lamz	iij li. vj s. viij d.
Item sold to Scrivener and Wryght xl^{ti} cullyng yews and lx lamz at iij s. iiij d. the pece. Sum	xvj li. xiij s. iiij d.
Summa Clxxv li. xix s. vj d.	

Memorandum my wolle of this yeres growyng sold and delyvered to Mr. Kyrton and Whettell at xxv s. iiij d. a pec	Clxxx li.

[20] For Henry Makepeace's annuity see p. 148.

Item the fedyng and grasyng of bestes this yere (endyd (at)[er] after to este ... may)[er]	xxxv li.
Memorandum left in the pastur at Martylmas [*11 Nov.*]	Mj[c]xvij yews
Item xxxiiij[xx] and iiij hogrells and x rame hoges. Item xxxij old ramz.	
Summa totalis xvij[c]xxiij [= *2063*]	
Item sold to Warner j ryke of heye for ix li.	

71 f. 62 v.[21] Wether hoges, bareg yews and other cullyng sheep and lamz sold at Ester and after anno 5 regni regis Edwardi vj [*1551*]

Inprimis sold to Mr. Marow vj yews bareg	xlv s.
Item sent my brother Bartylmew[22] iiij yews	
Item sold to Robyns of Tachebroke and his brother xij[xx] wetherhoges	lxxviiij li. vj s. viij d.
[*margin*] Resceyved xxxix li. vj s.	
Item sold lxxx cullyng wether and chilver hoges in the wolle to Haskens of Renford[23]	xxj li. vj s. viij d.
[*margin*] Resceyved vij li. vj s. viij d. Item resceyved vij li.	
Item sold at Banbery xx baren cullyng yews.	vij li. xvj s. viij d.
Item sold to the Lame Taker iiij yews	xx s.
Item he toke for the Kyng lij lamz	v li. iiij s.
Item sold more to Hasken xx cullyng hogrells	iiij li.
Item sold to Slade ij lamz	vj s. viij d.
Item sold to ij buchers of Banbery xij yews shorne	iij li. xj s. iiij d.
Item sold to them more vj yews shorne	xxxvj s.
Item sold to them more of the same viij yews	xlviij s.
Item sold to them more xx[ti] yews	vj li.
Item sold to Mr. Marrow xiiij yews	iij li. xiiij s. viij d.
[*margin*] Resceyved of Hyginson the sayd iij li. xiiij s. viij d.	
Item sold to Powell lxxxij yews	xx li.
Item sold to hym more vj[xx] and x (lam)[er] cullyng lamz	xxvj li.
[*margin*] Resceyved xiij li.	
Item sold to Mistris Chamberlen lxxxiij cullyng yews	(xvij li. viij s.)[er] xiiij li. x s.
Item delyvered to Herytage and Hyerne of Rodway vj[xx] and j lamz	xxvj li.
[*margin*] Resceyved xiiij li. xiij s. iiij d.	
Item gevyn to Knyght x collyng lamz	
Item gevyn to a hynd toward hys losse by fyer vj lamz	
Item sold to the Clerke ij lamz	vj s. viij d.
Item to Frepase ij blacke lamz	viij s.
Summa ij[c]xxvij li. (x)[er] v s. vij d. and xiiij s. viij d.	

[21] Reproduced as the Frontispiece.
[22] Bartholomew Jekyll; see Pedigree 4 (p. 25).
[23] Perhaps Romford, Essex, where a large stock fair and market was held.

Item fedyng and fe[24] gresse sold for hey and gystment thys yere — xl li.

Memorandum my wolle of this yere sold and delyvered to Mr. Marshe at xx s. the tode abatyng xl s. in the holle and over and above the allowance of iij li. to the sacke — Cxxx li. x s.

Item delyvered to the said Mr. Mershe xvij tode and halfe at xx s. the tode. Summa xvij li. x s. of tythe wole and bought wolle.

[*margin*] Item sold the remanment of a ryck of hey for xl s.

[*margin*] Item left ij ryckes of old hey, about xxv lodes. Sold the same ij ryckes in Marche anno vij Edwardi vj [*1553*] for xiij li. xj s. viij d.

Memorandum left in the pastur at Martylmas xj^{c} and v^{xx} yews and xij yews to kyll in the howse, in hogrells vj^{c} and xiiij, and rame hogrells xlix and iiij rygylls to kyll, in old ramz xxxiiij.

Summa xviij^{c}lxiij of the gret tale [= *2223*],[25] and in fels xx^{ti}, wherof bought of Water Frekylton vij^{xx} yews and v ramz at vij s. the pec, for l li. and xv s. at Mychelmas. Qd ... for they were not worthe halfe the money the next [?yere].[26]

72 f. 44 v. A — [*Undated stock sales*]

Sold to Gysby xlvij stews at xviij d. a pec	iij li. x s. vj d.
Sold Gysby ij bullokes at xvij s. the pec	xxxiiij s.
Sold to Gysby ij bullokes	xxxix s. viij d.
Sold to Gysby j hoge prec'	v s. viij d.
Sold [*blank*]	

73 f. 45. B

Sold to Gamon xxx ews at xx d. the pec — l s.

FIELD ACCOUNTS AND FLOCK COUNTS

74 f. 11. B — [*1544*]

xxxvj li.	Charges de Heritage Feld anno xxxvj [*1544*]
Woll	xxx li.
iiij^{xx} wetherhoges	xv li.
ix^{c}xxviij felles	[*blank*]
colly ews	viij li.

24 i.e. for fee.

25 The correct total is 2253.

26 Squeezed in at the bottom of the page and partly illegible.

75 f. 4 v. B *[1540s year I]*[27]

The yerly revenews of Herytag Feld

The woll of xxxviij^{xx} yews and xl rams	xxxvj li.
The lamene xxvj^{xx}	xxxix li.
The collyd yews	vj li.
Item viij mylche kyne	*[blank]*
j mare	
dage lockes	
wyndyng lockes	
sheryng lockes	

76 f. 5. B *[1540s year II]*

The Hyls[28] iij^{c}liiij acres j rode xiiij polle	The yerely charges of my pasture comonly callyd Erytage Feld	j^{c}lxxxvj acres iij rode viij pole
Fyrst the yerely rent there of ys		xxvj li.
Item for the tythe there off		iij li. x s.
For the sheperdes wagis and his lyverey		xxv s.
Item his borde		(iij li.)^{er} lxvj s. viij d.
Item for hardels		vj s.
Item for wasshing the shepe		v s.
Item for sheryng the[m]		x s.
Item the woll wyndyng		x s.
Item for pyche and ter		viij s.
Item for hey makyng and mowyng		x s.
Item for reperacions and thackyng		v s.
	Summa xxxvj li.	

The revenews therof

Woll of xxxvj^{xx} shepe and xl rams	xxxvj li.
xxij^{xx} lamz	xxx li.
Cully yews iij^{xx}	iiij li.
xij mylche kyne	iiij li.

77 f. 5 v.	The yerely charge of my feld calyd Hals Feld and Old Lesse	iiij^{c}lxix acres ix pole
The rent and tythe		lxvj li.
Sheperdes wages and vj kyene and j mare[29]		xliij s. iiij d.
Item for hurdels		vij s. vj d.
Item washyng		x s.
Sheryng		xx s.
Wyndyng		xx s.

[27] By elimination, these estimates may be for 1545 and 1546, as 74 is for 1544.
[28] Why this field is noted is unclear, as the details cover only Heritage Field.
[29] Probably a grazing right.

Piche and tere	xvj s.
Hey makyng and mowyng	xxvj s. viij d.

lxxiij li. xij s. vj d.[30]

The yerely revenews of the feld afore syde

The wol of xij^{c} shepe	lxx li.
The lams xxxvj^{xx}	liiij li.
Colye yews vj^{xx}	ix li.

j^{c}xxxiij li.[30]

viij geldyng x runtes[31]

Somer xxx bullock

[*margin*] Memorandum now I have provyd that this pownd wyll not kepe x^{c} shepe and there fore[32]

78 S.1.D [*Flock counts, late 1550s years I and II*][33]

Halsfeld	yews	vj^{c}
Old Leys	lams	iij^{c}xl
medow and Heelskote [*Arlescote*?] Close	thevys	C
Herytage Feld (vj^{c})^{er}	lamz	j^{c}xxxx
Halsfeld	thevys	C
Ramz Close	ramz	lx
Yews		xvj^{c}
(yews)^{er} chylverhoges		iiij^{c}lx
wetherhoges and ramzhoges		iiij^{c}lx
thevys		ij^{c}
ramz		lx

Summa totalis MMvij^{c}lx [= *3300*]

wherof to sell		
cullyng lamz	iij^{c}	lxxx li.
culyng yews	iij^{c}lx	lxx li.
wetherhoges	iiij^{c}	Cxl(iiij)^{er} li.
(to shere at x the tode)^{er}		
to shere at xj the tode MMCCC [= *2760*] 230 todes		200 li. 10 s.

CCCClxxxx(iiij)^{er}v li. x s.[34]

[*Year II*]

Yews	MMCCCClx
chylver hoges	vj^{c}lx
wether hoges	v^{c}lx
thevys	iij^{c}
ramz	lxxx
Summa totalis	MMMMxx [= *4820*]

30 In the right margin, bracketed against the preceding figures.

31 After a short gap.

32 Nothing more written.

33 In three paragraphs of continuous text in the original, set out here in columns for clarity.

34 The corrected total requires £145 for the sale of wether hogs, but the sum given is £140, corrected from £144 which gives a cost per sheep of 6s. 0d.

wherof to sell		
cullyng lamz	viij^{c}	Clx li.
and cullyng yews	(v^{c})^{er} iiij^{c}lx	lxxxx li.
wether hoges	v^{c}	Clxxx li.
to shere	MMMCCCClxxx [= *4160*]	
at xj the tode	374 todes	327 li. v s.
	[*total*]	vij^{c}lvij li.

79 [S.1. E] [*Late 1550s, year III*]

Cxxxij tode at xvij s. vj d. the tode	Cxv li. v s.
v^{c}lx lamz at iij s. iiij d.	Cx li.
Clxxx yews	xxxiij li. vj s. viij d.

80 S.6. A [*Sheep, 1562–3*]

A reconynge of the shepe left in the charge of John Sheperde at Mycaelmas even, anno 1562. This reconynge was taken the ixth of June anno domini 1563. Fyrst for the xxxij^{tie} score and v sh hogges left then. He doth thus recone: viij^{xx} of them are nowe, even the date of this present reconyng with Westley. iij^{xx} of them were sold about Martlemas [*11 Nov.*] to one Lysle and Goodwin of Ancor [?]. One Allen bought xx^{tie} of them more about the xxth of Marche. Ther were of them gyddy and dead xiij^{ten}. Ther doe remayne nowe, even the sayd ixth day of June, in Heritage Feld xix^{teen} score and xiiij^{teen}. So hath he accompted for them all and ij more, which is by reason that ij cade lames were sold and now reconed and not apon the other accompt, even for hogges.

The viij^{t} cullinge yewes were all kylled.

Of the xxvij^{tie} wethers, xiiij^{teen} kylled, j dydd and xij remayne, and so even.

Of the lxix rames, v dydd and iij^{xx} and iiij yet remayne.

Of the xxviij^{ti} ram hogges, j was kylled, the rest remayne.

So John Sheperdes accompt is even and falles out well.

A reconyng of the shepe left in the charge of Hacocke on Mycaelmas even, anno 1562. This reconyng was taken of hym the ixth of June, anno domini 1563.

For the lj^{ti} score yewes and v shepe ther are now remayning in Halles Feld and Old Lease vij^{c}viij [= *848*], xvij^{tene} dead, viij^{xx} remayn in Heritage Feld, so even.

For the xiij^{teen} score and j hogge left in hys charge then, xiij^{xx} he sold to Duncobe [?] and the other was kyllyd, and soe even.

So his accompt falles out well.

4. *Peter Temple: Wool*

The tale of Peter Temple's own wool clip is simply and profitably told (summary in Table 4.1). From £30 in 1544, his income rose to almost £300 in 1549. A fall followed, the result partly of a smaller

Table 4.1: *Wool sales and purchases*

(A) Sold from Peter Temple's own flock

Year	Sheep shorn	Amount[a] (tod)	Price per tod	Value	Buyer: comments	Ref.
1543				£43	Probably includes bought wool	208
1544	(535)[b]	48 tod 19 lb.	12s. 8d.	£30 3s. 4d.	Robert Temple	81 (see also 74)
1540s (I)	800	(57)[c]		£36	Perhaps for 1545	75
(II)	760	(57)		£36	£116 total; perhaps for 1546	76
	1440	(110)		£70		
1546	101			£2 12s. 4d.	Wool of some Welsh ewes	55
1546		11 tod 25 lb.	13s. 0d.	£7 14s. 7d.	Anthony Ashefeld	223
1547		(242)[d]		£181 13s. 4d.	Robert and Cuthbert Temple	82
1548	(2470)	224½	22s. 0d.	£246 19s.	Thomas Lee	83
1549	(2670)	242½	24s. 0d.	£291	Anthony Cave (excluding bought wool)	84
1550	(1560)	142	25s. 4d.	£180	Kyrton and Whettell	70
1551	(1890)	171½	15s. 6d.[e]	£130 10s.	Marshe	71
1550s (I)	2760	230	17s. 5d.	£200 10s.		78
(II)	4160	374	17s. 6d.	£327 5s.		78
(III)	(1452)	132	17s. 6d.	£115 5s.	Presumably incomplete	79

(B) Purchases

Year	Amount	Price	Total paid	Comments	Ref.
1543			£6	Laid out for Robert Temple	221
1544	11		£6 19s. 4d.	Sold at 12s. 8d.	81
?1546–7		15s. 4d.			85
1548	290	19s. 10d.	£285 3s.	Excluding 10 tod from previous year	86
1549	71½	19s. 10d.	£77 15s. 6d.	Also 9 tod tithe wool	90
1550	12	21s.	£12 6s.		92
1551	17½			Bought wool sold for 20s. per tod	71

[a] 1 sack = 13 tod of 28 lb.
[b] Assuming 11 fleeces per tod.
[c] Assuming a price of 12s. 8d. per tod.
[d] Assuming a price of 15s.
[e] Notionally 20s. a tod, but reduced by £3 per sack (i.e. £10 for 13 tod) and then by £2 overall.

clip, and partly of a considerable drop in the price.[35] However, by the later 1550s, even with the lower price, the predicted income was over £300. Thus, the sales of wool brought in a sum comparable

[35] This is also available in the national compilation of prices, *Ag. Hist.*, p. 842.

to that from sheep sales—more when wool was up in 1547–8, and rather less in the 1550s. The direct costs were minimal, £4 5s. for 2,200 sheep (**76**).

Frustratingly, though we know either the total weight of wool *or* the number of sheep shorn for the whole period, only the predictions in the 1550s give the vital figure of the weight of wool from each sheep. It was then recorded that eleven sheep gave one tod, or 28 lb.[36] of wool, i.e. $2\frac{1}{2}$ lb. each. In the 1540s, if the price given in 1544 can be used, each fleece weighed just over 2 lb. (thirteen sheep to the tod).[37] These figures fully confirm the reputation of the Midlands and the Cotswold sheep for big fleeces. In Norfolk, the average weight was just one half of this.[38]

Peter Temple's wool trading had another side. In his earliest accounts (for 1543, **221**), he spent £6 buying wool for his brother Robert, and later he also bought odd lots of wool for resale (e.g. **85**). But in 1548 came an astonishing change. Between 6 and 17 April, he made a tour through twenty-seven villages and towns, mostly north of Burton Dassett (Fig. 5). There he contracted with sixty-five villagers to buy the wool they would shear in June, to a total of 298 tod.[39] More important, in contrast to the opportunist picking up of odd parcels of wool for cash, this needed a major capital investment, as the wool was mostly paid for in advance (in instalments), totalling no less than £285 (19s. 10d. per tod).[40] When sheep-shearing time came, not everyone could produce all their promised wool, but others had extra; the 4 tod and 25 odd pounds lacking was more than replaced. Unfortunately, we do not have a record of the resale price, which was presumably not more than the 22s. a tod that Peter received for his own wool. This would indicate a gross profit of £31.

36 For some wool bought in 1549 there is a note that each tod was either $28\frac{1}{2}$ or 29 lb., but this seems not to have affected the price paid.

37 There is also one figure for bought wool, 24 tod from 240 sheep or 2 lb. 13 oz. per fleece (**86**, f. 69 and 67 v).

38 Allison, op. cit. (on p. 78), pp. 105–6. Finch, 1956, estimates nine to ten fleeces to the tod, but without extensive evidence. One Heritage entry in the account book (**98**) gives twelve fleeces per tod, but these are of unknown origin and quality.

39 A further 31 tod was expected, but the contracts were cancelled. Rather later evidence (1580), from the only detailed tithe account for Northend and Knightcote, shows that the wool Peter Temple collected was only a small fraction of that produced. Even in these common field villages, no less than 175 tod were shorn (Wotton Accounts, Bodleian Library, Broxbourne, MSS. 84.15/R267). Figures for wool in the tithe accounts discussed in section 10 indicate a clip ranging from 32 tod in 1537 (**153**) to 76 tod in 1557 (**162**), but it is possible that part of the clip was paid for separately.

40 Just when he paid is not clear; the only recorded date is 1 June, but this was in 1550.

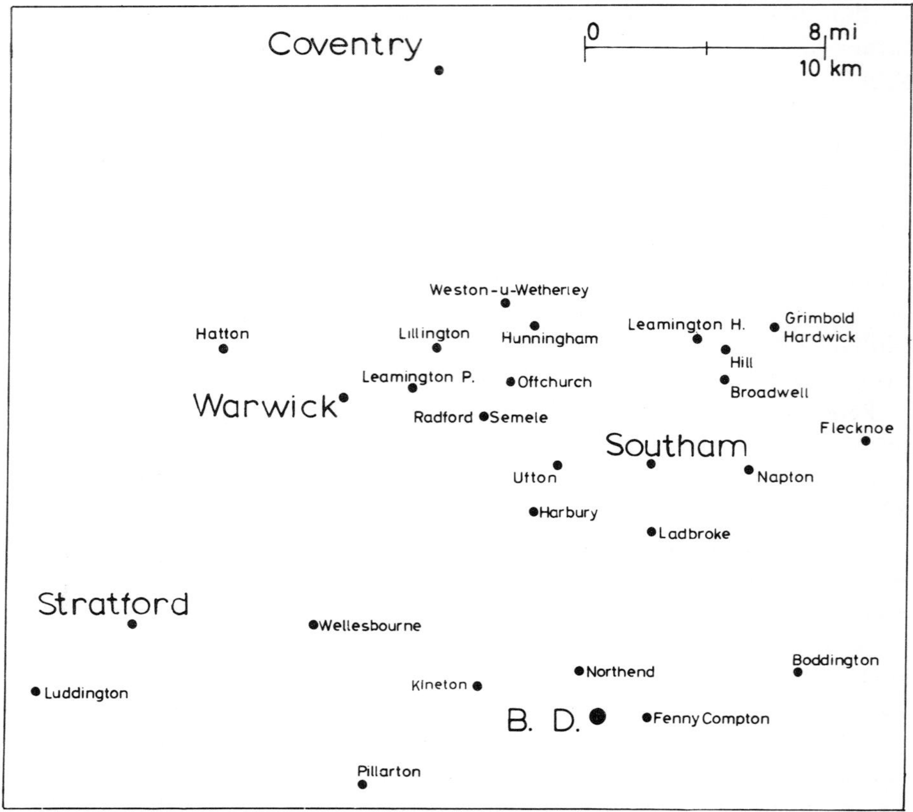

Fig. 5. Wool purchases, 1548–9: locations. Leamington H. = Leamington Hastings; Leamington P. = Leamington Priors.

Next year saw a repetition, but on a smaller scale, with only 78 tod bought, in six places. Though he paid the same price, the selling price of wool was higher·and the profit perhaps £17. However, that ended this endeavour, and the next years saw only oddments bought. Did Peter Temple anticipate the coming fall in wool prices, or was there just too little profit in this enterprise? It is also not clear why he started. It could have been an experiment, or he may have blundered in his dealings with the people buying his own wool, and contracted to supply for two years larger quantities of wool than his own flocks could provide.

Peter Temple's role here is immediately recognizable as that of the 'wool brogger', the small-scale wool dealer of Tudor England, perpetually blamed for all the ills that affected the wool supply.[41] Of

[41] Bowden, 1962, *passim*.

their activities little is known except by inference, though they seem to have combined their dealing with agriculture or other trades. However, their wool buying must surely have followed the same pattern as his. They too would have needed to arrange their dealings in April or May, when the villagers could estimate their clip quite well, collect it in June and then resell. They would also concentrate on particular areas. Indeed, as Peter Temple ignored the villages to the south of Burton Dassett, another dealer was probably buying there. The scale of his activities, with a profit of £20–30 might also correspond to those of a small brogger; however, the evidence suggests that they would probably deal on credit, or expect a rapid turn-over of their capital, rather than lay out the considerable sums that Peter Temple could afford.[42]

The background to Peter Temple's sales of wool is much clearer, mainly because he was dealing with men of considerable importance, who are thus well-recorded.[43] Robert Temple, of course, was a clothier, and no doubt put his purchases directly to use. However, four of the other buyers were themselves middle-men, Merchants of the Staple, supplying wool particularly to the Flanders cloth industry. Anthony Cave was established as a sheep farmer at Tickford, Buckinghamshire, as well as running his wool business.[44] Anthony Ashefeld, a few years after his dealing with Peter Temple, appears as a very prominent dealer, holding (and abusing) one of the few licences to market wool for export.[45] Kyrton and Whettell can be recognized as Stephen Kyrton and Richard Whethill; both of them were London merchants, with houses of surpassing magnificence.[46] Indeed, it is not surprising to find that anyone able to deal with the major graziers, with wool clips worth several hundred pounds, was himself a man of great resources.

WOOL

81 f. 60. B Anno xxxvj [*1544*]

Delyvered my brother in woll of my pastur xlvij[ti] tode xix[li] at xij s. viij d. the tode. Summa	xxx li. iij s. iiij d.

[42] Ibid., pp. 79–80.

[43] Particularly because of the survival of the John Johnson papers (Winchester, 1955); many references to these are printed in *L. & P. Henry VIII*, XIX–XXI.

[44] Winchester, 1955, *passim*.

[45] Bowden, 1962, pp. 127–8.

[46] John Stow, *Survey of London*, cited by Winchester, 1955, p. 211.

Item delyvered my brother in woll that I bought of Stonley xj tode at xij s. viij d. the tode			vj li. xix s. iiij d.
Lent hym by Jack			xiij li. vj s. viij d.
Delyvered Thurwood	iiij li.	Resceyved by Cutbart	iiij li.
Delyvered Cutbart	xvj li.	Resceyved by Wyll	xvj li.
Delyvered my brother	vij li.	Resceyved of hym	iij li.
		and of Cutbard	iiij li.

[223 *of 1546 includes*: Delyvered to Mr Anthony Ashefeld xj tode xxv^{lb} at 13 s. the tode 7 li. 12 s. 6½d.]

82 f. 74. B Anno primo Edwardi 6 [1547] money that I have resceyved of my brother apon my woll, as well for hys self as for Cuthbart.

Delyvered to Thomas Spenser for me	viij li.
Item resceyved of Wylliam	xl li.
Item the sayd Wylliam delyvered Thomas Spenser for	xl li.
Item I resceyved of my brother	vj li. xiij s. vj d.
Item more of hym	xl s.
Item my brother promised to delyver Thomas Spenser	xx li.
Item resceyved of Wylliam	lxv li.

83 f. 78. B

Receyved of Mr. Temple the xxij^{ti} daie of September anno secundo Edwardi sexti [1548] ix sacke of woolle

Thomas Lee

Recyved of Mr. Temple the xxiiijth of September anno secundo Edwardi sexti xvij sackes three toode a halfe and (two)^{er} one pound of woole at xxij s. the todde, amountyng in the hoole to the soome of xij^{xx} and six poundes nyntyne shyllynges of currante monney.

The which monney is to be paid within six daies after the date herof.

Thomas Lee

84 f. 64. B [*Wool, 1549*][47]

Delyvered to Mr Anthony Cave by his servant Georg Peres xviij sack viij tod and halfe at xxiiij s. the tode. Summa of the holle ij^{c}lxxxxj li.

[47] Dated partly by elimination, and partly by its following the 1549 sheep sales (**66**).

WOOL DEALING

85 f. 70 v. C[48]

Delivered to Profyt of Northend in part of payment for hys woll at xv s. iiij d. per tode	xxvj s. viij d.

86 f. 69 *[1548]*[49]

Bought of William Brokes of Dasset xxiiij tod woll at xix s. the tode	Delyvered in hand xl s.; delyvered x li. delyvered xiiij li.
Item bought of Parkyns of Honyngham xx[ti] tode at xix s. the tode	Delyvered in hand xix li.
Bought of Thomas Burbery de Dasset xviij tode of woll at xvj s. the tode	Delyvered xiij li. viij s.
Bought of Rychard Mercot of Harbery ij tod at xix s.	Delyvered xxvj s. viij d.
(Bought of Mr Hykman the woll of xij[xx] shepe at xxj s. the tode to be paid at Candlemas [*2 Feb.*] next)[er]	
Bought of Reynold Messenger, smyth, of Harbery ij tode woll at xix s. the tode and vj d. over	Delyvered xxxviij s. vj d.
Rychard Mylls of Harbery ij tod bought at xix s. the tode	Delyvered xxxviij s.
Bought of James Clerke of Compton the vj[th] of Aprill at xx s. the tode, abowte xv tode	Delyvered xj li.; iij li. viij s.
Bought of Jhon Nychols of Lylington ij tode at xx s. the tode the vij of Aprill	Delyvered xl s.
Bought of Jhon Ansty of Honyngham j tod at xx s. the tode	Delyvered xx s.
Item of a woman of Honyngham di. tode	x s.
Bought of Edward Quiny of Ufton ij tode at xx s. the tode and di. and di. li. [$2\frac{1}{2}$ *tod* + $\frac{1}{2}$ *lb.*]	Delyvered xl s.; x s. iiij d.
Bought of Jhon Smyth of Brodwell the ix[th] of Aprill j tode at xx s. the tode	Delyvered xx s.
Bought of Harry Garrett of Hyll in Lemyngton parishe the ix[th] of Aprill iij tode at xx s. the tode	Delyvered iij li.
Bought of Rychard Curteys of Brodewell the ix[th] of Aprill iij tode at xix s. the tode	Delyvered lvij s.

[48] An early year from the price.

[49] This item was written in reverse, the right side of each opening before the left, from f. 69 to f. 67 v, and is continued by the 'wool received' (**88**) on ff. 67–66 v (identifiable from the correspondence of names and amounts). The dating follows from (i) dated items for 1549 and 1550 (**90–92**), (ii) its preceding the 1548 sheep accounts (**65**, f. 66. A), (iii) the reference to Rychard Myls of Harbury, with 'Myls widow' in 1549 (**90**).

Bought of Jhon Hygyns of Brodewell iij tode at xix s. the tode the ixth of Aprill	Delyvered iij li.
Memorandum[50] that Sawll of Pyllarton oweth me j tode woll, and Rychard Myls of Harbery xxiiij s. iiij d., and Rychard Mosse of Radford owes for wol lackyng x s., and Burchols xxj s. iiij d., and Dycke Sheperd xiij s. iiij d. I delyvered Jamz Clarke vj s. viij d. for Dycke, which I must have agayn of Jamz.	

[f. 68 v.]

Bought of Thomas Mekoke of Napton iij tode at xx s. the tode the ixth of Aprill	Delyvered xxx s.; delyvered x s.; delyvered xx s.
Bought of Jhon Curteis of Brodwell j tode (di)^{er} at xx s. the tode the ixth of Aprill	Delyvered xx s.
Bought of Rychard Savage of Bodyngton, the mother ij tode at xx s., ixth of April	Delyvered xx s.; xx s.
Bought of Rychard Cattell of Hyll in Lemyngton j tode at xix s. viij d. the tode eodem die	Delyvered xix s. viij d.
Bought of Dycke Sheperd of Priors Lemyngton the ixth of Aprill at xx s. the tode, vij tode	Delyvered vj li. xiij s. iiij d.; xx s.; vj s. viij d.; iiij d.
Bought of Mr. Rey, Bayly of Warwyke[51] the xvth of Aprell x tode at xx s. the tode	Delyvered x li.
Bought of Thomas Saull of Pyllarton the xvth of Aprell at xx s. the tode xiij tode	Delyvered vij li.; delyvered vj li.
Bought of Jhon Heritage of Kyngston iiij tode woll at xx s. the tode the xvth of Aprell	Delyvered xl s. and xxx s. and he oweth me x s.
Bought agayne of Jhon Nychols of Lylington at Southam ij tode more at xx s. the tode	Delyvered xl s.
Bought of Thomas Nychols of Lodbroke ij tode at xx s. the tod the xvijth of Aprell	Delyvered xl s.
Bought of Jhon Carpenter of Napton j tode	Delyvered xx s.
Item of Thomas Ancester of Napton j tode	Delyvered xx s.
Bought of Jhon Stonele of Ofchurch iiij tode at xx s. the tode the xvijth of Aprill	Delyvered xl s.; delyvered x s.; xxx s.
Item of Rychard Wynter of Lodbroke di. tode	Delyvered x s.
Bought of Robart Amors of Coventre, whittawyer, iiij tode at xx s. the tode eodem die	Delyvered iiij li.

[50] After a slight gap.

[51] John Rey was Bailiff of Warwick (strictly the Principal Burgess) in 1549–51: Thomas Kempe, *A History of Warwick and its People* (Warwick, n.d.).

Bought of Jhon Oldfeld[52] of Napton j tode	(Delyvered xx s.)[er]
Bought of Edward Hancocke of Weston iiij tode at xx s. the tode	Delyvered iiij li.
Of Wylliam Smyth of Brodwell j tode	Delyvered xx s.
Of Wylliam Cattell of Brodwell j tode	xx s.

[f. 68]

Bought of Thomas Bisshope of Welsburne iiij tode at xx s. the tode, delyvered to Saull for hym	Delyvered iiij li.; capt. lix di
Bought of Rychard Qyinnye of Flekenho at xxj s. the tode (xxiij tode)[er] xviij tode di., the xvij[th] of Aprill	Delyvered ix li.; Delyvered x li. xviij s. vj d.
Bought more of Wylliam Brokes vj tode at xxj s.	Delyvered xl s.; delyvered xl s.; xl s.
Bought of Jhon Medes of Radford iiij tode at xx s. the tode. Delyvered to Baldwyn Ward for hym	Delyvered iiij li.
Bought of Rychard Brasse of Harbery j tode	Delyvered xx s.
Bought of Thomas Grenwey of Harbery j tode at xx s. the tode. Delyvered to Messenger for hym	xx s.
Bought of Oliver Croftes of Harbery j tode	Delyvered xx s.
Bought of Hugh Palmer of Hatton v tode at xx s. the tode	Delyvered v li.
Bought of Rychard Mosse of Radford iiij tode at xx s. the tode	Delyvered iiij li.
Bought more of Thomas Burbery of Dassett x tode at xx s. the tode	Delyvered x li.
Bought of Leonard Masse of Kynston iiij tode. Delyvered to Saull Thomas[53] for hym	Delyvered iiij li.
Of Wylliam Basse of Hyll in Lemyngton j tode at xx s.	Delyvered xx s.
Of Wylliam Perkens of Honyngham iiij tode at xx s. the tode	Delyvered iij li.; xxx s.
Bought of Thomas Chebse of Lodbroke iiij tode at xx s.	Delyvered xl s.
Of Robert Man of Honingham ij tode di. at xx s. the tode	Delyvered xx s.; xxx s.
Of Wylliam Canternell of Feny Compton iij tode at xx s.	Delyvered xl s.; xix s.
Of Roger Brafeld of Ofchurche ij tode at xx s.	Delyvered xl s.
Of Rychard Langley of Sowtham j todd and ij flysshes [*fleeces*] at xx s. the tode	Delyvered xx s. viij d.

[52] Absent from the list of wool received (**88**).

[53] For Thomas Saull.

Of Wylliam Davy of Feny Compton j tode at xx s. the tode	xx s.; v s. viij d.
Of Thomas Garret of Hyll in Lemyngton j tode	Delyvered xx s.
Of Wylliam Clerke of Feny Compton j tode, to James delyvered	xx s.
Of Robert Hyll, servant to Henry the smith of Feny Compton j tod	Delyvered xix s.

[f. 67 v.]

(Bought of Jhon Gefferys of Stratford xx^{ti} tod at xxj s. the tode. Delyvered Saull by Leonard Herytage for hym	iiij li.)^{er}
Bought of (William)^{er} Rychard Hunt of Luddyngton ij tode at xx s. the tode. Delyvered Saull by Leonard Herytag	Delyvered xx s.; xx s.
Bought of Leonard Herytage of Kyngton j tode and iij^{li} at xx s. the tode	Delyvered xx s.; ij s. j d.
Bought of Edward Petyfer my servant vij tode at xx s. the tode	Delyvered xl s.; my wife delyvered xx s.; item delyvered iiij li.
(Bought of Wylliam Palmer of Chadshunt xiij tode at xx s. the tode	Delyvered xiiij li.)^{er}

[*margin*] I must have of Wylliam Palmer xvj li.; iij li vij s. viij d.; xiij s. iiij d.

(Item delyvered to Sawll for Hunt xx s. at Warwyke Fayre and at home vj s. viij d.)^{er}	
Bought of Robert Stonle of Ofchurch ij tode	xl s.
Bought of Rychard Parr of Northend ij tode xxij^{li} weight at xxij s.	Delyvered xx s.; xx s.; iiij s.
Bought of Profyt of Northend viij[54] tode at xxij s.	Delyvered ix li. xviij s.
Bought of Mr. Hyckman xxiiij tode at xxj s. the tode and j yowe her lamz in the woll over	xxv li. iiij s.
Item of hym more ij tode di. at xxij s.	Delyvered xxxiij s.

87 f. 69 v. D ij^{c}lxxxiij tode[55]

88 f. 67 Woll resceyved anno [*1548*][56]

Resceyvyd of Bawdwyn Ward for Jhon Medes of Radford	iiij todes

[54] *Sic*, though the payment and delivery were for 9 tod.

[55] Written in the top right margin facing the first page of wool purchases and probably giving an estimate of the total wool bought.

[56] See footnote 49. The date is blank in the MS.

Resceyved of Rychard Mose of Radford	iij tode and di.; remayneth unpayd x s.
Resceyved of Edward Quiny of Ufton	ij tode and di. and di.^{li}
Resceyved of Jhon Stoneley of Ofchurche	iiij tode lacks di.^{li}
Resceyved of Robert Stele[57] of Ofchurche	ij tode
Resceyved of Reynold Messengr of Harbery	ij tode
Resceyved of Rychard Savage of Bodyngton	ij tode
Resceyved of Rychard Brace of Harbery	j tode
Resceyved of Thomas Grenwey of Harbery	j tode
Resceyved of Thomas Chebsey	iij tode
Resceyved of Rychard Wynter of Lodbroke	di. tode
Resceyved of Thomas Nychols of Lodbroke	ij tode
Resceyvyd of Thomas Bysshop of Welsburne	iiij tode lackes di.; and di.
Resceyvyd of Rychard Hunt of Luddyngton	ij tode
Resceyvyd of Saull for hymself	xij tide (di.)^{er}
Resceyvyd of Leonard Herytag	j tode iij^{li}
Resceyvyd of Jhon Smyth of Brodwell	j tode
Resceyvyd of Wylliam Smyth of Brodwell	j tode
Resceyvyd of Wylliam Cattell of Brodwell	j tode
Resceyvyd of Rychard Cattell of Hyll	j tode lackyng iij^{li}
Resceyvyd of Jhon Curteys of Brodwell	ij tode
Resceyvyd of Wylliam Laysse[58] of Hyll	j tode lackyng di.^{li}
Resceyvyd of Rychard Curteys	iij tode lack ij^{li} quarter
Resceyvyd of Jhon Hygynse of Brodwell	iij tode lacks j^{li} quarter
Resceyvyd of Thomas Garet of Hyll	iij tode (lack quarter)^{er}
Resceyvyd of Harry Garrett	iij tode
Of Mors[59] of Coventre	iiij tode
Resceyvyd of Thomas Perkyns of Honyngham	xx tode
Resceyvyd of Robart Man of Honyngham	ij tode di.
Resceyvyd of Wylliam Perkyns of Honyngham	iiij tode di.
Of Anstye of Honyngham	j tode
Item of a woman ther	di. tode
(Resceyvyd of Edward Petyver (and)^{er} my man	vij tode lackyng v^{li})^{er}

[f. 66 v.]

Resceyvyd of Thomas Mecoke of Napton	iij tode
Resceyvyd of Jhon Carpender of Napton	j tode
Resceyvyd of Rychard Quiny senior of Flekynho	xviij tode di.
Resceyvyd of Thomas Burbery of Dasset	xxvj tode and x^{li}
Resceyvyd of Merkot of Harbery	ij tode
Resceyvyd *[blank]*	Summa *[blank]*
Resceyvyd[60] of Edward my man	vij tod lack v^{li}
Resceyvyd of Myls of Harbery	j tode lack iij^{li}

57 Stonle in **86** (f. 67 v).
58 Basse in **86** (f. 68), Base in **89**.
59 Amors in **86** (f. 68 v).
60 After a small gap.

Resceyvyd of Palmar of Hatton	v tode lacks di.
Resceyvyd of Oliver Crofts of Harbery	ij tod lacks di.^{li}; paid
Resceyvyd of Robert Hyll, servant to Hary Smyth	ij tode
Resceyvyd of Wylliam Clarke of Feny Compton	j tode
Resceyvyd of Jamys Clarke of Feny Compton	xv tode
Resceyvyd of Thomas Ancester of Napton	j tode lacks di.^{li}
Resceyvyd of Edward Hancoke of Weston	iiij tode lack iiij^{li} di.
Resceyvyd of Dycke Sheperd of Leamyngton	vij tode
Resceyvyd of Jhon Nychols of Lylington	iij tode
Resceyvyd of Par Rychard of Northend	ij tode ij^{li} di. lacks ij^{li}
Resceyvyd of Davy Wylliam of Feny Compton	j tode x^{li}
Resceyvyd of Wylliam Chanternell[61] of Feny Compton	iij tod lacks iij^{li}; paid
Thexecutors of Bramfeld of Ofchurche	ij tode
Of Leonard Masse of Kynston	iiij tode
Resceyvyd of Jhon Herytage of Kynston	iiij tode
Resceyvyd of Mr. Raye of Warwyke	x tode
Resceyvyd of Rychard Langley of Southam	j tode j^{li} di.
Resceyvyd of Profyt of Northend	ix tode
Resceyvyd of Wylliam Brokes	xxx tode and di.
Resceyvyd of Mr. Hykman	xxiiij^{ti} tode
Item of hym more	j tode di.
Item of the last yeres bying	x tode

89 L. 31 b. C [*Wool lacking on delivery, 1548*][62]

Rychard Curteys	ij^{li} qr
Wylliam Base of Hyll	di.^{li}
Rychard Cattell of Hyll	iij^{li}
Thomas Byshop de Welsbourne	j^{li} di.
Jhon Stonle of Ofchurche	di.^{li}
Edward Hancoke de Weston	iiij^{li} di.
Wasover [?] de H[arbury?]	. . .[63]
Mylls of Harbery	[*blank*]

90 f. 49 Woole bought in anno iij^{tio} regni regis Edwardi vj^{ti} [*1549*] and money in payment there of aforehand by Peter Temple as followeth

Inprimis bought of Thomas Burbery of Dassett xxvj^{ti} tode woll xxix^{li} weyght [*per tod*] at xx s. the tode	Delyvered hym in part of payment ther of xvj^{li}; item more vij^{li}; iij li.

[61] Canterwell in **86** (f. 68).

[62] An incomplete list, written on a slip of paper.

[63] In a crease and partly illegible, unidentifiable in **86**.

Item bought of William Brookes of Dasset abowt xxviij todes wooll (xxij)^{er} xxviij^{li} di. weyght at xx s. the tode	Delyvered hym in part of payment there of xx li.
Item bought of [*blank*] Elwall of Napton ij tode wool xxviij^{li} di. weyght at xviij s. the tode	Delyvered xxxvj s.
Item of Jhon Nichols of Lilington j tode	Delyvered xxj s.
Bought of Jhon Colyns of Napton halfe a tode (29)[64] at xix s.	Delyvered ix s.
Bought of Wylliam Smythe of Napton ij tode (29) at xix s.	Delyvered xxxviij s.
Bought of Edward Hancoke of Weston vj tode (29) at xviij s.	Delyvered iiij li.
Of Jhon Byddell of Grymbold Hardwyke in Lemyngton j tode (29)	Delyvered xviij s.
Of Rychard Brasse of Harbery ij tode (29) at xx s.	Delyvered xij s.; delyvered xviij s.
Bought of Thomas Swayne vj tod	Delyvered vj li.
Bought of Pare of Northend ij tod at xxij s.	Delyvered xx s.
Bought of Myls wydow j tod at xxj s.	Delyvered xxj s.
(Bought of Nychols j tode xxj s.	Delyvered xx j s.)^{er}[65]
Resceived by Jamz Clarke of Hawke j tode	Delyvered xx s.

91 f. 49 v. Woll resceyved in anno tercio regni regis Edwardi vjth [*1549*]

Resceyved of Thomas Burbery	xxvj tode	paid xxvj li.
Resceyved of Wylliam Brokes	xxxj tode	paid xx li.; xj li.
Resceyved of Thomas Swayne	vj tode	paid vj li.
Resceyved of Jhon Nychols of Lylington	j tode	paid xxj s.
Resceyved of Byddell of Grymbold Hardwyke	j tode	paid xviij s.
Resceyved of Rychard Brasse of Harbery	j tode di. iij^{li} di.	paid xxxij s. viij d.
Resceyved of Myls wydow j tode Harbery		paid xxj s.
Resceyved of Par of Northend	ij tod di. and viij^{li}	paid iij li. xiiij d.
Resceyved of tythe woll	ix tode	paid ix li. xviij s.
Resceyved of Hawke by Jamz Clarke	j tode	paid xx s.
Resceyved of Elwall	j tode di.	paid xxvij s.
Resceyved of Collyns	di. tode	paid ix s. vj d.
Resceyved of Wylliam Smythe	ij tode	paid xxxviij s.
Resceyved of Edward	vj tode di.	paid vj li. xiij s. iiij d.

64 Superscript, indicating the number of pounds to each tod.
65 Already entered above.

92 f. 50 Woolle bought in anno quarto regni regis Edwardi vj^{ti} [*1550*] and money delyvered by Peter Temple as followeth

Inprimis bought of Thomas Griffyn of Feny Compton xij tode wolle at xxj s. the tode, di.^{li} weyght[66]
Delyvered hym the 1 day of June in part of payment there of x li.

5. *Thomas Heritage: Wool and Other Trading* (Pl. IV)

Peter Temple's wool trading is complemented by that of Heritage, who is the exemplar of the London merchant, buying wool in bulk from country producers, and shipping it out to France. We see him as well, in another role that must have been typical of the wool merchants; he sent all sorts of exotic goods from London to his country clients, usually in part payment for their wool. On the negative side, unfortunately, these accounts are technically poor, with only a rudimentary approach to credit and debit balances.[67] They are also obviously incomplete, and dated items are found only for 1533 to 1534;[68] they were presumably recorded because the transactions were not completed at one time. What we have then are vignettes of his activities. To judge from the samples, which show investments of £100-200, he was dealing on a substantial scale, though not up to the level of the greatest merchants of the kingdom. This corresponds well to the status indicated by his admission a couple of years earlier to the Fraternity of Corpus Christi, the social élite of the Skinners' Company.

His purchases (Table 5.1) came from the Midland counties, Gloucestershire, Northamptonshire and Warwickshire; relatives were, of course, prominent among the sellers. The wool was carried to Leadenhall in London, the place where all wool was weighed and bargains were struck.[69] One recorded sale (**104**) is intriguing: a lot of 1,800 sheepskins (fells) was sold to a group of Scottish merchants, Deryke Hobynson and his Company, of Leith, carriage paid to Calais. This was almost certainly an illegal transaction, as

[66] Presumably for $28\frac{1}{2}$ lbs. per tod.

[67] Contrast, for example: Jean Vanes (ed.), *The Ledger of John Smythe, 1538–1550*, Bristol Record Society, **28** (for 1975). He was a Bristol merchant, mainly in the overseas trade.

[68] Other Heritage items are dated as late as 1540.

[69] E. M. Power and M. M. Poston (eds.), *Studies in English Trade in the 15th Century* (London: Routledge, 1933 (1966 edn.)), p. 56.

Table 5.1: *Thomas Heritage: Wool dealings*

Date	*Buyer/seller*	*Quantity*	*Rate*	*Cost*[a]	*Ref.*
(a) Purchases					
18 Mar. 1533	William Wylnor	164 tod	11s. 6d.	£94 6s.	**93**
16 Dec. (1534)	William Wylnor	100 tod	12s.	£60 6s.	**96**
25 Aug. 1533	John Medley	302 tod	13s. 4d.	£202 2s.	**99**
4 Oct. 15 ...	Mab Palmer	12 tod	12s.	£7 4s. 4d.	**100**
16 June 1534	Thomas Godes	450 summer fells	£5/100	£21	**101**
		498 winter fells	£3 13s. 4d./100	£17 9s. 4d.	
(1534?)	John Glover	413 fells	£4/100	£16 6s. 8d.	**102**
(b) Sales					
31 Aug. (1534?)	Deryke Hobynson	1800 fells	£5 3s.4d./100	£93	**104**
Aug. ...	Robert Raymand	800 fells	£4 6s. 8d./199	£35 3s. 4d.	**107**

[a] Excluding transport, etc.

the sale of wool to aliens was forbidden by statute, and the export of wool to Calais was restricted to Merchants of the Staple.[70]

Of the goods that Thomas Heritage sent back from London to his country customers, some obviously filled special needs in sheep farming: tar and pitch for treating scab, alum for other ailments,[71] and canvas and net for packing the wool. With this went leather work, saddlery (and probably a hide), and also a harness and bows. He provided cloth: say, russett, powyck and black cotton, some of it made up as bed testers and curtains, a hat and tippett. Most prominent were the fish: sprats, red herring, stock fish and whale oil, the hogsheads of claret and the exotic groceries: almonds, rice, sugar, figs, raisins and spice.

Of all this heterogeneous collection, including the wool (and the iron considered later), only the hat and the tippett could possibly be part of a skinner's usual stock-in-trade. This is not, however, unexpected. During the sixteenth century (and particularly from the 1520s on), the Skinners' Company underwent a radical change.

[70] Ibid., p. 55. As Thomas Heritage did not describe himself as a Merchant of the Staple, he was surely not one. However, John Johnson's great account book (P.R.O. SP1/185, ff. 100–27; 196, ff. 97–226) contains one double page (SP1/196, ff. 101v–2) of accounts with Thomas Eritage, Merchant of the Staple, in 1534–6. It also mentions Dericke Hobinson of Leith (ibid., ff. 204v–5).

[71] Bowden, 1962, p. 17.

The majority of its important members turned from practising skinners to general merchants, as a consequence of a decline in the fur market and an increase in overseas trade. Merchants also needed membership of a London livery company to give them the freedom of the city, allowing them to trade directly with men from the provinces.[72] Thomas Heritage fits precisely into this pattern. As an inland trader he appears exceptional, but this is no doubt because only overseas merchants are well recorded (in customs documents).

Included with this section are a few financial memoranda, showing debts being paid off in stages (**106–111**). They are similar to those relating to the sheep and wool purchases, but without more information cannot be fully understood. The first, however, gives the only direct information we have about Thomas Heritage's father—that he had a house 'without Cripplegate', i.e. in the parish of St. Giles, London.

More important is the substantial transaction in Spanish iron in 1532 (**112–18**, Table 5.2).[73] Heritage must have been led to this by the elder Thomas Heritage, through the latter's involvement with the building trade; the other man named, Nolly Gachon, was perhaps the Spanish supplier. The iron was shipped in bar form, and the length in yards, as well as the weight, is specified in the account. Rather than being a single 60 foot long strip weighing $\frac{1}{4}$ ton, the iron must have been in yard-long bars, each weighing about 25 lb., and the lengths given indicate the number of bars to provide the 5 cwt. of each sum. From this information, the cross-section of a bar can be calculated at 2·5 sq. in. (say 1·5 in. square or $3 \times \frac{3}{4}$ in.).[74] Of those purchasers whose names have survived, two were smiths,[75] but a third was Robert Temple, no doubt intending his iron for re-sale in Witney. The prices for this deal in iron are puzzling. It was sold for £4 16s. 8d. to £5 a ton, but the purchase price was £5 6s. 8d. a ton. However, this was only to be paid after a three year delay, in 1535, so no doubt Thomas Heritage succeeded in making a profit on it. A counterbalancing sale may have been linked with this purchase, showing sufficient profit to offset the direct loss on the iron.

[72] E. M. Veale, *The English Fur Trade in the Later Middle Ages* (Oxford: Oxford University Press, 1966), p. 181f.

[73] From other merchants' records, Spain was the major source of iron at this period, e.g. J. Vanes, op. cit. John Smythe did not record the lengths of his iron.

[74] Assuming a density of 7·86 $g\,cm^{-3}$ for iron.

[75] Rickmansworth, the home of one, includes the manor of More, where Thomas Heritage had part of his Hertfordshire land.

Table 5.2: *Iron sales*

Buyer	*Quantity*	*Length (yds)*	*Price per ton*	*Total*	*Item*
–	3 t. 122 lb.	265	£4 16s. 8d.	£14 15s. 3d.	**113**
–	(4 t.	–	£4 16s. 8d.)	£19 6s. 11d.	**113**
Thomas Kakefyld	2 t.	178	£4 16s. 8d.	£9 13s. 4d.	**114**
Thomas Dene	1 t. 72 lb.	98	£4 16s. 8d.	£4 19s. 3d.	**115**
Rychard Saffag	1120 lb.	45	£5	£2 10s.	**115**
Robert Temple	1 t.	86	£5	£5	**116**
Kyrstofer . . .	2 t.	.[a]	£5	£10	**117**
–	2 t. 1344 lb.	272	£4 16s. 8d.	£12 12s. 10d.	**118**

[a] Only one surviving item, giving 116 lb. for 9 yards.

THOMAS HERITAGE: WOOL AND OTHER TRADING

[*Accounts with William Wylnor and others*]

93 f. 3. A

Memorandum that I Thomas Herytag bowght off my cosson William Wylnor off Ryton[76] the xviij day of Marche anno 1532 [*/3*], viij^{xx}iiij tod off woll at xj s. vj d. every tode	iiij^{xx}xiiij li. vj s.
Item paid for pakyng off the said woll	ij s.
Item geven in rewardes	xij d.
Item paid for xxiiij elles[77] off canvas at iiij d. qr. a nell	viij s. vj d.
Item paid for my costes	v s.
Item payd for the caryag off the same woll to London	xlvj s. viij d.
Item paid for the caryag off yt to Lodon Hall[78]	[*blank*]

[*Bottom margin*][79] 4^{xx}17 li. 9 s. 2 d.

94 f. 4[80]

Forst payd my cosson Wylnor in hand	xiiij li. vj s.
Item paid to my cossons sestur at London	x li.
Item paid to Hary Over	x li.
Item paid to hym selfe at Mydsomer in dokettes	xx li.

76 Ryton-on-Dunsmore, Warwickshire.

77 1 ell = 45 inches [*O.E.D.*].

78 Leadenhall.

79 This is the sum of all the priced items above. The figures *5 s. 9 d.* are also written in the centre of the page, in Heritage's hand.

80 The total of this page is £95 17s. 4d., corresponding closely to the previous account. The figures 228 (113)^{er} **140** are in the top margin.

Item delyveryd to hym the iiij day off September by the handes off Mr Thomas Wytell	x li.
Item send him the xxvij day off September by Rychard Gooder	x li.
Item sent hym a barell off tare prisse	iiij s. viij d.
Item sent to hym ij barelles of tare by Barow prysse the barell iiij s. viij d.	Summa ix s. iiij d.
Item paid to hym my selfe a fore Kyrsmas	x li. vj s. viij d.
Item sent hym a sadell prysse	vj s. viij d.
Item paid for a bolt of canvas to pake in the sadell	iiij s.
Item paid to his systur the iiij day of Aprell	x li.
Item sent to hym a barell of piche prysse	vij s.

95 f. 4 v. A[81]

Item I paid for lyse and coller x d., and a dobull hedstall, a rayn and apperrell xxij d.	ij s. viij d.
Item sent to my cosson William Wylnor of Ryton by my sarvand Rychard Kyrbe on Corpus Cryst eve in the xxvj yere of the reyne of Kyng Harry the viij[th] [*3 June 1534*]	xx li.
Item paid for a tester off a bedd with cortens[82]	xxiij s. viij d.
Item paid for a nother tester and cortens and ij pecesse of say[83]	vj s.
Item for spysse	[*blank*]
Item paid hym sens at London and at Coventry my selffe	xxx li.
Item for a Spaneshe skin[84]	v s. iiij d.
Item paid for a balt of vyter vandlas[85]	v li. xiij s. iiij d.

96 f. 9 v. A

Memorandum that I Thomas Herytag skiner of London bowght of my cossen William Wylnor of Ryton the xvj day of Dessember vij sakes ix tod off woll at xij s. the tode.	Summa iij[xx] li. vj s.

97 f. 83. A

Mony layd owt for my cosson Wylliam Wylnor off Ryton Forst payd for ij bowys for hym	v s. iiij d.
Item for canvas and nett	iiij d.
Item for canvas	vj d.
Item for vj[li] off almons	xviij d.

[81] The credit portion of this account may be the next item. The page total is £57 11s. 0d.
[82] The canopy over a bed, here presumably the cloth rather than its frame.
[83] A fine serge-like cloth [*O.E.D.*].
[84] Spanish leather?
[85] A bolt of strong canvas from the town of Vitne in Le Vendelais, Brittany [*O.E.D.*].

Item[86] I lent to John Saffag off Ikeman[87] the last day off May to be payd at Lamas [*1 Aug.*] in this yere of Kyng Henry the viijth xxv [*1533*] — iij li. x s. plus v s.
Recyvyd of John Croftes — vij s. vj d.
Item for a tobnet[88] of fygges for hym — xxij d.
Item for a nell off [? *canvas*][89] — iiij d.
Item for the cariage of your fyges — [*blank or rubbed*]

98 f. 82 v. B.[90]

Item sent to my cosson William Wylnor off Ryton by Barow a barell of tare pych — iiij s. viij d.

99 f. 10. A[91]

Memorandum that I Thomas Herytage, skinner off London, bowght and wayid with Mr. John Medley the xxv day off August anno 1533 xxiij sake and iij tode di.[92] off brockeres woll[93] at xij mark x s. the sake. — Summa ij^{c}ij li. ij s.
and ther ys left in reffise woll[94] j sake and iiij tode xvij^{li} woll which ys ij^{c}xvij flessys
Item recvyd from Brynton[95] the same tyme x tode iij^{li} off woll
Item bowght more at Brynton ij tod j^{li} of woll

100 f. 14. A

Memorandum that I Thomas Herytage paid to my cosson Mab Palmer the iiij day of October anno 15 [*blank*] for xij tode of woll at xij s. the tode — vij li. iiij s. iiij d.

[*Accounts for purchase and sale of fells, 1534*]

101 f. 11. A

Memorandum that I Thomas Herytage, skener of London, bowght of Thomas Godes of Cowton[96] the xvj day of June anno 1534 iiij^{c}l somer felles at v li. every C.
Summa xxj li. 22 li. 20 d[97]

[86] After a small gap.
[87] Perhaps Rickmansworth, Hertfordshire; cf. the arable account 132.
[88] Tapnet, a basket of rushes in which figs were imported [*O.E.D.*].
[89] Blank in MS.
[90] Opposite the last, in the margin of another Heritage note (**110**).
[91] Reproduced as Plate IV.
[92] *d* only in MS., almost identical to the abbreviation for *and*.
[93] Presumably broggers' wool, i.e. not bought directly from graziers.
[94] Refuse or poor quality wool?
[95] Probably Brington, Northamptonshire.
[96] Probably Coughton, Warwickshire.
[97] The arabic figures perhaps include some costs.

Item bowght more of the same Thomas Godes iiij^{c}iiij^{xx}xviij wynter felles at iij li. xiij s. iiij d. the C	xvij li. ix s. iij d.
	17 li. 13 s. 6 d.
Item paid for the caryag of these same felles to London	xv s.
Item geven in rewardes	xiij s. viij d.
Wher of ys to be payd at Myclmas a peryng by my byll	vj li.

[102 f. 11 v. A]

Item bought of John Glover of Brad Campden[98] iiij^{c}xiij felles and iij tode skyens after iiij li. the C	xvj li. [vj s. viij d.]
Item paid for the cariag of the same felles to London by me Thomas Herytag	xvj s. viij d.
Memorandum that I Thomas Herytage delyvered to John Glover in ernest	x s.
Item paid to John Glover by my aunte Allys Pamer	xiij li. vj s. viij d.
Item sent to hym iij hoghedes of Claret wyen at xx s. xx d. the hoghead	iij li. v s.
Item sent hym ij hoghedes at xxiij s. iiij d. the hogehead	xlvj s. viij d.
Item paid to the portars and for spenyng and caryage to the waynes the sayd v hoghedes	viij s. viij d.

[103 f. 12. A]

So that John Glover oweth to me Thomas Herytage	iij li. xiij s.
This parselles following sent to John Glover of Camdon the xiij day of January anno 15 [*blank*]	
Forst sent to hym half a C of allam[99]	ix s.
vj^{li} of almons	xv d.
ij^{li} of rysse	iij d.
iiij^{li} of sugar	ij s.
ij topenes of fyggs	ij s. vj d.
ij kad[1] of red heryng	x s. iij d.
a kad of sprattes	xv d.
half C stok fyshe[2]	
xiij gallons a quart of well howell[3]	xiij s. vj d.
for a barell for the same owell	x d.
for a kare to kary it to the kart	iiij d.
Summa	lj s. x d.
Item sent to hym a harness	x s.
Item ij hoghedes of wyne	xlvj s. viij d.

[98] One mile south-east of Chipping Campden, Gloucestershire. This item is probably also of 1534.

[99] Alum.

[1] A barrel of fish, especially herrings, containing 500 or 700 fish [*O.E.D.*].

[2] Dried cod from Scandinavia.

[3] Whale oil?

Item a barell of pyche and tare	xij s.
Summa	ix li. viij s. vj d.
	iiij s. viij d.[4]
Item for a bot' of rasyn[5]	iiij li. xiij s. iiij d.
[*total sum*]	xiiij li. ij s. viij d.
Paid	xxj li.

104 f. 12 v. A

Memorandum that I Thomas Herytage sold Deryke Hobynson and his company off Leyth the last daye of Augost xviij^{c} felles at v li. iij s. iiij d. sterling tabull the C	iiij^{xx}xiij li. sterling tabull

Memorandum that ther ys xxiiij felles to reken
Item recevyd of my felles xxviij li. sterling tabell fer at weys sterling in angeles [?]

[**105** f. 13. A]

The costes off the xviij^{c}xxiiij fells from London to Calles	
Forst paid for the frayt the iiij pakes j^{c}xxiiij felles at vj s. vj d. the pake	xxix s. vj d.
Item paid for pynag[6] of iiij pakes ij^{c}xxiiij fells at ij d. the pake	ix d. qr.
Item paid to the hede man of the cartars j d. of a C	xviij d. qr.
Item paid to the howsars[7] j d. of C	xviij d. qr.
Item paid at Lanton gat[8] iiij d. of every C	vj s. j d.
Item paid to Thomas Lasse for fetcyng, koping, castyng and mendyng of felles	ij s. qr.
Item paid for howsse rome	[*blank*]

[*Miscellaneous accounts and memoranda*]

106 f. 59 v. A [*Account for £108 owed to Robart Raymand*]

Memorandum that my wyff delyvered to Robart Raymand at my farme called Oxsay Hall the vj day of Marche	iij li.

[4] Uncertain significance; not included in the total.

[5] Probably raisins, though the container is unidentified. The price should be £4 13s. 8d. for the total to be correct.

[6] Possibly 'shutting up' from 'pind' [*O.E.D.*].

[7] Obscure. E. Power and M. M. Postan, *Studies in English Trade in the 15th Century* (London: Routledge, 1933). p. 59 cite 'houshire' at Leadenhall from the Cely papers, apparently suggesting the hiring of space for wool storage. However, this meaning is unlikely here.

[8] London Gate? Followed by a small erasure.

Item paid to Thomas Goodes of Cowton for you apon the rest of your felles bought of hym — ix li. xiij s.
Also you showyd me that you had recevyd from John Johnson[9] your man sarvand for me — ix li.
Item delyvered to you by John Sandors — x li.
Item delyvered (hym)[er] you more by John Sandors (which)[er] what I delyvered to John Sandors in Cheppesyde — xv li.
Item delyvered (hym)[er] you the same tyme at my fathors housse with owt Crpullgat. Memorandum my father and my mother and my wyffe beyng by — xij li.

[107 f. 60. A]

Item delyvred to (hym)[er] you in Augost viij[c] felles at iiij li. vj s. viij d. the C and x s. forther in the holle — xxxv li. iij s. iiij d.
Also you showyd me that you had recevyd of one John Johnson your man sarvand for me — ix li.
Item delyvred to you by John Sandors the vj day of Septembre — v li.
Item delyvered (hym)[er] you iiij crakyd crans[10] — [*blank*]
Item delyvered to (hym)[er] you in the pressens of (hys)[er] your wyffe — iiij s.

108 f. 74 v. A

Mony owyng to me Thomas Herytag by my unkyll Mr. Herytage and layd owt at hys commandyment as folowys and ys not in my acowynt
Foryst my unkyll owyth me a peryng by hys owne hand wrytyng in hys bok and also in myne — xxj li. vj s. v d.
Item delyvered to my cosson Thomas Spenser at my unkyll comandyment — xvj li. x s.
Item to my cosson Robart Tempull — v li.
Item bowght of my brother Rychard further be lx wethers at ij s. a pece — vj li.
Item bought of Westers and Lay iij[xx] hogrelles at xx d. a pece — v li.
Item ther was of my owen shepp whych were in Maskat[11] feldes iiij[xx] shepe

109 f. 82. A

Memorandum that I Thomas Herytag sent to my brother Rychard Frythorn the xvj day of September anno 1533 x barells of tarr at viij s. a barell and he most pay the caryage xx s. — xliij s. iiij d.

[9] Presumably not the Merchant of the Staple (Winchester, 1955).
[10] Reading clear, but meaning obscure.
[11] Uncertain reading; unidentified, though Arlescote, Warks., is possible.

Item sent to Mr. Parson of Adylstrop the same tyme iij yardes of Rosset[12] at v s. viij d. a yarde	xvij s.
Item vij yardes of blake cotton at vij d. a yarde	iiij s. j d.
Item for a typpet[13]	xviij d.
Item for a hat and a hatbande	ix d.

110 f. 82 v. A

Forst I most receve of my aunt Spenser for my cosson Thomas Spenser	iij li.
Item for ij yardes iij quarter of black powyk[14] at vij s. the yarde	xix s. iij d.
I must resceyve of Mistris Bykars servant of Warwyke the next weke	xj li. viij s.
Item delyvered to my cossen Thomas Knyght a peryng by a byll of hys hande	v li.

111 f. 83 v. B

Memorandum that Mr. Thomas Wyttell a greyd with John Norrous for such mony as he owyd to Mr. Hary Pyfford to be payd iiij li. in viij yeris, that ys x s. a yere	
Forst payd to Thomas Herytage for ij yerys	xx s.
Item payd by Robart Vensent when Mr. Wytell delyvered hym Sir Roger Norrous indentur	xx s.
and the said Robart must pay Mr Wytell more	xl s.

112 f. 5. A [*Dealings in Spanish Iron*]

Jesus

Anno 1532

Item bowght the xij day of June off Master Bryon Towke[15] xviij tone off Spanyshe iron for v li. vj s. viij d. a tone. Summa	iiij^{xx}xvj li.
and I moste pay for yt the xij day off June in the yere off ower Lord God xv^{c}xxv, aperyng by a (byll off)^{er}.	
Nolly[16] Gachon and my Unkyll Mr. Herytage hath sellyd therto	lxxxxvj li.

[12] Russet cloth.

[13] A strip of cloth or a cape, usually of fur [*O.E.D.*].

[14] Pewke: cloth dyed with woad or madder, the colour ranging from russet to black (*Ledger Book of John Smythe* [op. cit. on p. 112]).

[15] Probably Sir Brian Tuke, Treasurer of the King's Chamber, *L. & P. Henry VIII*.

[16] *Nobly* is a slightly preferable reading, but *Nolly* (= Oliver) is a more obvious interpretation.

113 f. 6. A[17]

[*weight*][18]	[*length or number of bars*]	
v^{c}vij^{li}	qt.[19]	xxj yerdes
v^{c}viij^{li}	qt.	xxiij yerdes
v^{c}xxij^{li}	qt.	xxiij yerdes
v^{c}iiij^{li}	qt.	xxj yerdes
v^{c}xxix^{li}	qt.	xxij yerdes
v^{c}x^{li}	qt.	xxij yerdes
v^{c}xviij^{li}	qt.	xxj yerdes
v^{c}	qt.	xxj yerdes
v^{c}iiij^{li}	qt.	xxvj yerdes
v^{c}iiij^{li}	qt.	xxiij yerdes
v^{c}vj^{li}	qt.	xxiiij yerdes
iiij^{c} di. xxvj^{li}	qt.	xvij yerdes
qr. xij^{li}	qt.	j yerdes

Summa: iij tones j^{c}x^{li} off iron, at iiij li. xvj s. viij d.
a tone — xiiij li. xv s. iij d.
Summa totalis — xxxiiij li. ij s. (iij d.)^{er} ij d.

[**114** f; 6 v.]

Item sold to Thomas Kakefyld smeth the xxiiij day off June (Spanys)^{er} iron as foloyth

v^{c}	qt.	xxiij yerdes
v^{c}	qt.	xxij yerdes
v^{c}	qt.	xxiiij yerdes
v^{c}	qt.	xxij yerdes
v^{c}	qt.	xxj yerdes
v^{c}	qt.	xxij yerdes
v^{c}	qt.	xxj yerdes
v^{c}	qt.	xxij yerdes

Summa: ij tones, at iiij li. xvj s. viij d. a tone — ix li. xiij s. iiij d.
Wheroff ys payd — iiij li. xvj s. viij d.
Rest to be payd at Kyrsmas — iiij li. xvj s. viij d.

[**115** f. 7. A]

Item sold to Thomas a Dene, smith off Rekemansworth the xxiiij day off Augost as foloyth

iiij^{c} iij^{li}	qt.	xvij yerdes
iij^{c} qr. ix^{li}	qt.	xviij yerds
iij^{c} qr. xxij^{li}	qt.	xviij yerdes
iij^{c} xij^{li}	qt.	xiiij yerdes

[17] From the collation (p. 249), two leaves are missing somewhere after f. 4 and before f. 7. One of them, between ff. 5 and 6, must have carried the start of the iron sales.

[18] 1 ton (2,240 lb.) = 20 hundredweight (*c* or cwt.); 1 cwt. (112 lb.) = 4 quarters (*qr.*).

[19] Probably *quantum*, how much.

iij^{c} xx^{li}	qt.	xv yerdes	
iij^{c} qr. xxv^{li}	qt.	xvj yerdes	
Payd by my unkyll			
Summa: a tone di.^{c} vj^{li}, at iiij li. xvj s. viij d. a tone			iiij li. xix s. iij d.
Item sold the same day to Rychard Saffag of Lambeth as foloyth			
v^{c}	qt.	xxij yerdes	
v^{c}	qt.	xxiij yerdes	
Summa: x^{c}, at v s. a C			l s.

[**116** f. 7 v. A]

Item sold to my cossen Robart Tempull of Wytney a tone of Iron the xij day of Augost aperyng by a byll of hys hand			
v^{c}	qt.	xxij yerdes	
v^{c}	qt.	xxj yerdes	
v^{c}	qt.	xxij yerdes	
v^{c}	qt.	xxj yerdes	
Summa: j tone, at v li.			v li.

[**117** f. 8][20]

Item sold to Kyrstof [er . . .]			
the xxvj day off A[ugust . . .]			
j tone to be payd v[^{c} *on 31 May*]			
next foloyng, other v[^{c} . . .]			
iiij^{c} iiij^{qr} xv^{li}	. . .		
iij^{c} iij^{qr}	. . .		
iij^{c} iij^{qr} iiij^{li}	. . .		
iij^{c} iij^{qr} xviij^{li}	qt.	. . .	
iij^{c} iij^{qr} xxiij^{li}	qt.	. . .	
iij^{c} iij^{qr} xij^{li}	qt.	. . .	
iij^{c} iij^{qr}	qt.	. . .	
iij^{c} iij^{qr} viij^{li}	qt.	. . .	
iij^{c} iij^{qr} viij^{li}	qt.	. . .	
iij^{c} iij^{qr} viij^{li}	qt.	. . .	
j^{c} and xvj^{li}	qt.	ix y[erdes]	
Summa: ij tones, at v li. a tone			x li.
Recevyd the xvj day off Marche			liij s. iiij d.
Recevyd the last day of May			xxvj s. viij d.
Recevyd by Lenard Gavy			xx s.
Recevyd more at Mychelmas			xxxiij s. iiij d.
Item recevyd the xxvj day of Februarye			xx s.
Item recevyd the laste day of May			xx s.

[20] Cut away on the right side, to three quarters down the page.

[**118** f. 8 v. A][21]

... the xvj day off
... as folowyth
... ton

	...	xvj yerdes
...	qt.	xix yerdes
...	qt.	xix yerdes
...	qt.	xix yerdes
...	qt.	xxj yerdes
...	qt.	xviij yerdes
...	qt.	xviij yerdes
.. iiij^{li}	qt.	xxij yerdes
.. xij^{li}	qt.	xix yerdes
[iii]j^{c} x^{li}	qt.	xvij yerdes
iiij^{c} ij^{li}	qt.	xxij yerdes
iiij^{c}	qt.	xxxvj yerdes[22]
iij^{c} qr. xiiij^{li}	qt.	xxvj yerdes

Summa: ij tones xij^{c} (xxviij^{li})^{er} xliij^{li}, at iiij li. xvj s. viij d. the tone xij li. xij s. x d.

6. *Thomas Herytage: Stock*

A few items show Thomas Herytage raising stock. In 1533, as was Peter Temple's practice later, many of the sheep were being kept at neighbouring villages (298 from a total of 477), and the two John Heritages were particularly concerned. By September (apparently in the same year), Thomas had 668 sheep in Heritage field, mainly ewes and lambs. He also had 100 head of cattle in the 'Grett Pasture' (presumably a field at Burton Dassett).

In the next year, he seems to have started a partnership with Nicholas Freckleton, by which he paid £75 for 300 ewes with lambs. They were jointly responsible for the rent and the tithe composition. The shepherd, who was another Heritage, Humphrey, received 26s. 8d. wages, but he also was allowed to keep thirty couples of sheep, a mare and three cows of his own. Finally, in 1536, the same arrangement seems to have been in operation, and Thomas Heritage had 718 sheep in the pasture.[23] This represents a substantial level of farming and capital investment, and it is not surprising that he found a local partner useful. This enterprise

[21] Cut away on the left side.

[22] Perhaps in error for 16 yards.

[23] A further undated reference in **108** mentions his buying sixty wethers and sixty hogrells, and having eighty other sheep in an unidentified field.

continued up to his death, when he had 646[24] sheep in his Burton pasture.

THOMAS HERITAGE: STOCK

119 f. 80 v.

Money left with Sir John Harte, paryshe preste of Harbery by Rychard Kyrbe and Thomas Fellypis the xxj day off May anno 1533	ix li. vij s. j d.
Item sent to hym by John Palmer	xl s.
A remembrans that I have recyvyd from hym xj kyne and a boll.	
Geff hath in Aven Dassett (x)^{er} iiij^{xx}xvj wether hoges, wherof on ys ded.	
Herytage of Kyngeston had vij^{xx} and ij Welshe yews wherof he hath sent home[?] ij skyns	
Herytag of Rodowey had iij^{xx} Welshe yews wherof he hath delyvered (home)^{er} x to Weste[?].	
Ther must remayne in my pastur viij^{xx} and vj Welshe lamz.	
Ther must be in the pastur xiij Welshe wethers.	

120 f. 81. A[25]

Ther remaneth in Herytag Feld the xxth of Septembre in yews and lamz	xxx^{xx}v
and in the same close in old ramz	xxiij
and in rame shere hoges	xx
and in ram lamz	xiij
and in wethers	vij
Ther remayneth in the Grett pastur the xxiiijth of Septembre	v^{xx} besse
and at Kyngston	xvj (besse)^{er} oxen
and my brother hath calves	xj

121 f. 64. A

Memorandum that I Thomas Herytag, skener of London, hath bargyng and bowght the xvj day of June in the xxvj yere of ower Soveren Lord Kyng Henry the viijth [*1534*] ij^{c}lx yowys and ij^{c}lx lamys which go in a pastur in Byrton callyd Herytag Pastur

[24] Or 726 if the count was by great tale; N.R.O. Temple Stowe, Box 40, Inventory of Thomas Heritage.

[25] Presumably also of 1533, and a continuation of **119** facing it.

Forst I the sayd Thomas Herytage moste pay to the sayd Nykolas Frekylton for the ij^{c}lx copolles, that ys to say f)r the yow and hyr lam as for every copull. Summa — iij^{xx}xv li.
And I most have vj^{xx} to every C.
Item the sayd Thomas bowght more the same tyme of Nykolas Frekylton xviij collyng sheppe at xvj d. the pece. Summa — xxiiij s.
Wherof I have payd — xlj li.
and xix li. most be payd with[26] a monyth and the rest at May Day next comyng — xxxiiij li. xiiij s.

122 f. 64 v. A[27]

A remembrans that Nycolas Frekylton and Thomas Herytage most pay to my Lady (Belnoke)^{er} Belnope for ower pastur every yere as long as we okapy it — xxvj li.
Item we most pay for ower tythe woll and lamz with other — iij li. x s.
Item we most pay to Homfray Herytage ower shepart — xxvj s. viij d.
Item xxx yowys and lamys goyng in the same pastur tyll Stratford Fayer.[28]
Item he must have goyng in the pastur a mare and iij mylshe kyne.
A remembrans that Nycolas Frekylton and Thomas Herytage moste bere all maner of charges lyke in the pastur, to wytt Herytage dyscharg the shering and all other thynges nessary.

123 f. 45. A

Memorandum that I Thomas Herytag, skiner of London, left in my pastur the xxj day of September in the xxviij yere of Kyng Henry the viijth [*1536*] and delyvered Humfray Herytag the tayelles and left my tayells with Mistres Frekylton.

Item in yowyes	xxix^{xx}	xxxv^{xx}xviij yowys lams and rames
Item lames	v^{xx}ij	
Item xvij old ramys and xix ram hoggettes		

Item delyvered to Humfray a gedy yow and vj lames of the worste.
Item left in my pastor a colte and a sorell geldyng.

[26] For *within*.

[27] Presumably a continuation of **121** facing it. However, the rent is an increase over that specified in the original lease, which only expired in 1538 (see p. 33). Between 1521 and 1547, Dame Alice was entitled to the profits of Heritage Field (see p. 29).

[28] Probably allowed to the shepherd, as in the next entry.

7. *Miscellaneous Farming: Hay, Pasture Letting and Arable*

These three topics complete the record of the two cousins' farming. Peter Temple must have cut hay on the Dasset meadows every year (see p. 37), but most of this obviously went to his stock in the winter. Only occasionally was there enough left in the spring to be sold to those less well supplied—£7 worth in 1549, a rick in 1550 (**70**) worth £9, and in 1553 two ancient ricks, eighteen months old, which only fetched £6 16s. each (**71**). More cautiously, in 1548, he sold odd loads of hay to local villagers, some on condition that they repaid him in kind at hay time (**124**). Just how big was a load of hay is not clear, though it may have been about half a ton;[29] from the prices, a rick contained about thirty loads.

The letting of pasture was a significant part of pastoral farming, as there were often occasions when the owner could not fully stock his land. In a couple of years, Peter Temple nearly paid his rent with the proceeds of 'fedyng and fee grasse sold for hey and gystment',[30] £40 in 1551 (**71**) and £35 in 1550 (**70**). This was connected with his problems in buying store cattle (see p. 45). Somewhat earlier, he was receiving both money and corn in exchange for pasture for cattle and horses. The rate was 3d. a week per head, or half a 'stryke of wheat' probably for four weeks, the period of the money rents. For someone doing no arable farming, the receipt of rent in the form of corn would have been a useful security against grain shortages, which were a frequent problem in the later 1540s.

Thomas Heritage leased out the meadows of his Hertfordshire property; his rate was similar, $2\frac{1}{2}$ to 3d. a week per head. The tenants were very varied—a local butcher and a 'butterwife', other people from Ruislip, the next village, and two more important figures, 'Mr. Comptroler of My lord Prinsy's housse' and 'Mr. Baldwyn, Chaplain to my lady Maryre', members of the households of the future Edward VI and Queen Mary Tudor. The King's children were almost certainly staying at Moor Park, the manor of More (in Rickmansworth, Hertfordshire); although this visit is not recorded,[31] the court was there in September, 1539.[32]

[29] Cf. N. W. Alcock, 'An East Devon Manor in the late Middle Ages', *Trans. Devonshire Ass.*, **102** (1970), 158.

[30] Agistment, i.e. grazing right; fee grass = grass sold for a fee.

[31] Their usual residences, Ashridge and Hunsdon, Herts., and Hampton Court, Middlesex, are all a long way from Rickmansworth and Oxhey. W. K. Jordan, *Edward VI: the young King* (London: Allen and Unwin, 1968).

[32] *L. & P. Henry VIII*, **14** (ii), 183.

The very first entries made by Peter Temple in the account book, in 1541 (**134–8**), concerned his only essay in arable farming. This followed on directly from Thomas Heritage, not at Burton Dassett but in Hertfordshire. Curiously, the single Heritage item for arable farming covers the harvest costs for one summer,[33] while Peter Temple's account starts at Michaelmas, 1541, and runs on through winter and spring, but omits the harvest. As often, therefore, an excellent description of the processes emerges, but with less information on the land sown, the yield and the profit.

Starting in the autumn, the first job was the ploughing and sowing of the winter corn (wheat and rye); later, the spring corn (oats) was sown; this was a particularly important crop in Hertfordshire, through which much horse traffic passed to and from London. Peter Temple sowed no barley in the spring of 1542, though some had been harvested, and he did not plant peas either. Throughout the winter, the last year's crops were threshed, and there were hedges to be mended and gates to be made.

In the summer, Thomas Heritage had paid the mowers for cutting his hay, and then his wheat, barley, peas and oats. The hay had to be made (turned as it dried in the sun), the wheat and oats bound in sheaves and 'shocked' (or set up in stooks of three sheaves), the barley 'cocked' (apparently the same as 'shocked'), while the peas were hockled (their stems cut and raked up). Finally, a thatcher was needed for the ricks of corn. The harvest workers were given food as well as wages, and a bullock, a sheep and other meat were bought for them.

The sale of one year's crop is recorded (probably that threshed by Peter Temple in 1541). Three of the buyers came from the farm workers, including the major purchaser, Williams, while John Popy was also connected personally with the estate as lessee of Hamper Mill (see below). Some overall view of the finances of this farm can be achieved (Table 7.1), indicating that about 30 acres were being cropped.[34] The costs were about £11, apart from some work done by permanent servants. The previous year's crop was worth £37, but we must doubt that this had been grown on the same area. This would indicate a net yield of 35 bushels per acre, or 40 bushels allowing for tithe (which was always removed as sheaves in the field); in terms

[33] The year is unstated, though 1540 is possible. It cannot be much before his death in early 1541, from the recurrence of the names mentioned in the 1541/2 accounts. No doubt Millicent Heritage had undertaken the 1541 harvest.

[34] They may well correspond to the 35 acres, surveyed in 1556. P.R.O. E315/391 (Augmentation Office Miscellaneous Books), f. 18.

Table 7.1: *Arable farming summary*

Ploughing:	Pecyfeld	17s. 8d.
	Ladyfeld	12s. 6d. at 1s. per acre—12½ acres
	Pecyfeld	17s. 8d. 17½ acres estimated[a]
Sowing:		3s. 6d.
	Pecyfeld	5 qr. wheat, 1 qr. 5 b. rye } at approx. 3 b./acre
	Ladyfeld	4½ qr. oats at almost 3 b./acre
Threshing:		£2 15s. 7d. for 121 qr. 3½ b. at 5½d. per quarter and 5 qr. 2 b. not paid for.
Other costs (1541)		£2 5s. 3d.
Harvesting (earlier year):		£3 19s. 1d.
	Total cost:	£11 11s. 3d.

Crop	*Produced qr. b.*	*Seed qr. b.*	*Recorded sales qr. b.*	*Receipts £ s. d.*	*Average price (per qr.) s. d.*	*Total value[b] (excluding seed)*
Wheat	35 2	4 6	26 3	11 15 11	8 11	£13 12s.
Rye	8 0½	2 2				£2 1s.
Barley	45 6	– –				£14 10s.
Oats	44 2	4 4	30 4	5 6 4	3 6	£6 18s.
Total:	133 2					£37 1s.

[a] This could well be the 18-acre field of wheat that was cut for Thomas Heritage (132).
[b] Assuming prices of 7s. 2d. and 6s. 4d. for rye and barley, derived from the ratios between the prices for 1539–40 in *Ag. Hist.*, vol. IV, Appendix Table 1, pp. 817–8.

of seed sown, this represents a thirteen-fold yield. On either calculation, this is probably too high; there are very few recorded yields for the sixteenth century, but an average estimate was made of five to eight-fold yields by the end of the seventeenth century.[35]

HAY

124 f. 73. B Primo die Aprill anno ij[do] regni regis Edwardi sexti [*1548*]

Delyvered to Thomas Barnard and Thomas Cokes	j lodde heye
Delyvered to Jhon Mylls and Wylliam Wryght	j lodde heye
Delyvered to Harry Worall and Jhon Chambers	j lode

[35] M. K. Bennett, 'British Wheat Yields per acre for Seven Centuries', *Economic History*, III.10 (1935), p. 12.

Delyvered to Harry Byrd	j lode
Delyvered to Rychard Lodbroke and Jhon Garlyke	j lode heye
Delyvered to Rychard Mecotte	j lode heye
Thes vj lode of heye to be delyvered me agayne at hey tyme	
Delyvered to Elys Smyth, Jhon Creke, Jhon Garlyke and Rychard Lodbroke ij lode of hey for	xj s.
to be paid at Stratford Faire next comynge[36]	
Delyvered to Thomas Barnard and Reynold Messenger	j lode hey v s. vj d.
wherof resceyved of Reynold Messenger for his half lod	ij s. ix d.
Delyvered to Henry Weroll and his brother	j lode hey v s. vj d.
Delyvered to R. Brasse for Mylls	j lode hey v s. vj d.

PASTURE LETTING

125 f. 81v. B [*Peter Temple: Pasture Letting, 1540s*][37]

Wagstaffe	xxxij kyne and x jades[38] and xx^ti	stryke[39] whett
Jhon Brokes	vj jades	iiij stryke
Robert Profett	xiij[40]	vj stryke
Yonge Knybe	ij kyne	j stryke
Thomas Swayne	vj kyne and iij jades and	v(j)^er styke whet
Knybe of Knyghtcott	iiij kyne	ij stryke whett
Thomas Gryffyne	xx^ti kyne	viij stryke
Hyerns wyffe	x kyne at iij d. the weke a pece	x s.; resceyved iij s. vj d.
Jhonsonn	ij kyne at iij d. the pece	ij s.
Mylls	iiij at iij d. the pece	iiij s.

126 f. 82. D [*Payment for pasture letting*]

Wagstaff	viij stryke
Brokes	iiij stryke
Profett	iiij stryke
Knybe	ij stryke
Knybe	j stryke

[*Thomas Heritage: Pasture Letting, 1539?*][41]

127 f. 70. A

Memorandum that I Thomas Herytage let a medow to Mr. Comtroler of my

[36] Of the various Stratford fairs, this may have been that on 29 June.

[37] The style and lack of heading indicate an early date. It clearly relates to **126**, which may be the amounts not received; the latter post-dates f. 82. B (**213**), of 1545.

[38] A poor quality horse.

[39] A measure of corn. Normally 2 strike = 1 bushel, but see **135** and note 55.

[40] *Kyne* understood.

[41] Items **127–31** in volume order, seem to run through one summer, perhaps 1539 as in **129**.

Lord Prynsys howsse[42] off v akors or ther abowght for v s. a naker the Saturday after Myssomer Day [*28 June*].
Received iiij geldyngs of Mr. Comtrowlers the same day
[*Margin*] iiij dayes
Item recevyd the morow after j geldinge
[*Margin*] iij dayes

[128 f. 70 v. A]

Recevyd the Saturday after Myssomer Day a wytt geldynge and a gray of Mr. Baldwyns, chaplyn to my Lady Maryes grasse [*grace*].[43]
Recevyd the vj day of July a bay geldynge.
Recvyd of Mr. Marshalles and Mr. Sevars [?] ij geldynges the Sonday after Myssomer Day.
Recvyd a geldynge of Mr. Peryas of the wyne seller.

129 f. 73 v. A Besse and Horssys takyn in to my pastur seyns Myssomor in the xxxj yere of Kyng Henry the viijth [*1539*]

Item resevyd of Mower of Ryslyp for iiij oxsons grasse at ij d. ob. a pesse	ij s. viij d.
Item for a mares grasse	ij s. ob.
Item of Mr. Hatry for xv bees a wyke	[*blank*]
Item the now[?] bocher for ij young besse for a quarter of a yere	v s.

130 f. 79 v. A Mowers[44]

Recevyd of hym and Nox ij kyne the morow after Seynt Marges[45] day at ij d. a pec a wyk Item recevyd of hym a geldynge the same day at iij d. a wyk	iiij s.
Recevyd of my botu^{r} wyffe[46] iij kyne on Seynt Lawrens day [*10 Aug.*] at ij s. a pec	iij s. vj d.
Recevyd of Rychard Prest of Rysselype on Seynt Laurans day ij kyne at ij d. a wyke a pece	ij s. viij d.

[42] Prince Edward's household was set up in March 1538, with Richard Cotton as Controller. *L. & P. Henry VIII*, 13 (i).
[43] Richard Baldwyn, appointed chaplain to Princess Mary in 1536. *L. & P. Henry VIII*, **10**, 1187.
[44] Presumably the same man as in **129**. There is a jotting by Peter Temple in the top right corner, *The ixth of J.*
[45] St. Margaret, 20 July.
[46] Butterwife? i.e. someone who sells butter.

Recevyd of my Mersse [?] the Sonday after Seynt Bartylymewys day [*24 Aug.*] or the Sonday afore ij hoxson at ij d. a pec	xx d.

[131 f. 80. A]

Recevyd of Hyll of Lowyeston[47] the Monday byffor Saynt Mathowys day [*21 Sept.*] ij hoxson and a kow at ij d. a pec a wyke	iij s. iiij d.
Mr Hawtrey (xv bollykys xv)^{er} bollockys a wyke	ij s. vj d.
Recevyd of Mr. Hautry the xij day of Augost xiij bollokys and a nold kow, and delyvered them the x day of September to hys servand and William Amberys servantes xij bollokys	

ARABLE FARMING

132 f. 1. A[48] The charges of my [*Thomas Heritage*] corn and hay in[49] redy mony and mete

Item paid to my mowers	vij s. x d.
Item paid to work fokes for makyng of hay	vij s. ij d.
Item paid to iij wemen for cokyng of barle and bindyng of owttes and shokyng and hoklyng of pessen	ij s.
Item paide to Passo and his fellow on wyk [*one week*]	ij s. v d.
Item paid to Wyllyams for fellyng of xviij akors of wet [*wheat*], bindyng and shokyng	xxj s.
Item to Hokt	xiij s. iiij d.
Item paid to Paysso and hys fellow the sekond wyke [*Superscript*] Passo on payd	ij s. vj d.
Item paid to iiij wemin the same wyke	ij s. vj d.
Item paid to mawyers for mowyng of my barlay and wottes	iij s. vj d.
A bulloke	vj s. viij d.
A shyppe	ij s. vj d.
Mete bowght	vj s. viij d.
Item paid to a thecher for iij dayes	xij d.

133 f. 84. A [*Thomas Heritage: memorandum about corn*]

Roger Haydon a bosshell whet and rye	xvj d.
Allys a boshell rye	xiiij d.
Left at Allys the towyess day afore Krysmas[50] in all vij quarter viij bosshells rye	

[47] Probably Leavesden, part of the parish of Watford, Hertfordshire, until 1853.
[48] For discussion of the date see note 33 on p. 128.
[49] The page is defective after *in*, but no text seems to be lost.
[50] Two days before?

[*Right margin*] Lent to Foster 10 s.
Bowght off Watur Cowper briklayer the xiiij daye off July j^{c} quarter wottes

[*Peter Temple: Arable Farming*]

134 f. 47. A Anno 1541 a Festo Sancti Michaele
The Pecyfeld

Sown vj quarters v bushels v quarters whet; xiij bushels rye	
To the Goodman Whelar paid for ploughyng	v s. vj d.
To Goldhurst for plowyng	v s. x d.
To Thomas Whaler for ploughing	iiij s.
To Hugh	(vj s.)^{er} ij s. iiij d.
To Wylliams for thressyng vij quarter: iiij quarter vj bushels in seed whett and ij quarter ij bushels in rye	iiij s. viij d.
For a quarter seed whet bought	xj s. x d.
For v new gates makyng	iij s. iiij d.
For lokes	ij s. iiij d.
For whyt lether	iiij s.
For a bryer hoke	x d.
The hedgers (in ernest)^{er} for hedgyng	x s. x d.
To Wheler for thresshyng vj quarter iiij busshells whet	iiij s. viij d.[51]
To Wheler for thresshyng iij quarter (xv busshels)^{er} barley	xij d.
Ralf thressyd ij bushells di. of (barly)^{er} rye	[*blank*]
Too Wheler for thresshyng xx quarter otz	vj s. viij d.
Rauff thressyd in rye j quarter v bushels	[*blank*]
To Wylliam Arber for thressyng x quarter di. of otts (vij quarter)^{er}	iij s. iiij d.
To Edward for the rack makyng	ij s.
(To Pygin for tythe corn)^{er}	
(Awes[?] had j bushel whett[52]	ij s.)^{er}
To Arber for thresshing ix quarter iij bushels barley	iij s. ij d.
To Arber and Skelton for ij days worke	xvj d.
Too Haukyns for hedgyng	iiij s. viij d.
Rauff thressyd ix bushels rye	[*blank*]
To Mors for hyem work at Our Lady Day [*25 March*]	viij s. ix d.
To Father Pace for thresshing x bushels rye	x d.
To Father Pace and Savag for thresshing xij bushels rye	xij d.
(For)^{er} To Wheler for iij quarter iij bushels barley thresshyng	xvij d.
To Rauffe for hys sow[ing]	iij s.
To the smyth	vj s. viij d.

[51] Followed by erased sums: *xij d.; iiij s. iiij d.; xx d.; iiij s. x d.; Summa x s. x d.*
[52] Marked in margin *sol'*, paid.

[f. 47 v. A]

Too Wylliam Arber for thressyng viij quarter barley	ij s. viij d.
To Arber for a quarter whet thressyng	viij d.
(Paid)^{er} Cokedell thressyd v busshels whett	v d.
To Father Pacoe for thresshing vij quarter vj bushels di. ottes	ij s. vj d.
To Rychardson for plowyng the Lady Feld at xij d. the acre	xij s. vj d.
Sowyn in ottz there iiij quarters di.	
To Father Pacoe for sowyng my ottz	vj d.
To Father Pacoe for thresshing ij quarter whett	xvj d.
To Father Pace for thresshing ij quarter ij busshels whett	xviij d.
[*Margin*] Refuse j[53]	
To Father Pace for thresshing ij quarter vj bushels whet	xxij d.
Mors had ij bushels whett	
To Father Pacoe for thresshing ij quarter vj bushels whet	xxiij d.
[*Margin*] Refuse j	
Too Father Pace and Savage for thresshing v quarter vj bushels whet	iij s. xj d.
Too Pace for thresshyng (vj quarter vij bushels)^{er} whett	vij s.
[*Margin*] Refuse v	
Too Pace and Savage for threshing xxij quarters barley	vj s.

135 f. 47 v. B[54]

Summa in whett and rye	xliij quarters ij stryke di.
Summa in barley	xlv quarters vj stryke
Summa in ottes	xliij quarters ij stryke[55]

136 f. 48 v. A

Delyvered to Fynche in barley xj quarters and di.
Delyvered to Fynche in whet iij quarter ij bushells
Delyvered to Fynche in whett vj quarter

137 f. 45 v.[56]

Sold to Wylliams vj quarter (di.)^{er} j bushell whett at x s. the quarter	iij li. (xv s.)^{er}
Sold to Wylliams xx quarter otz at iij s. v d. the quarter	iij li. viij s. iiij d.
Sold to Ryve of Bushe[57] iiij quarter otes at iiij s. the quarter	xvj s.
Sold to Hadwell iiij quarter otz at iiij s. the quarter	xvj s.

[53] Perhaps 1 bushel of rubbish.

[54] Written across the top corner of the same page as the last item.

[55] If 1 strick is taken as 1 bushel, the first two sums are correct, including seed corn, but the oats should total 38 quarters $2\frac{1}{2}$ bushels.

[56] The amounts of oats sold correspond to those threshed, indicating the year 1541–2.

[57] Bushey, Hertfordshire, just east of Oxhey.

Sold to Jhon Popy v bushels whet	vj s. iij d.
Sold to Wheler ij quarter di. otz	vj s.
Sold to Jhon Popy xv bushels whett	xviij s. ix d.
Sodl to Jhon Popy xv bushels whett	xviij s. ix d.
Sold to Jhon Popy xviij busshels whett	xxij s. vj d.
Sold to Jhon Popy xxij bushels whett	xxvij s. vj d.
Sold to Warren v quarter whett	xlvj s. viij d.
Sold to Mors j quarter	ix s. iiij d.
To Savage 1 bushel	(xij)[er] xiij d.
[Sold] to [*blank*] ij quarter whett	xviij s. viij d.
Sold to Hadwell xiiij busshels whett	vj s. iiij d.

138 f. 46. A[58]

Delyvered to Anthony	xx d.
(Delyveryd to Rauff	xx d.)[er]
Delyvered to Wylliam Sheperd for a shert	xij d.

To Rauffe

Delyvered to Rauffe	xiij s. vij d.
Delyvered to Rauffe	xxij d.
Delyvered to Rauffe	vj d.
Delyverd to Wylliam Sheperd	iiij s.
Delyvered to Rauffe	xx d.
Delyvered to Wylliam Sheperd for shepe skyns	ij s.
Leyd owt for Wylliam Sheperd for his cote	viij s. iiij d.
Delyvered Wylliam Sheperd at Lundon	iij s. iiij d.
Delyvered hym the same tyme there	xij d.
Delyvered to Rheve for certen charges cumyng up	x s. viij d.
Delyverd to Rave in whett	iiij bushels
Delyverd hym in rye	v bushels
Delyverd him in malt	ij busheles and ij quarters

SECTION B: RENTS AND ESTATE ADMINISTRATION

8. *Introduction*

Apart from his Burton Dassett land inherited from his father, Thomas Heritage had an interest in three groups of property. He himself built up a small estate in Hertfordshire, while through his wife's first husband he had the use of a group of properties in Coventry and another in Stepney, east of London. All these reached Peter Temple through his cousin's widow, and were owned in her right; the assured revenue must have been an important factor in his early years at Dassett, though he later disposed of the Hertfordshire estate. The

[58] Presumably also of 1541–2, from its position between **137** and **142**.

record of these properties in the account book is fairly short, but a much longer section illustrates the administration of another estate. It was compiled by Peter from 1548 to 1551,[59] when he acted for the co-owners of Burton Dassett as bailiff, and also as receiver for their Warwickshire lands. These accounts cover both the estate rents and the tithes of Dassett; the proceeds of considerable sales of wood from one of the Warwickshire properties are recorded separately.

9. *Rents*

Hertfordshire

The Hertfordshire property seems to have contained three components (Table 9.1). One was a copyhold of the manor of More,[60] called 'Pipers and Bakers', consisting of enclosed land (perhaps about 30 acres).[61] Hamper Mill was a water mill, with 47 acres of good quality land, while the most substantial was Oxhey Hall, a sub-manor, or portion of the manor of Watford (acreage unknown).[62] All were held on lease, and as well as the quit-rents, other outgoings are recorded in the accounts. Most unusual is the dredging of the moat at Oxhey and the mill stream, while Thomas Heritage had to repair the mill extensively. Payments were also made in lieu of tithes, and for taxes.[63] The copyhold only produced £2 clear, but the mill fetched £12 or £13, while Oxhey Hall was worth £60 to Peter Temple when he leased it.

To Thomas Heritage, however, it was the nucleus of a country estate, whose fields he ploughed, and on whose meadows he pastured his neighbour's stock. He must also have lived at Oxhey, at least occasionally, from one reference in his accounts (**106**). The pattern is very much that expected for a rising London merchant, setting himself up with a country estate,[64] though Heritage's early death cut it short. His involvement in Hertfordshire is first seen in 1532, when he obtained the lease of Hamper Mill. It is a likely guess that his

[59] Some earlier and later accounts survive on loose sheets.

[60] Otherwise known as Moor Park, in the parish of Rickmansworth.

[61] Applying a letting rate of 2s. per acre estimated for the Hamper Mill land in 1556 (P.R.O. E315/391, f.18). It is probably for this holding that a late fifteenth-century copy of court roll survives (ST Manorial box 18). It was granted by the Abbey of St. Albans from their manor of More, and included a 'new close extending from Oxey Lane to the warren of the manor'.

[62] Of the various Oxhey estates, Thomas Heritage's was probably Oxhey Walround; *V.C.H. Hertfordshire*, vol. II, p. 454 (London, 1908).

[63] In **142**, the *quindeme* (quindecim) or fifteenth (*O.E.D.*) and probably also the *sherriff's shott*.

[64] Among many parallels, John Johnson, the Merchant of the Staple, could be cited. He leased the manor of Glapthorn, Northants, in the early 1540s. Winchester, 1955, p. 90f.

Table 9.1: *Hertfordshire lands*

Property	*Acquired*	*Disposed*	*Annual income*	*Annual outgoings*	*How held, and nature*
Pipers and Bakers	post 1521[a]	10 March 1547[b]	1542: £3 6s. 8d.	21s. 4d.	Copyhold of Manor of More. Enclosed land perhaps 30 acres
Hamper Mill	4 May 1532[c]	1546[d]	1536: £8 13s. 4d. 1542: £12 1545: £13 6s. 8d. (213–4) Probably the mill itself without land	£13 6s. 8d.[e] (mill and land)	Lease, 31 years from 1532. (Mill plus 35 acres arable, plus 4½ acre meadow)
Oxhey Hall	?	1543	1543: £60 (208) from Oxhey Hall and Hamper Mill (probably all the lands)	Uncertain	Probably Oxhey Walround, manor in Watford[f]

[a] Not in P.R.O. S.C.2 178/5 (Rental of Manor of More).
[b] P.R.O. E326/12003, surrender to Crown.
[c] P.R.O. E315/391, f. 18, recites the lease to Thomas Heritage.
[d] No later references in the accounts; the lease was probably assigned.
[e] Receipt 10 May 1541 by George Zouche, ST L9 A1, Temple Accounts, 9, for £6 13s. 4d. for half year's rent.
[f] V.C.H. Herts. II, p. 487. A lease by St. Alban's Abbey for forty years expired at Michaelmas, 1546; P.R.O. E303/4.75 (f. 49).

interest started abruptly then, for in the spring of that year his uncle, Thomas Heritage the parson is first recorded in the King's service, working on the manor house at the More.[65] What more likely than for him to pass on a tip to his nephew, about some land that could be profitably acquired?

The dispersal of the estate came in 1546, when the lease of Oxhey Hall expired, and Peter Temple surrendered the More Park copyhold.

[65] *L. & P. Henry VIII*, V, no. 976. He was reporting to Sir John Russell on the decayed state of the park there (Tuesday, 30 April 1532). Two further letters, from Russell to Cromwell about Heritage's work are in VI, nos. 347 and 426; they are only dated 16 April and 1 May, and are assigned to 1533, but must surely also be of 1532.

He probably also assigned the lease of Hamper Mill, which does not appear in later accounts. By this time, the development of his Warwickshire interests must have made the administration of this property more trouble than it was worth.

Stepney

When Hugh Radcliff, gentleman of the Middle Temple, made his will on 8 November 1531, he bequeathed 'to Mylisen my wyfe' all his lands and tenements in the parish of Stepney in London, or elsewhere.[66] She was to hold them for life, and then they were to pass to 'her children of my body'. These un-named children we know to have been two daughters, Alice and Margaret. What finally befell fifty years later, when Millicent died, is considered later. After 1531, however, Millicent was very soon remarried, to Thomas Heritage the skinner. He recorded a half-year's rents in 1533, perhaps the first he had received,[67] but thereafter the account book is silent, apart from a few notes among the financial memoranda; a sheet of paper has survived with a scribbled list of rents that Peter Temple made in 1550 (**146**).

After Peter's death, the Stepney estate came back to Millicent herself, but she agreed to let it to John Temple in return for an annuity, the use of part of the house at Dasset, and her maintenance.[68] The land then passed to Hugh Radcliff's eventual heirs, the children of John Acland and John Brett.[69] They, with some difficulty established just what the property contained 'by scrutiny of rolls of court', and their copy of court roll provides the only clear description.[70] It consisted of one freeholding of 50 acres, recognizable as the so-called 'Manor of Horstall' (**144**), though in reality it was only a large house in North Street, Stepney.[71] It was accompanied by some smaller free holdings, and several copyhold tenements. Thomas Heritage received £11 6s. 8d. a year from six tenants (perhaps not a complete list). In

[66] P.R.O. PROB 11/24, 11 Thower (f. 18 v). Probate was on 28 November 1531, by his widow. The overseer of the will was Stocker Jekyll, Millicent's brother. These lands lay partly in Stepney itself, and partly in its adjacent hamlets of Limehouse and Poplar.

[67] It is puzzling that this item, though written in the first person like Thomas Heritage's other items, is in a formal hand, quite different from his usual one.

[68] ST Deeds, List 2, Box 27 (no. 84); see pp. 196–7.

[69] See Pedigree 4, p. 25.

[70] Devon R.O. 1148M (Acland family)/T/1 London and / Add. 9/25.

[71] In 1550 (Warde's house, **146**), it was lived in by John Ward, who collected some of the rents for Peter Temple, and also paid the quit-rent (ST L9, piece 27, 29 September 1552, receipt by Lord Wentworth for quit-rent paid by John Ward).

the 1540s, Peter Temple received £15 (**209**), and by 1550 there were eleven or twelve holdings with an annual rent of £20 17s. 10d.[72] In 1580, John Temple collected £39 6s. 8d. from his lands in 'Poplar, Lymehouse and Stepne',[73] then, as earlier, having to pay out £2. 1s. 9d. for quit-rents.[74]

Coventry

The history of the Coventry property was considerably more complex than for Stepney, but it is much better recorded.[75] It originated as the estate of Adam Hyton, a dyer and one of the most wealthy men in Coventry in the 1420s. The descent to the Temple family was complicated, marked by disputes at every turn, and with more than one partition.[76] Hugh Radcliff became the owner in due course of a portion of the original estate, and this passed with his Stepney land to Millicent. The later development is also confused, particularly as two vital documents are only referred to incidentally. The difficulty arises because in 1578 Peter was possessed of the Coventry property, while after Millicent's death, we find John Temple as owner, rather than Hugh Radcliff's proper heirs; this contrasts with the Stepney estate, which descended normally (though possibly only to Margaret Radcliff's heirs). The Coventry estate was, however, subjected to a perpetual rent charge of £6 13s. 4d., payable to Alice Radcliff. What may have taken place is a division of Radcliff's estate, so that Margaret and her heirs received Stepney and Alice had Coventry. Their rights, however, remained subject to Millicent's life interest, and Alice must therefore have surrendered her eventual ownership to the Temple family, in exchange for the annuity. This was formally implemented by a deed dated 14 February 1565, but the account book shows that the annuity was already being paid in 1554. The family

[72] Assuming that one item left blank was the same for each half-year; a more serious doubt must be whether items were omitted from either half-year's list.

[73] ST L8, Box 4. Temple Land, Bucks.-Leics., 13 February 1579/80.

[74] This comprised 39s. 1d. to Lord Wentworth, to whom the manor of Stepney was granted in 1550 (receipts in ST L9 A1, Temple accounts, pieces 27 and 51), and 2s. 8d. (Mr. Sandars and Mr. Morrow in 1550, 'heirs of Draner' in 1580). A receipt for 5s. 4d. by the Crown for quit-rent for Kildavy (cf. **146**) must be the same sum, even though it is said to be for one year, not two. (ST L9 A1, Temple accounts, piece 9.)

[75] As well as deeds proper, experience showed that among the miscellaneous boxes of the Stowe archives, any crumpled fragment of medieval appearance was almost certain to relate to Coventry. They must have made up the most substantial group of early documents that Peter Temple preserved.

[76] A full examination is out of place in the present study, but it is hoped to consider the estate further elsewhere.

partition was formalized on 3 May 1589; again, this probably confirmed an existing situation.[77]

The Coventry estate was valuable by the time John Temple inherited it, with annual rents rising from £24 in 1580 to £36 by 1600;[78] the main outgoing was the £6 13s. 4d. to Alice Radcliff. In Peter Temple's time, the summary accounts from 1551 to 1555 (**147–50**) show an income of about £14, of which Alice's annuity formed a larger proportion. The lands were managed by Thomas Hyginson,[79] and he received a fee of 13s. 4d., while there were also repair bills to be paid.

Table 9.2: *The Coventry estate in 1578*[a]

Property	*Comments*
Quarter tenement in Smithford Street	City property
Second tenement in Smithford Street	
Cottage + five small closes, called Cross Tavern	
Tenement in Spon Street	
Garden called 'Malt Mill Ground'	
Tenement by gable of Gaol Hall	
Half tenement in Earl Street	
Tenement in Cook Street	
Three tenements in Gosford Street	
Tenement at Broad Gate	
Plot of land in Catesby Lane	
10s. 8d. rent from Chapel of St. James	Chief rents
6s. 8d. from tenement at Jordan Well	
Over Crabtree Field: 15 acres	Grazing land outside the city wall on the south-west side
Nether Crabtree Field: 19 acres	
Pitfield	
Quarrel Field: 9 acres	
Swans Close	
Mill Meadow: 4 acres	
Crow Mote	
Paradise Field	

[a] As recorded in Peter Temple's *Inquisition Post Mortem* (ST L9 D4).

[77] Both dates are given in the draft copy of John Temple's *inquisition post mortem*, ST L9 D4, Temple Inquisitions Post Mortem, but an extended search has not discovered copies of either deed.

[78] ST L8 B4, Temple Land, Bucks., 13 February 1579/80; ST L9 B9, Temple Accounts, O/S 6, 13 September 1581 (£32 gross); ST L8 B9, Temple Land, Warws., 20 April 1600. These would fully support the sale values of £660 in 1627, ST Deeds, List 2, Box 36.

[79] Before him by Foster (**221**).

The nature of the property is made clear in Peter Temple's *inquisition post mortem*,[80] and is summarized in Table 9.2. The most valuable pieces were the extra-mural fields, because such land was in great demand for grazing, and they contributed particularly to the rising rent roll.

HERTFORDSHIRE PROPERTY

139 f. 75 v. [*Thomas Heritage, Rent of Hamper Mill* [?], *1536*]

Memorandum that I Thomas Herytage hath lett my myll
to John Waker at owr Lady Day in Lent for iij s. iiij d.
a wyke and to pay monethly

Item he howyth me for xij wykes apon Trynetesonday[81]	xl s.
Item for his bord v wykes	ix s.
Summa	xlix s.
Where of payd by hym for mendyng my cog wyll	iij s.
Item I most alow hym for standyng of the myll vj wykes	xx s.
Item paid for hokys and hynges for the gatt	viij d.
Summa	xxiij s. viij d.
Soo rest to me Thomas Herytage by sydes hys kott and hys hosse	xxv s. iij d.

[*Peter Temple, Hertfordshire Property*]

140 f. 17. B [*1538, but written in about 1545*][82]

Flesher Joyner came to Oxsay Hall the Monday afore
Myssomer Day, which was the xvij day [*of June*]
xv^{c}xxxviij

141 f. 44. A [*1542*]

Rescyvyd of Roger Wynter for the half yers rent of Pipers and Bakers endyd at the Annunçyacyon of Our Ladye last past anno xxxiij^{o} Henrici octavi and xxviij die Marcii [*1542*]	xxxiij s. iiij d.
Resevyd[83] of Jhon Popi for a quarters rent for Hamper Myll (end)^{er} dew at the Annunciacion of Our Lady last past anno xxxiij^{o} Henrici viij and ij die Aprilis	iij li.

[80] Draft in ST L9 D4, Temple Inquisitions Post Mortem. This states that Peter had bought the property from the heirs of [Hugh] Radcliff.

[81] Trinity Sunday was therefore about 11 June, with Easter about 10 April, as in 1536; 1533 (Easter, 13 April) is possible, but less likely.

[82] A marginal note on a page of 1545 accounts in Peter Temple's hand.

[83] *Reseseyvyd* in MS.

142 f. 46 v. [*Expenses for Hertfordshire Property: perhaps 1542*][84]

For dragyng the ryver of Oxe Hall	iij s.
For the dragyng of Hamper Myll	v s.
For the sheryffes shott	iij s.
For bere	xix s.
For the quiet rent of Pypers and Bakers	xxj s. iiij d.
For hey tythe	xv s.
To Robyn	xx d.
To Pygyn for corne tythe[85]	x s. viij d.
The quindame	iij s. iiij d.
To Adams for rent endyd at Our Lady Day	viij s.

143 f. 18. A[86]

(Resceyvyd of Edward Phylyps for Hamper Myl | iij li.)[er]

STEPNEY

144 f. 78 v. A[87] [*Thomas Heritage: Stepney, 1533*]

Quittancys that be belonging to my lande at Stepney and other plassys

Thys bylle made the xij daye of Apryel the xxv[th] yere of the raine of King Henry the viij [*1533*] wytnessithe that I, Thomas Herytage, skenar of London, have recevyd of John Barns, gentylman, iiij li. for halfe a yeres rent for the manor of Horstall in the Norte Strete of Stepney, dewe at the feist of the Annuncyacyon of Our Lydy last past, writen the day and yere abow seyd.

Thys byll made the xij daye of Apryel (the)[er] in the xxv yere of the raine of Kyng Henry the viij wytnessith that I, Thomas Herytage, skennar and cystesyn of London, have recevyd of John Edgose vj s. viij d. for halfe a yeres rent of a serten gronde lying in Stepney March dew at the Annunciacyon of Ower Blesid Lady, writen the day and yere above seyd.

Memorandum that I Thomas Herytage, skennar of London, have recevyd of Geffrey Hakys iiij s. for halfe a yeres rent for a closse that lyeth in the Est part of a certen grond that bolongyth to the Manor of Horstall, dewe at the feast of Annuncyacyon of Our Lady last past, in witness wherof I, the seyd Thomas, have sete to my hand the xij daye (and yere)[er] of Apryel the xxv yere of the raine of Kyng Henry the viij.

[84] In a group of Hertfordshire accounts from 1541 to 1542 (ff. 45–48 v).
[85] Cf. the erased entry in **134**; Pygyn is unidentified.
[86] Date unknown.
[87] The hand is much more formal than the other Thomas Heritage items.
[88] The stub of a missing leaf between ff. 78 and 79 shows no trace of text.

[145 f. 79][88]

Thys byll made the xij daye of Apryel in the xxv yere of the raine of King Henry the viij wytnessith that I, Thomas Herytage, cytesin of London, have recevyd of Wylliam Jaymes viij s. iiij d. for a quartors rent of a tenement in Lymost,[89] dewe at the feist of the Annuncyacyon of Your Lady laste past, written the daye and yere abowe seyd.

Thys bylle made the xij daye of Apryel the xxv yere of the raine of King Henry the viij wytnessith that I, Thomas Herytage, cytesin and skennar of London, have recevyd of Walter[90] Blake vj s. viij d. for a quartors rent (dewe at)[er] for a tenement and a close lying in the Norst Stret in Stepney Parishe, and vij d. for a certen ground that abuttet into the hyewaye, dewe at the Annuncyacyon of Your Lady last past, written the daye and yere abow seyd.

Thys byll made the xiij daye of Apryel the xx[v] yere of the raine of King Henry the viij wytnessith that I, Thomas Herytage, skennar of London, have recevyd of Alexandr Lee vj s. viij d. for halfe a yereies rent of a tenement that lyeth in Stepney of the nort parte of the Church dore, at the Annuncyacyon of the Ower Lyday last past, wryten the day and yere above seyd.

146 S2.[91] [*Peter Temple: Stepney, 1550*]
24 April anno regni regis Edwardi vj[ti]

Resceyved of the house in the churche yard	xj s. viij d.
Item for Kyldavy[92]	iiij s.
Resceyved for Wardes house and the Mershe	v li. x s.
Summa	vj li. v s. viij d.
Wherof allowed Ward for quit rent to my Lord of And'[93] dew at Michelmas last	xxxix s. j d.
Item ij s. vj d. dew to Mr. Sandars and Mr. Morrow die dicte[94]	
Resceyved of Stevyns for his howse in Lymehose	v s.
Item the sandpit	ij s. vj d.
Item ij lytyl tenements[?]	vj s. viij d.
Item of hym more for a house in Popler[95]	xxij s. vj d. dew then ut supra
Memorandum there ys to resceyve of Bateman [?]	xxv s.
Of Calton	v s.
Of Colman	v s.

[89] Limehouse, part of Stepney.

[90] Reading uncertain, due to a worm-hole.

[91] A very roughly written slip.

[92] A location in Stepney. Cf. W. P. W. Phillimore (ed.), *London and Middlesex Note-book* (London, 1892). p. 218.

[93] This should be Lord Wentworth. The significance of *And'* is unclear; there was no Lord Andover until 1622 (*Peerage*).

[94] Given as 2s. 8d. in other items.

[95] Another part of Stepney.

[*Dorse; probably Michaelmas rents*]

Resceyved of Ward for his half yeres rent of Hurstals dew at Michelmas	[*blank*][96]
Item resceyved for Kyldavy lykewyse then dew	v s.
Item for Urlod of Lymbre[?]	xviij s.
Wherof allowed Ward for quit rent dew to the Lord at Mychelmas anno regni regis 4 Edwardi vj	xxxix s. j d.
Resceyved for the howse in the church yard	xj s. viij d. dew at Mychelmas
Resceyved of Bateman	xxv s. dew then
Resceyved of Calton	x s. dew then
Resceyved of Stephins dew then	xl s. x d.

COVENTRY

147 f. 62. A[97] [*1551*]

[gale?] xiij d. resceyved and for the reperyng of Jhonsons house	iiij s. ij d.
and for the decaye of the rent of the bakeshowse	vj s. viij d.
and for the howsell at the geoll hall[98]	iiij d.
and for mureg[99]	ij s. vj d.
and for Chelsmore[1]	xij d.
and for hys [*Hyginson?*] fee	xiij s. iiij d.
and for the howse in the shepe market	v s.
Summa totalis receptis et allocatis pro integro anno finito in festo Annunciacionis Beate Marie in anno v^{to} Edwardi vj^{ti} [*25 Mar. 1551*] ut superius patet	xiiij li. xij s. vj d.

148 f. 62. B.[2]

Resceyved of Higinson for our rent at Coventre iij li. that he delyvered for me to Mr. Lavendre, and for a wayne cum pertimenciis, wherof I delyvered my dowter Alis for her husband at Whitsuntyde	iij li.

[96] Sum blank, but likely to be £5 10s. as above.

[97] The stub of a missing leaf before f. 62 can be seen to have been written, and this item probably runs on from it. It is in continuous text, but has been set out in separate lines for clarity.

[98] Gayll Hawl in 1581, i.e. the gaol.

[99] Payment for repair of the city walls.

[1] Quit-rent to the manor of Cheylesmore.

[2] Probably 1552 or 1553.

149 f. 62. C [*1554*]

Memorandum that I have delyvered Mr. Sheldon at dyvers tymes vj li. vj s. viij d. fore one holle yere rent for his part of the landes in Coventrye, dew at Mychelmas and at Lady Day last past. Wrytten the xx^th^ of Maye anno domini 1554.

150 f. 62. D[3] [*1555*]

Memorandum that resceyved for Coventre rent dew for one holle yere endyd at the Annunciacion of Our Lady last past.

In primis Hygyns delyvered me at Lundon at Barthilimewtyde	xl s.
Item to Lavendre for me at Hallowtyd	iij li.
Item allowed hym for (Jhonsons)^er^ the Bakehowse	vj s. viij d.
For mureg	ij s. vj d.
and for Chelsmore	xij d.
and for his fee	xiij s. iiij d.
and for Jhonsons howse quia (vacat)^er^ a retro[4]	viij s.
For the malt myle croft in Spone Stret	vj d. quia vacat
and xvj s. iiij d. allowed hym for overplus payd afore in the last yers accompt	
Item resceyved of hym at Hallowes	vij li. xij s.
[*Margin*] Memorandum xij s. ys yet in hys handes to paye	
Summa totalis	xiiij li. xvj s. iiij d.

receptis et allocatis pro integro anno finito in festo Annunciationis Beate Marie in anno 1555 and so remayn

Whyrof delyvered Mr. Sheldon at Hallowtyd	iij li.
Item delyvered hym at Whytsontyd	iij li. xiij s.
Item for hys part of old tyle	vj s.
and so evyn at Whytsontyde anno 1555	

151 f. 82 v. E [*Undated memoranda*]

Delyvered to Mr. Sheldon at Coventre	iij li.
Delyvered hym in the parlor	xl s.
Delyvered hym at ij tymes	xl s.

152 f. 83. B

Resceyved for Coventre Lady Daye rents of Thomas Hygynson	iiij li. xij s.
Whereof delyvered to my dawghter Als	xlv s. vj d.

3 Rearranged from continuous text.

4 I.e. as noted on the missing opposite leaf.

10. *Bailiff for the Lords of Dassett*

None of the three co-owners of Burton Dassett, Cooke, Dannet and Wootton, lived near Warwickshire, and so they needed an agent to administer it and the other property that they had inherited from Sir Edward Belknap (see p. 29). This lay in several places further north in Warwickshire, with one outlier in Leicestershire, and a modest town estate in Banbury (**168**) including the Swan Inn and the former Hospital of St. John[5] (see Fig. 6, p. 177). The co-owners also took a lease from the Crown in 1537 of the profits of the parsonage of Burton Dassett (formerly the property of Erdbury (Arbury) Priory) which they later bought outright.[6]

Peter Temple became involved with the administration of the estate in 1548, on the death of the former bailiff, John Petifer.[7] He acted as bailiff proper for Burton Dassett, and as receiver-general for the other estates, which had their own bailiff, a man called Wase (or Wast); his fee was 52s., and he also received 26s. 8d. for acting as bailiff for the parsonage, the same sum that Wase was paid. These were modest fees, as Peter Temple himself noted in his lawsuit with Anthony Cooke.[8] The account book shows no obvious bribes or the like, but undoubtedly influence was to be gained in Burton Dassett—enough to make the job worthwhile. He was, indeed, accused by Cooke of filling the ranks of the Dassett leaseholders with his relatives, but this was an exaggeration; Giles Spencer was the only one, and he already had strong family connections with Burton Dassett.[9] Overall, Peter Temple's post as bailiff was one of the levers he used to raise himself from among his fellow yeoman tenants toward the landed gentry. He lost the post in 1560, at the start of his dispute with Cooke.[10]

Peter Temple recorded his receipts and outgoings in detail in the account book, but in a rather confused form. The parsonage and estate accounts are mingled, while the payments are apparently

[5] *V.C.H. Oxon.*, **10**, p. 49. Curiously, the Banbury property is not referred to in the 1557 account, even though Cooke at least did not sell his portion until 1580 (P.R.O. C54/1110; also fragment in Sterling Memorial Library, Yale, Eng. Misc. MSS. Folio 4 (series 2)).

[6] Crown lease: 1 July 1537; P.R.O. E315/209, f. 107. Sale to Duke of Suffolk, 30 September 1538. *L. &P. Henry VIII*, **XIII**, 1182 (18m). The sale by Suffolk to Cooke, Dannet and Wootton is not recorded, but probably took place before 1548, and certainly before 1557.

[7] The date is inferred from the tentative 1548 account notes (**172**). Cf. also Gay, p. 376.

[8] Gay, 1938, p. 380; see p. 243.

[9] Ibid., p. 383; see p. 19.

[10] Ibid., p. 381; see p. 240.

recorded from Michaelmas to Michaelmas but the receipts from Lady Day to Lady Day; this may have been caused by John Petifer's death falling just after he had collected the Michaelmas rents. The clearest picture therefore comes from two separate sheets of accounts, one for the parsonage in 1537–8,[11] made by a previous bailiff, Thomas Burbery (**153–4**), and one of 1557 by Peter Temple for both parsonage and estate (**162**). The main sequence of Peter Temple's accounts series starts with a draft for 1548 (**155**) and continues with separate receipts and payments until 1551–2. As well as the separate account for 1557, there are two sheets for 1560, in which Peter Temple calculated the final reckoning between him and his successor, Elise Burbery; the latter countersigned the account. By this year, Peter was himself the owner of one-third of the manor.

The evidence is completed by brief rentals for Banbury and Wappenbury, and lists of points to be remembered (**167–172**); most of these date from the start of his work in 1548, and they include a reminder to discover what arrangements the former bailiff had made (**172**). A special account concerns the Burton Dassett beacon (**173**). The beacon was made from five trees, built up with hurdles, with pitch to help it burn. It stood on the end of Burton Hill, and would have been visible for many miles. Beside the beacon itself, stood (and stands) the fifteenth-century circular Beacon Tower, which would have sheltered the watchers.[12] The beacon may have been Peter's concern as bailiff, but the most likely occasion for it to have been needed is 1545, when a French invasion was feared.[13] If so, he must have been acting on behalf of the village community, as one of its prominent members. Similarly, he wrote the draft of a letter (**174**), probably to a local arbitrator, setting out the facts of a dispute at Fenny Compton over the interpretation of a 'homely writing'. He may have been asked to deal with this because he was bailiff, but it was not directly part of the job. In the same way, in 1551–3, he wrote the accounts for the churchwardens.[14]

The Estate

The accounts for the estate proper are fairly simple. In 1557 (**162**), Burton Dassett itself produced a clear £238, while the rest of the

[11] The first year after the co-owners leased the tithes.

[12] It has, however, been suggested that it was in origin a windmill, and only became a look-out tower later. N. Pevsner, *The Buildings of England: Warwickshire* (London: Penguin, 1966).

[13] *L&P. Henry VIII*, **XX** (i), p. 52; **XXI** (i), p. 1137. Sheriffs were also ordered to set up beacons in May 1548 (*Cal. State Papers Domestic, Edward VI*, **I**, p. 7).

[14] British Library, Stowe MSS. 795, ff. 5–6. These are two sheets from a lost volume.

estate added another £56. One heriot was paid that year on the death of a tenant, and the other accounts also record some entry fines. Overwhelmingly, the largest contributions came from the rents of the large pasture closes at Burton, ranging down from £66 a year. Peter Temple's two leases made up the largest individual payment of £87, but this was only a third of the total rent.

Among outgoings were the bailiff's and other fees, and some quit-rents, payable by the free-holder to the lord of the manor or another landlord. A number of annuities had to be paid, some clearly long-established, such as that to the former Abbey of Leicester. The most important one from Burton Dassett was that of 36s. 8d. to the 'heirs of Makepeace'. This had been established by Edward Belknap in 1505, payable to Edward Odyngsele, and was transferred to Henry Makepeace in 1522.[15] Finally, to close the account, the proceeds were divided and paid over to the three co-heirs or their representatives.

The Parsonage of Burton Dassett[16]

The principal income of the parsonage came from tithes, in three main forms. Most important were the tithes paid for the pasture lands of Burton. As these were often used for fattening stock reared elsewhere, there might not be any tithable young beasts, and at some date before 1538 it had been agreed that the tithes should be commuted for a money payment calculated at 8d. for each noble of rent paid (6s. 8d. or 80d.).[17] This brought in £16 in 1538 and £28 in 1557. The difference arose mainly because in 1538, the tithes for part of the land were subject to a separate lease made in 1530 by

[15] It was split before 1591 into two-thirds and one-third. W.R.O. CR457, Box 5, Loose B, covers the larger portion in a splendid original bundle. A deed of 1757 has folded within it the earlier deeds to the annuity, back to the original of 1505, all in pristine state. W.R.O. CR920/1–3 is a rather less complete sequence for the remaining third, with an abstract of title from 1591, and a deed of 1770 by which this third of the annuity was extinguished. The Makepeace heirs are only naned in the Wotton accounts for 1580, as Thomas Petiver and William Neale, whose wives were the daughters and coheirs of Henry Makepeace, Bodleian Library, Broxbourne 84.15/R267. N.R.O. Temple Stowe, Box 4/1B/20 is a grant for life by Elizabeth Neale, of her two-thirds of the annuity (1614).

[16] Or lay rectory, i.e. a monastic rectorial estate which had passed into lay hands after the dissolution. I thank Kevin Down for advice on these accounts.

[17] The freeholders' tithes were also commuted. In 1580 (Wotton accounts, op. cit.), John Woodwarde paid 9s. 4d., and this sum can be identified throughout the accounts. The Underhill freehold paid nothing in 1580, perhaps because the tithes had been bought out, but it may be represented by the 6s. 8d. which Leonard Savage paid in 1537 (153) and later, which regularly follows John Woodwarde's payment. The other 1580 payment was of 8d. from John Wilkins, for the freeholding formerly belonging to Sir Davy Owen. This must be 'The Mylner's Close' in 1537, but cannot be recognized in Peter Temple's accounts.

Erdbury Priory to Thomas Try, who rented some of the fields; he paid £10 10s. a year until 1544, when he surrendered the lease.[18] The tithes of corn from the arable of Northend and Knightcote were also converted to cash, being leased for £8 a year.[19]

The remaining tithes were principally the 'small tithes',[20] with pigs, geese, eggs, hens and pigeons named; these tithes were often retained by the vicar when a church was appropriated to a monastic house, but at Burton, Erdbury Priory owned them. Various other tithes were also received from Northend and Knightcote, including those for 'foreign sheep', i.e. sheep from other villages being pastured there, and 'Easter tithes'; these were paid by many, perhaps most, of the villagers, but it is not clear just what they concerned.[21]

'Spiritual' income came from offerings at the principal festivals, at marriage and death and for wedding bells. Finally, the church wardens paid 2s. 2d. for the 'holy' or 'holy loffe' candle, which may have been a candle burning on the rood loft.

The parsonage had considerable outgoings. Indeed, in 1537 the rent of £23 10s. ½d. left a net profit of only 15s. The next year was rather better, producing a surplus of £4. However, the Crown did cover the individual payments due from the lay rector, later the responsibility of Cooke, Dannett and Wootton themselves. The largest sum was the vicar's stipend of £12 a year (cf. p. 36), while the clerk had 16s. and Peter Temple, as bailiff, 26s. 8d. A tenth of the notional income of the rectory[22] went to the Crown, while the archdeacon collected *proxies* or procurations[23] and *synods* or synodal dues.[24] Communion (housling) wine and bread were bought, oil for the lamps,[25] wax and yarn for candles, and the great Easter

[18] The original counterpart lease is P.R.O. E303/17. Warws. Conv. Leases, no. 258; the surrender is ST Deeds List 2, Box 36, 26 June 1544.

[19] PRO E303/17, Warws. Conv. Leases, no. 238, 14 June 1520 for twenty years and ST L9 B1, Temple Bucks. transcript book, 23 April 1540, for seventeen years.

[20] In contrast to the great tithes normally of corn, hay and wood (though the division was not always firm). E. J. Evans, *The Contentious Tithe* (London: Routledge and Kegan Paul, 1976).

[21] They may have been some form of formal Easter Offerings, which were sometimes described as tithes.

[22] As calculated in 1535 in the Valor Ecclesiasticus.

[23] In origin, payments in lieu of the obligation to entertain the archdeacon on his visitation. Simon Pegge, *The Parson's Counsellor* (London, 7th ed., 1820), p. 367. Nominally, the 7s. 6d. was made up of 1s. 6d. for the archdeacon and his horse, and 1s. for each of his attendants and their horses, ibid., p. 373, but in reality many different sums were paid for proxies. P. Heath, *Medieval Clerical Accounts*, St. Anthony's Hall Publs., 26, York, 1964.

[24] Another fixed payment, apparently originally connected with attendance at diocesan synods. Simon Pegge, op. cit., p. 370.

[25] Sacramental oil is less likely, as this was usually called *chrism*.

candle itself, the Paschal.[26] In 1548-9, Erasmus' *Paraphrases of the New Testament* was bought; every church had been ordered to obtain one in 1547, but only 'half' could be bought as the second volume was not published until 1549.[27] The rectory was also responsible for the chancel of the church, though the only payment recorded was for the windows in 1557.

BAILIFF'S ACCOUNTS

153 S. 3

[*Endorsed*] Thomas Burberies acount for the Parsonage of Dorset The 30th of Henry 8 [*Michaelmas 1536–Michaelmas 1538*]

[f. 1] Thomas Burberyes accompt of the parsonag[e of] Dorset for one yere endyng at Mychel[mas] anno xxix° Henrici VIII [*1537*]

Oblacio die Sancti Michaelis archangelis	ij s. ix d.
[*Margin*] Festum Sancti Martini [*11 Nov.*]	
Recepi de Henrico Makepeace senior pro decimi averia in campis de Knightcote et Northend	iiij s.
Item de Willelmo Brokes pro consimili	iiij s.
Item de Henrico Makepeace junior pro consimili	ij s. vj d.
Item de Thoma Burbery pro consimili	ij s. vj d.
Oblacio ad obitum Margarete Petifer	xvj d.
[*Margin*] Festum Nativitatis domini	
Oblacio die Nativitatis domini	ij s. ix d.
Oblacio ad obitum Agnete Brokes	vj d.
[*Margin*] Festum Pasche [*1 April*]	
Oblacio die Pasche	vj s. vij d.

Easter Tythes

Primo de Willelmo Hunt	xx d.
De Johanne Palmer	xix d.
De Willelmo Knight	vj d.
De Willelmo Wagstaff	v s.
De Johanne Profett	iij s.
De Willelmo Leyborne	xx d.
De Willelmo Richardes	xviij d.
De Thoma Bas	iij s.
De Thoma Colyns	ij s.
De Willelmo Swayne	iij s. iiij d.
De Johanne Higyns	xviij d.

[26] This may be the candle for which the churchwardens paid.

[27] R. W. Dixon, *History of the Church of England* (London: Routledge and Sons, 1887), vol. II, p. 451.

De Johanne Lodbroke	ij s. iiij d.
De Thoma Profett	ij s. ix d.
De Henrico Makepeace	ij s.
De Henrico Bas	xiiij d.
De Roberto Stacye	ij d.
De Johanne Brokes	iij s.
De Elizabethe Whytehedd	xiiij d.
De Henrico Davye	ij s.

Festo Invencionis Sancti Crucis [*3 May*]

Recepi de Willelmo Brokes pro ovibus in campis de Knightcotes	iiij s. vj d.
Item de Henrico Makepeace senior pro consimili	iiij s. vj d.
Item de Henrico Makepeace junior pro consimili	vj d.
Item de Thoma Burbery pro consimili	iiij s.
Summa	iiij li. xxij d.

[S. 3: f. 1 v][28]

Oblacio die Nativitate Sancti Johannis Baptiste [*24 June*]	ij s. ix d.
Oblacio ad nuptias Johanne Dom[?]	ij s.
Oblacio ad nuptias Beatrice Fever	xiij d.
Tythe lambes xiiij, every of theym the pece xviij d.	Summa xxj s.
Tythe wolle, three toddes and vj poundes, xj s. the tod	Summa xxxv s.
Tythe pygges and geas xlj[29]	Summa x s. iiij d.
Tythe egges vj^{c} and three score[30]	ij s. ij d.
Tythe pegyns ij doson[31]	viij d.
Tythe hay of small closis in Northend	xij d.
Of John Brokes for odd tythes	ij s.
Of Nicholas Frekylton	xx d.
Of the halilof candell[32]	ij s. ij d.
Summa	iiij li. xxj d.
Summa totalis	viij li. iij s. vij d.

The tythe of therbage per annum

[*Margin*] These tythes be certen yerly	
De Williemo Brokes and Elizabethe Makepeace	xxvj s. viij d.
Of the same Elizabethe for small closes	vj s.
Item the lesowes that John Burbery did hold	Cxlviij s.

[28] At base of last page, *verte*.
[29] 3d. each.
[30] 4d. per hundred.
[31] Three for 1d.
[32] See p. 149.

Item of Thomas Burbery — xvj s. viij d.
Of Nicholas Freklton for the Hilles, the conyes and Haydwyke per annum — liiij s. viij d.
The myll per annum — iiij s.
John Wilkyns — ix s. iiij d.
Leonard Savag — vj s. viij d.
The mylners close — viij d.
Tythe corne per annum — viij li.
Summa parcellas xvj li. xij s. viij d.

[S. 3: f. 2]

The totall profett of this present yere amountith to — xxiiij li. xvj s. iij d.
Wherof is paid for farme of the said parsonag to the Kynges grace yerely — xxiij li. x s. ob.
Item to be abated for that [*defective*] inhyghed[?] in the herbage — x s. viij d.
So restethe due by Thomas Burbery unto us apon thaccompt for this yere — xv s. vj d. ob.
Recyved the iij^{d} day of July anno xxxj Henrici viij [*1539*] my part of the above said xv s. vj d. ob.
Anthony Cooke

Receyvyde the iij^{de} daye of Julye anno xxxj Henrici viij my mothers part of the abovesayde xv s. vj d. ob.
John Dannett

154 S. 3: f. 3

Thomas Burberyes accompt for the parsonage of Dorset for one yere ending at Mychelmas anno domini regis Henrici 8 xxx^{o} [*1538*]

Oblacio die Sancti Michaelis archangelis — iij s.
[*Margin*] Festum Sancti Martini
Receyved of William Brokes for tythe of certen shipe goyng in Knightcote Feld — ix s. viij d.
Item receyved of hym for foure score — xij d.
Item receyved of Elizabeth Makepeace for certen shipe in Knightcote Felde likewyse — vj s. viij d.
Item receyved of Thomas Burbery for certen shipe likewyse — iiij s.
Oblacio ad obitum Henrici Makepeace senior — xx d.
Item his mortuary[33] — x s.
Oblacio die Natalis domini — ij s. viij d.
[*Margin*] Festum Pasche [*21 April*]
Oblacio die Pasche — vij s.

[33] Payable to the church on death. 10s. implies goods worth £40 according to the statute 21 Henry VIII. c. 6. Sir Simon Degge, *The Parson's Counsellor* (London, 7th ed., 1820), p. 424.

Easter Tythes

Recepi de Willelmo Hunt	ij s.
Item de Johanne Palmer	xiij d.
Item de Willelmo Palmer	xvj d.
Item de Willelmo Knight	vj d. ob.
De Willelmo Swayne	iij s. vij d. ob.
De Ricardo Walshe	x d.
De Thoma Bas	iij s.
De Thoma Proffett et Roberto	iij s. ij d.
De Willelmo Richardes	xxiij d.
De Willelmo Leyborne	xv d.
De Thoma Pomphrey	x d.
De Johanne Blakehurst	ij s.
De Roberto Clarege	xviij d.
De Willelmo Wagstaff	v s. iiij d.
De Johanne Lodbroke	iij s.
De Thoma Colyns	ij s.
De Johanne Hygyns	ij s. iiij d.
De Johanne Brokes	iiij s.
De Henrico Bars	iij s.
De Johanne Proffett	ij s. xj d.
De Thoma Whytehed	xvj d.
De Henrico Davye	xx d.
Summa	iiij li. xv s. v d.

[S. 3: f. 3 v][34]

Festum Inventionis Sancti Crucis	
Recepi de Willelmo Brokes pro certis ovibus in campis de Knightcote	iij s.
De Elizabethe Makepeace pro consimili	ij s.
De Thoma Burbery pro consimili	ij s. vj d.
De Agneto Makepeace	xij d.
Oblacio die Nativitatis Sancti Johannis Baptiste	iij s.
Recepi de Thoma Hyron	ij s.
Recepi de Willelmo Palmer	viij s.
Oblacio ad nuptias Willelmi Tomkyns	vij d. ob.
Receyved of John Symes for certen shipe that went in Northend Field	xx d.
Tythe lambe xxx^{ti}, every lambe xvj d. Summa	xl s.
Tythe wolle iij toddes and di. todd, price le todde xij s. Summa	liiij s.
Tyth egges viij^{c}	ij s. viij d.
Tythe pygges and geace xl	x s.
Piggins ij doson	viij d.
Tythe hempe	iiij d.

[34] At base of page *verte*.

The haliloff candell	ij s. ij d.
Summa	vj li. vj s. iij d. ob.
Totalis summa	xj li. xx d. ob.

[S. 3: f. 4]

The totall of this present yere amountethe to	[xxvij li.] xiiij s. iiij d. [ob.]
Wherof ys paid for farme of the said [parso]nage to the Kynges Grace yerely	xxiij li. x s. ob.
Item paid by Thomas Burbery unto us in readye money the [*blank*] day of [*blank*] anno 1538	xl s.
So is due apon this accompt as apperethe by the same Thomas Burbery	xliiij s. iiij d.

Receyved the iij[de] day of July anno xxxj Henrici viij [*1539*] for my part of the abovesaid xliiij s. iiij d.

Anthony Cooke

Receyvde the iij[de] daye of Julye anno xxxj[o] Henrici viij[i] my mothers part of the abovesayde xliiij s. iiij d.

John Dannett

155 L. 31 b. B [*Notes for Bailiff's Accounts, 1548*][35]

For quit rent	xij s. (j d.)[er]
that is to saye of Jhon Higins	iij s.
Of Thomas Makepec	xij d.
Wylliam Whithed	ij d.
Thomas Swayne	vj s. viij d.
Jhon Colyns	iij s.
Jhon Knebe	iij d.
Rychard Colman	viij d.
Wylliam Hunt	xvj d.[36]
Jhon Palmer of [Rodwey][37]	xx s.
Rychard Colman of Rodwey	xx s.
Water Frekylton	xxxv s. viij d. for tythe
The same Water for wood	xvij s. ix d.
Woodward[38]	ix s. iiij d.
Savage[38]	vj s. viij d.
Item for a heryot dew in Petyvers tyme	xviij s.
Item tholy loffe candell	ij s. ij d.
Hacoke	v s. iiij d.
Sir Anthony Cope[39]	(vj li.)[er] iij li. vj s. viij d.

[35] The same date as L. 31b. C (89); Mills was dead by 1549. Cf. 167–71.
[36] 15d. elsewhere. This error is no doubt why the total was changed.
[37] For rent, as in other years.
[38] For tithe. Cf. 153, f. 1v, 162 and p. 148.
[39] Of Hanwell, near Banbury.

[*Right Margin*] Memorandum to aske a reconyng of my brother for iij li. ij s. ix d. my Lady Spenser for hym	
Myls of Herbery for hey	vj s.
Item a rekenynge	
Mr. Hyckeman for a felly[40]	xiij s. iiij d.
Palmer of Chadshunt	xxx s.

156 f. 59[41] Money paid and delivered by Peter Temple for the Lordes of Dassett in anno ij^{do} et iij^{tio} Edwardi vjth [*1548–9*] as followeth

Inprimis paid to the vicar of Dassett for his pencyon endyd at Martylmas [*11 Nov.*] (the purification of Our Lady)^{er} anno ij regni regis Edwardi vjth	iij li.
Item paid for Mr. Loves charges and myne at Warwicke at your wood sall	xij s. iiij d.
Item for the one half a paraphrasis[42]	vj s.
Item to the vicar of Dasset for his pencyon dew at the Purification of Our Lady [*2 Feb.*] in anno iij^{ti} regni regis Edwardi vjth	iij li.
Item delyvered to the clarkes boy for howslyng wyne[43]	xij d.
Delyvered the clarke for Christmas and Our Lady Day	xj s. iiij d.
Paid for ij tapers	xij d.
Item for a pownd of wax[44]	vj d.
Item weyke yarne[44]	j d.
For oleum[45]	iiij d.
Bred at Ester	j d. ob.
Item paid to Mr. Guyes for his rent dew at Mary Ann'	iiij li. ij s. iiij d.
Item paid to the vicare of Dassett for his pencion dew at the Invencion of the Holy Crosse [*3 May*]	iij li.
Item paid the heyrs of Makepese	xxxiij s. iiij d.
Item paid to Wast for Mr.[46] Forster of Balsell	iij li. xj s. viij d.
Item paid to Mr. Cooke for hym selfe and Mr. Wotton as apperyth by his byll	j^{c} li.
Item to hym more as aforeseyd by Mr. Grey	xxj li. (vj s. viij d.)^{er}
(Memorandum there ys xx li. ij s. yet in Mr. Grey his handes)^{er}	
Item paid to Mr. Thomas Dannett for his mother as apperith by his byll	lvj li. xiij s. iiij d.
Item paid to Mr. Coke as apperith by his byll for hym selfe onely	xvj li. x s.

[40] Filly?
[41] These accounts follow almost consecutively in the book, written inverted.
[42] See p. 150.
[43] See p. 149.
[44] Probably for candles.
[45] See p. 149.
[46] Or *Mistress* as elsewhere.

Item paid to the vicar of Dasset for his pencion dew at the fest of Seynt Peter ad[47] Vincula [*1 Aug.*]	iij li.
Item paid to Mrs. Forster of Balsall	iij li. vj s. viij d.
Item paid for synodes and proxies[48]	vj s. vj d.
Item paid for Banbery cheffe rent	ij s. iij d.
Item for the Spittell thier[49]	viij d.
Summa	ij^{c}xix li. xv s. v d.

[f. 58 v.]

Item paid to theyrs of Makepese[50]	xxxiij s. iiij d.
Item paid for ij tapers	xij d.
Item for 1 pownd waxe	vij d.
Item the clerke's wagis at Mydsomer	iiij s.
Item paid the churche wardens	xiij s. iiij d.
Item paid the clark's wagis at Mychelmas	vij s. iiij d.
Item for synodes	ij s.
Item to the churche wardens	xiij s. iiij d.
Item paid to Mr. Cooke as apperyth by his byll[51]	lxxxv li.
Item paid to Sir Edward Wotton aperyng by hys byll	lx li.
Item paid to Mr. Seeton [?] for the fee of Mr. Sadler	liij s. iiij d.
Summa	j^{c}lj li. viij s. iiij d.
Item paid to Anthony Cooke	xxv li. ix s. iiij d.
Item paid to Wylliam Hokes for theyrs of Norrys	iiij s.
Item paid to George Petyver for Henry Cranes aunte	xl s.
Item my wyffe to Mr. Guyes	iij li. ij s. iiij d.

157 f. 56 b.v Resceyved by Peter Temple for the Lordes of Dasset, dew at the Annunciacion of Mary to May Day anno iij^{tio} Edwardi vjth [*1549*]

Resceyved for thofferyng at Mychelmas	ij s.
Item for Chrystmas	ij s. viij d.
Weddyng of bells	vj d. ob.
Thoffring at Ester	v s. vij d.
Resceyved for the hedgyng at Bubnell Spryng[52]	xij s. vj d.
Resceyved of Wase	iij li. xiij s. iiij d.

[47] *the* in error before *ad*.

[48] See p. 149.

[49] Also a chief rent, for the Hospital of St. John (see p. 146; 168).

[50] ST L9 A1, Temple Accounts, Box 1, piece 11 is the receipt by Barnabas Holbeche of Feningley [Fillongley, Warwickshire], yeoman, for this annuity, due to Richard Makepeace, son and heir of Henry Makepeace; there are other receipts for later years.

[51] Ibid., piece 13 is Cooke's receipt, dated 20 April 1549.

[52] See p. 178.

Ester

(resceyved for)[er] Part of parvi tythes[53]	(viij s. vij d.)[er]
Resceyved for Lyse rent	xliiij s. xj d.
Of Elyse for vj elms	xj s. iiij d.
Of Weston[54]	vj s. viij d.
Of Davy[54]	vij s. iiij d.
Memorandum that Wase delyvered to Hygins	xx li.
Item he delyvered to Thomas	iiij li.
Item resceyved of Petyver for his rent and tythe at Dasset and Rawlyns Close	vij li. iij s.
Item resceyved for the rest of Banbery rent	xlvj s. j d.
Item resceyved of Wylliam Brokes for his rent and tythes of his part of a pasture in Dasset	iij li. xiij s. iiij d.
Item for his part of the tythe corne	xl s.
Item resceyved of Waste	xxix s. j d.
Item resceyved of Wase	x li. xix s. x d.
Item resceyved of Wylliam Makepec for his part of a pasture in Dasset for the rent and tythe therof	iiij li. xv s. iiij d.
Item of hym for hys part of the tythe corn	xl s.
Item resceyved of Elys Burbery for the rent and tithe of his part of a pasture in Dasset	vj li. xij s.
Item of hym for the corne tythe of Rodwey	xx s.
Item of hym for part of his fine	xx li.
Item resceyved of Thomas Burbery for the rent of his pasture in Dassett	v li.
Summa	lxxxxix li. xiij s. xj d. ob.

[f.56 b]

Item resceyved of Mistris Frekylton	xv li. xvj s. viij d.
and for tythe dew at Maye Daye	xxxv s. viij d.
Item resceyved of Mr. Wylliam Shelden for the rent and tyth of the Grett pastur in Dasset dew at Mayday last	xxxvij li.
Memorandum my owne rent and tyth for Hals Feld and Old Lease dew for Christmas and Our Lady Daye last past	xxxiij li.
Item for Herytag Feld for Candelmas and May Day	xiij li.
Item for the tythe of Herytage Feld dew at Lammas for a holle yere then endyd	iij li. x s.
Item resceyved of Wast for Mr. Newpert[?]	viij li.
Item resceyved of Bosworth and Wagstafe for wood	vij li.
Item resceyved of Bosworth and Wagstafe ageyne	iiij li.
Memorandum my owne rent and tyth for Hals Feld and Old Lesse dew for Mydsomer and Mychelmas	xxxiij li.

[53] See p. 149.

[54] Banbury rent.

Item for Herytag Feld dew for Lamas and Martylmas	xiij li.
(Item resceyved for tythes of lame and	vij s. ij d.)[er]
Item of Wagstaff for Ester tythes	(v s. viij d.; v s. viij d.)[er]
Item resceyved of Bosworth and Wagstaff for wood	xxxj li.
Item resceyved of Bosworth and Wagstaff for wode	xxxj li. vj s. viij d.
Item resceyved of Bosworth and Wagstaff for woode	iij li. vj s. viij d.
(Item resceyved of the Clarke for Ester tythes	xxiij s.)[er]
Item resceyved of Lane of Honyle for one holle yere endyd at Mychelmas	vj s. vj d.[55]
Item resceyved for Wrothes house for on holle yere	xiij s. iiij d.
Item resceyved of Mr. Raye for woode	xxxv s. vj d.
(Item of Wase for Ulthorpe and Bubnell	xiij li. xj s. vij d. ob.)[er]
(Item resceyved for tythes	xv s. ij d.)[er]
(Item resceyved for tythe wooll of Robart Waraner	xv s.)[er]
Item resceyved for Banbery rent	iij li. j d.
Item of Rychard Over for land in Honyle for a holl yere	iij s.
Item resceyved of Wase for certain smalle parcels of wood	v li. iij s. viij d.
Item resceyved of Wase for rentes	xxij li. xviij s. viij d. ob.
Item resceyved of Jhon Brookes for quit rent	xiij s. j d.
Summa pagine	ij^{c}lxx li. iiij s. ij d. ob.

[f. 56 v.]

Item resceyved of Wase upon Hall Halow Daye	xj. li. xvij s. ij d.
Item resceyved of Thomas Hall for tythe rent	xliiij s. xj d.
Resceyved for Ester tythes	xlix s. iiij d.
Item for 1 tythe lamz	l s.
Item for odes[56]	ij s. v d.
Item for tythe of foren shepe	iiij s. iiij d.
Thoffryng at Mydsomer	xxiij d.
Thoffryng at Myhelmas	ij s. ij d.
Thoffryng at the weddyng	iij d.
Tythe hey of small closes	xxj d.
Resceyved for part of Wylliam Brokes fyne	xx li.
Item of hym for tythe of foren shepe	ix s.
Item for the tythe of pyges gese pygeons and egges	xiij s. iiij d.
Item for ix tode woll	ix li. xviij s.
Summa	l li. xiij s. ij d. ob.
Item resceyved of Wylliam Brokes for hys rent of the tythe	xl s.
Item of hym for hys rent and tythe of Dasset	iij li. xiij s. iiij d.
Item resceyved of Rychard Petyver for the rent and tythe of his occupying in Dasset	vj li. xij s.

[55] Marginal note *no* [for *nota*?] *vj s.*

[56] Probably odd tithes, e.g. for incomplete tens of lambs; cf. **161**, f. 53 v.

Item of hym more for the rent and tythe of Rawlyns close	xj s.
Item of Wylliam Makepece for the rent and tythe of hys occuping in Dassett	iiij li. xv s. iiij d.
Item of hym for the tythe corn	xl s.
Item resceyved of Water Frekylton	xv li. xvj s. viij d.
Item resceyved of Thomas Burbery	vj li.
Item of Elys Burbery	vij li. xj s.
Item resceyved of Jhon Croker esquier for rent and tythes	xxxvij li.

158 f. 58. Money paid by Peter Temple for the Lordes of Dasset (after)[er] dew after the fest of Saynt Mychell in the iij[d] yere of Edward the vj[th] untyll the fest of Seynt Mychell in the iiij[th] yere of the sayd Kyng [*1549–50*]

Item paid to the vicar of Dasset for his pencyon dew at Martylmas last past	iij li.
Item paid to the sayd vicar for his pencyon dew at Candell Lammas	iij li.
Item paid to Thomas Gryffyn for theyrse of Makepes dew at the Annunciacion	xxxiij s. iiij d.
Item for ij tapres	xij d.
Item the Clarkes wages at Christmas	iiij s.
Item paid for a li. of waxe	vij d.
Item paid for oyle	iiij d.
Item the Clarkes wages at Ester paid	vij s. iiij d.
Item paid to Mr. Guyes for Our Lady Daye rent	iiij li. (i)[er]ij s. iiij d.
Item paid to Mr. Dannet the xth of May[57]	lxvj li. xiij s. iiij d.
Item paid Mr. Wotton the xth of Maye[58]	lxvj li. xiij s. iiij d.
Item paid to Mr. Coke the xth of Maye	lxvj li. xiij s. iiij d.
Item paid to Mr. Coke for hym selfe then	xvj li. x s.
Item paid theirs of Norrys dew at [Mydsomer?]	ij s.
Item paid the vycar for May daye	iij li.
Item paid to Mrs. Forster at Maye Daye	iij li. vj s. viij d.
Item paid the vicar of Dasset for Lammas	iij li.
Item paid the Clarkes wages dew at Mydsomer	iiij s.
Paid to Thomas Gryfyns son for theyrs of Makepece	xxxiij s. iiij d.
Paid Mr. Guyes esquier for Mychelmas rent	iiij li. ij s. iiij d.
Paid the Clarke for his wages dew at Mychelmas	vij s. (vj d.)[er] iiij d.
Paid to Mistress Foster at Mychelmas	iij li. vj s. viij d.
Paid to Mr. Wygston and Jhon Rawlyns for their fees	iiij li.
Paid to Mr. Burnbye	xj li. xiij s. iiij d.
Paid to the King for quit rent at Honyle	iij s. vj d.
Paid to My Lord Marques Dorset	x s. iiij d.
Paid to the late Abbe of Leycester	iij li. iij s. iiij d.

[57] Op. cit. (note 50), piece 15 is in the receipt.
[58] Ibid., piece 16.

Paid to Mr. Culpeper	iij s.
Item allowyd Wast for his fee	xxvj s. viij d.
Summa	ij^{c}lxviij d. xj s. iiij d.

[f. 57 v.]

Item paid to Sir Anthony Coke the xvijth of Novembre	lxxxj li.
Item paid to Mr Wotton for hymself and Mistris Dannet[59]	j^{c}lxij li.
Item paid to Sir Anthony Coke for hymselfe	xvj li. vij s. vij d.
Item paid to theyres of Norrys for Mychelmas	ij s.
Item delyvered to Mr. Water Frekylton for the fee of [Hirane?]	xl s.

159 f. 56. Money Resceyved by Peter Temple for the Lordes of Dasset dew at the Annunciacion of Our Lady and Ester in the iiijth yere of the raygne of Kyng Edward the vjth as followeth [*1550*]

Inprimis resceyved of Wast for Bubnell	vj li. viij s. x d.
Item of hym more for Ulsthorpe	vj li. xj s. ix d.
Item of hym for Nunseton	lvj s. viij d.
Item (for)^{er} of hym for Stokyngford	ix li. xvij s. viij d.
Item of hym for Wapenbery	x li.
Item resceyved of Banbery rent dew at the Annunciation	iij li. j d.
Item resceyved for thofferyng at Mychelmas	ij s. ij d.
Item thofferyng at Christmas	xxj d. ob.
Item thofferyng at Ester	v s. vj d.
Item resceyved for Tyso rent	xliiij s. xj d.
Item resceyved of Wylliam Brokes for his rent dew at May	iij li. vj s. viij d.
Item of hym resceyved for the tythe therof then	vj s. viij d.
Item of hym resceyved more for the tythe corne	xl s.
Item resceyved of Wast for Barnacle	iij li. xiij s. iiij d.
Item resceyved [of] Wase for the rest of Wapenbery, etc.	xxxviij s. viij d.
Item resceyved of hym for Stretton	iiij s. ob.
Item resceyved of Elyse Burbery for the last part of hys fyne	xx li.
Item of hym more for the rent and tythe of Dasset and Rodwey	vij li. xij s.
Item resceyved of Mr. Frekylton for the halfe yeres rent of a pasture in Dasset dew at Maye Daye last	xv li. xvj s. viij d.
Item resceyved of Wylliam Makepece for the rent and tythes of a pasture in Dasset dew at Maye Daye	iiij li. xv s. iiij d.
Item of hym for part of the tythe corne dew then	xl s.

[59] Ibid., piece 17.

Item resceyved of Thomas Burbery for the rent and tythe of a pasture that he occupieth in Dasset dew at May Day	v li. x s.
Item resceyved of Rychard Petyver for the rent and tythe of pastur that he occupieth in Dasset dew at Maye Daye	vij li. iiij s.
Item Mr. Frekylton for the tythe of his pastur dew at Maye Daye	xxxv s. viij d.
Item resceyved for the offeryng at Mydsomer	iij d.
Item my owne rent and tythe for Halls Feld and Old Leese for one holle yere dew at Mychelmas	lxvj li.
Item my rent and tythe for Herytage Feld dew at Martylmas	xxix li. x s.
Item the rent and tythe of Rawlyns close dew then	xxij s.[60]
Summa	ij^{c}xiij li. iiij s. v d.

[f. 55 v.]

Item resceyved of Wase the xxth of Octobre for rentes dew at Mychelmas	xxxj li. iij s. iiij d.
Item resceyved of hym for Warwyke	xiij s. iiij d.
Item of hym more for a heryott at Bubnyll	xxiiij s.
Item Wast paid for me to Mistris Forster	iij li. vj s. viij d.
Item he paid for me to Mr. Wygston and Jhonnis Rawlyns for the fees	iiij li.
Item he paid to Mr. Burnebye for me	xj li. xiij s. iiij d.
Item he paid to the Kyng for quit rênt at Honyle	iij s. vj d.
Item he paid to My Lord Marques Dorset	x s. iiij d.
Item he paid to the late Abbe of Leycester	iij li. iij s. iiij d.
Item to Mr. Culpeper he paid	iij s.
Item he reteyneth in hys hand for his fee	xxvj s. viij d.
Item resceyved of Jhon Palmer of Rodwey	xx s.
Item of Rychard Colman	xx s. viij d.
Item resceyved of Wylliam Hunt for chefe rent	xv d.
Item resceyved at Banbery	iij li. j d.
Item resceyved at Tyso	xliiij s. xj d.
Item resceyved of Rychard Petyver	vij li. ij s.
Summa	lxxj li. xvij s. v d.
Item reseyved of Wylliam Makepese	vj li. xv s. iiij d.
Item resceyved of Mr. Frekylton	xv li. xvj s. viij d.
Item Edward resceyved of Hygyns and Colyns and the Weyner and Jhon Knebe	vj s. v d.
Item I resceyved of Wylliam Brokes the rest of his fine	x li.
Item I resceyved of hym for rent and tythes	v li. xiij s. iiij d.
Item for foren shep resceyved of hym lykeweys	viij s.
Item resceyved of (Jhon)^{er} Thomas Swayne for chef rent	vij s. viij d.

60 Figure altered.

Item resceyved of Thomas Swayne for viij lamz	v s. iiij d.
Item resceyved of Elyse Burbery for his rent and tythes of Rodwey dew at Mydsomer[?]	vij li. xij s.
Item resceyved of Mr. Frekylton for his tythes dew at Martylmas	xxxv s. iiij d.
Item resceyved of Thomas Burbery for rent and tythes dew at Martylmas	v li. x s.

160 f. 51 v. Money paid for the Lordes of Dassett (for)[er] in the vth yere of Kyng Edward the vj[th] [*1551*]

Inprimis paid to theyres of Henry Makepe[ce] dew at Christmas	xxxiij s. iiij d.
Item paid to Mr. Guyes for Bubnell dew at the Annunciacion	iiij li. ij s. iiij d.
Item paid to the vicar for hys pencyon dew at Martylmas and Candelmas	vj li.
Item paid to Mistress Foster at Balsall dew at the Annunciacion	iij li. vj s. viij d.
Item paid to Mr. Vicar for his pencyon dew at May Daye	iij li.
Item paid to Mr. Medle for Mistris Dannet	lx li.
Item paid to Mr. Wylliam Wotton for his father	lx li.
Item paid to Mr. Cooke	lx li.
Item paid to Mr. Cooke	xvj li. x s.
Item paid to Wagstafe for the churche wardens	xiij s. iiij d.
Item paid for Norrys	ij s.
(Memorandum that I sent to Mr. Cooke xiiij oxen prised at	xxix li. xx d.
Item for their charges before they came to my howys	ij s.
Item I paid Anstye for the charges of them to Rumford	xj s.)[er61]
Item paid the vicar of Dasset for his pencion dew at Lammas	iij li.
Item paid to the archedecon for (fyne)[er] proxies[62]	vij s. vj d.
Item paid for Banbery chefe rent	ij s. iij d.
Item paid for the Spittell at Banbery for chef rent	iiij d.
Item paid to Sir Anthony Coke at Hallowtyd	lvj li.
Item paid to Mr. Wotton then	xxxv li.
Item paid for Norrys quit rent	ij s.
Item paid to Mr. Coke the xxvij[th] of Novembre	xxx li. iiij s. iij d.
Item to hym then	xxvij s. x d.
Item paid to Mr. Thomas Dannet for his mother then	l li.
Item paid to Mr. Wylliam Wotton for his brother then	xxxj li. iiij s. iij d.
Item paid to Mr. Dannet agayne for his mother	xvj li. iiij s. iij d.

[61] Cf. **42**.

[62] Op. cit. (note 50), piece 19 is the receipt by Randolph Coxe for 'pension due'.

Item paid to Mr. Clement Smythe for his fee	xl s.
Item paid to Mr. Guyes for Bubnell dew at Mychelmas	iiij li. ij s. iiij d.
Item paid to Mistress Foster for Balsall dew at Mychelmas	iij li. vj s. viij d.
Item paid to Rawlyns by Wase for his fee	xl s.
Item paid by Wase to Mr. Wigston	xl s.
Item paid by Jamz Clark to Makepes heyrs dew at Mydsomer	xxxiij s. iiij d.

161 f. 54 v. Money resevyd for the Lordes of Dassett dew at the Annunciacion and after in the vth yere of Kynge Edward the vj[th] as folowethe [*1551*]

Inprimis resceyved of the Clarke for Ester tythes	xvj s.
Item resceyved of Wase for Wolstrop dew at the Annunciacion	vj li. xj s. ix d.
Item resceyved of hym for Bubnell dew then	vj li. viij s. x d.
Item resceyved of hym for Barnacle dew then	iij li. xiij s. iiij d.
Item resceyved of Wase for Stockyngford dew at the Annunciacion	ix li. xvij s. viij d.
(Item for Ethrop dew from [*blank*]	vj li. iij s. iiij d.)[er]
Item for a house in Stretton	iiij s.
Item for Wapenbery, Ethrop and Honyngham dew then	xj li. xvij s. vj d.
Item of Hyneton[63] dew then	lvj s. viij d.
Item resceyved for Tyso rent	xliiij s. xj d.
Item resceyved of Wase opon the wood money	xx li.
Item resceyved of Mr. Wylliam Sheldon for his part of the rent in Dasset dew at the Annunciacion last past	xviij li. x s.
Item resceyved of Wase more for Woode money	xx li.
Item my owne rent and tythe dew then for Hals Feld	xxxiij li.
Item my owne rent and tythe for Herytage Feld	xiiij li. xv s.
Item resceyved for Banbery rent[64]	xlij s. iiij d.
Item of Wylliam Makepece for rent dew at the Annunciacion wher he delyvered iij li. vj s. viij d. to Petyver	vj li. xv s. iiij d.
Item resceyved of Wylliam Makepece for hys part of wode	xxvj s. viij d.
Item resceyved of Wylliam Makepece for Mr. Frekyltons part of wode	xxxv s.
Item resceyved of Mr. Hykman for wode	iij li. xviij s.
Item resceyved of Thomas Burbery for rent and tythes	v li. x s.

[63] For *Nuneaton*?

[64] Omits one item, which is on the next page.

Item resceyved of Wylliam Broks for rent and tythes which he delyvered to Henry Petiver — iij li. vj s. viij d.
Item of hym for the tythe therof and tythe corne — xlvj s. viij d.
Item of hym more for his part of woode — xxvj s. viij d.
Item resceyved of Mr. Croker for his rent dew then — xviij li. x s.
Item resceyved of the Goodman Wagstaffe for wood — iij li.

(Summa Clxxxx li. xij s. ix d.)[er]
Summa CC li. xiij s. ix d.

[f. 54.]

Item resceyved of Mr. Frekylton for rent and tythe dew at the Annunciation last past — xvij li. xij s. iiij d.
Item resceyved of Elyse Burbery for rent and tythe of Dasset dew then — vj li. xij s.
Item of hym more for Rodwey tythe dew then — xx s.
Item of hym for woode money — iij li. iij s. iiij d.
Item resceyved of R. Petyver for his rent and tythe dew then — vij li. iij s.
Item resceyved of the Clarke for Ester tythes — x s.
Item resceyved of Thomas Makepec for woode — v li. xvj s. viij d.
Item xvj s. viij d. Lebourne must paye — xvj s. viij d.
Item resceyved of Thomas Griffin for woode — xxxvj s. viij d.
Item resceyved of the Swanne[65] — xvij s. ix d.
Item resceyved of H. Petyver for woode — xxxv s.
Item resceyved of Wase more for woode money — xj li. xij d.
Item resceyved of Wase more for woode sold at Bubnell — xl s.
Item resceyved more of hym for Mr. Haulops wode — xiij s. iiij d.
Item my owne paid of wode xx[ti] okes xx[ti] elms — v li.

[*Margin*] Summa lxv li. xvij s. (ij d.)[er] ix d.

Item resceyved of Wase the ix[th] of Octobre for Ulsthorpe — vij li. ij s. ix d.
Item resceyved of Wodeward for hys tythe dew at Mychelmas — ix s. viij d.
Item resceyved of Wase for Barnacle — iij li. xiij s. iiij d.
Item of hym Wase for Nunseton — xxix s. ob.
Item of hym for Bubnell — vj li. viij s. x d.
Item of hym for Stockyngford — vj li. xiiij s. vij d.
Item resceyved of the Clarke on St. Lukes daye [*18 Oct.*] for lamz — xxxiij s.
Item my owne rent and tythes dew at Mychelmas for Halfeld — xxxiij li.
Item my owne rent and tythe for Herytage Feld — xv li. vij s.
Item resceyved for Tyso rent dew at Mychelmas — xliij s. x d.
Item resceyved for Banbery rent — iij li. j d.

[65] In Banbury, omitted before.

Item resceyved of Bothe for rent and tythe dew at Martylmas — vij li. xiiij s.
Item resceyved of Jhon Brokes for chef rent — xiij s. j d.
Item of hym for tyth woll and lamz — x s.
[*Margin*] Summa lxxxx li. 3 d.

[f. 53 v.]

Resceyved of Wase more — vij li. xvj s.
Item a byll that he leyd owt for me — xvj s. vij d.
Item resceyved of Mr. Croker and Shelden their rent and tythe dew at Martylmas for their occupiing in Dasset — xxxvij li.
Item resceyved of[66] Wast for Warwyke — xiij s. iiij d.
Item of hym for Honyle — ix s. vj d.
Item resceyved of the Clarke for tythe lames — xxxj s.
Item resceyved of Wylliam Brokes for rent — iij li. vj s. viij d.
Item of hym more for the tythe therof and for tythe corn — xlvj s. viij d.
Item resceyved of hym for tythe of foren shepe — vj s.
Item resceyved of Wylliam Makepes for rent and tythe — vj li. xv s. iiij d.
Item resceyved of the Clerke for tythe money — xij s.
Item resceyved of Elyse Burbery for rent and tythe — vij li. xiiij s.
Item for the tyth of Rodwey — xx s.
Item resceyved of the Clarke for tyth — xvj s.
Item of T. Makepes for his quit rent — xij d.
Item resceyved of Rychard Petyver for his part of rent dew for the Hyls — xix li. xv s. ix d.
(Item resceyved of hym more for the rest of the sayd rent — x s. v d.)[er]
Item resceyved of the Clarke for Colmans quit — xx s. viij d.
Item resceyved of hym more for Huntes quit rent — xv d.
Item resceyved of hym more for j tythe lame and odes of Colman — xxiij d.
Item resceyved for Jhon Palmers quit rent — xx s.
Item of hym for on tythe lame and v d. odes of Palmers — ij s. j d.
Item resceyved of the Clarke for the Weyner and Jhon Knebes quit rent — v d.

162 S. 4: f. 1 The acompt of Peter Temple, gentleman, for the parsonage of Byrton and Dasset for one holl yere endid at Mychelmas anno domini 1557 et regnorum Philyppe et Marie quarto et quinto

Imprimis the offrynges at Mychelmas, Chrysmas, Ester and Mydsomer — xij s. xj d.

[66] *of* repeated.

Item for Ester tythes	xlv s. ij d.
Item for xxx^{ti} tythe lames	xlv s.
Item for vij tode di. iij^{li} of tythe woll	v li. xix s.
Item for tythe of foren shippe	ix s.
Item for ode tythes of woll and lame	vij d. ob.
Item for tythe pyges, gese, pygions, eges, etc.	xiij s. iiij d.
Item for tythe hey in small closis	xv d.
Item for ofrynges, weddynges and puryfyc[ations]	nyhill
Summa	xij li. vj s. iij d. ob.
Item resceyved of John Brokes esquiere	viij li.
Item of Peter Temple	ix li. xij s.
Item of Ane and Rychard Petyver	iiij li. xj s. iiij d.
Item of Thomas Burbery	xx s.
Item of Gyles Spencer	xxviij s.
Item of Eles Burbery	xxviij s.
Of William Brokes	xiij s. iiij d.
Of William Makepec	xvij s. iiij d.
Of John Woddward	ix s. iiij d.
Of Leonard Savage	vj s. viij d.
Of William Brokes and William Makpece for tythe corne	viij li.
Of Elise Burbery for tythe corne in Rodwey	xl s.
Of the church wardens for holly candell[67]	ij s. ij d.
Summa	xxxviij li. viij s. ij d.
Summa totalis receptis	l li. xiiij s. v d. ob.

[S. 4: f. 1 v]

Wheroff paid to the vicar of Birton for his stypend for one holl yere endid at Lammas anno domini 1557	xij li.
Item to the Clarke for his wagis for the holl yere endid at Mychelmas anno domini 1557	xvj s.
Item for synodes by yere	ij s.
Item for proxes	vij s. vj d.
Item for wyne and bred	xx d.
Item for oyle	iiij d.
Item for the pascall[68]	xij d.
Item for waxe and yarne[69]	ij s. viij d.
Item the bayley his fee[70]	xxvj s. viij d.
Item for the mendynge the glace wyndowes in the chancell the last yere	xij s.
Item for the tenthes of the parsonage dew to the Quene at Mychelmas last[71]	iij li. x d. ob.
Summa	xviij li. x s. viij d. ob.
And so remaneth clere	xxxij li. iij s. ix d.

[67] Cf. 153, note 32.
[68] See p. 150.
[69] For candles.
[70] Peter Temple himself.
[71] See p. 149.

[S.4: f.2]

The acompt of Peter Temple, gentleman, for one holl yere endid, part at Mychelmas and part at Martylmas, anno domini 1557 et regnorum Philippi et Marye quarto et quinto, for the Great Dasset and other landes in the county of Warwyke and Lecestre, where one iij[d] part late pertenyng [*to Sir Anthony Cooke, but now to*][72] Nycolas Bacon and George Medley esquiers, by vertue of a lese therof mayd too them[73] and the other tow partes pertenynge to Thomas Wotton, Esquire and Mistris Mary Dannet, widow.

Inprimis of Peter Temple for one holl yers rent of Hawlesfyld and Oldylesse endid[74] at Mychelmas	lx li.
Item of hym for Herytage Fylde and Rawlyns close for one holl yere endid at Martylmas last	xxvij li.
Item of John Brokes for a holl yeres rent off Travers Fyld then endid	lxvj li.
Of William Makpec for a holl yers rent then endid	viij li. xiij s. iiij d.
Of William Brokes for his rent lykwys	vj li. xiij s. iiij d.
Of Thomas Burbery lykwis	x li.
Of Gyles Spencer lykwis	xiiij li.
Of Elise Burbery lykwis	xiiij li.
Of Ane and Rychard Petyver	xlv li. xiij s. iiij d.
Item for quit rentes in Northend, Knyghtcot and Rodwey	
Inprimis of John Brokes xiij s. j d., of Harry Higuns iij s., of Thomas Makepec xij d., of Wylliam Peerson ij d., of Thomas Swane vj s. viij d., of William Collyns iij s., of John Kneb iij d., of Rychard Colman viij d., of William Hunt xv d. In the holl	xxix s. j d.
Summa	CCliij li. ix s. j d.

[S.4: f.2v.]

Wherof payd to Sir John Sayntlow	xx s.
Item to theres of Harry Madpec[75]	iij li. vj s. viij d.
Item to the vicar of Dasset	xl s.
Item to the Clerke there	vj s. viij d.
Item to the churche wardens ther	xxvj s. viij d.
Item to Harry Crane	xl s.
Item payd Mr. Wigson his fee	xl s.
Item paid the bayle his fee[76]	lij s.
Summa	xiiij li. xvj s.
And so remanethe clere	CCxxxviij li. xiij s. j d.

[72] Marked for an insertion after *parteyning*, but none made. The probable text is supplied.

[73] *too them* interlined in Peter Temple's own hand, rather than that of the scribe of these sheets.

[74] *endided* in MS.

[75] For *Makepeace*.

[76] Peter Temple himself.

Bubnell[77]

Item the rentes there by yere	xiiij li. iiij s. iiij d.

Barnacle

Item the rentes there for the holl yere	vij li. vj s. viij d.
Summa	xxj li. xj s.
Wherof paid to Mr. Guyes for one holl yere	viij li. iiij s. viij d.
Item for the fee of the woddward	xx s.
Item for the decay of Bubnell myll	vj s. viij d.
Item for the purches of Lampacre[78]	xxiij s. iiij d.
Item for the wrytynges	iij s. iiij d.
Summa	x li. xviij s.
And so remaneth clere	x li. xiij s.

Warwicke

Item the rent there for the yere	xiij s. iiij d.

Stretton

Item the rent there dew for the yere	viij s.
Summa	xxj s. iiij d.

Honeley

Item of William Lane x s., and of ode iij s.	xiij s.
Wherof paid to the Kynge for chefe rent	iij s. vj d.
Item to Mr Feres[79] for Gage Grove	xij d.
Summa	iiij s. vj d.
And so remaneth clere	viij s. vj d.

[S. 4: f. 3]

Ulstrope

Item the rent there this yere	xiij li. xiiij s. vj d. ob.

Wapinbury

Item the rent there by yere	xv li. ij s. ij d.

Ethrope

Item the rent there by yere	xij li. xvj s. xj d. ob.

Honyngham

Item the rent there by yere	viij li. iiij d.
Summa	xlix li. xiiij s.
Wherof paid to Master Burnby	xxxj li. xiij s. iiij d.
And so remaneth clere	xviij li. viij d.

77 The place names are in the margin in the MS.
78 Probably land charged with the cost of lighting a lamp in the church.
79 Probably Ferrers of Baddesley Clinton.

Tyso	
Item resceyved of Thomas Hall	iiij li. ix s. x d.
Summa	iiij li. ix s. x d.
Rodwey	
Item of John Palmer	xx s.
Item of Rychard Colman	xx s.
Summa	xl s.
Stockingford	
Item resceyved there for the holl yeres rent	xxj li. xv s. vij d.
Wherof paid to the manor of Ashaw[80]	x s. iiij d.
Item to the late Abbe of Lecester	iij li. iij s. iiij d.
Item Mr. Culpeper for a quit rent	iij s.
Item to My Lord Barklet[81]	xij d.
Item for the bayley his fee	xxvj s. viij d.
Item for the tenthes of Stockingford	xxviij s. j d. ob.
Summa	vj li. xvij s. v d. ob.
And so remaneth clere	xiiij li. xviij s. j d. ob.
Nunsetun	
Item the rentes there yerely	v li. xiij s. iiij d.
Wherof paid to Mr. Connstable	xxvij s. vij d. ob.
And so remanethe clere	iiij li. v s. viij d. ob.
Summa totius oneris omnium terrarum	CClxxxxiiij li. x s. iij d.
Item for the parsonage	xxxij li. iij s. ix d.
Item for the harret of Thomas Westle	xl s.
Summa totalis clare	CCCxxviij li. xiiij s.

Wherof every iij^{d} part comethe to Cix li. xj s. iiij d.

[S. 4: f. 3 v.]

Unto which iij^{d} part dew unto Thomas Wotton esquiere must be addide one iij^{d} part of the manor of Stockingford for one holl yere endid at Mychelmas last past, anno domini 1557, which ys iiij li. xix s. iiij d. ob. and so the iij^{d} part of the sayd Thomas Wotton amownthe in all	Cxiiij li. x s. viij d. ob.
Wherof paid to the sayd Thomas Wotton esquire the xxxth day of May 1557 last past	l li.
Item paid to the sayd Thomas Wotton esquire the xxijth day of Novembre at the fynishinge of the accompt	lxiiij li. x s. viij d. ob.
Summa paid unto hym for his iij^{d} part	Cxiiij li. x s. viij d. ob.

And so even

Received by Thomas Wotton[82]

[80] For *Ashley*, as **164**.

[81] For *Berkeley*, who received the property of the Marquis of Dorset after the latter's execution in 1554. Earlier, however, the latter had received 10s. 4d., the sum paid to the manor of Ashley.

[82] Autograph.

From which iij[d] part dew unto Mistris Marye Dannet, widowe, must be deducted for the iij[d] part of the manor of Stockingford iiij li. xix s. iiij d. ob., for that she hathe nothing therin, and so hir iij[d] part amounth but to	Ciiij li. xj s. xj d. ob.
Wherof paid to Mr. Medley to the use of the sayd Mary Dannet the xix of May last past anno domini 1557	l li.
Item paid unto the said George Medley to hir use also the xxiiij[th] of Novembre at the fynishinge of this accompt	liiij li. xj s. xj d. ob.
Summa paid to hir for hir iij[d] part	Ciiij li. xj s. xj d. ob.

And so even.

Receaved by me George Medeleye to the use of the seyd Mistris Dannett due at anno supradicto. George Medeleye[82]

[S. 4: f. 4]

Memorandum that this last iij[d] part aperteneynge to Sir Anthony Coke and now to Nycolas Bacon and George Medley esquires for certen yeres amownth to Cix li. ix s. iij d. as ys aforesayd	Cix li. xj s. iiij d.
Wherof paid to Robart Badby the xiiij[th] day of May last past, anno domini 1557 to the use of Nycolas Bacon and George Medley esquires	l li.
Item paid to the sayd Robart the xxiiij[th] day of Novembre to the use of Nycolas Bacon and George Medley esquirs at the fynishing of this acompt	lix li. xj s. iiij d.
Summa paid for this last iij[d] part as aforesaid	Cix li. xj s. iiij d.

And so evyn

Receyvyd by me Robert Badby[82]

[S. 4: f. 4 v.]

Memorandum that at the ende of this acompt, the sayd Peter Temple did delyver thes acquittances under wrytton to Master Thomas Wotton aforesayd

Inprimis delyvered to the said Mr. Thomas Wotton, one acquittance of iiij li. xiij s. for the tenthes of Stockingford and Dasset, dew for one holl yere endid at Mychelmas last past.

Item ij acquittances of Burnby for xxxj li. xiij s. iiij d. for one holl yere then endid for the manor of Wapynbury.

Item one acquittance of Mr. Over for iij li. iij s. iiij d. gouing out of Stockingford dew to the Quene for one holl yere then endid[83]

[83] The rent paid to the 'late Abbey of Leicester'.

Item acquittance of Edward Povy, bayley to Mr. Connstable for xxvij s. vij d. ob. for landes in Nunsetun for one holl yere dew at Mychelmas last.
Item one acquittance of William Whetley, reve to Mr. Chamberleyne for x s. iiij d. gouing out of Stockingford for one holl yere then endid.[84]
Item one acquittance of John Ramston for iij s. for landes in Stokingford dew to Mr. Culpeper lykwise then endid.
Item one acquittance of Water Strepe, servant to Mr. Clement Throgmorton for iij s. vj d. dew to the Quene then lykwise for landes in Honeley.
Item one acquittance of Mr. Wigson for his fee.
Item one acquittance for Mr. Feres for xij d. for Gage Grove.
Item ij acquittances of Thomas Guyes for viij li. iiij s. viij d. for landes in Bubnell dew then lykwise.
Item ij acquittances of theres of Harry Makpec of iij li. vj s. viij d. for landes in Dasset dew to them at Chrysmas and Mydsomer last.
Item one acquittance for xij li. dew to the Vicar of Dasset for his pencion for one holl yere endid at Lammas.
Item one acquittance of Rychard Hawse, bayley to Sir John Sayntlow, knyght, of viij li. dew for viij yeres rent endid at Mychelmas last anno 1557.
Item the indenture of the bargayne and sale of the Lampacre in Barnacle.
In witness wherof the sayd Thomas hathe subscrybed to these presentes at the fynyshyng of this acompt aforesayd.
Item[85] delyvered one acquittans of Henry Crane for xl s. dew to hym at Mychelmas last past.

Receaved by Thomas Wotton[86]

163 S. 1. B[87]

Bubnell and Barnacle	xx li. iiij s. iiij d.
Warwyke and Stretton	xxj s. iiij d.
Honyle	viij s. vj d.
Wapenbery etc.	xviij li. viij s.
Summa xxxix li. [xiiij s. xj d.],	
the 3rd part therof ys	xiij li. iiij s. xj d. ob.
Stokyngford	xvj li. (xviij s. j d. ob.)er xj s iiij d.
the 3rd part ther of ys	(iiij li. xix s. vij d. ob.)er v li. x s. v d.
So the hole sum of a thyrd part is	xviij li. (xij s. vij d.)er xv s. iiij d. ob.

164 S. 1. C[88]

Stokyngford rent at Our Lady Day	x li. ij s. x d.
and at Mychelmas	x li. ij s. x d.

[84] The rent to the manor of Ashley.
[85] Added in Peter Temple's own hand.
[86] Autograph.
[87] Date uncertain. It does not quite match the 1557 account.
[88] Not necessarily the same date as **163**, but certainly later than the execution of Dorset in 1554. The figures are the same as in **162**, except for the omission of a tithe charge.

and chef rent ther	xxix s. x d.
[*Total*]	xxj li. (xiij s. j d.)^{er} xv s. vij d.
Wherof to the quene	iij li. iij s. iiij d.
Item to the manor of Asheley	x s. iiij d.
Item to Culpeper	iij s.
The balyes fee	xxvj s. viij d.
To the Lord Barkeley	xij d.
[*Total*]	v li. iiij s. iiij d.
So the clere totall sum ys	xvj li. xj s. iiij d.

165 S. 5[89] [*Draft Account, 1560*]

Hole yeres rent one third part of Bubnell and Barnacle	iij li. xix s. x d. ob.
Warwike and Stretton lykwise	vij s. j d. qr.
Honeley	ij s. x d.
Rodwey	xiij s. iiij d.
Wattenbury, Ethrope, Honingham and Ulstrope	vj li. ij d. ob.
Tyso	xxix s. xj d. qr.
Nun Eaton	xxviij s. vij d.
Summa	xiiij li. xxij d. qr.
Wherof half yeres rent	vij li. xj d. qr.
Item Guyes rent for half yere	iiij li. ij s. iiij d.
Mistris Dannettes third part is as appereth for the hole yere endid at Michelmas 1560	xiiij li. xxij d. qr.
Item for Guyes rent half a yere	iiij li. ij s. iiij d.
Item the third part for half a yere	xxvij s. v d. qr.
Item I doe owe hym for the rest of xx li. repayd by twoe bylles and so restes to hym	ix li. xj s. vij d. ob. qr.
which ix li. xj s. vij d. ob. qr. is dewe to Mr. Dannett for the rest of hys rentes dew at Mychelmas anno 1560, which I have allowed hym apon the backsyde of one of hys billes of l li. dew to me, wherof he must alow me back againe xxxxiiij s. lij d. ob. for money delyvered by suvuvor[?], as appereth in Ellice reconynge, that ys to say for the iij^{d} part of Rodwey xiij s. iiij d., for Tyso xxix s. viiij d., for [*Ullesthorpe*?] xxvij s. vj d. ob. Summa	iij li. xj s. x d.

wherof I must allowe Mr. Dannet for the iij^{d} part of iij li. iiij s. vij d. dew for iij hariotes in Wattenbury and Ethrope xxj s. vj d. ob. and for wood by me bowght vj s., and soe must Mr. Dannet restore to me clere xxxxiiij s. iij d. ob., and so Mr. Dannet shold have cleere but vij li. vij s. iij d. ob.

[89] The original is in running text.

166 S. 6. B *[Final Reckoning, 1560]*

The holle somme of the rent in Dassett for one halfe yere endyd part at Mychelmas and part at Martylmas resceyvyd by Peter Temple and Elyse Burbery ys	Cxxij li. ix s. j d.
besyde Thomas Burberys rent	
wherof the iij[d] part ys	xl li. xvj s. iiij d.
Item Elys must have of Peter Temple for the tythe of Traversfeld dew at Mychelmas last for d.ydes	iiij li.
Item for the tythe of Halsefeld [*and*] Old Lesse lykweys	iij li.
Item for the tythe of Herytagefeld lykewys dew then	xxxvj s.
Item for the tythe of Rychard Petyver dew then	xxxiij s. iiij d.
[*Total of above*]	x li. ix s. iiij d.
Item for the heyrs of Norrys xvj d. (and to the clerk in)[er]	
Item for the clerke for one hole yere endyd at Mychelmas last	iiij s. v d.
Item to the churche wardens for one hole yere endyd at Mychelmas last	xvij s. j d.
Summa	lij li. viij s. vj d.
Wherof Elys hath resceyvyd of Makepece for his half yers rent endyd at Martylmas	iiij li. vj s. viij d.
Item of Brokes lykeweys	iij li. vj s. viij d.
Of Spenser	vij li.
Of Elys hymselfe	vij li.
Of An Petyver	vj li. iij s.
And for quit rent	xxix s. j d.
[*Total of above*]	xxix li. v s. v d.
Item Elys hath resceyved for a quarter's rent of Halfeld	v li.
Item he must allow for [my?] Lady Seintlow	vj s. viij d.
And for the heyres of Makepec	xxij s. ij d. ob.
And for the vycars besse	xiij s. iiij d.
And for ij partes of Guyes rent for di. yere endyd at Mychelmas	liiij s. x d. ob.
Wheras he hath resceyved the holle half yeres rent for all the owt landes dew at Mychelmas anno 1560, he must allow for ij partes of certen of them	xiij li. xviij s. j d.
And for ij partes of iij heryottes	xliij s. j d. ob.
Summa	lv li. iiij s. viij d. ob.
And so Elys must paye to me lvj s. ij d. ob. and for Thomas Burberys rent for one holle yere endyd at Martylmas anno 1560, v li.	vij li. xvj s. ij d. ob.

[*dorse*]

Which vij li. xvj s. ij d. ob. I have resceyved of Elys this xxj[th] of Novembre anno 1560, and so he ys allowed a full iij[d] part of all the rent in Dassett dew at Mychelmas and Martylmas last, and for all the tythes dew for the sayd pastur for halfe a yere endyd at Mychelmas last. He ys also allowed for the iij^{d} part of al the owt landes for di. yere endyd at Mychelmas last, and all the hole yere of Tyso, Rodwey and Nuneton.

In wytnes whereof the sayd Peter and the sayd Elys have subscrybyd this byll the xxjth daye of Novembre anno 1560.

By me Peter Temple
By me Elys Burbery[90]

BAILIFF'S MEMORANDA

167 f. 79 v. B[91] [*1548*]

The old rent of the half of the Hyls	xiij li. xvj s. viij d.
The new rent therof	xviij li. xv s. viij d.
The old rent of the other halfe of the Hyls with the wynd myll and waren	xxj li. xvj s. viij d.
The new rent therof	xxvj li. xvj s. viij d.

168 f. 44. B Banbery rent for thalf yere

Inprimis the Swane	xvij s. ix s.
Item the howse of Jhon Wyse	xl s.
Stephanie Wykes	v s.
Davy his howse	vij s. iiij d.
Westons howse	vj s. viij d.
The Spytell[92]	xiij s. iiij d.
Summa	iij li. j d.
Wherof deduct for quiet rent to the bayly there	ij s. iij d.
Item for the Spyttell	iiij d.

169 L. 56 a.[93] Thys ys the over rentes of Wappenbury and Honyngam [*1548*]

Roger Bromfyld by hys promys that he made to you	iij s. vj d.
Nycolas Myells for Northoull	xx d.
Thomas Bambery	xvj d.
Master Cocken	iiij d.
Master Rychard Newporth	ix li.
vj li. for the close	
iij li. for iij haweyeres rentes	

[90] Autograph.

[91] A new lease of half the Hills was made in 1548, ST L9 E1, Temple Land, Bucks.

[92] Cf. note 49.

[93] 1548, from the reference to Roger Bromfyld, whose holding was taken over by Newport (**169**). This note was written on a slip of paper, perhaps by Wase, and was kept in the account book among the bailiff's accounts.

170 L. 31 a. B[94] [*Probably 1548*]

A remembrance for the fees of Mr. Sadler and Mr. Smythe
Remembre Colets heryott / Hacok for v s. iiij d.
Memorandum to resceyve of Mr. Newpert iij s. vj d. for Bromfeldes land / and viij li. per annum for the landes he holdeth in Honyngham and xl s. dew for the last yere endyd at Mychelmas /
Item he must paye vj li. for the agreement with the Lordes /
Remembre to take of Banbery of Wapenbery xx s. (wherof)[er] by cause ij s. for the lampe lyght ys extynguished /
Remembre Wrothes house

171 f. 82. C[95]

The fees of Mr. Sadler and Mr. Smyth / Colet / Hacocke
Mr [Newport] iij s. vj d. for Br[omfeldes] and xl s. dew the last yere, vj li. for j [*rent of*?] Banbery of Wapenbery [*for*?] Wrothes house

172 f. 64 v. B[96] [*1548*]

Memorandum that the tenements of Bubnell repay the mony the theyes [?] paid for hedgyng the springe
Item to speke with Mr. Sanders, Ansley and Wast what ordre Jhon Petyfer dyd take for the rentes of Weston dew at Mychelmas next after my Lady Belknaps dethe
Item to speke with Colet of Bubnyll fot the heryott of hys brother Colett, prec' xvj s.
Item Hacoke for the woode that he feld in Weston in Smyths grownde
Item speke with Elys Burbre concernyng the tythe
Item repayrd the chancell
Item the widow at Warwyke
Item the wood salle the lessys of Wapenbury

173 f. 81. B [*Perhaps 1545*][97]

Resceyved for the beacon	iiij li. xiij s. vj d.
Layde owth to Belle and the wayener for watching.	
Summa	xxxij s.
Item paid to to carpenters of Farneborow for the makyng therof	vij s.
Item payd to Mr. Rawleygh[98] for v treese	xvj s.
Item allocat' ville de Dasset	x s.
Item pytche and hurde[*l*]s	viij d.

[94] Generally consistent with 1548. For Hacock, see 155. Other items on L. 31a are of 1549. Punctuation here is by solidus.
[95] A jotting of the same notes as the last.
[96] Dated by the reference to Colett's heriot (172).
[97] See p. 147.
[98] Lord of Farnborough, a near-by village.

174 f. 73 v. B [*Letter draft, undated*][99]

Ryght worshipful sir, my dewtye rememberyd this . . .[1] ys to certefye yow that acordyng to yor letter dyrectyd to me concernyng the mater in controversy betwene (Gybyns)^{er} Tod and Gybyns, I have examyned both the partyes. Wherapon hit aperyth that one Rychard Makepes was sesyd in fe (for xl)^{er} of a cotage with a close in Feny Compton and therof bying seysyd mad theroff a lesse for terme of yeres (be wyt)^{er} to the sayd Gybbyns before certen wytnes and causyd a homely wrytyng to be mad requesting the sayd agrement, in the which wrytyng ther aperyth no condicion of forfeture, but only to dystreyne for the arrerages, and after this lesse so made, the sayd Rychard Makepese (made)^{er} (dyd sesse)^{er} dyd alyenate the sayd cotag with thapertenances to the above namyd Tode and after the rent was behynd unpayd by the space of a moneth, by reson wherof the sayd Tod suposed the lesse to be forfett, wher in dede ther ys no suche condicion expressyd in the sayd wrytyng, never the lessee whe[n] because I cold not persuade the sayd Tode to . . . that he . . . to be at a . . . .[2] ys to enioye his [losse?]. I thought it met and convenyent to certefye yow of the holl matter, certifying surely that he that shall here how you declare the truthe unto the thei . . . satysfy[ed] shall rather give credens unto so worshipful a man.

11. *Wood Sales*

Even by the early sixteenth century, woodland was very scarce in South Warwickshire, in the open-field 'Felden' area. As an example of this, neither Burton Dassett nor Northend and Knightcote had any appreciable area of wood. Much more was available in the north-west of the county, the former Forest of Arden, and this ended in a thick belt of woods just east of the Avon, from Ryton-on-Dunsmore through Wappenbury to Weston-under-Wetherley. For the three years, 1549–1551, the lords of Dassett exploited their wood at Wappenbury very vigorously, and realised from it about £100 each year; Peter Temple recorded the details of the sales in special entries in the account book, separate from the main estate receipts. The exact sums received are not certain because some of the money was entered twice. The details are:

Year	*Main accounts*	*Wood sales*	*Wood money received*
1548	£1	—	—
1549	£63	£93	—
1550	Nil recorded	£107	£117
1551	£79	—	—
1557	Nil recorded	—	—

[99] The next item on the page (228) is of 1549.
[1] One word obscure.
[2] Words lost in earlier text.

What was taking place was probably not clearance felling but organized woodland management,[3] because the wood was divided into at least 25 *hags* (separate enclosures or coppices[4]), and within each a number of the best trees were reserved. There is no indication,

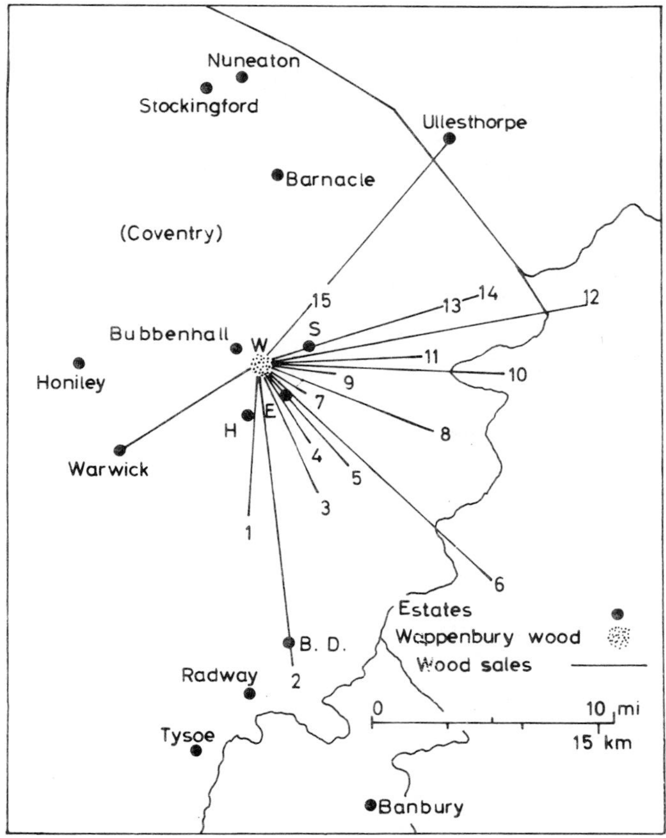

Fig. 6. Bailiff's work, 1548–60: location of estates and wood sales. Large dots indicate the property of Cooke, Dannet and Wotton. E = Eathorpe, H = Hunningham, S = Stretton, W = Wappenbury. Lines show the destinations of wood from Wappenbury: Warwick, Harbury (1), Burton Dassett (B.D.), Avon Dassett (2), Southam (3), Bascote and Long Itchington (4), Eathorpe (E), Stockton (5), Charwelton (6), Marton (7), Grandborough and Sawbridge (8), Draycote and Frankton (9), Onely, in Barby (10), Dunchurch (11), Yelvertoft (12), Stretton (S), Rugby (13), Clifton-on-Dunsmore (14), Wolston (15), Ullesthorpe. County boundaries are also shown.

³ Following the normal contemporary method of coppicing. O. Rackham in E. Duffey and A. S. Watt (eds.), *The Scientific Management of Animal and Plant Communities for Conservation* (Oxford: Blackwell, 1971), pp. 563–80.

⁴ *O.E.D.*

however, that only a section of the wood was being worked—necessary if the profits were not to be very erratic. Individual trees were sold for between 1s. and 2s., while the larger *hags* fetched £7, smaller ones ranging down to £1. The bark was always reserved, and sold separately to a tanner, Hartlet (177).

The value of this woodland to the farmers of the treeless Felden is made very clear from its purchasers. They came from some twenty-five villages, almost all to the south-east of Wappenbury, and up to 15 miles away, well into Northamptonshire (Fig. 6).[5] Some of the Burton Dassett villagers were also included; they, no doubt, had a good opportunity to negotiate purchases, as well as needing to go a considerable distance for wood.

WOOD SALES

175 f. 2 v. C Wood sold this yere of anno iij[tio] Edwardi VI [*1549*] for the Lordes of Dassett etc. as foloweth

Inprimis a grett parcell of the hye wood in Wapenbury sold for	lxxvj li. xiij s. iiij d.
Item a pece next the same sold to Mr. Ray, Water Frekylton and Thomas Harrys for	iij li.
[*Right margin*] Memorandum Walter ys to pay	
Item to Mr. Wygston for a parcell of a hedgero	xx s.
Item to Thomas Gedle for iij treese	vj s.
Item to Ellys Burbery viij tres	xiij s.
Item the myller of Sowtham for iiij tres	vij s.
Item at Ulsthorpe for xxxij[ti] ashe tres	iij li. vj s. viij d.
Item to Jhon Anstye and Jhon Theay	x s.
Item to Lapworth	ij s.
Item my selfe	[*blank*]
Item for a corner withowt the hedge	xxxvj s. viij d.
Mr. Wast payd to the hedgers of the gret sals sprynge[6]	
Note of thes rest I have allowed Wast xvj s. viij d. for sawyng, so resceyved clere	v li. iij s. viij d.
Item I paid myself for fellyng and sharyng[7]	iij s. iiij d.
Memorandum that the Clarke oweth me x s. vij d. ob. for the rekenyng of the tythe.[8]	

[5] This is a characteristic pattern, seen also for example in wood sale books of the 1580s for the Stoneleigh estate, a couple of miles west of Wappenbury (S.B.T. DR18).

[6] Probably the big pool on the parish boundary, between Wappenbury and Bubbenhall; cf. 172.

[7] Meaning obscure.

[8] More in the nature of bailiff's jottings.

176 f. 60 v. Wood sold at Wapenbery in January yn the iij[d] yere of the reygne of Kyng Edward the vj[th] [*1550*] by Peter Temple gentleman, as followeth

Inprimis sold to Cutbard Whene, gentleman, on hagge next unto the hedge of the south syde at	vij li.
Item sold the next hagge to the same to Clarke and Wescott of Sowtham, reservyng v of the best tres and the barke	vj li. xiij s. iiij d.
Item sold the next hagge to Henry Frost and Wylliam Smyth of Onele in Barbye parishe,[9] reservyng iiij of the best trese etc., at	vij li.
Item sold the next hagge to Wylliam Edwardes and Rychard Porter of Clyfton,[10] reservyng j tre of the best etc., at	vj li.
Item sold the next hagge to Mr. Wylner[11] and Mr. Medlee at	vij li.
Item sold the next hagge to Mychel Wylkyns and Rychard Westlee of Frankton, reservyng v of the best tres etc., at	vj li. vj s. viij d.
Item sold the next hagge to Edward Corbet of Dunchurche, reservyng xj of the best tres with the barke at	v li.
Item sold the next hagge to Jhon Haw and Jhon Denell of Wolston, reservyng ix tres etc., at	iiij li. x s.
Item sold the next hagge to Thomas Cheyls and Jhon Olever of Sawbryge,[12] reservyng viij of the best tres etc., at	iiij li. x s.
Item sold the over gore next the same hagge unto Wylliam Fyrle of Long Ychyngton, reservyng iij of the best tres, at	xxiij s. iiij d.
Item sold the nether gore next the self same hage to Jhon Alen and Jamz Garet of Dunchurche, reservyng x of the best tres, at	iij li. vj s. viij d.
Item sold the fyrst short crosse hagge on the west syde, reservyng 1 tre, to Jhon Anstye at	iij li.
Sold the next hage to Wylliam Makepes and Brokes, reservyng ij of the best tres, at	xl s.
Sold the next hag to Wapenbery men, reservyng v of the best tres, etc., at	xx s.
Sold the next crose hage unto Wylliam Mabe of Rokebye[13] reservyng iij of the best tres, at	xxiij s. iiij d.
Sold the vth hage, reservyng iiij tres, unto Jhon Geydon of Barscott, at	xxvj s. viij d.

[9] Northants.
[10] Clifton-on-Dunsmore.
[11] Perhaps Thomas Heritage's cousin, of Ryton-on-Dunsmore.
[12] In Wolfhampcote, Warks.
[13] Rugby, Warks.

Sold the next hage, reservyng iij tres unto Thomas Reve of Yelvertoft, in Northamptonshire, at	xxvj s. viij d.
Sold the next hage, reservyng iiij tres unto Jhon Weyner of Granboro, at	xxiij s. iiij d.
Sold the next hage unto Jhon Jenkyns of Long Ychington, reservyng iiij tres, at	xxiij s. iiij d.
Sold the next hage unto Jamz Smyth of Marton, reservyng vj tres, at	xxx s.
Sold the next hage, reservyng iij tres to Mr. Hykman, at	xx s.
Sold the best long crosse hage, reservyng iij tres etc., to Jhon Hygyns at	xl s.
Sold the next hagge to the same, reservyng vj tres, to Jhon Alen and Wyllyam Audley of Brawg[14] at	xxx s.
Sold the fyrst crosse hagge from the sowthe hedge, reservyng viij tres, to Thomas Genys of Marton at	xxiij s. iiij d.
Sold the next hage to the same, reservyng vj of the best tres, to Robyt Hoke of Stockton at	xv s.

[177 f. 61]

Sold unto Mr. Androws of Charlton,[15] Mr. Shukborow and Mr. Dyxwell j^c^xx tres at	xxiij li.
Item sold to Hychecoke iiij tres	x s.
Item sold to Jhon Byrton vj tres at	xvj s.
Item sold to Byrd of Rokby iiij tres	vj s. viij d.
Item sold to Frankton and Gardner ij lode	ij s. viij d.
Item sold to Runtes in Northamptonshire[16]	v s.
Item sold the barke of this sayd woode to Hartlet for	iij li

178 L. 61 a. *[Note of wood sales sent to Peter Temple, 1550?]*[17]

Item one hacke for Knyghtcote men	x s.
Item one hacke for Avenderset men	x s.
Item John Bodyngeton of Harbore for x polles	xvj s.
Item the vicare of Wattonbury for vj polles	vj s. viij d.
Item the vycare of Marton for ij tres	iij s. iiij d.
Item Henry Smyth of Dracot for ij polles	iij s.
Item Callway of Streton and Baulle for ij tres	iij s. iiij d.
Item for Etherope men v tres	vj s. viij d.
Item Thomas Wayse of Etherope	xx d.
Item John Hyhernes	xviij d.
Summa	iij li. ij s. ij d.

[14] Unidentified.

[15] Charwelton, Northants.

[16] Blank for place.

[17] Probably sent by Wase, and likely to be in his hand. It was kept in the account book with the wood sales. Its dorse (**179**, in Peter Temple's hand) refers to 1550, from a comparison with **180**.

Off thys I have paed Wylliam Dowse xl s. for hegynnge
And I have paed vj s. for the court denner
And I have paed Wylliam Aller iij s. iiij d. for sawynge
And I have paed Rychard Wellche ij s. for mendynge of the hege

Remaynynge beheynde x s. x d.

179 L. 61a. v [*Notes by Peter Temple, added to last sheet, 1550*]

Memorandum there ys to resceyve of Mr. Wygston	xx s.
Item of Elyse Burbery	x s. and xiij s. iiij d.
Item to resceyve of Swayne	xvj s.
Item at Stretton	xviij s.
Memorandum that I lack of Sowtham men	xiij s. iij d.
wherof the parson of Harbery must pay	viij s.

180 f. 61v. Money resceyved by me Peter Temple for wood sold the yere of anno quarto regni regis Edwardi vjth [*1550*] as foloweth

... of ... for barke	iij li.
Item resceyved of Wase the xixth of May for wood	xx li.
Item of hym more by thandes of Mr. Shukborew, his servant	vij li. xiij s.
Item of hym more the Mondaye after Trinite S[*unday*] [*17 June*]	xxix li.[18]
Item of hym then that Hygynson had for Mistris Forster[19]	iij li. vj s. viij d.
Item of hym then that he resceyved of Mr. Corbet[20]	v li.
Item resceyved of hym at Sowtham the vjth of Julye	x li.
Item resceyved more ther then of Sowtham men	vj li.
Item resceyved more of hym at my howse	xviij li. xx d.
And he hath apoynted me at Mr. Hyckman	xx s.
and of Makepece	x s.
Item resceyved of Wast for Stretton	xviij s.
and for Mr. Wygston	xx s.
Item resceyved of Wylliam Brokes and Makepes[21]	xl s.
Item resceyved of Mr. Hyckman	xviij s.

[18] *xixx* in MS.
[19] Cf. 159 (f. 55 v.).
[20] Cf. 176.
[21] Cf. 176.
[22] Wood sales seem the only likely reason for making this list of people from three Northamptonshire villages.

181 f. 82 v. F *[Possible Wood Sale]*[22]

Names	Place
Jhon Bafeld Symond Aryse Wylliam Baseley Wylliam Bodyngton Jhon Tayler	Over Catsbye[24]
Jhon Bayle, senior Edward Gardner, senior Henry Smith, senior	Stareton[23]
Thomas Bulles Richard Skyner, senior Symond West, senior	Helydon[25]

SECTION C: PERSONAL MATTERS

12. *Introduction*

This section brings together the last major portions of the account book, coming closest to Peter Temple's own life, day by day and year by year. Brief but informative summaries give the cost of a year's supplies for his household, with one or two related items, such as London shopping lists. He wrote down lists of the traditional New Year chickens, gifts from all those who looked to him for favour. His servants' wages are recorded for several years, as his establishment gradually grew in size. Thomas Heritage also used the book for regular accounts of payments to his servants.

An informative group of accounts cover the building of a new house by Peter in 1548–9, though the house itself regrettably does not survive.

A large and complicated section deals directly with Peter Temple's finances. In most years, he put together lists of debts due to him, and intermittently he also wrote down all his realizable assets. Unfortunately, these accounts are confused in places and cannot be completely understood in detail. Their overall picture is, however, clear: Peter Temple's sheep and his other enterprises prospered and his wealth increased.

Finally, in the most personal section of all, the jottings and pen trials with which Peter adorned many pages of his account book, tell something of him as a person rather than a businessman. They make a final vignette of that part of his life which we can observe through his account book.

[23] Staverton, 3 m. S.W. of Daventry.
[24] 1 m. S.W. of Staverton.
[25] 1 m. S.W. of Over Catesby.

13. *Household expenses* (Pl. V)

The two summaries of the yearly household costs, probably for 1543-4 (**182**) provide most important evidence. Of the total of £35 for the first year, more than a third went on grain, mostly barley, some of it malted for beer; white bread was also prominent. Fish and meat took up another third, and of the remaining sundries, heat and light cost the most. With their small household, Peter and Millicent Temple must have lived very well, eating about a sheep a week (cf. **61**), with eight or ten pounds of bread.

In the following year, Peter Temple revised his calculations, to give a lower total of £26, likely to be a more accurate figure as he used it again in 1561 in his financial summary (**236**). The household costs continue with lists of the servants' wages, (**182c–e**), to complete the summary of his outgoings.

The account book also provides one detailed reckoning for fish (**183**), probably a year's supply; one must hope that at least one of the salmon was fresh. The fishmonger also brought soap, in two grades, ordinary (probably coarse and brown) and white.[26] Two lists of more exotic groceries, were compiled on separate pieces of paper; one (**185**) is almost certainly a shopping list for Peter Temple in London, and the other (**184**) also has a London association.[27] He was buying sugar, spices, dried fruit, and also shoes and hose (stockings).

Two accounts from the early 1560s and two miscellaneous items (**186–9**) also illuminate the household and its life. One concerns money probably laid out for John Temple,[28] including buying gloves and 'points' as well as something for him to gamble with. The second details the expenses of a rapid journey by one of Peter's servants, Townsend, from Leicester to Mansfield and back to Lutterworth, a distance of 79 miles, covered in three days, including the time to transact his business. He then went on to Warwick, apparently meeting his master, and they rode back to Burton, dining at Harbury in considerably more style than during the journey.

An odd half-page was used for a prescription (**188**)—clearly for someone very sick. The least that can be said is that it should have done the patient no harm, while the 'nourishable meates' can be

[26] This item is written as if Peter Temple was receiving the payment for the fish, and it may be that he was supplying it to someone else.

[27] The slip has six items on it, but the first is an address in London.

[28] In 1560, John went up to Lincoln's Inn, at the age of 18.

positively commended. It was probably intended to cure either measles or smallpox.[29]

An inventory of silverware in Thomas Heritage's hand presumably referred to his property. Plate, of course, had its use at the merchant's table, and these pieces must have been very decorative, but its value was just as important. It was a repository for spare cash, that could immediately be pawned or sold, and Peter Temple's own chain is listed among his assets in 1549 (**231**).

New Year Gifts (**190–192**)

Lists were compiled for three years of the poultry received by Peter Temple on New Year's Day.[30] As well as a useful contribution to the household, the names in the lists show that the gifts had a considerable social role. The givers are immediately recognizable as those who were trading with Temple in sheep and wool; the chickens and ducks were the sixteenth century equivalent of the Christmas bottle of whisky. The gifts listed were from Peter Temple's business inferiors, and we do not unfortunately have a list of his own gifts. It is noticeable that over the three years, the numbers of donors rose from eight (?1548) to fifteen (1550) as the sheep farming expanded.

Servants (**193–203**)

Both Heritage and Temple kept reckonings of their servants wages, because they were paid quarterly, and also often received small advances. From Heritage's accounts, his household contained one or two men servants, and in 1538 a maid as well. The men received between 20s. and 32s. a year, and also had clothing in kind, usually a coat cloth,[31] the maid had 16s., a kirtle (gown) cloth and shoes. Two other men were paid more, but were not ordinary servants. Lovet in 1536 was apparently the miller, presumably at Hamper Mill (see p. 136), while Father Pasco, with 1s. a week, was employed as a farm worker at Oxhey.

One item records Peter Temple's servants while he was still in Hertfordshire (**138**); four people are named, of whom two, Rauff

[29] I thank E. J. Freeman of the Wellcome Institute for the History of Medicine for advice on this recipe.

[30] The traditional day for gift-giving in the 16th century, M. Girouard. *Life in the English Country House* (New Haven: Yale University Press, 1978), p. 24.

[31] The five shilling sword for Thomas Wyllor (1538, **194**) was taken out of his wages.

and Wyll Sheperd, were clearly servants.[32] In the first year at Dassett (probably 1543), Peter's household was quite small with two men (paid 30s. and 26s. 8d. a year) and a girl (16s.), together with the shepherd, who was paid rather more (36s. 8d.); these wages included a money payment in lieu of *livery*, in this case clothing, as the servants must have lived in. A couple of years later, the establishment had grown to two women and four men, and by 1547 included six or seven men. The wages seem to have been generally similar, though for 1546–8, the totals are not given. In the last entry of all (*circa* 1555, **203**), three men received considerably higher wages (33s. 4d. to 40s.), but the 'sheep pasture' that two of them enjoyed, suggests that they may have been shepherds, who were often given the right to run some of their own sheep with those of their master.[33]

HOUSEHOLD EXPENSES

182 f. 9[a][34] Charges of Howsold

Fuell	iij li. vj s. viij d.	
xv quarter malt	v li.	
xij quarter barle	iiij li.	
iij quarter whett	xl s.	
whitte bred	xl s.	
candells	xx s.	
salt	xiij s. iiij d.	
ote mell	viij s.	
venyger	iij s. iiij d.	
mustard	iij s. iiij d.	
fleshe wekly iiij s.		
Summa per annum	viij li. xvj s.	
Fyshe in the Lente	xl s.	
Fyshe owte of Lent	xl s.	
1 Mertylmas besse	xx s.	
and iiij bacons	xxvj s.	lviij s. viij d.
j braiver[35]	viij s.	
x mylche kyne	[*blank*]	
	xxxv li.[36]	

[32] Wyll Sheperd is mentioned later, and so may have moved to Warwickshire with Peter Temple.

[33] Bowden, 1962, p. 19; cf. 122.

[34] Written in sections, apparently year by year. The year of **e** may be 1546, as **198**, but is more likely to be 1545, suggesting dates 1543 (**a**, **c**), 1544 (**b**, **d**), 1545 (**e**). Reproduced as Pl. V.

[35] Unidentified.

[36] The correct sum is £34 5s. 4d.

[b]

bred and drinke		xij li.	xxvj li. xiij s. iiij d.[37]
fuell		xl s.	
candells		x s.	
salt		xiij s. iiij d.	
otemell		viij s.	
veneger	(iij s. iiij d.)er	vj s. viij d.	
mustard verges aleger[38]			
fleshe		(wek)er x li.	
fyshe			

[c][39]

Wagis and lyvere for Wyll Robyns		xxx s.
Wagis and lyvere for Lytill Wyll		xxvj s. viij d.
Wag and lyvere for An		xvj s.
The sheperdes wages and lyvere	(xlij s. viij d.)er	xxxvj s. viij d.
	[*total*]	v li. ix s. iiij d.

[d] Wages

Lytl Wyll Gryffyn[40]	iij li.
Mother Medham, Elysebeth	xxxij s.
Wyll Sheperd	xxxiij s. iiij d.

[e]

Mother Medham	xvj s.
Annys	xiij s. iiij d.
Edward	xxx s.
Archer	xxvj s. viij d.
Gryffyn	xx s.
Hys [*lyvere*][41]	vij s.
Nycholas	xij s.
His lyverey	viij s.

183 f. 69 v. C [*Purchase of Fish, possibly 1548*][42]

A quarterne of lynge[43] iij li.

[37] The correct sum is £25 18s. 0d.
[38] Unidentified.
[39] **c, d, e** form a second column in the MS; **c** is crossed through.
[40] i.e. two people.
[41] Apparently omitted.
[42] The date of the remaining items of f. 69 v.
[43] North Atlantic fish, usually salted.

A quarterne of habardyne[44]	xvj s. viij d.
di. hundreth of stockefyshe[45]	xv s.
A fyrkyne of sope	viij s. v d.
ij cakes whit sope	xv d.
mate and cords[46]	x d.
The caryag being iiij^{c} di.[47]	xj s.
Item towardes his chargis	ij s. vj d.
	Sum v li. x s. viij d.
Wherof resceyved in part of payment	iij li. vj s. viij d.
Item for iij salmons	vij s.
Item j strike di. of pese	iij s.
Item for a quarter of malt	xv s. iiij d.
Item resceyved	iiij s.
Item resceyved on Ester Sunday more	iij li.
and so remayn . . .	. . .

184 L. 31a. D [*Shopping list on loose slip*]

Peper gres[?] resynges[48] and fiall crose and iaces[?] sanders[49] j d. dates di. li. craftes shues for Anthony and my wyffe hose for my wyffe

185 S. 6. I [*Shopping list, 1562?*][50]

Sugar	j lofe
resenes	xx li.
prunes	xij li.
currans	vj li.
figgs	a topnet[51]
almons	vj li.
pepper	ij li.

cloves mace
biskeles[52] carowes[53]
stramm[54] and ginger
sucker[55] marmales[56]
saunders[49]
lose shewes slippers for my wyfe

[44] Salted or sun-dried cod.
[45] Dried cod.
[46] Probably for a bed.
[47] 4½ hundredweight.
[48] Raisins.
[49] Sandalwood [*O.E.D.*].
[50] The adjoining item (237) is of 1562.
[51] Basket for figs; cf. p. 117.
[52] Biscuits.
[53] Carroway [*O.E.D.*].
[54] Uncertain.
[55] Perhaps 'suckers', sucking sweets [*O.E.D.*], though the recorded references are later.
[56] Probably marmalade, then meaning a preserve of quinces [*O.E.D.*].

186 S.6.G [*About 1560*]

Recevyd of you	vij li.
Inp. .	[*blank*]
Item payd to Master Cunnet for ij weekes comeng	xxxvj s.
Item payd to the potycary	xviij s.
Item payd to Harry for ij quarter of reye	viij d.
Item delyvyared you to play at tables	[x s.?]
Item payd for a payer of gloves for you	iiij d.
Item payd for a dosen of poyntes for you	iij d. ob.
Item payd for a quyer of paper	vj d.
Item payd to Harry for [?blue] beard	vij d.

187 S.6.C [*Expenses of a journey, 1561*]
Townsend[57]

Item payd for horse meatte at Lester	iiij d.
Item pade for my dennar there	vj d.
Item payd for my super at Nottyngham	vj d.
Item payd for hoarse meatte ther the sayme nyght	viij d.
Item payd for my denner at Manncefeld	iiij d.
Item payd for hoarse meatte thear	iiij d.
Item payd for showyng the whyghte nage j showe and a remove payd together	iiij d.
Item payd for horse meate at Manncefeld	iiij d.
Item payd for my supper at Nottyngham the same nyght	vj d.
Item payd for horse meatte ther	x d.
Item payd for my denner at Lester	iiij d.
Item payd for horse meatte ther	iiij d.
Item payd for my super and breckefeaste at Lyterworthe	viij d.
Summa	vj s.
Item payd for horse meate at Skyltes[58]	viij d.
Item payd for horse meatte at Warwycke	iiij d.
Item payd for your supper at Harborowe	ij s. iiij d.
Item payd for horse meatte there	xviij d.
Item gave to Master Spencer man	iiij d.
Summa totalys	xj s. ij d.

Which[59] I have payd hym the xxviij[th] of September 1561.

188 f17.C [*1545 or after*]

Rec[*eipt*]: Water imperiall[60] j sponfull, as muche triacle[61] as 2 walnuttes, a penyworth of clove, maces as muche of the powder as vj whetcorns wyll

[57] Added in Peter Temple's hand; the main hand is not found elsewhere.

[58] Not identifiable as a place between Lutterworth and Warwick; it was perhaps an inn in Coventry.

[59] Added by Peter Temple.

[60] A drink made of cream of tartar, flavoured with lemons [*O.E.D.*].

[61] Theriac, a medicinal antidote, possibly but not necessarily made of molasses [*O.E.D.*].

way, a peny weight of powder of soll ammoniake.[62] Boyle all thes together in good stall all and gyve the pacyent to drink as shortly as ye may open the infection, and yf he be sore gone as ye think past remedy, take a garlycke hede, pyll hit and stampe hitt small with a lytill safron, sinamon, lang peper[63] and temper hit with stronge oil and hole maces, and drink hit and hell hym warme and make hyme to swatt, and yf the spottes do appere all in the sheetes, make a nother bede quickly and a freshe paire of shetes warmyd, and do hym to that bed, and give hym good nouriseable meates and drinkes. Also geve him possetes made with sorell. Also let hym hold the levys of sorell in hys mouthe.

189 f. 16. A [*Thomas Heritage: Plate*]
111 li. 2 s. 6 d.

A salt parsoll gylt waying xij oz. and a quarter at iiij s. the oz.	37 li. 11 s.[64] [3 d.?]
Item lassor[65]salt parsell gylt waying vij oz. iij qr. at iiij s. the oz.	[*blank*]
Item ij harnes gyrdelles and crosse[66] wayinge v oz. iij qr. at iij s.	[11 li.] 7 s. 11 d.
Item iij gobelet parsell gylt with a cover wayinge v[?] oz. at iiij s.	[*blank*]

NEW YEAR'S GIFTS

190 f. 2 v. B [*New Year's Gifts, possibly 1548*][67]

W. Brookes	ij capons
Stonely	j capon
Thomas Gryffyn	ij capons
Jhon Herytage	ij capons
Horrod	ij capons
Jhon Savage	ij kokerls
Profytes wyf of Knighton	j capon and j pullet
Wagstaffe	ij capons

191 f. 76 v. B New Yeres Geyftes resceyved ij^{di}
Edwardi vjth [*1549*]

Resceyved of Godwyf Petyver	ij capons	iiij d.
Resceyved of Stonley of . . .[68]	ij capons	iiij d.

62 Ammonium chloride.

63 Long pepper, from *piper longum*; M. Ogden (ed.), *Liber de Diversis Medicinis*, Early English Text Society, 1938.

64 These calculations do not seem to tally.

65 Lesser.

66 Harness girdles: belts or chains [*O.E.D.*].

67 These are clearly New Year gifts; the year presumably precedes the next items; from the MS. it is after 1544, and 1548 can be suggested.

68 Apparently not Offchurch (as in **86**).

Resceyved of Colman of Rodwey	ij capons	iiij d.
Resceyved of Mr. Hikman	j capon and j drake	ij d.
Resceyved of Thomas Gryffyn	ij capons	iiij d.
Resceyved of William Brokes	ij capons	iiij d.
Resceyved of Jamz Clarke	ij hens	iiij d.
Resceyved of Jhon Herytag	ij capons	iiij d.
Resceyved of Horwood	ij capons	iiij d.
Resceyved of Herytage of Rodwey	ij hens	[*blank*]
Of Hary Petyver	j capon	iiij d.
Of Thomas Haws	ij capons	iiij d.
Of Godard of Wapenbury	ij capons	
Of Wyll Robyns	ij capons	

192 f. 76 v. C New Yers Geyftes anno iij^{to} regni regis Edwardi vj [*1550*]

Of Rychard Colman	ij capons
The Weyner of Knyghtcott	j capon
Horwod of Weston	ij capons
Gryffyth of Compton	ij capons
Clarke of Compton	ij capons
William Makepece	ij capons
Elyse Burbery	ij capons
Henry Petyver	ij capons
R. Warner	j capon
Herytage of Rodwey	ij capons
Leyborn	j hen
Herytage de Kyngston	ij capons
Godard	ij capons
Wylliam Colyns	ij capons
Wylliam Brokes	ij capons

SERVANTS

193 f. 81 v. A [*Thomas Heritage, 1536–7*]

At Kyrsmas anno xv^{c}xxxvj	
Item paid to Lovet for his quarter wages	x s.
Item lent to him	iij s. iiij d.
Item halffe a bosshel of whet and rye	(vij d.)^{er} xvj d.
Item halfe a bosshell of maltte	(vj d.)^{er} iiij d.
Item for hys howsse rent	xx d.
Item for his chyld	xx d.
Item for met	v d.
Item — Ester	vj s. viij d.
Item in renk corne a busshell	x d.
Item paid to my myeller	ix s.

Item paid to the myller	v s.
Hyrd John Clark at Halloltyd for viij nobullys [*26 s. 8 d.*] a yere and a cott cloyth and a payer of hosse cloyth	
Item delyvered to John Clark	iij s. iiij d.
Item to him at Ester	iij s. iiij d.
Item delyvered him his hosse clothe	
Item delyvered him apon Seynt Laurans day [*10 Aug.*]	vj s. viij d.
Item for Roger	(ij s.)er

194 f. 75. A [*1537*]

Hyred Father Passo at Holoutyd for a yere for xij d. a wyk
Item hyred my servand Thomas Wheler in the xxix yere of our soverain lord Kyng Henry the viijth [*1537*] at Hollowtyd for a yere next followyng for xxiij s. iiij d. and a kott clorth whych I have delyvered hym.
Memorandum I Thomas Herytage owyth to Thomas Wyllor my servand xxiij s. iiij d. for a holle yeres wages endyng at Hallowtyd in the xxx yere of our soverain lord Kyng Henry the viijth [*1538*]

Item I how more to the seyd Thomas Wyllor	ix s. viij d.
Wheroff payd hym apon Seynt Kators Day [25 Nov.]	vj s. iiij d.
*[*Inset*] So rest to hym with his wages	xxvj s. viij d.
Item delyvered hym at Krysmas	v s.
Item delyvred hym in the Krismas hally dayis to by hym a sworde	v s.
At Shrofted	v s.
Item delyvered hym at Ester	v s.
Item at Myssomer	v s.
Item paid for makyng of his cotte	xiiij d.
Item delyvered to hym when he wente for Geny Borby	xij d.
[*Margin, at * above*]	
To a dowber	ij s.
for a nox	xx s. viij d.
John Owens [?]	ij s.
show maker	
whott ys	

195 f. 76 [*1538*]

Hyred Thomas Fypis at Mycellmas in the xx yere [*1538*] for xxvj s. viij d. a yere and a kote clorth	
Item delyvered hym at Krismas	v s.
Item delyvered hym at Estar	v s.
and his kott cloyth	
Item delyvered to hym at Mysomer	v s.
Item delyvered to hym at Mycelmas	v s.
Item delyvered hym by Thomas Felpis	vj s. viij d.

Hyred Wylliam the same tyme for xx s. a yere and a kott cloyth

Item delyvered hym at Kyrsmas v s.
Item delyvered hym at Estur v s.
and his kott cloyth
Item delyvered hym at Myssomer v s.
Item delyvered hym at Mycellmas v s.

196 f. 76 v. A [*1538–9*][69]

Hyred my mayd the same day for xvj s. a yere and a cyrtyll clothe
Item I delyvered hyr at Estur iij s. iiij d.
Item paid for a payer of showyes for hyr by Thomas Whellor x d.
Item delyvered hyr the last day of July ij s.
Item delyvered her at Wyssontyd her kyrtell cloyth
Item delyvered hyr at Mycellmass to hyr and hyr father ij s. vj d.
Item delyvered hyr ganst Kyrsmas v s.
Item delyvered hyr at Shroftyde v s.
Item delyvered her at Myssomer ij s. iiij d.

Item hyrd Wyllyam at Mycellmas[70] in the xxxj yere of Kynge Henry the viij[th] [*1539*] for xxiij s. iiij d. and his cote cloyth
Delyvered hym at Estur v s.
Item delyvered hym hys kotte
Item delyvered hym by Willor and Horst ij s.
Item delyvered hym at Watford Fayer [*blank*]

197 f. 77. A [*1540*]

Hyred raffe Gardner at May the xxxij yer of ower sovereyn lorde Kynge Henry the viij[th] [*1540*] for a yere and to Mycelmas next foloyng for xxxij s. and a cott cloyth
Paid to hym at Myssomer ij s.
Delyvered hym when he was syke iij s. iiij d.
Item delyvered hym hys kott cloyth
Item paid for makynge his kott and lynyng [*blank*]
Hyerd Hary the last day of May for viij s.
Paid for a payer of showyes for hym x d.
Delyvered hym by my wyffe iij d.
Delyvered hym for a shortt xiij d.
Item for redy mony in the kechen vj d.

[*Peter Temple*][71]

198 f. 17 v. January anno xxxvij[o] Henrici viij[ti] [*1546*]

[69] Continuing from the opposite page (**195**).
[70] MS. *Myellmas.*
[71] For earlier years see **138** and **182c–e**.

Mother Medham hath resceyvyd for wages	iij s.
Blanche hath resceyved	xx d.
Mother Medham rescyvyd at Our Lady Day	iiij s.
Nycholas resceyvyd at Our Lady Day	viij s.
and so he ys payd for Mydsomer quarter.	
Gryffyn ys payd for Our Lady Daye and hath rescyvyd for Mydsomer quarter	ij s. iiij d.

A Festo Sancti Michaelis anno xxxviij° Henrici viij^th [*1546*]

Memorandum that I have paid all my servantes their wages being dew at Mychelmas last except v s. which I owe to Mother Medham at the sayd fest.[72]

Inprimis delyvered to Annes apon her wages	xx d.
Item to Gryffyn apon hys wages	ij s. viij d.
Item to Nycholas apon his wagis	iij s. iiij d.

199 f. 22 v. [*1547*]

Servantes wages payd anno primo Edwardi sexti [*1547*][73] ut patet infra

Inprimis payd to Wylliam at Christmas	vij s. vj d.
Item to Townsend the same tyme	v s.
Item to Dove then	vij s.
Item to Gryffyn	vj s. vij d.
Payd to Edward	vij s. vj d.
Payd to Archer	vj s. iij d.
Payd to Harry	v s. ix d.

Annunciacion of Our Lady

Payd to Wylliam then	vij s. vj d.
Payd to Gryfyn then	vj s. viij d.
Paid to Townsend	v s.
Paid to Dove	v s.
Paid to Edward then	vij s. vj d.
Paid to Archer in part of his bord and wages	vij s. viij d.

Mydsomer and Mychelmas

Paid to Wylliam Lucas then	vij s. iiij d.
Item to Gryffyn then	vj s. viij d.
Item to Thomas Townsend then	iij s. iiij d.
Item To' [?*Thomas*] Dove	xvj s.
Item paid to Archer in part of his wyfs bord and wages	vj s.

[72] Margin *soll'*.

[73] This complete year is presumably 1547, though 1 Edward VI actually began on 28 January 1547.

Item paid more to Archer for hys bord and wages	xx s.
Item Edward delyvered to Archer	xx s.
Item Edward delivered to Archer	xx s.

200 f. 23 Servantes wages payd at Christmas anno ij^{do} regni regis Edwardi vj^{ti} [*1548*]

Delyvered too Edward then	vij s. vij d.
Delyvered to Anthonye	vj s. viij d.
Delyvered to Horwood	vj s. vij d.
Item to Thomas	vj s. viij d.
Item to Fause then	vj s. viij d.
Delyvered to Dove at Banbre	iij s. iiij d.

Annuncyacion of Our Lady

Delyvered to Edward	vij s. vj d.
Delyvered to Anthony	vj s. viij d.
Delyvered to Horwod	vj s. viij d.
Delyvered to Thomas	vj s. viij d.
Delyvered to Robart Vause	vj s. viij d.
Delyvered to Dove	ix s.

Mydsomer

Delyvered to Anthony at Banbery fyrst fayre[74]	v s.
Delyvered to Thomas at Whitsontyd	vj s. viij d.
Delyvered to Dove at Warwyke	vj s. viij d.
Delyvered to Vawse	v s. xx d.

Mychelmas

Delyvered to Dove	vij s. vj d.
Delyvered to Thomas	vj s. viij d. at Stratford
Delyvered to Vawse	vj s. viij d.
Delyvered to Horwood	xiij s. iiij d.

201 f. 12 v. B [*Undated*][75]

Delyvered Gryffyn iij s. iiij d. his wages endyd at the Annunciacion of Our Lady
Lent Gryffyn xx d.; lent hym allso ij s. viij d.
Gryffyn ij d.

[74] Ascensiontide [10 May]; *V.C.H.*, Oxon., **10**, p. 58.
[75] Gryffyn was employed from 1544 to 1547.

202 f. 59 v. B

Thomas Wylner	iiij d.
Hues[76]	ix d.
Horsemet	vj d.
lynen clothe xvj d.; lynnen cloth vj s. viij d.	
Wyll and Gryffyn for dyvers rekynyngs	xviij d.
My wyffe	xx d.

203 f. 47 v. C [*Shepherds' wages, post 1554*][77]

Hyred Phylyp Rawlyns for xl s., vj shep pasture and a payre of old bottes
Hyred Wylliam Bowghton for xxxiij s. iiij d. and iiij shep pasture
Hyred Edward Sponor for xxxiij s. iiij d.

14. *Building Work*

Thomas Heritage noted only one small building expense, putting windows into his shop, but this reference illuminates his life in London and shows that he was retailing goods as well as trading in the provinces. The windows themselves were carpenter's work only, and therefore unglazed.

In contrast, for Peter Temple's new house a very complete record is given. The work took two summer seasons, nineteen weeks in 1548, from 2 June to 13 October, and about twelve weeks from 1 June the next year. In the first year, most of the work was shared between the master mason, Kytchin[78] and the carpenters, Wylkyns and then Turkeyn. Kytchin always had his boy and one or two other men, while there were usually two assistant carpenters and also a couple of sawyers.[79] After a brief visit in week seven, the tilers came in earnest from the fifteenth week to the end of the first season. The house can be recognized as of the characteristic style found in the Banbury region,[80] (Pl. III), a shell of the local yellow-brown ironstone with the interior walls, floors and roof-structure of timber. The roof

[76] Hughes?

[77] Dated by the changed shillings symbol (see p. 250). There is a jotting *20d.* at the top of the page.

[78] A local man, as he bought eleven ewes from Temple the same year.

[79] One, of course, needed on top, and one in the saw-pit.

[80] R. B. Wood-Jones, *Traditional Domestic Architecture in the Banbury Region*, Manchester, 1963.

was tiled with at least 3,400 plain tiles,[81] three dozen crest tiles and seven dozen gutter tiles.[82] Brick was also used, probably for the chimneys, where limestone would be decomposed by the heat,[83] and special stone lintels were bought from the Hornton Quarries, 4 miles to the south. Most of the stone was free of charge, presumably cut by Kytchin and his men from Burton Hill.

In the second season, the inside was finished. The hinges for the doors must have been superior as they were bought at Banbury Fair and Warwick,[84] not made by the local blacksmith, though he was also employed. The major work that year was done by the daubers, on the partitions of wattling (wynding rods) with lime plaster, while windows in the parlour and the kitchen were glazed.

The total recorded cost of the building was £39 12s. 9d., but this did not include the bulk of the materials. The stone was effectively free, but the great quantity of wood must have been bought. The wage rates for the craftsmen can only be guessed, because when the days worked were listed, the wages were not itemized and *vice versa*; however, carpenters seem to have received up to 2s. 2d. a week, tilers and sawyers about 1s. 6d.

The impression of the whole house is that it was of high quality, with its use of tiles and bricks, glass in the windows even in the kitchen, and two proper chimneys at a date when most houses in the region retained open hearths. What the accounts do not reveal is how big the house was, its rooms or its plan.

Later probate and other inventories[85] describe the principal house on the Temple estate at Burton Dassett. However, the first information that certainly relates to Peter's own building comes from an agreement made just after his death by Millicent Temple. She agreed

[81] Unfortunately the first large purchase of tiles does not give details.

[82] The gutter tiles were probably for valleys between two roofs (e.g. main roof and wing) with a concave curve. The use of tiles rather than thatch is significant as they are now widespread in south-east Warwickshire, but have been supposed to be eighteenth century replacements for thatch (Wood-Jones, op. cit., p. 159). Clearly this tradition is much older than has been believed.

[83] Brick was used nearby in the early sixteenth century in three prestige houses, Hanwell Castle (1495), Wormleighton (1512) and Compton Wynyates (1520), but does not appear in smaller dwellings until the beginning of the nineteenth century (Wood-Jones, op. cit., p. 244).

[84] These were probably made in Birmingham, already a centre for iron work. It is particularly interesting to find hinges as worthwhile commodities for chapmen to take to fairs. See M. B. Rowlands, *Masters and Men*, Manchester University Press, 1975.

[85] ST L9 D5, Temple Inventories. Among the wealth of early inventories that the collections contain, the only major absence is that of Peter Temple himself. There is one for Millicent, taken in 1582, but it is short and has no information about the Dassett house.

to resign her third share in his lands in favour of their son, John, in exchange for £40 a year, food and drink for herself and two maids, and the use of 'two chambers, one studye now newly builded under the gallerye, and one maydes chamber at the stayre head wherin a presse nowe standeth'.[86]

Peter Temple, of course, built his house on the land he leased, on 'The Grove', at the north-east corner of Heritage Field (see p. 38 and Fig. 1).[87] After the 1576 partition, this was assigned to Sir Thomas Wotton, and the original manor house became the main Temple house, standing just south of the church (now Church Farm). However in 1580, John Temple was still the tenant of The Grove and its house, let to him at will by Thomas Wotton.[88] We do not know when this tenancy was resigned, and it is probable that John Temple was still in occupation at his death in 1603. Certainly, the description in his inventory does not match that of the 'house neare the church', of 1630 (Table 14.1), and the Gallery and the Presse Chamber are reminiscent of the 1578 agreement.

Of the house before Peter rebuilt it, there is firmer evidence, from Roger Heritage's inventory of 1495 (Table 14.1); it is unlikely to have been much altered during the intervening period, when its tenants were absentees. In 1495, it was clearly a house of quality, though by 1550 it would have been old-fashioned. John Temple's inventory (if it can be validly cited) confirms what we would expect, that Peter made of the old house one eminently suited to be a gentleman's home.[89]

After the 1576 partition, the house remained associated with Heritage Field, and is to this day called 'The Grove'. Further study has regrettably been prevented by its destruction by fire on 28 January 1920. No photographs of it have been discovered, and the sole and tantalising description come from the newspaper report of the fire,[90] that the dining and drawing rooms contained some fine oak panelling and stencil work. The stone walls, rebuilt after the fire,

[86] Dated 3 August 1578, ST Deeds List 2, Box 27, no. 84.

[87] The 1546 lease of Heritage Field included 'a certain house that Peter Temple dwells in', ST L9 E1, Temple Land, Bucks., book of leases.

[88] Wotton Accounts, Bodleian Library, Broxbourne 84.15/R267.

[89] He claimed later that his lease of Heritage Field was on condition that he dwelt at Burton, to 'keep hospitality there' and to repair and rebuild a house likely to cost 200 marks (£130). Cited by Gay, 1938, p. 380, probably from ST Temple Law case 212.

[90] *Banbury Guardian*, Thursday, 29 January 1920. I am most grateful to Anthony Temple for providing a copy of this report.

Table 14.1: *Houses in Burton Dassett*
(rooms in order, as listed in the inventories)

Roger Heritage's inventory: 1495[a]	*John Temple's inventory: 1603*[b]		*House near the church: 1630*[c]	
Halle	Hall	Buttry and Celler	Parler	Milne house (for malt mill)
Parleur	Parler	The Old Hall	Little Chamber	Chamber over the Parler
(Inner?) Chambre	Parler Chamber	Kitchin and Larders	Hale	Two Bed Chambers
Over Chambre	Inner Chamber	Brewhouse and Boulting house	Little Hale	Chamber over the Hale
(*One heading lost,*	Greene Chamber	Cheese Chambers	Buttery	Chamber over the Little Hale
perhaps Linen)	New Chamber		Kitchinge	Chamber over the Buttery
Servantes Chambre	Presse Chamber		Bolting House	Chamber over the Kitching
Bakhous	Gallery over the Parler and Chamber		Larder	Chamber over the Brewhouse
Dyehouse			Dayrye House	Old Studye
Kechyne			Seller	Apple Chamber
			Brewhouse	Cockloftes
				Corne Chamber

[a] P.R.O. PROB. 2/457.
[b] ST. L9 D5 Temple Inventories.
[c] Ibid., annotated: 'Inventory of goods in the house where Henry Rose dwelled, 9th March, 1629[/30], neare the church of Dassett in Com. Wa., and heretofore next before dwelled Thomas Temple, son of me Sir Thomas Temple, kt., bart.'

apparently follow the original foundations at least in part, and suggest that the core of the house was of three bays. Beyond this, there is nothing.

BUILDING WORK

[*Thomas Heritage*]

204 f. 83 v. A Costes off the wyndawys in the shoppe

Item for ij pere of granandes hokys[91]	ij s.
Item for v^{c} v d. naylls	xx d.
Item for the carpenter for his wages and quarters	x s.
Item for bordes	[*blank*]

[*Peter Temple*]

205 f. 72 The charges of my buyldyng in anno ij^{do} Edwardi vjth [*1548*]

Inprimis delyvered to Kyttchyn in ernest	iij s. iiij d.
Item delyvered to the sayd Kytchyn at dyvers tymes	iij li.
Item paid for tyle and brycke	iij li.
Item for lyme paid	v s. vj d.
Item for Horndon[92] stone for my oven and mantell tre paid	vj s. viij d,
Item delyvered to Wylkyns the carpenter the fyrst Saturdaye [*9 June*]	xx d.
Item delyvered to Wylkyns the next Saturday	ij s.
Item to ij sawyers then	(ij s.)^{er} xx d.
Item delyvered to Wylkyns the iij^{d} Saturday	ij s.
Item to ij sawyers then	iij s. x d.
Item to j carpenter	xxij d.
Item to ij carpenters	iij s. x d.
Item the iiijth Saturdaye to ij sawyers	ij s. viij d.
Item to ij carpenters then	ij s. viij d.
Item to Wylkyns the vth Saturdaye	ij s.
Item to Wylkyns the vjth Saturdaye	ij s.
Item to ij carpenters then	iiij s. iiij d.
Item to ij sawyers then	ij s. viij d.
Item to Wylkyns the vijth Saturdaye	ij s.
Item to ij carpenters then	iiij s. iiij d.
Item to ij tylers then	iij s. ij d.
Item to Wylkyns the viijth Saturdaye	xx d.
Item to ij carpenters then	iij s. viij d.
Item to ij sawyers then	ij s.

[91] Probably T-shaped 'garnet' hinges; L. F. Salzman, *Building in England down to 1540* (Oxford: University Press, 1966), p. 298.

[92] Hornton, a village 4 miles to the south.

Item to Wylkyns the ixth Saturdaye	ij s.
Item to ij carpenters then	iiij s. iiij d.
Item to ij sawyers then	iiij s.
Item to Wylkyns the xth Saturdaye	ij s.
Item to ij carpenters then	iiij s. vj d.
Item to iij sawyers then	iiij s.
Item delyvered to Kytchin	xx s.
Summa	xj li. vj s. viij d.

[f. 72 v.]

Item to Wylkyns the xjth Satrday	xx d.
Item to ij carpenters then	iij s. viij d.
Item to ij sawyers then	xvj d.
Item the xij Satrday [*25 Aug.*] being the next morow after Saynt Bartylmewtyde [*24 Aug.*] to Wylkyns	xvj d.
Item to Turkeyne the carpenter and his man then	ij s. ij d.
Item the xiijth Satrdaye to Wylkyns	xvj d.
Item to Turkeyn and his man	iiij s. iiij d.
Item the xiiijth Satrdaye to Wilkyns	xx d.
Item to Tyrkyn and hys man	iij s. viij d.
Item to ij sawyers	iij s. iiij d.
Item to Kytchyn the mason	xx s.
Item the xvth Saturday, morow after Stratford Fayre [*14 Sept.*] to the sawyers	iiij s.
Item for lyme	v s.
Item for iiij^{c} bryke	v s.
For lath naylles	xij d.
Item to Turkyn and his man	iij s. iiij d.
Item to ij laborers	xvj d.
Item to the tylier and his man	iij s.
Item at Stratford Fayre v^{m}v^{c} lathe nayles and vj^{c}l v-peny nayll and j^{c} vij-peny nayle	viij s. viij d.
Item for vj^{c} tylle delyvered[93]	(iij s.)^{er} ij s. viij d.
Item the xvjth Saturdaye to Wylkyns the carpenter	xvj d.
Item to Turkeyn and hys man	iij s.
Item to the tyler and hys man	ij s. iiij d.
Item[94] for 5^{c} tyle, v dosen gutter and j dosen crestes	[*blank*]
Item to ij laborers	xij d.
Item the xvijth Saturdaye, morowe after Michelmas to Turkeyn	iij s. viij d.
Item to the tyler	x d.
Item the xviijth weke, the fyrst Monday after Mychelmas for iiij^{c} brykes delyvered	v s.
Item iiij^{c} bryke (and ij dosyn gutter tyll)^{er} delyvered	v s.
Item to Kytchyn delyvered	xxvj s. viij d.

93 Meaning 'paid over', not 'sent to Burton Dassett'.

94 Line inserted.

Item vij^{c} tylle delyvered	x s.
Item di.^{c} v-peny nayl and v^{m} lath nayll	v s. vij d.
Item to Turkeyn and hys man	iij s. viij d.
Item to the tylor	ij s. vj d. and iiij d.
Item to ij plasteres	iij s.
Item tylle ij^{m} vj^{c}, ij dosen crestes and ij dosen gutter tylle delyvered	xiiij s.
Summa	vij li. xij s. xj d.

[f. 69 v. B][95]

Item the xixth weke, the ij^{d} Saturday after Mychelmas [*13 Oct.*] to Kytchin and his boy	iij s. iiij d.
Item to Turkeyn and his man	iij s. iiij d.
To the tylers	ij s. vj d.
To the plasterers	iij s.

206 f. 80. B [*Masons' Work, 1548*]

Kytchin the fyrst weke with hys boye and j man	v hole dayes and di.
Item the second weeke with hys boye and j man	iiij hole dayes and di.
Item the iij^{d} weeke with hys boye and ij men	v holle dayes
Item the iiijth weke with j man and hys boye	iij holle dayes
Item the vth weke with his boye and ij men	iiij holle dayes and di.
Item the vjth weke with his boye and ij men	v holle dayes
Item[96] the viijth weke with his boye and j man	ij hole dayes and di.
Item the ixth weke with his boye and j man	iiij hole dayes and di.
Item the xth weke with his boye and j man	v hole dayes (and di.)^{er}
Item the xjth weke with his boy and man	v holl dayes
Item[97] the xiijth weke with his boye and man	iiij holle dayes and di.
Item the xiiijth weke Kytchin and Hynd and hys boye and iij men	iiij hol dayes
Item the xvth weke, beyng Stratford Fayre, Kytching and Hynd the boy and iij men	ij hol dayes
Item the xvjth wek Kytching and his boye and ij men	j holle daye
Item the xvijth weke Kytchyng, his boye and ij men	iiij holle dayes and di.
Item the xviijth weke v holl dayes with his boye and ij men	

207 L. 31 a. A [*Probably 1549*][98]

At Banbery Fayre [*30 May in 1549*] for hinges and nayls	x s.
At Warwyke for hinges, yron and nayls	iiij s.

95 F. 72 v. clearly continues on f. 69 v. B, but a sheet is cut out following f. 72, that did carry text.

96 Week 7 absent.

97 Week 12 absent.

98 This must follow on from the 1548 accounts, and so is of 1549.

Item in vj-peny nayll	v s.
Item for j^{c} x-peny nayl	xx d.
Item Edward paid for naylls	ij s. iiij d.
Item ij^{c} vj-peny nayll and ij^{c} x-peny nayll	vj s. viij d.
Item iiij^{c} vj-peny and ij^{c} x-peny nayll	iij s. viij d.
Item paid the carpenter and his man for to holle weks	xxx s.
Item another carpenter	iiij s. (viij d.)[er]
Item to Belle	ix s. iiij d.
For glasyng the ij windows in the parlor and j window in the [new?] qutchen	[ ]
Item to the sawyers for sawyng ij^{m} ij^{c}bord and gyftes	xx s.
Item for wyndyng roddes	v s. iiij d.
Item viij^{c} lath	ij s. viij d.
Item wynd rodes	v s. iiij d.
Item lyme	xij s.
Item iij daubers j weke	vj s.
Item lath nall	vj s.
Item lathe iiij^{m} and spars lxxx	xxij s. viij d.
Item lath nayl and 10-peny nayl	v s. viij d.
Item iij dawbers xxij dayes	xxij s.
Item sauers [*sawyers*?]	iij s.
Item Belle	xiij s. iiij d.
ij dawbers ij wekes	viij s.
[*Total*]	xj li. iij s.

[L. 31a: f. 3]

ij carpenters iij wekes	xj s.
iiij^{m} lath nayle	v s. viij d.
ij^{c} iiij-peny nayll	viij d.
ij^{c} vj-peny nayll	xij d.
iiij^{c} vj-peny nayll	ij s.
The smyth	xx d.; item ij s.
Delyvered the carpenter	xiij s. viij d.
iiij^{c} vj-peny nalle	ij s.
The smythe	iij s. iiij d.
The carpenters	v s.
Delyvered Bell	x s.
Paid to laborars	vij s. ij d.
Item to laborars	ij s. iiij d.
Item to the carpenter	iij s.
Paid to Belle	viij s.
Item the smythe	iiij s.
Summa[99]	iiij li. xviij s.

99 Sum written on L. 31a: f. 2.

15. *Finance* (Pls. IV, VI)

The numerous items in the account book relating directly to Peter Temple's finances are the most complicated of all, and can only be understood incompletely. They run from 1543 to 1549, while others on loose sheets for the 1560s include a remarkable and important summary for 1561. Four types of account were recorded. The simplest were the transactions with an individual; that with James Clarke in 1548–9 started with his purchase of twelve cattle and sixty-one sheep in the autumn of 1548, whose price was paid off in various ways over the following year.[1] Similar accounts relating only to particular subjects have already been covered in their proper places. Secondly, outstanding debts were listed in most years, James Clarke's debt appears in its place in the 1548 list. More rarely, Peter recorded his own payments. Finally, on two or three occasions, he tried to strike a balance of his resources, between the money he could hope to receive, whether from debts, farming or rents, and the payments he had to make. In the early years especially, these are accompanied by numbers of rough drafts; they mostly lack any headings, but can be identified from their contents.

We can add to the picture of Peter Temple's finances by collecting estimates of the annual receipts from his various enterprises, worked out from the specialized accounts (Table 15.1). The results, both for income and expenditure, can only be minimum figures, but to some extent they quantify the success of his farming. Another view of this comes from the debts due to him, whose totals rise from £175 in 1545 to an impressive £1,074 in 1564. As these usually included his cash-in-hand, they really describe his realizable assets, and give a measure of his accumulation of capital, or rather the liquid part of it. A full analysis is impossible, as we known nothing from the accounts of money invested in property, whether for the purchase of freeholds, or as entry fines for leaseholds. Nor is it easy to calculate the rising assets represented by the flocks; the cattle are more straightforward, as they were sold off year by year. It is clear though, that a good proportion of Peter's capital was kept as cash or on short term loan. Presumably interest contributed to his income, though no direct reference is made to this in the accounts. However, one of the miscellaneous items (242) in this section does show that lending money was not always straightforward, with Mr. Wade both unwilling and unable to repay his debt on time.

[1] This account is remarkable for the eight separate items that refer to it (29–31, 61, 221, 226–8).

Table 15.1: *Financial summary*

	1543	1544	1545	1546	1547	1548	1549	1550	1551
Estimated profits									
Cattle			£32	£79	£67	£50	£46	£14	
Sheep			£32	£60	£75	£138	£176	£212	£175
Wool grown	£43	£30	£36?	£116?	£181	£246	£291	£180	£130
Wool bought						£31[a]	£17[a]		
Hay sold							£7	£9	
Pasture sold								£35	£40
Rents									
Herts.[a]	£60	£60	£60	?					
Stepney[a]	£20	£20	£20	£20	£20	£20	£20	£20	£20
Coventry[a]	£8[b]	£8	£8	£8	£8	£8	£8	£8	£8
Total	[£131]	[£118]	£188	£283	£351	£493	£565	£478	£373
Direct costs									
Burton rents	£96	£96	£96	£96	£96	£96	£96	£96	£96
Household	£25	£25	£25	£25	£25	£25	£25	£25	£25
Wages	£6	£6	£7	£7	£7	£7	£7?	£7?	£7?
Sheep bought			£94	£163					£50
Total	£127	£127	£222	£291	£128	£128	£128	£128	£178
Flock value[c]						£368		£361	£450

[a] Net profits.
[b] Probably £14 in earlier years before Alice Radcliff's marriage.
[c] Calculated at 3s., 3s. 6d. and 4s. per head for 1548, 1550 and 1551 respectively.

From the summary, despite its crudity, it is very clear that the sheep provided the backbone. With the breeding herd built up, the net income might have approached £400 a year. Alternatively, the debt values of £175 in 1545 and almost £500 in 1549 can be compared. Adding the value of his sheep, £360 in 1549, and a rough guess of £100 in 1545, suggests that over four years, Peter's capital resources might have trebled. But the effect of inflation must be remembered, even though it had not yet reached its peak. Allowing for a debasement of about a third, Peter's wealth increased some $2\frac{1}{4}$ times in real terms.[2] The whole calculation is crude, though probably the best that can be achieved with the available information. It does give an indication at least of the profits of his enterprise.

Considered in more detail, the financial entries interpret the broad picture, though they also contain many puzzles. The 1543 accounts

[2] *Ag. Hist.*, p. 848.

include a good summary of receipts (totalling £433) and payments (apparently £349 3s. 4d.) (**208**), though other sums appear in two further items (**209** (Plate IV), **210**) which only partly duplicate **208**. However, the main problem with this year's account is that it predates almost all Peter Temple's material in the account book, and no explanation is possible for many of the larger entries. The payments include the purchase of stock and the rent of Halls Field and Heritage Field, while most of the rest may be money laid out as loans. On the credit side, the £24 from Dycheford, Strille and Cornforth probably represented the repayment of debts, as may also the £160 from Hangers.[3] The receipt of £100 from *Alys* (Alice Radcliff, Peter's stepdaughter) balanced by a payment of £13 6s. 8d., is puzzling because it seems unlikely that at this time she would have had independent resources. Thus, although the account shows an overall credit balance of £80, this cannot be identified as a profit for the year.

For 1544, only a couple of accounts exist (neither certainly dated), relating to cattle and to money received from Robert and Cuthbert Temple, perhaps for buying wool (**211**, **212**). However, 1545 is represented by at least eight items. A list of receipts totalled £271 (or £300), while payments came to £277 (**213**). Again, debts are apparently represented, but the outgoings are much clearer than in 1543. A summary of debts dated 15 August (**214**, **215**), divided them into larger and smaller amounts (£167 17s. 4d. and £8 14s. 4d.).[4] Several similar lists (**216–17**) were presumably drawn up at different times in the year. Finally, an item started on 29 March (**218**) shows £71 as cash in hand and begins to list expenditure; however, it then seems to become another list of debts or repayments.

For the next three years, the main item is a continuing list of debts, marked off as they were repaid, from 4 October 1546 to after 24 October 1548 (**221**). With many other contemporary accounts in the book, more of the entries are recognizable, usually being overdue payments for buying stock; it is noticeable that most of the sums are quite small. The largest debts involved Cuthbert Temple, for whom Peter settled more than one substantial bill. Apart from a couple of

[3] *Hangers pane* is, however, mentioned again in **209**, in the context of a list of outgoings, mainly from lands. Strille might be Sir Nicholas Strelley (see p. 23).

[4] A puzzling entry is the £20 for a fine from Ashefeld (Asheford), paid in two parts (**214**, **218**). The only land that Peter Temple is known to have had available is Hamper Mill, but its rent was still being received (**213**), while Ashefeld had Warwickshire connections, both buying wool and collecting taxes (**223**).

individual accounts with Anthony Ashefeld and James Clarke (223, 226) the only other significant item in these years is a note of 'ready mone' for March 1547, rather similar to that for 1545 (224). It included £17 for gold in hand, and some debts that presumably could be called in immediately, and also the remaining profit on the previous year's cattle, and the money that had already been passed on to Thomas Hyginson (Hygins) to buy new stock. Thus the total, £229 15s. 3d., is only a very rough approximation to Peter's working capital.[5]

The three accounts for 1549 are the clearest of the series. On 6 May Peter Temple collected up the major and minor debts (231, 232) to a total of £590 and £24. His nephew, Cuthbert, was again by far the most indebted, owing a total of £360, but Peter also kept his eye on smaller matters, down to the couple of shillings he had lent to Mr. Dannet's servant. His own debts were also recorded, mainly for rent due and for his uncleared account as bailiff,[6] giving him £492 in net available capital, excluding any cash in hand. A month later, on 4 June, Cuthbert had repaid £150, some of which Peter had passed on, leaving the total little changed at £469, without the small debts.

The account book contains no later dated financial items, though most of the individual series continue for several more years.[7] Among the loose papers are a couple of lists of debts (234, 235), mostly from unidentified people, but showing that the connection with William Gyfford, the sheep and cattle dealer, was being maintained fifteen years after he was first recorded. More interesting is a full summary of debts and cash on 1 January 1564 (238), totalling no less than £1,074 (including about £210 in cash).[8] However, the list which Peter made a couple of years earlier (236; Plate VI) is of far greater significance because he annotated it with the intended use of the money. At Candlemas 1562, his total assets amounted to £1,175, including £336 in gold and silver, but against this had to be set his own debts of £387. Of the total, the first priority was for £606 for buying Frankton.[9] Then, £217 was allocated for stocking

[5] An earlier draft of this item, probably dated 21 January 1547, dealt almost entirely with the cattle, and is included under that heading (20). It gives a total of £164, including £53 cash-in-hand.

[6] The £46 for the latter does not appear obviously in 157, and it possible that it is the same £46 that he owed in rent.

[7] None of the undatable financial items are likely to be of the 1550s.

[8] The end of this piece is very roughly written, and not all the final entries can be deciphered; the last five seem to be for cash and the like.

[9] In the event this idea was abandoned, probably because by April, he was in prison (see p. 243).

Morebarne Fields, Leicestershire, for which a long lease had just been granted (p. 233); this might have bought 400 ewes and lambs,[10] and was clearly essential to guarantee the income for the coming year.

Of the remainder, £48 was earmarked for his own expenses for the half-year March to September, 1562; presumably by autumn the farming money would have come in. The final £303 included £120 which the wool was expected to bring, and was to cover Peter Temple's own debts. The deficit, noted as £88, had to be found from other resources, presumably by fresh loans.[11]

What makes this account remarkable, and indeed perhaps unique among contemporary documents, is its anticipation and control. We can see Peter Temple moving towards this with the earlier listing of assets and how they should be deployed, and the gradual acquisition of this skill makes it no surprise that from his small beginnings, Peter was able eventually to employ his wealth to best advantage. This sheet comes close to being the financial balance whose absence from previously known Tudor accounts has made their study the more difficult.[12] Clearly, by this time, Peter's long practice had brought his accounts into as clear a state as those of any of his contemporaries.

FINANCE

208 f. 9 v. B Resceptes anno Henrici viij xxxv^{o} [*1543*]

Oxehall and Hampermyll	lx li.
Hangers	j^{c}lx li.
Alys	j^{c} li.
Dycheford	x li.
Strille	x li.
Cornforth	iiij li.
Wether hoges	xv li.
To Spenser shepe sold	xxx li.
Woll	xliij li.
	Summa iiij^{c}xxij li.

Leyd owt therof

Cawket	lxxx li.
Halsfeld and Old Lesse	lx li.

[10] Allowing a price of 10s. per couple.

[11] This is the precise balance between resources and debts, but it omits the £25 required for Peter's own household. This may have been included in his own £48.

[12] A. Simpson, *The Wealth of the Gentry: 1540–1660* (Cambridge: University Press, 1961), p. 12.

Clerke for Wheston	xl li.
To Jhon Spenser	xx li.
Besse	xx li.
Wylliams	(l li.)[er] xiij li.
Fynche	(xxvj li. xiij s. iiij d.)[er] xiij li. vj s. viij d.
Spenser for shepe	xviij li.
Wether hoges	xij li.
Brother vj li. for wooll bought	
Paid for my brother Gekel[13]	vj li.
Paid for Als[14]	xiij li. vj s. viij d.
Paid for rent of Herytag Feld and other charges	xxx li.
To Petifer	xl s.
My Lady Belknap	xj li.
To Mr. Bryges	xl s.
To Peny for wethers	(xvij li.)[er] viij li.

209 f. 10. B [*Draft Notes, 1543*][15]

[*Top margin*]

Johanni [*Spencer?*]	xx li.
Halls	lx li.
Bulockes [*beasts bought*]	xx li.

[*Centre left margin*]

Phips	xx s.
Mylls	xx s. xl d.
Brokes	iij li. xv s.

[*In gaps in f. 10. A*]

	iij[c]xxxiiij li. xiij s. iiij d.		
	liij li. xiij s. iiij d.	ix s. iiij d.	
Wylliams	xiij li. iij s.	my brother	xl li.
Strille	xiij li. vj s. viij d.	Spenser	xiij li.
		Item Fynche	xiij li. vj s. viij d.

[*Below A*]

Popler	xv li.	Hangers pane	xviij li. vj s. viij d.
Coventre	vj li. xiij s. iiij d.	(Al)[er] Popler	xv li.
Whestun	x li.	Coventre	xiij li. vj s. viij d.
(Old Lesse	x li.)[er]	Hamper myll	vj li.
		Pipers Bakers	liiij s. iiij d.
		Oxe Hall	iiij li.
		Alys	xiij li. vj s. viij d.
			Summa lxxij li.

[13] Jekyll (Pedigree 4).

[14] Peter's step-daughter Alice Radcliff (Pedigree 4). She is probably also the Alys in the first part of this account.

[15] This corresponds to the tidier version **208**, on the facing page. It is written around f. 10. A, and in its gaps. Reproduced in Pl. IV.

210 f. 1. B [*Receipts, 1543?*][16]

[*Top of the page*]	
Halsfeld	lx li.
Herytage Feld	j^{c} li.
Cawket	lxxx li.
Wheston	xl li.
Smithe[17]	(xxvj li.)^{er} xiij li. v s.
Spensr	xvj li.
(Penser [?*Spenser*]	xj li.)^{er}
Stirle	xiij li. vj s. viij d.
Bullockes	xx li.
woll	xx li.
Wylium	xiij li.
Ego[18]	xx li.
Styrle	xiij li. vj s. viij d.
Wylium	xiij li.
Spensr	xiij li.
[*Base of the page*]	
Stirle	ij^{c}lxiij li. vj s. viij d.
Suffes	xl li.
Alys	j^{c} li.
Oxehall hampermyll	lx li.

211 f. 1v. B [*Perhaps for cattle, 1544?*][19]

Resceyved of Byker by his man	vj li.
Item by Gryffyne	xl s.
Item by Townsend	iij li.
Item by Griffin	xx s.

Item by Gryffyn a geldyng, price xxxiij s. iiij d. and xvj s. viij d.

212 f. 3. C [*Perhaps 1544*][20]

Resceyved at Lamas[?] by the handes of Jhon Barnaby of my brother and Cutbard	xxvj li. v s. iiij d.
Item	ix li. xiij s.
Item	xliiij li. v s.
Summa totalis	lxxx li. iij s. iiij d.

213 f. 82. B Money resceyvyd the xxxvijth of Henry viij^{o} [*1545-6*]

Inprimis in my owne handes	lx li.
Item for (a)^{er} xx^{xx} wether hoges	xl li.

[16] Very similar to **208-9**.

[17] Not in **208**.

[18] This word also occurs in **213** and **215**, where the best reading is *ugo*; despite this, the likely significance is *ego*, 'for myself'.

[19] F. 1v. A is 1544, concerned with cattle, and this may relate to it.

[20] F. 3. B is of 1544.

Item of Clarke	xl li.
Item of Throkmorton[21]	j^{c} li.
Item of Jhon Pople[22]	xiij li. vj s. viij d.
Item of Mr. Anthony Cope[23]	v li.
Item gotte by shep bought of Mr. Ashefeld[24]	xiij li.
Summa	iij^{c} li. vj s. viij d.[25]

Unde Soluto

[*Second column of payments*]

For shep	lx li.
For Herytage Feld	l li.
For the Old Lesse	xl li.
Ego	xxxvj li.
I suppose the besse	lxxx li.
Wagstaffe	iiij li.
Gyfford	vij li.

214 f.10 v. Debtes dew unto Peter Temple anno xxxvij^{t} Henrici viij^{ti} [*1545*] 15 die Augusti

Anthoni Cope esquier	xiij li. vj s. viij d.
Ward for besse bowght	v li.
Mr. Ashefeld for the rest of hys fyne	xx li.
My brother	xj li.
Buchare	iiij li. x s.
Mr Wylliam Gyford owes for xxx kyne and xij wethers that Benet his bayle bought[26]	xxxix li. x s. vj d.
[*Margin*] Rest unpayd iiij li. x s.; for xl wethers vj li.	
Wyliam Fynche and Johanni Popule[27]	xiij li. vj s. viij d.
	Summa j^{c} li. xliiij s. viij d.
Memorandum Wylliam Gyfford owes for xx kyne and xxx^{ti} oxen liij li. vj s. viij d. and xxx s. that he left unpayd of the last reconyng.[26]	Summa liiij li. xvj s. viij d.
[*Margin*] Resceyved xx li.; item xiij li. vj s. viij d.	
Item Benet his man ows for a cow[26]	xvij s.

[21] Presumably Throckmorton of Coughton, Warwickshire.

[22] Probably for Hamper Mill. He is recorded as lessee in the 1550s (*V.C.H., Herts.* II, p. 452), and may be identical to John Popy (**141**).

[23] Of Hanwell, Oxfordshire, 5 miles south of Burton Dassett.

[24] This corresponds precisely to the transaction recorded in 53, though that took place in the first days of 38 Henry VIII, on 28 April 1546.

[25] The correct sum is £271 6s. 8d. The obvious explanation for the error would be that *xiij li.* has been written for *xlij li.*, but this seems unlikely as both £13 entries can probably be identified. It may be that one entry has been omitted.

[26] All these can be recognized in 13.

[27] Probably for Hamper Mill (cf. 213). Finche is also named in 1543 (208), but in relation to a payment.

215 f.11. D Petyt debtes eodem die [*15 Aug. 1545*]

Greffyn	x s.
Jhon Brokes of Knyghtcott	(lv s.)er xxxv s.
Henry Petyver	xxxv s.
Myls	xxiij s. iiij d.
Foster	xxj s.
(Frencley	xl s.)er
Thomas Makepes	xx s.
[*Separate on page, but perhaps continues*]	
Brother	xlvj li.
Strelle	xiij li. vj s.
Mershe	vj li. x s.
Sturdye	x li.
Ego	xxx li.
Fynch	xiij li. vj s. [viij d.]
Farwaye	[*Blank*]

216 f.13. B[28] [*Probably 1545*]

Gryffyn Compton	xl s.
Petyver[29]	xxv s.
Myls	xxiij s. iiij d.
Brokes[30]	lv s.
Thomas Makepec	xl s.
Stonle	iiij li.
Spenser	xl s.
[*Separate, but probably connected*]	
Spenser	(xx li.; xx li.)er xxxij li.

217 f.13. C

Stev'	v s.
Ward	v li.
Clerke	v li.
Jas wyf	xx [*s.*]
Wodward	xxij s. x d.

218 f.13. D [*1545*]

In the whit lether bage the xxixth daye of Marche in gold and sylver	lxxj li. xv s. viij d.
and leyd owt for xx kyne[31]	xij li. vj s. viij d.

[28] The items on this page (**216-8**) are probably all notes for the 1545 accounts.
[29] Cf. **221** (1546), when he was forgiven 25s.
[30] Cf. **215**.
[31] On 27 March 1545 (**12**).

and for iij kyne[32]	xxxviij s.
Of Jhon Marshe	vj li. x s.
Of my brother	xj li.
Of Strylles	[*blank*]
Wetherhoges	[*blank*]
Asheford[33]	xx li.; xx li.
Perynall	[*blank*]
Gryffyn	xl s.
Felles[34]	xxvj s. iij d.
Woll	xx li.; ix li. vj s. viij d.
Of Forster[35]	iiij li. xij s.

219 f. 74 v. B [*1545*][36]

[*Top margin*]	
Anthoni Cope	viij li. vj s. viij d.
Jhon Popill	xiij li. vj s. viij d.
[*Top left corner*]	
Throkmorton	xl li.
Gyfford	xij li. xij s.
Marshe	xiij li. vj s. viij d.
My brother	v li. ij s.
Gyfford	vij li. xij s. viij d.
[*Bottom left, in two columns*]	
Hygyns	ij^{c} li.
Throgmorton	(lxx li.)^{er} xl li.
Marshe	xiij li. vj s. viij d.
Gyfford	xxij li. xij s. viij d.
(Grey	x li.)^{er}
Gyfford	vij li. xij s. viij d.
Mr. Anthony Cope	viij li. vj s. viij d.
[*Second column*]	
Rent to my Lady	vj li. [x] s.
Item Mr. Cok	xv li.
For tythes	iij li.

220 f. 12 v. C [*Payments, 1545*][37]

Delyvered my cosyn Thomas Spenser in part of payment of iiij quarter of whet the xv daye of Marche at xvj d. the stryke	xl s.

[32] On 20 March (**12**).
[33] Presumably the two halves of a fine, one being still unpaid in **214**.
[34] Cf. those sent to Badbye (**51**), whose value is given as xxvj s. ij d.
[35] Perhaps from Coventry, cf. **221**.
[36] Several entries match with **213–4**.
[37] Datable from the Benevolence, collected in the first few months of 1545; *L. & P. Henry VIII*, XX, passim.

Delyvered the vijth of Aprill to Frysby for rent for my Lady Belknap	xl s.
Item the xxth of Marche to Burbery for the Kyng (hys)^{er} for my benevolence	xxx s.
Paid to my Lady Belknap for rent dew at Mydsomer	vj li. x s.
Paid for the subsydye	x s.

221 f. 71.[38] Dettes dew unto Peter Temple at and after the iiijth of Octobre in the xxxviijth yere of Kyng Henry the viijth [*1546*]

*Inprimis Father Carter oweth for x wethers	xx s. xx d.
Item[39] Henry Petyver oweth (for)^{er} money to hym lent	xxv s.
[*Margin*] Memorandum I have forgeven hym	
*Item lent to Jhon[40] Brokes	xxviij s.
Item Nycholas Myles oweth for a horse	xxiij s. iiij d.
*Item Jhon Foster my baly at Coventre apon a byll	xxx s.
Item Thomas Gryffin of Compton oweth	xx s.
Item Wylliam Robyns	iij s. iiij d.
Item Jhon Herytage of Kingston	xxx s.
Item lent unto Stele of Ichington	iij li.
Item lent unto Wagstaffe	iij li.
Item lent unto Cutbart Temple	xx s.
Item lent hym money that I payd to Mistris Onle for hym	xxxv li. vj s. viij d.
Item Mr. Wylliam Gyfford oweth	xij li. xij s. viij d.
[*Margin*] Resceyved x li.	
Item delyvered to Thomas Gryffyn for my brother	xx s.
Item Rychard Griffin my servant ows for xxviij yews cullyng[41]	lvj s. viij d.
[*Margin*] Resceyved xxj s. viij d.; item xiij s.	
Item the x of October remayneth of myne in Higs handes	iij li. vj s. viij d.
and for a cow that came not to my handes	xiij s. iiij d.
and my brother Jukell[42] delyvered Hygyns	xl s.
Item delyvered to Thomas Gryffyn for my brother	xxxiij s.
(Item Worle[?] of Harbery ows me	xx s.)^{er}
Item Profytt ows	iiij s.
Item Thomas Phelps oweth for v^{xx} and j wether yews[43]	x li. ij s.
[*Margin, with a pointing hand*] Resceyved xx s.	
Item lent Cuthbert the last of Octobre	viij li.
Item lent Jhon Petyfer the xvjth of Decembre	xx li.
Item lent to Thomas Gryffyn the xixth of Decembre	xx s.

[38] Most entries are marked in the margin +, presumably as they were paid off. Those not so marked are asterisked here.

[39] Pointing hand in the margin.

[40] Repeated in MS.

[41] Cf. 58.

[42] Jekyll (Pedigree 4).

[43] Cf. 55.

[f. 71 v.]

Item lent to Stoneley the xxvijth of Decembre	iij li.
Item lent to Thomas Makepes the xvjth of January [*1547*]	xl s.
Item lent to Clarke of Compton by Gryffin	iiij s.
Item lent to Cuthbard the xxviijth of January	iiij li.
Item lent to [*blank*] Haws the xxvijth of Febryary	liij s. iiij d.
Item lent to the warenner the iij^{d} of Aprill	iij s. iiij d.
Lent to Profett apon hys woll at ij severall tymes	iij li. vj s. viij d.
Item to the same Profet apon his said woll	xxxiij s. iiij d.
*Delyvered to Thomas Burbery for v^{xx} lamz	xij li. x s.
Layd owt the xvjth of May for my brother for a bull	xvj s.
Layd owt for Cutbard to my Lady Spenser	xx s.
Lent to Thomas Phelps the [*blank*] of August	iij li.
Leyd owt for the churche for Wagstaff[44]	iij li.
Lent to Thomas Makepes the xxiijth of (Octobre)^{er} Novembre	xl s.
Wylliam Palmer of Chadeshunt	xxxv s.
James Clerke of Compton for xvij wethers	xxxxj s.
Lent to Haws the xxviijth of (October)^{er} Novembre	xl s.
*Delyvered to Wagstaff, paid the churche chalyse	xij s.
*Item delyvered to Wagstaff, Thomas Makepes and Wylliam Brokes the resydew of the money for the sayd chalyce	iij li. vj s. viij d.
Delyvered to Messengre to ley owett for woll	iiij s.
Lent to Thomas Makepese the xxvij of Novembre	l s.

[*1548*]

Lent to Mr. Hickman the xxiiijth of Octobre anno ij^{do} regni regis Edwardi vj [*1548*]	xl s.
Jamz Clerke oweth me for xij kyne[45]	ix li. xvij s. vj d. qr.
Resceyved in part of payment of xl s. and for a saddell iiij s., and for Jhon Temples bord vj s. viij d.	
Item Jamz oweth me for a blake pyed cow	xix s.
Item Thomas Hygynson oweth	xxj s.
Item lent to Cuthbard Hauwes of Eathrop [?]	xl s.
(Item lent to James Clarke	xx s.)^{er}

222 f. 75. B [*Debts due, 1546*][46]

[*Column 1*]

Cayster [? *Carter*]	xx s.
Gryffyn[47]	xxx s.

[44] He was probably one of the churchwardens.
[45] Cf. 29 and 226.
[46] Apart from one entry (Spenser), these are in 221.
[47] *xx s.* in 221.

Robyns	iij s. iiij d.
Herytag	xxx s.
[*Column 2*]	
Petyver	xxv s.
Jhon Brokes	(xxxv s.)^{er} xxviij s.
Myls	xxiij s. iiij d.
Foster	xxx s.
[*Column 3*]	
Stoneley	iij li.
Spenser	xxij s.
Cutbart	xx s.

223 f. 74. A [*Account with Anthony Ashefeld, 1546*][48]

Delyvered to Mr. Anthonye Ashefeld xj tode xxv lb. at xiij s. the tode	vij li. xij s. vj d. ob.
Item vj li. x s. dew at the Annunciacion of Our Lady [*25 March*] anno xxxvij Henrici viij [*1546*] remayneth unpayd for a quarters rent of the Old Lesse	vj li. x s.
Item paid for Mr. Anthoni Ashefeld for the quindysume[49] of the Old Lesse dew anno predicto	viij s.
Item vj li. x s. dew at the fest of Syent Johanne Baptiste [*24 June*] xxxviij Henrici viijth remaynth unpayd for a quarters rent of the Old Lesse	vj li. x s.
Item I payd for the sayd grownd at Mychelmas	vj li. x s.
Item payd at Christmas for the same	vj li. x s.

224 f. 70. B Redy Mone the xxth of Marche anno regni regis Edwardi primo [*1547*]

Delyvered to Hygyns at dyvers tymes[50]	lxvij li.
Mr. Gyfford for my brother and Cuthbard oweth	xx li.
Mr. Grey	xx li.
and the same Mr. Grey	xiiij li.
Cosyn Spenser	xx li.
Phelps[51]	x li. ij s.
In gold	xvij li.
In besse of the last yers as I suppose	xlv li.
Of my wyfes	iij li. vj s. viij d.
For my sorell colt	iij li.
Of Mr. Anthony Cope	xlvj s. viij d.
From Hygyns for Coventre rent	viij li.
	Summa ij^{c}xxix li. xv s. iij d.

[48] As well as buying wool, he seems to have been collecting rent for Lady Belknap.
[49] Tax of one fifteenth part.
[50] As in **21**.
[51] For sheep (**71**).

225 f. 82. E [*Probably 1547–8*]

De Spenser	xvij li.
De Grey	xx li.
To Mr. Coke	xvij li. x s.[52]
To dod[53] Belknap	xiij li.
Et sic remanet	l s.

226 f. 70. C [*Account with James Clarke, 1548*]

Scriptum xxiiijth die Martii anno regni regis Edwardi vjth iij^{do} [*1549*][54]

Memorandum that Jamz Clarke oweth me for xij kyne	ix li. xvij s. iiij d.
Item for xlj yews at ij s. vij d. the pece. Summa	v li. ix s.
Item for xx^{ti} yews at ij s. the pec	xlj s.
[*Total*]	xviij li. vj s. iiij d.
Item for my nether Rame Close dew at Christmas last	xx s.
Item for my nether Rame close dew at Lammas	xvj s. viij d.
[*Total*]	xxxvj s. viij d.[55]
Resceyved in part of payment herof	xl s.
Item for a saddell and Jhon Temples bord	x s. viij d.
Item v kyne	iiij li.
Item iij tode wolle	lj s.
Item resceyved di. quarter barley	iij s. iiij d.
Item resceyved vj quarter malt	xxx s.
[*Margin*] Item resceyved v qr. malt at xj s. viij d. the quarter and j quarter at xv s. iiij d. the quarter. Summa	iij li. xiij s. viij d.
Item for the overplus of a noxe	x s.
Item for mowing the medow	xx s.
Summa (xij li. iiij s.)^{er}	xv li. xvij s. viij d.

227 f. 74. C

Resceyved of Jamz Clarke di. quarter barle	ij s. iiij d.
Item vj quarter of malt	xxx s.

228 f. 73 v. C

Memorandum that all thinges recevyd and accompyt and allowed betwene Jamz Clerke and me the xxth of Marche anno iij^{o} regni regis Edwardi vjth [*1549*], he oweth vij li. xij s. iiij d.

229 f. 69 v. A [*1548, probably early in the year*]

Lent to Thomas Spensr	xxx li.

[52] This is the best reading, but it is possible that the figure was amended to *xxj li. ij s.*, which would give the correct final total.

[53] For dead? Lady Belknap probably died in June 1547 (p. 29).

[54] The account, however, refers to 1548; see **61**.

[55] *xxvj s. viij d.* in MS.

Lent to Thomas Makepes	xl s.
Lent to Mistrys Wylls	v li.
Leyd owt for my brother	x li.
Delyvered Hygyns[56]	xlix li. x s.
Delyvered to Wyll Brokes against his woll[57]	xl s.; x li.; xiiij li.; xl s.
Paid to the men of Harbery	xlvj s. vij d.
Lent my brother	x li.
Lent Wylliam Phelps	xx li.

230 f. 77 v. B [*Account with Cuthbert Temple, 1548*]

Resceyved of Cutbart Temple	lxxx li.
Wherof delyvered to Mistris Onele for hym	(xxij)^{er} xxij li. xiij s. iiij d.
Item to Mistris Onele for hym more	xx li.

Item there dothe remayne in my hand the ixth of Octobre anno ij^{do} Edwardi vj^{ti} [*1548*] xxxvij li. vj s. vij d., as apperyth by hys byll of reconyng datyd the daye and yere above sayd, wherof he borowed agayne of me the same daye iij li.

231 f. 24 v. B Dettes dew unto Peter Temple the vjth of May anno iij^{tio} regni regis Edwardi vjth [*1549*]

Inprimis Cutbart Temple oweth me as apperyth by iij severall obligacions	j^{c}lxxxxij li.
Item[58] the sayd Cutbard oweth me as apperyth by a nother byll of hys hand	(j^{c})^{er} lxx li.
Item Bryan of Wytney oweth me	xxviij li. xiij s. iiij d.
Thexecutors of Jhon Petyver owe me[59]	x li.
Jhon Warner of Ratle oweth me	(xl li.; xxvj li.)^{er} x li.
viij oxen of the last yere	xvj li.
Delyvered Hygyns to by besse	(lvij li.)^{er} lxxxxj li. 3s. ij d.
Delyvered for woll	lvj li.
Mr. Hyckman oweth me[60]	xl s.; item xxvj s. viij d.
Leyd owtte my selfe for besse about[61]	xiij li.
Robyns of Tatchebroke oweth me for shepe	(xx li.)^{er} x li.
My cheyne in Mr. Geys handes[62]	xxv li. x s.
Item ther ys owyng me for cullyng shepe of the last yeres as apperyth in the end of the boke[63] about	(lxv li.)^{er} xxxiij li.
Summa	v^{c}lxxxx li.

[56] On 25 March 1548 (**26**).

[57] See **86**.

[58] This and the next entry boxed together with the erased sum *xvij li. ix s. viij d.* written against them.

[59] Cf. **221** (f. 71).

[60] Cf. **221** (f. 71 v).

[61] Cf. **33**.

[62] Boxed, with *liij s. iiij d.* against it.

[63] Probably f. 65. B (**62**).

Whereof:

I owe unto the Lordes for rent past	xlvj li.
Item for rent which shalbe dew at Mydsomer next	xxv li.
Item to Mr. Hyckman	xxv li. iiij s.; paid vij li.
Item I owe the Lordes apon my accompt	xlvj li.
Summa j^{c}xxj li. iiij s. and so rest clere	iiij^{c}lxviij li. xvj s.

232 f. 24. C Petit dettes dew unto Peter Temple the vjth of Maye anno iij^{tio} regni regis Edwardi vjth [*1549*]

Jhon Myls of Harbery and the other men with hym owe me for hey[64]	xxx s.
Item the same Myls oweth apon a recnyng	xxiiij s. iiij d.
Jamz Clark[65]	xxxv s.; resceyved j oxe, xxiiij s. iiij d. and viij d. in money
(Memorandum Sir Anthony Cope oweth me	v li.)^{er}
Sawll of Pyllarton oweth	xx s.
(Thomas Haws)^{er} Robart Haws of Ulthrop[60]	xl s.
Thomas Makepes	xxvj s. and [*blank*]
Wylliam Palmer of Chadshunt[60]	(xxxij s. viij d.; iiij li.)^{er} xx s.
Jhon Warner of Ratle for heye	xxxvj s. viij d.
(Mr. Hyckman and Horwood of Marsheton for hey	liij s. iiij d.)^{er}
Dyck Shepard[66]	xiij s. iiij d.
Herytage de Kyngton	xx s.
Mr. Hyckman for hey	xvij s. ix d.
Paid to my Lady Spenser Wormleygton for my brother	iij li.
Item lent my cosyn Thomas Spenser	v li.
Lent Grene, Mr. Dannetes man	ij s.

233 L. 31 a. E 4 die June anno iij^{tio} Edwardi vjth [*1549*][67]

Cutbard	xvij li. ix s. viij d.
Petyver	x li.
Jhon Warner	xl li.
viij oxen	xvj li.
Mr. Hickman	xl s.; xxvj s. viij d.
[Rob]yns de Tachebroke	xx li.; x li.
Leyd owt for woll	lvj li.
Leyd owt for besse	xj li.
Delyvered Hygyns for by besse	lxxiij li.
For cullyng shepe	lvj li.
Cutbard	Clxxxxij li.
Mr. Grey	liij s. iiij d.

[64] Cf. **155**.
[65] Cf. **226** for the ox.
[66] For wool, cf. **86**.
[67] A revised version of the preceding item.

Item I have in gold	xx li.
Summa	v^c xvj li. iij s.
Unde:	
I owe to the Lordes for rente which shal be dew at Mydsomer next	xxj li. x s.
Item to Mr. Hickman	xxv li. iiij s.
Summa	xlvj li. xiij s.
Et sic rest clere	iiij^c lxix li. ix s.

234 S. 6. D [*About 1561*]

Sens Mychelmas

Resceyved Hugh Haryson	
In redy money	iij li. (x s.)[er] ij s.
Of Gyfford	xxvij li.
Of Medes	xiij li.
Sp'	xl s.
Ottes	iiij li.
Fels	ix s. iiij d.
Brodgat	vj li.
Larrell	xv s.
Of Wryght	x s.
	51 li. 16 s. 4 d.

235 S. 6. F [*About 1561*]

Aken	iij li. vj s.
Bracebryge	vj s. viij d.
(Medes	xiij li.)[er]
Hyerns	iij li. v s.
Densfeld	iiij li.; resceyved x s. and iiij quarters befe
(Fox xl s.)[er] Fox	v li.
Letherborow	iiij li.
Mecote	vj li. xv s.
Dentun	xiij li.
(Gyfford	xxvij li.)[er]
lent back to Chaple xvj s.	
Capenherst and Lane	xx li. x s.; resceyved ...
Love	iiij li. x s.
Smythe	v li.
Habone and Corton	vj li. xiij s. iiij d.
Wylworth	xxx s.
Erytage	xl s.
Ottes	iiij li. xiij s. iiij d.
Lent Wylkyns	xx s.
	18 li. 1 s. 8 d.
	90 li. 7 s. 8 d.
	6 li. 14 s. 4 d.

236 S. 6. H[68] Candlemas [*2 Feb.*] 1561 [*/2*]

Thys is for	In gould	CClvj li. ij s.
the purchase	Item in sylver	lxxx li.
of Francton	Item of Spenser	Cxxxiij li. vj s. viij d.
	Item of Laddge	Cxxxvj li. x s. *C li.*
	Summa	vj^{c}vj li. iij s. viij d.
	Carpender oweth	xxviij li. *xviij li. to be paid at May Day*
	Oneleye and Newsam	l li. *x li.; vj li. xiij s. iiij d.*
This must	Butterfeld	xlj li. vj s. viij d. *xiiij li. (xiij s.)^{er}; xiij s. iiij d.*
serve for the		
storinge of	Byshoppe	v li.
Morebarne	My heyffers owe me	xxx li.
	Carter	xl li. *xv li.*
	Carpender *at May Daye*	xiij li. vj s. viij d. *and at Mychelmas vj li. xiij s. viij d.*
	Humferye	x li.
	Summa	CCxvij li. xiij s. iiij d.
	Item my wether hogges	[*blank*]
	Welsborne	v li.
	Hudmith in the lac	x li.
Thys is to serve	Stevens	liij s. iiij d. *Resceyved xliij s. iiij d. Resceyved x s.*
for parte of		
my expenses	Alen	xliij s.
between Our	Eritage	liij s.
Lady Daye and	Hause	xl s.
Mycaelmas	Westeleye	xl s.
Day	For barlye	ix li.
	Delyvered Rychard for my brother	vij li.
	Frayne	vj li. vij s.
	[*Sum*]	xlviij li. xvj s. iiij d.
	Item of Burbery	*v li.*
	My heye	*(vj li.)^{er} xiij li.*
	The Petiver close and croft	*iiij li.*
	[*Sum*]	xv li.
	A hyppt cowe	*xxxv s.*
	The geldyng	*iij li.*
Thus much	I owe Pope	xl li. *Item paid hym*
I owe	To Megge	x li.
	To Petiver	xxviij li.
	Mr. Lee	CC li.
	[*Sum*]	CClxxviij li.

[68] The numerous alterations and additions are in paler ink, and are shown here by italics. Reproduced as Pl. VI.

	To Rychard	*xxxj li. x s.*
		CCCix li. x s.
	Shakerley Alis	*xlviij* [*li.*]
	Mr. Coke	*xl li.*
	Shakerlye and Cok	*lxxxviij li.*
	Summa	CCClxxxviij li. x s.
And thus much I have to discharge the premises[69] and the remenaunt for the kepinge of my house which is xxv li.	To resceive of Bysshoppe	lxxx li.
	Of Newsam	xliij li.
	My woll owes me by estimacion	Cxx li.
	Bysshoppe	xl li.
	Mr. Lyght	xx li.
	[*Sum*]	CCCiij li.

So I have to fynd my howse and for other expenses as it may appere by this accompte iiij^{xx}viij li. xvj s. iiij d.

. . . *of Mr. Lee*	*v li.*
. . . . . .	*vij li.*

237 S.6. H: dorse Money resceyved sens I came from London videlicet at Candelmas time anno 1561[/*2*]

Inprimis of Stephyns	xliij s. iiij d.
Item the money that Rychard had which Hyggynson sent me for Coventre rent dew at Mychelmas last	vij li.
Item of Botrefeld	xxvij li. xiij s. iiij d.
Item my Lady Welsborne	v li. xiij s. iiij d.
Item of Carpender	x(iiij)^{er} li.
Item resceyved of Mr. Shakerley the vjth of Aprill	xiij li.
Resceyved of Rychard for a hypt cowe	xxxiij s. iiij d.
Resceyved of Mr. Lodge	xxxvj li. x s.
and for Rychard	xxxj li. x s.

[S.6. H dorse][70]

Carpender	vj li. xiij s. iiij d.
Frayn	vj li. vj s.
Butterfeld	vj li. xiij s. iiij d.
Byshop	xiij li. vj s. viij d.
Shakerley	xlij li. and v li. x s.
Newsam	xliij li.
Horsman	viij li.
S.okers rent	xj li.

[69] Perhaps the debts just listed.

[70] The primary use of this page was the shopping list S.6.I (**185**), in a column down the left side. The part of **237** up to this point is written in a block to the right of **185**. It apparently continues in the following section, written in a column below **185**; none of the names here duplicate those in the earlier part.

Hawse	l s.
Warnder [?]	iiij li.
Bramfeld	iiij li.
besse	[*blank*]
Mr. Lyght	
Westley	
Lylworth	
rent at Dassett	

238 S. 6. J[71] Dettes dew primo Januarii 1563[*/4*]

[*Margin*] Nota that Whetell dyd owe then lxxx li. whych ys now paid

Shakerley	Cxx li.
Newsam	iij li.
Lyght	xv li.
Busshoppe	xx li.
Butterfeld	iij li. vj s. viij d.
Frayne	vj li. vij s.
Hiernes in [*or* and] Westeley	xiij li. x s.
Tyrell	xxvj li. xiij s. iiij s.
Dannet	l li. and xiij li. xix s.
Woll	Ciiij^{xx} x li.
Bease and Brokes	x li.
Williaston	xxvj s. viij d.
Onley	lv li.
Allen	vj li. vj s. viij d.
Carpender	xvij li. x s.
Allen eres[72]	xxvij li.
Duncombe	x li.
Throkmorton	C li.
Pergiter [?]	xxv li.
Cotesford	xv li.
In specijs	C li.
spennde	xl li.
In money	lvj li.
In spece in Lunsar [?]	iij li.
Ryser [?]	vij li.

Summa Mlxxiiij li. (xix s. iij d.)^{er} xiiij s. iiij d.

239 f. 3 v.[73] [*Undatable*]
[*Legal Charges*]

[Ch]arges	vij li. xiij s. iij d.
To the Kyng	xx li.
To Pawlet for his mat^{r}ess	xiij li. vj s. viij d.

[71] In running text in the MS.

[72] Heirs?

[73] Badly rubbed. This is probably an early account, from its position in the volume. The transaction to which it refers has not been identified.

Indenturs of bargain for the Kyng	xxvj s. viij d.
Letters Pawles	xliij s. iiij d.
Byl assyred	iij s. iiij d.
Then.ollyng	ij s. iij d.
Charges of ryding to Mr. ...	xl s.
Indenturs betwene Pawlot and Tuke	vj s. viij d.
Summa	xlvj li. (vj)^{er} iij s. iiij d.
Item x li. over and above al thes charges to be payd to Mr. Tuke	x li.

240 f. 70 v. B

Gardener of Kyngston owes me	ij s. x d.
Lodbroke of Compton oweth me	xij s. vj d.
A man of Rodwey	xviij d.
Profyt of Northend oweth for a quarter of a cow	ij s. viij d.
Item Thomas Griffyn for the same	ij s. viij d.
Colman of Radwey[74]	viij d.

241 f. 82 v. G

Mistris Oneley	j^{c}lviij li. xiiij s. ix d.
Mr. Lee	j^{c}ij li. xij s.

242 L. 43. a [*Letter to Peter Temple*]

Cosyn Tempel thes be to sartyfy yew that I wos wytt Mr. Wade for the mone [*money*] so that at thes tyme he can not help yow to no mone, for hall ys mone is in is costemors handes thell [*till*?] it be Lords Ester and[75] then he wol make spede for yow if there be no remede, bot he wolde fane have it yere hout.

243 f. 6. B [*Draft bond, perhaps provided by Peter Temple*][76]

That yf the within bownded Thomas Marten his heires, executors, or assignes do discharge acquite and save harmeles the (seyd)^{er} within namyd Nycholas Frekelton and Alis his wyff, (against all men)^{er} their heires, executors and assignes, against all men of for and concernyng all maner of dettes, dutyes and demandes comyng or growyng be reson of eny act or actes done by Thomas Underhill of Shustock in the county of Warwyke, gentleman, decessyd, be reson wherof the sayd Alys shold or myght in eny wyse be

[74] *Of* repeated in MS. This is probably for quit-rent (cf. 155).

[75] *And* repeated in MS.

[76] The identity of Thomas Underhill is rather uncertain. The family has been studied in great detail (J. H. Morrison, *The Underhills of Warwickshire* (Cambridge: privately printed, 1932)). There was no Thomas of Shustoke, and the subject must either be *William* of Hunningham, who had estates in Shustoke and whose will was proved on 2 May 1544 with Thomas Martin as one of the executors, or *Thomas* of Hunningham, died *c.* 1520, whose will was the subject of a dispute in the Court of Common Pleas in 1545–6.

chargid as executor unto the seyd Thomas Underhill, and also yf the sayd Thomas Marten do satisfye, content and paye all suche sums of money as (was dew to eny man by)^{er} (the seyd)^{er} Thomas Underhill [dyd] at the tyme of his dethe or eny tyme before, and also yf the sayd Thomas Marten do (performe and delyver)^{er} satisfye, content and paye all suche legacyes and bequestes comprised in the last wyll and testament of the sayd Thomas Underhill, accordyng to the true intent and meanyng of the same (...)^{er}, that then this present obligacion to be voyd and of none effecte or weight[?].

16. *Jottings*[77] (Pl. IV)

Peter Temple's account book is not completely made up of formal accounts and less formal memoranda. Many pages have disjointed phrases and Latin tags, written in a more formal style than Peter's usual cursive hand, but occasionally running on without change of ink into reckonings in his normal writing. We must see him sitting at his table, turning the pages, while considering other matters, and lighting on a margin or gap which he might fill equally with a jotting or a scribbled note of reckoning.

Through them we get our only glimpse of Peter Temple the man, behind the business-like grazier. He remembered particularly, and perhaps with nostalgia, the old Latin liturgy with which he had been brought up,[78] and he had a feeling for the resounding titles of his sovereign (f. 84b). His thoughts strayed back to his schooldays, to his Latin irregular verbs (f. 78 v. B), and perhaps to his writing exercises (f. 74. D). When John leaned over his shoulder to say 'Write my name, father', he provided 'Jhon Temple ys a good boye' (f. 64 v. C). He scribbled scraps of doggerel (f. 74 v. C; f. 82. G) and he liked the sound of bagpipes (f. 82. G); perhaps they reminded him of the time he spent as organ scholar at Oriel.

[77] References in this section are to the folios within item **244**. I would like to thank Kevin Down of the University of Birmingham for going to considerable effort to identify the Latin phrases for me.

[78] It was superseded in stages between Easter 1548 and Whit Sunday 1549, though it was restored by Queen Mary.

JOTTINGS

244[79] [f. 1. D]

Dominus vobiscum. Et cum spiritu tuo[80]
Dominus vobiscum[80] In dominio[81]
Consider without eny dobte he that ys yn stockes
lege peccatorum[82] 14 li.; 15 li. Dominus vobiscum[80]
Johannis Spensar In domino confido[83] Dominus vobiscum[80]
Dominus vobiscum
Ryght honorable Et gloria[84] Ryght honorable
honor domine nobilis, domine honorabilis[85]
Idem spiritu Huius Idem Quatu'[86]
Henry Yardley of Rodford

[f. 6. C]

Henery the eight
Be hit known to all men by these presentes that I Peter Temple have resavyd of Rychard

[f. 7. B]

xlviij li. xviij s. ij d. (xl)[er] lxxxj li. xv s. v d.

[f. 7 v. C]

Fenite exultemus domino[87] domini

[79] These are collected under one item number, as they neither show any distinction in character, nor are individually datable. Most are difficult to read, and it is not always certain that they reproduce the Latin texts without idiosyncratic spellings.

[80] Versicle and response found throughout the Mass and Office.

V. *Dominus vobiscum.*	'The Lord be with you,
R. *Et cum spiritu tuo.*	And with thy spirit.'

[81] 'In demesne'.

[82] Not precisely identified, but probably an echo of Ps. 1, v. 1:

'*... Et in via peccatorum non stetit*'	'Nor stood in the way of sinners'

[83] Ps. 10, v. 2 (Vulgate):

'*In Domino confido,*	'In the Lord put I my trust;
quomodo dicitis animae meae:'	how say ye then to my soul?'

[84] The end of the Canon of the Mass

'*omnis honor et gloria*'	'All honour and glory.'

[85] 'Noble lord, honorable lord'.

[86] These words (the third of which is probably *quatuor*), were repeated with *coquine*, and perhaps represent a standard writing exercise. *Jhesus* and *Maria*, also frequent, were commonly used as dedications at the top of pages at this period.

[87] Ps. 94, vv. 1–2 (Vulgate); this psalm, interspersed with an antiphon, made up the Invitatory, said at the beginning of the night office (Matins or Nocturns).

'*Venite, exultemus Domino*;	'O come let us sing unto the Lord;
Jubilemus Deo salutari nostro;	Let us heartily rejoice in the strength of our salvation.
Preoccupemus faciem ejus in confessione,	Let us come before his presence with thanksgiving;
Et in psalmis jubilemus ei;	And shew ourselves glad in him with psalms.'

[f. 8 v. B]

Deus in adiutorium meum intende domine ad adiuvandum me festina
Gloria patri et filio et spiritui sancto[88]
Venite exultemus domino[87]
[*transverse*] Deus in adiutorium meum intende domine ad adiuvandum me festina. Gloria patri et filio et spiritui.[88] Fiat[89]

[f. 10. C][90]

In adiutorium[88]

Predictus Henry the viijth by the grace of God, of England, France and Ireland, Kyng, Defender of the Faithe and in erthe the Supreme Hede of the Churche of England

Henrico	Preoccupemus faciem eius in confessione et in psalmis jubilemus [*ei*][87]
Henrico octavi dei gratia Rex	Venite exultemus domino
octavo Rex	Jubilemus Deo salutari nostre[87]

x li.; xx li.; xxxiij li. vij s. viij d.; lxvj s. xiij s. iiij d.
The bay mare; the bay colte; Lyard; whit curtoll; Lase; the bay geldyng; the brown bay clot;[91] the grey nage

Sursum corda	Habemus ad Dominum[92]	
Et in psalmis jubilemus[87]	Oremus preceptis[93]	
et in	Dominus vobiscum[80]	Preceptis[93]
Exultemus domino[87]	Jubilemus[87]	Dominus vobiscum[80]
Deo salutari[94]	Cum spiritu tuo[80]	
Jhone Nashe	xj s. iiij d.	

[f. 11. E]

Be hitt known unto all menn

[88] The versicle and response at the beginning of all the hours of the Divine Office.

'V. *Deus in adiutorium meum intende,*	'O God come to my aid.
R. *Domine ad adiuvandum me festina.*	O Lord, make haste to help me.
Gloria Patri et Filio et Spiritui Sancto.'	Glory be to the Father, and to the Son, and to the Holy Ghost.'

[89] 'Let it be'.

[90] Reproduced on Pl. IV.

[91] For *coit*. This series is in a column down the right side of the page; it might be a list of horses taken in for pasture.

[92] Versicle and response in the introductory dialogue of the Preface of the Mass.

V. *Sursum corda*	'Lift up your hearts.
R. *Habemus ad Dominum*	We lift them up unto the Lord.'

[93] Introduction to the Lord's Prayer, immediately following the Canon of the Mass.

'*Oremus. Praecepitis salutaribus moniti*'.	'Let us pray, taught by the precepts of salvation.'

[94] An echo of the piece quoted in footnote 87.

[f.12 v. D]

40 li. 7 s. 9 d. 181 li. 13 s. 4 d.	194 li. 14 s. 11 d.

[f.14. C]

[iij s.] iiij d.; ij s. viij d. iiij li. xv s. v d.	Jhesus Maria xxxv li. iiij s. vj d.	xl li. viij s.

[f.16. C]

Dominus vobiscum[80]

[f.18. E]

Dominus	Mariam

[f.20. B]

Jhesus

[f. 24 v. D]

Venite exultemus Domine[87]

[f. 44 v. B; also f. 47. B]

Jhesus

[f. 46. B]

Jhesus Maria Amen	Dominis vobiscum[80]	Dominus vobiscum

[f. 48 v. B]

Jhesus Maria

[f. 59 v. C]

Jhesus Marias Annunc'	xx d.; xij d.; xx d.

[f. 64. C]

Jhesus

[f. 64 v. C]

Jhesus xxxvj li. xv s.	Dominus vobiscum Jhon Temple ys a good boye	Et cum spiritu[80]

[f. 70. D]

The tyme may come that I shall

[f. 73 v. D]

The tyme may — Dominus vobiscum et cum spiritu tuo[80]
Henry the viijth
Dominus vobiscum et cum spiritu tuo
by the grace of God, Kyng of Inglond

[f. 74. D]

Huius Item Quatu' Quatu' Jhesus Coquine Huius Item Quatu' Jhesus Coquine Jhesus[85]

[f. 74 v. C]

In Domino confido[83]
Withowt eny dobte the catte ys in the cage. She came nott owt
In Domino confido[83]
Withowt eny dobt the catte ys in the cage. She came owt
Herytag

[f. 75. C]

Dominus vobiscum — Et cum spiritu
Domino oremus[95] — Dominus vobiscum

[f. 76 v. D]

Henry the viijth

[f. 77. D]

Henry Makepec

[f. 77 v. C]

Exultemus Domino[87]

[f. 78 v. B]

Dominus Deus[96]		fi finis			
Sum	I am[97]	Es	Thow art	Est	Hie ys
Sumus	We bie	Sont	They bee		

[95] 'Let us pray to the Lord', not in the Liturgy.
[96] 'Lord God'.
[97] Conjugation of *Sum*; *sont* is correctly sunt.

[f. 79 v. C]

The ixth of J . . .

[f. 82. F]

Memorandum that I James
Memorandum
Bullockes
Cum spiritu tuo[80]
Dominus vobiscum

Boll bolloke
Dominus vobiscum[80]
Noble quod
In Dei nominum[98]

Jhesus Maria
Bulluk
Dominus vobiscum
Spiritu tuo vobis

[f. 82. G]

viginti sexti
todullodull bagepypes
Noddye hoddy doddy, se the apishe [busi?] bodie

[f. 83. C]

Be hitt knowen unto all men by these presents

[f. 84a. B]

Unto the Father

[f. 84b.]

Henrie the viijth tres noble, honorable Emperor du Grand Brittayne, Roy d'Engleterre, de France, Ireland et Schottland, le puissand defenc' de Christen' et le supreme [tete] de l'aglise d'Angleterre, Ireland, [vicheng?] et totes les lieges.
Henri the viijth by the grace of God, King of Inglond, France and Irelond
Temple

[98] 'In the name of God', the standard beginning for a will.

PART III: THE LATER YEARS

1. *Branching out: Tenant to Landowner*

AFTER 1550, Peter Temple gradually gave up using his account book, and apart from the few accounts on loose sheets, we lose their direct evidence for his farming and his finances. However, the pattern had been set, and his sheep continued to make their profit year by year.

He chose to put this profit into land, and it was this investment that transformed Peter Temple from a tenant to a landowner. His son John completed the build-up of the family estate.[1] The evidence of the transactions is very scattered, and Gay[2] feared that all trace might have been lost for some of them. However, after a wider search, almost all the purchases can be described fully. With at least two references identified for each, we can be reasonably confident that the picture is complete (with the possible exception of short-term loans). The table (p. 234) gives a brief chronological summary of the transactions, both by him and by John. This is brought up to 1580, when a rental compiled by John conveniently summarizes his holdings.[3]

Many of the early transactions involved Crown land, sales of which gave the outstanding opportunity for speculation and investment in the Tudor period. The first one of all shows just what a well-judged purchase could achieve. On 20 July 1549, Richard Fylde (or Field) and Ralph Woodward were granted a vast number of scattered pieces of land by the Crown. They included some property of the former Priory of Catesby, Northamptonshire, consisting of the rectory and tithes of Over Catesby. These brought in £17 6s. 8d. from a twenty-one-year lease made in 1537, but £13 17s. 0d. had to be paid out, principally for the vicar's salary. The price to Field and Woodward was calculated at twenty years' purchase, giving a total cost of £69 8s. 9d. On 20 January 1551, they re-sold it to Peter Temple. What he paid is uncertain as the deed merely states 'for good consideration', but it should not have enormously exceeded the cost to Field and Woodward, as they were certainly acting as regular middlemen in the transaction rather than as pure speculators.

[1] Gay, 1938, p. 384f. gives details of the later purchases.
[2] Ibid., p. 369.
[3] ST L8 B4 Temple Land, Berks.–Leics.

However, on 11 February 1553, Peter Temple sold it to a Northamptonshire man, Thomas Knight of Charwelton, for no less than £600. By now, of course, the twenty-one-year lease was nearing its end, and the clear annual value was probably £30 to £40, with the purchaser prepared to wait to get his profit when the lease fell in.[4]

Peter's next dealings in Crown lands were undertaken directly with the Augmentations Office, and show a consistent pattern. Each consisted of a substantial manor in Warwickshire, to which were appended a string of oddments. In 1554, for example, Peter Temple bought the manor of Oxhill (one of two in the parish), some land in Cropredy, Bloxham and Wardington (villages in north Oxfordshire and south Warwickshire), together with two houses in Buckingham, two in Warwick and a garden in Coventry. These at least were fairly near at hand, but other sales included land as far afield as Derbyshire and Kent. It may well be that the Augmentations Office was requiring prospective purchasers to take some odd lots off its hands as well as the major properties. On the other hand, all this property seems to have been sold off quite quickly.[5] Peter Temple may, therefore, have selected the properties himself, as suitable for re-sale The Warwickshire manors were dismembered, three or four smaller holdings being sold, presumably to their tenants, before the manor itself was disposed of. The exception was Marton (1557), where Peter Temple retained the manor, with some of the land.[6]

In all these transactions Peter Temple worked in partnership, once with his step-daughter's husband, Richard Petyfer,[7] and in the others with local gentry. Such partnerships are very characteristic of the principal dealers in Crown lands like Field and Woodward, who initially bought Over Catesby. Clearly, at this period we can count Peter Temple among them, after his first purchase made through intermediaries. Later dealings were perhaps not as spectacularly successful as his first, but no doubt they made satisfactory

[4] Particulars for Grant: P.R.O. E318/28/1608; Crown Sale: *Cal. Pat. Rolls Ed. VI* (ii), 351; Field and Woodward to Temple: P.R.O. C54/475, m. 16; Temple to Knight (counterpart) N.R.O. Temple Stowe, Box 40.

[5] Only a few of the sales required licences (recorded in the Patent Rolls), and details of the other sales have not come to light. However, apart from Marton and perhaps the Coventry garden, none remained with the Temples in 1580. The Buckingham houses they held then were acquired with their main Buckinghamshire property.

[6] His partner, Michael Cameswell, must certainly also have kept his own house, Newland, on the outskirts of Coventry, which was included in the last transaction. The full references are: Grants and Licenses to Alienate: *Cal. Pat. Rolls: Ed. VI*, 5, 75; *Philip and Mary*, 2, 227; 2, 229; 1, 363, 369, 482; 4, 216, 237, 242; *Elizabeth*, 2, 71; 1, 139. Quitclaim for Marton: Cameswell to Temple, ST Deeds List 2, folder 97 (2); recovery for same: ST L9 B9, Temple Land, Warws., 1561 (Easter 3 Eliz., R24).

[7] This relationship is slightly uncertain; see Pedigree 4.

profits. Just how much is not known. The purchase but not the selling prices are recorded; nor can we discover how much each partner contributed.

In between these Crown dealings, two concerned private individuals. The first was a rather curious transaction in which the Hampshire manor of Popham was bought for £540, and sold again six months later for £560.[8] There is no obvious reason for Peter Temple's involvement with this land, in contrast to the second. This involved four farms in villages very near Burton Dassett. They were bought in 1555, and three were sold quite soon, but a farm of half a yardland at Farnborough became the first property that Peter Temple kept.[9]

It was soon followed by much more important ones. The earliest followed the pattern of his original Burton Dassett interests, and was a lease of a large area of pasture. In this case it consisted of 542 acres at Morebarne Fields, near Lutterworth, Leicestershire.[10] In 1557, for a payment of £84, he obtained a forty-year lease at a rent of £37 a year.[11] This was not immediate, but was a reversion on the death of Frances, Duchess of Suffolk, which happened in 1561; it was then that Peter Temple made the allowance of £217 in his budget for stocking this property that has been discussed above (p. 207). This was certainly a very sound investment, and could be expected to produce £100 to £200 a year clear, like the Dassett lands. There is a suspicion that some sharp work underlay Peter Temple's acquisition of this lease. A copy of the text of a statute concerning unlawful retention by stewards is endorsed 'important for Morebarne Feilds', and an agreement was reached with the outgoing tenant, Edward Ferrys, Esquire, by which he should retain *the use* of half the land for two years.[12] It seems likely that Peter Temple had quietly obtained his lease, perhaps with the help of some special knowledge gained as steward to the Belknap heirs, when Ferrys had been confidently expecting to have it. The unusual agreement with him was probably undertaken as a compromise to avoid a legal battle. Twenty years later, in 1576, Peter was served in the same way by three Court hangers-on, all Grooms of the

[8] Both deeds were enrolled on the Close Rolls: P.R.O. C54/482, m. 6; C54/488, m. 39.

[9] Sold by Sir Thomas Vaux for £210; ST Deeds List 2, Box 36. Copy leases in ST L8 B9 Temple Lands., Warws., 1548; original in Deeds List 2, Box 36.

[10] ST L8 B4 Temple Lands, Leics., 1631, gives the area.

[11] *Cal. Pat. Rolls Philip and Mary*, 4, p. 15.

[12] ST L8 B4, Temple Land, Leics. The statute is given as 3 Henry VII, c12, but this seems to be incorrect, and the right reference cannot be identified.

Land Transactions Before 1580[a]

Date	*Place*	*Nature and Purchaser*	*Disposal (up to 1580) (1580*[b] *Rent in Parentheses)*
1551	Over Catesby, Northants.	Rectory (tithes); from Crown to Peter Temple	Sold, 1553
1552	Popham, Hants.	Manor; Peter Temple and Thomas Lee of Clatercote, Oxon.	Sold, 1553
1553	Butlers Marston and small properties in Middlesex and Kent	Manor; Crown to Peter Temple and Thomas Lee	Sold, 1553–5
1554	Oxhill and small properties in Warks., Bucks. and Oxon.	Manor; Crown to Peter Temple and Richard Petyfer	Oxhill sold 1559–61; others before 1580
1555	Avon Dassett, Farnborough, Northend	Four farms; Peter Temple	Farnborough retained (19s.); others sold before 1578
1557	Marton, Bubbenhall, Newland, lands in Derbys., Staffs. and Sussex	Manors (Marton and Sussex) and minor property; Crown to Peter Temple and Michael Cameswell of Newland, Coventry	Marton retained (£21); others sold (1557 in part).
1557	Morebarne Fields, Leics.	Reversion to lease of 500 acres pasture; Crown to Peter Temple	Entered on in 1561; retained (£7)
1557–60	Burton Dassett	1/3 manor; Peter Temple	Retained (£3 9s. 10d.)
1560	Burton Dassett	1/3 rectory; Peter Temple	Sold in 1560
1559	Bubbenhall	£8 6s. 8d. annual rent; Peter Temple	Sold, 1560
1565	Chadshunt	7 qr. wheat annual rent; John Temple	Retained; valued at £7 in 1580
1566	Henley-on-Thames, Oxon.	£20 mortgage; John Temple	Probably redeemed in one year
1566	Temple, Wolvey	£200 mortgage; Peter Temple	Probably redeemed in one year
1569	Hawling and Guiting, Glos.	£40 annual rent; Peter and John Temple	Disposed of between 1577 and 1580
1570	Hawling and Guiting, Glos.	£40 annual rent; Peter and John Temple	Retained (£40)

Land Transactions Before 1580[a] – continued

Date	Place	Nature and Purchaser	Disposal (up to 1580) (1580[b] Rent in Parentheses)
1571	Stowe, Bucks.	Lease of manor and lands; Peter Temple	Retained } (£105 16s.9d.)
1572	Lamport, etc., Bucks.	Lease of lands; John Temple	Retained }
1572	West Haddon, Northants.	£20 annual rent; John Temple	Retained (£20)
1574	Napton	Thirty acres land; Peter Temple	Sold by 1580
1577	Mollington, Oxon.	Lease of lands; Peter Temple	Retained (£1 6s. 8d.)
1578	Kineton	£12 annual rent; John Temple	Retained (£12)

[a] Detailed references in the text. When the vendor was the Crown, this is noted. Places are in Warwickshire if not otherwise stated.
[b] The 1580 rent is from ST L8 B4 Temple Land, Bucks.-Leics. It does not allow for any rents that had to be paid out, and it does not include the receipts from land kept in hand.

Bakehouse, who had obtained a reversion to Morebarne Fields and had to be bought out.[13]

The four years, 1557 to 1560, saw the most important transaction of all, which established Peter Temple as a property owner of manorial status rather than a tenant. He was able to buy one of the thirds of the manor of Burton Dassett itself, that belonging to the Dannet family. As well as the manorial rights themselves, which were not very valuable, this represented a third share in the 2,600 acres of the manor, which were bringing in £253 a year in rent. Mary Dannet had already divided her share, giving a portion to her younger son, Thomas;[14] it was this part that Peter Temple managed to obtain first, paying £972 13s. 0d. for it in 1557. The main transaction was completed in 1559 when Leonard Dannet, Mary's grandson, sold the remainder for £1,580.[15] One part of the manor was omitted from these sales, Hardwick, the former property of the Knights Hospitaller,

[13] P.R.O. C54/1009 is their quitclaim. E310/40/4 gives the Particular for Grant of the lease in 1576.

[14] Specified as Hallfield, Travers Field, and the lands occupied by William Broke. That it was her third share in the property is understood; ST49, f. 6.

[15] All these deeds are included in ST49 'Coppies of evidences concerning Burton Dassett', a volume written by Peter Temple. Related bonds are enrolled in P.R.O. C54/533, m. 46–46.

and Peter Temple obtained a third share of this in 1560.[16] In the same year he also bought Leonard Dannet's third part of the tithes of Burton Dassett, but this was almost immediately reversed, for reasons discussed in the next chapter.[17]

One property is missing from Peter Temple's purchases at this period, the manor of Frankton. As has been seen (p. 206), he allocated £606 to its purchase in 1562, but this was not the first interest he had shown in it. In 1557 it was included for him in Particulars for Grant provided by the Augmentation Office;[18] it was given an annual value of £19 8s. 10d., corresponding at the going rate of twenty-eight years' purchase to £544 7s. 4d. However, Frankton was crossed off the list before the total purchase price was calculated; no doubt Peter Temple could not afford it at that stage. His 1561 intention also came to nothing, and this we can connect with the problems he encountered at this period (see the next chapter). For the same reason, a clear gap developed between the conclusion of his purchase of Burton Dassett and his renewed activity of the 1570s.

The only investment by Peter Temple falling firmly into the 1560s is that involving Temple Hall in Wolvey, Warwickshire, which was of a very different type from the earlier ones. It consisted of a loan of £200, to be repaid in one year, secured on the land in question. John Temple also made a loan of this type, for £20, to one John Barnabye, who was perhaps one of his fellow students at Lincolns Inn; this also was to be repaid in a year.[19] The law and practice relating to mortgages was still rudimentary at this period, and the security of his lands to the mortgagor was very uncertain.[20] Thus these transactions, although properly drawn up in deeds of sale, must have been intended as short loans rather than as long-term mortgages. There is no evidence that either of these was not repaid. We should also note that these two deeds were enrolled on the Close Rolls, and

[16] P.R.O. C54/568; ST L8 B10, 11 May 1560. Thomas Wootton to Peter Temple. There are complications in the ownership of this land after its purchase by Cooke, Dannet and Wootton in 1553, not all of which are made clear in these deeds.

[17] P.R.O. C54/567: Leonard Dannet to Anthony Cooke. There is a remarkable valuation in ST L8 B10, Temple Land, Warws., *c.* 1560, which was probably made in relation to this. It suggested that the income from a third of the tithes would be £45 a year, by making some very optimistic assumptions, and by ignoring the out-goings. At forty years' purchase (an exceptionally long period), this gave a capital value of £1,832. In reality, in 1557, the full clear value had been £32 (see p. 166), giving the realistic value for one third at twenty years' purchase of £220, which was the actual price paid by Peter Temple.

[18] P.R.O. E318/42/2246.

[19] P.R.O. C54/721, item 51, Stayning to Temple: C54/709, item 12, Barnabye to Temple.

[20] Finch, 1956, p. 11.

if other such loans were not enrolled, then we could well know nothing about them.

In the 1570s, Peter and John Temple made use of a new form of investment, the purchase for a lump sum of a perpetual annuity. The first of these was bought in 1559, but was soon disposed of.[21] Next, in 1569, Peter and John received from Richard Stratford of Hawling, Gloucestershire, an annuity of £40 a year from his manors of Hawling and Guiting Power; six months later, for £500, he granted them a second £40.[22]

In the next few years, John Temple alone was involved in two similar transactions, securing £20 from West Haddon, Northamptonshire, for £200 and £12 from Kineton, Warwickshire, for £150.[23] As means of investment, these annuities had clear advantages. They were very secure, and the return of 8 to 10 per cent as good or better than could be obtained in other ways. They could, no doubt, be sold fairly easily, although most of these were retained for many years. They also must have been much easier to obtain than would be a manor or other property that was suitably placed and suitably profitable.

One annuity was of a different kind from the rest, the payment of seven quarters of wheat from the manor of Chadshunt. In the eighteenth century, a tradition was recorded:

> Some one of his Lordship's [Lord Cobham's] predecessors at Burton Dassett, and some one of Mr. Newsham's predecessors were merry together, and one of these Gentlemen was commending his Estate at Burton for Feding [feeding] the best of Oxen, the other for Growing the best of wheat at Chadshunt, upon which they thrown Dice that in case my Lord's predecessor won, Mr. Newsham's predecessor and his Successor(s) was to pay to the Temple family for Ever 7 Quarters of Chadshunt wheat, and in case Mr. Newsham's predecessor won, the Temple Family was to pay a fatt ox from Burton Dassett annually for Ever to the Newsham family.[24]

21 P.R.O. C54/576, Peter Temple to Anthony Cooke, reciting deed of 25 July 1559, Aurelius Gyles to Peter Temple. The following two deeds transfer parts of the same rent to Leonard Dannet and Thomas Wootton.

22 The second annuity is straightforwardly recorded in its purchase deed, ST Deeds List 2, folder 55, 10 February 1569/70. The first (17 September 1569) is only referred to in a re-grant by Henry Stratford of £20 and £19 19s. 0d. annuities, in exchange for the surrender in 1577 of the £40 (P.R.O. C54/1013; confirmed by George Stratford, N.R.O. Temple Stowe, Box 7/3A). This division must have been previous to its disposal, as in 1580 only the £40 was still received.

23 P.R.O. C54/897; C54/1052.

24 ST G Box 225 (43), letter from Leonard Lloyd to Mr. King, 1 January 1758. I thank George Clarke for this reference.

Confirmation from the original grant is impossible at it does not survive.[25] However, the fine of 1565 is between John Temple, then 23, and Walter Newsham, owner of Chadshunt. He was also a young man, perhaps only 20 and a fellow law student.[26] We can only conclude that the circumstances seem to fit the traditional tale, and that it is more plausible than the simple purchase of an annuity.

Not all Peter and John's investments in the 1570s were in annuities; Peter bought a small property in Napton, Warwickshire, described as a holding of 30 acres at his death, and obtained a lease of another in Mollington in north Oxfordshire.[27] However, much more important were two leases of land in Buckinghamshire, bought from one Thomas Gifford. They both related to former property of the Abbey of Osney, transferred at the Dissolution to the new see of Oxford, and the leases were for ninety-nine years, not due to expire until 1629. The first lease was for Stowe itself, the manor and rectory, and the other covered Lamport and Dadford (two other manors in Stowe parish) and other scattered property, including three houses in Buckingham.[28]

These leases provided one thing necessary for Peter Temple, a substantial property for his son John; indeed, the second lease was taken out by John himself. He settled at Stowe immediately, and thereafter the Burton Dassett land, though still important, played a less vital role. Looking ahead, John was able to buy the freehold of the Stowe leases in 1590. Similarly, in 1593 the spendthrift Anthony Cooke (the younger) sold to him the second third of the manor of Burton Dassett. With these purchases John completed the consolidation of the family estates.

For his second son, Peter Temple apparently made no particular provision in his lifetime. However, extremely little is known about Anthony's life, apart from its bare outline. He was born in the early

[25] The fine exists, N.R.O. Temple Stowe, Box 7/1, Hilary, 1565. Its endorsement by Sir Thomas Temple refers to the indenture, dated 6 February, 7 Elizabeth (1564/5).

[26] Walter's age poses a problem. Dugdale, p. 351, records that according to his tomb he was aged 76 in 1621, i.e. 20 in 1565. However, when his father, Thomas, died on 7 September 1557 (Inquisition Post Mortem, P.R.O. C142/112/164), Walter was said to be 24 years old. Can the jurors have misled the Escheator by twelve years? Certainly, his admission to the Middle Temple on 7 February 1561 would have been remarkably belated if he was then aged 28; H. A. C. Sturgess (ed.), *Register of Admissions to the Honourable Society of the Middle Temple* (London: Butterworths, 1949).

[27] Napton: *Cal. Pat. Rolls Eliz.*, 6, p. 828, license for James Platt to alienate lands to Peter Temple; i.p.m. ST L9 D4, Temple, Inquisitions Post Mortem. Mollington: ST Deeds list 2, folder 89, George Chambre to Peter Temple.

[28] ST L8, Temple Land, Bucks. These are discussed in more detail by Gay, 1938, p. 387.

1540s,[29] but most of the direct references occur near his death in 1581. By then he had settled in Chilvers Coton, near Nuneaton, in north Warwickshire. In 1567 he married Jane,[30] the widow of a wealthy local land-owner, Henry Acres.[31] She had been left a life interest in an estate called Temple Hall in Chilvers Coton[32] and it was there that Anthony was living before his death. When Peter died, in 1578, he left his second son £300 in cash and an annuity of £20;[33] this was 'in recompense of promises made to Anthony and Jane' on their marriage, which shows that he had not made them a previous settlement. This annuity was soon bought out by John for £580.[34] Anthony probably invested the money immediately, for by 1581 he held two long leases of the manor of Frankton, Warwickshire; these he left to his brother John in trust until his son Peter (II) was 18 years old, and should Peter die, they were to be sold for the benefit of Anthony's other children.[35] Peter may well have died, for there is no further record of him. Some time after 1589, the freehold of Frankton was finally acquired by the Temple family, bought by John; he left it to his younger son, John, founder of the line of Temple of Frankton.[36] It is unlikely that it was then still subject to Anthony's leases.

[29] John and Anthony were each left three silver spoons by their grandmother, Margaret Jekyll, in 1545; P.R.O. PROB 11/32, f. 196 (26 Populwell).

[30] The earliest parish register for Burton Dassett (W.R.O. PR 98/1) has the damaged entry '2 No[vember] 1567 [...] gent' and Joane Akers married', which must refer to Anthony.

[31] Will: P.R.O. PROB 11/50, f. 116 (16 Babington), dated 15 September 1567, proved 24 August 1568.

[32] Chilvers Coton lies near the Belknap estates in Nuneaton, but apart from this tenuous link there is no apparent connection between Anthony and the Acres family, nor is there evidence to indicate if he was there before 1567.

[33] Will; P.R.O. PROB 11/60, f. 192 v. (26 Langley).

[34] N.R.O. Temple Stowe Box 4/1a/10, 1579.

[35] Will: P.R.O. PROB 11/63, f. 169 (21 Darcy); the leases were not obtained directly from the Crown, but among them was probably the lease granted to Ralphe Staverton on 17 June 1579 (P.R.O. E310/40/7/21). Peter (II) had three sisters, mentioned in Millicent Temple's will (P.R.O. PROB 11/65, f. 41; 5 Rowe); one at least was sufficiently dowered to make a good marriage, to Thomas Judkin of Heyford, a relative of the Spencer family (H. J. Longden (ed.), *Visitation of Northamptonshire*, Harleian Society, 87 (1935)). Sir William Temple, ancestor of the Temple family of Ireland, was also by family tradition a son of Anthony Temple. This was recorded as early as 1646 in Kinloss 6, when Sir Peter Temple, baronet, noted 'Sir John Temple of Ireland desired me to enter this (*sc.* his pedigree).' However, Sir William was born in about 1555 and the chronological impossibility of this descent was pointed out in the *Dictionary of National Biography*. He was perhaps descended from the Buckinghamshire Temples or from a family recorded in Heytesbury, Wilts. (suggested by Anthony Temple).

[36] Dugdale, 291-2; it was sold to John Temple by Thomas Thornton and Thomas Woodcock (regular middlemen in sales of Crown land at this period) who bought it from the Crown on 17 October 1589 (P.R.O. C66/1351, m. 1-5). No early estate archives for Frankton survive to confirm the date of John's purchase.

Curiously, another Peter (III) appears at this moment in Chilvers Coton, but happily a contemporary record explains all:

> Peter Temple (was) a stranger in the contry unacquaynted and came purposlye to see and to be acquaynted with one Anthony Temple his nere kinsman. The same Peter often resorting to his said kinsmans house did growe in likinge with his now wyfe [Anne Akers], beinge one of the daughters and coheirs of Henry Akers deceased, whose wydowe the said Anthonye Temple did marye and take to wyfe.[37]

This Peter was the son of Cuthbert (see Pedigree 1),[38] and so he was Anthony's second cousin. He was earlier living in Sonning, Berkshire,[39] but after his marriage[40] he settled in Chilvers Coton, where his family owned property until 1642.[41]

2. *Controversy to Conclusion*

In 1560, Peter Temple could look back on twenty very successful years: marrying, settling at Burton Dassett, profitable sheep farming, becoming a landowner, and most recently purchasing a third share of the manor of Burton Dassett itself. Socially and financially his position was transformed.

However, his rise was not without opposition. For more than ten years, from 1560, he suffered the intense hostility of Sir Anthony Cooke, the co-owner of Burton Dassett, together with Sir Thomas Wootton and Peter himself. Although the overt cause was a dispute

[37] W.R.O. CR136. This collection, the archives of Newdigate of Arbury (in Chilvers Coton) contains very many poorly sorted sixteenth and seventeenth century estate papers, giving numerous incidental references to the Temple family. The document quoted, C1137 of about 1610, is a recital of the facts in a dispute about some lands that Peter Temple (III) had owned.

[38] According to the *Visitation* pedigrees, which there is no reason to doubt on this point.

[39] St. John's College, Oxford, Archives XV, 33-4, of 1570 (cf. p. 10, n. 16).

[40] His eldest son, Acres Temple, was born in 1577 (W.R.O. CR136/C1008, containing extracts from the lost Chilvers Coton parish register). The *Visitations* record Peter's wife's surname as Dakers, but this form is not found in contemporary sources. Her Christian name is given as Anne in a copy of court roll of 1583 (W.R.O. CR136/C1098) and in Peter's will 'to Anne my nowe wife'; this wording suggests the possibility of an earlier marriage, which is reinforced by the mention in Anthony's will in 1581 of Mistress Elizabeth Temple among the witnesses. It is hard to imagine who she could be other than Peter (III)'s wife. As Henry Acres' two daughters were called Elizabeth and Anne (from his will) and Peter (III)'s eldest son was clearly a descendant of Henry Acres, and was born before 1581, it seems that Peter must have married both daughters successively. Peter (III) died in 1614 and his will (dated 1609) was proved in the following year at Lichfield.

[41] W.R.O. CR136/C880, sale by Peter Temple, grandson of Peter (III).

over Peter Temple's purchase of his third share, the jealousy of an embittered old man for the successful youngster seems to have been at its root. Sir Anthony Cooke was a noted humanist and scholar, active particularly in the 1540s, when he was a tutor or companion to the future King Edward VI.[42] However, he spent Mary's reign in exile at Strasbourg. Although he returned on Elizabeth's accession, and took some part in public affairs, he did not again achieve high position. A deepening melancholy and moroseness seems to have started during his exile;[43] it may have been the bitterness and frustration of this period that underlay both his mood and the vindictiveness with which he pursued his quarrel with Peter Temple.

The dispute went through three stages. It apparently started when Sir Anthony returned in 1559 and discovered that Peter had bought Thomas Dannet's interest in Burton Dassett, and it was fomented by Peter's purchase soon afterwards of Leonard Dannet's share. What Anthony Cooke found offensive in these dealings was three-fold. He claimed to be planning himself to buy out the Dannet and Wootton shares in their Warwickshire property, and Peter, knowing this, should have made his purchase on behalf of Sir Anthony; secondly, Leonard Dannet had already promised to sell to Wootton and Cooke, but Peter Temple had secured his favour by a loan of £500 with interest, Leonard being a young man 'much given to play'; finally, Peter had made an offer which he then withdrew to surrender his purchase to Cooke.

The final accusation cannot be proved or disproved, but some truth certainly underlies the others. However, the balance of right can best be judged by the behaviour of the third party, Thomas Wootton. At first independent, he later threw his weight completely behind Peter Temple.

Sir Anthony Cooke was indeed investing considerable sums of money in land at this period. In 1564, in particular, he bought the Dannet share of Langport Manor, Kent, the Dannet and Wootton shares of Wappenbury and Eathorpe in Warwickshire, and also the manor of Hartshill, Warwickshire.[44] However, his first two purchases were in 1560, and both involved Peter Temple. In 1559, Aurelius

[42] His career has recently been surveyed in M. K. McIntosh, 'Sir Anthony Cooke: Tudor Humanist, Educator and Religious Reformer', *Proc. Amer. Phil. Soc.*, 119, 233–50. This passes over the thoroughly unedifying episode of the Temple quarrel. It is, however, dealt with in some detail by Gay, 1938, p. 378f., whose discussion is largely followed here. I thank Dr. McIntosh for much helpful information and guidance on the Cooke family in general, and their involvement with Burton Dassett in particular.

[43] McIntosh, op. cit., pp. 246–6.

[44] P.R.O. C54/655; C54/734.

Gyles had sold Peter an annuity of £8 4s. 8d. from his land in Bubbenhall, Warwickshire, and this Peter resold in equal shares to Cooke, Leonard Dannet and Thomas Wootton. The second involved the sale by Leonard Dannet of his third of the rectory of Burton Dassett to Peter Temple in 1560 for £220. This was immediately rescinded, and instead Leonard sold the same property to Anthony Cooke for £230. These transactions must have taken place after Cooke's first complaints against Peter, and it is hard not to see them as peace offerings by Peter to Cooke.[45]

For the most important purchase by Peter Temple, that from Leonard Dannet, a letter has survived, written by Peter to 'my sonne Jhon Temple at Lyncolnes Inn' telling him how to arrange the payment to Dannet.[46] John was to pay £600 in gold, of which he already had £229 in London, and Peter would send up the rest, with £100 in 'grosse money'.[44] Three hundred and thirty pounds was to be covered by a bond from Peter, probably to be paid in the following summer. The rest of the £1,580 total was money that Leonard owed Peter: a statute staple for £200, and bills for £260, and £40 (and £30 owed to John). This then was the £500 of Sir Anthony Cooke's complaint which indeed Peter Temple did not deny, although he claimed not to have received interest on it. The letter gives no indication of Dannet's use for the money, except in saying that John should make speed as 'Mr. Dannet hath losse in protractyng the same'.

All the further disagreements of the next decade stemmed from this original quarrel, with at least some reason on both sides. Sir Anthony's attacks very soon moved beyond anything that was either reasonable or legal, but Peter seems to have endured them with remarkable fortitude and little attempt at retaliation. However, the weakness of Sir Anthony's case in law, if not in equity, is indicated by the fact that he did not for a long time take legal action, not indeed, until he had provoked Peter Temple to react. Instead, his first approach was by petition to the Privy Council. This was undoubtedly where his social and political position would be most effective; three of his sons-in-law were members of the Council: William Cecil, Lord Burghley, Elizabeth's Secretary of State, Sir Nicholas Bacon, her Lord Keeper of the Privy Seal, and John, Earl of Bedford. The result must have been thoroughly to Anthony's satisfaction. Peter Temple was brought before the Council twice,

[45] P.R.O. C54/576; C54/567.
[46] ST T2021, dated 14 January (presumably 1560).

and following the second occasion was thrown into the Fleet prison on 19 April 1562, for his 'mysbehavour before your honours', i.e. for failing to admit doing any wrong to Sir Anthony Cooke.[47] There he stayed, until 30 June 1564, 'two yeres, two monthes and tenne dayes', as he recorded in his petitions and complaints. He sent in all thirteen petitions to the Council,[48] seeking all the time an ordinary trial of his quarrels with Cooke. He acknowledged in more and more abject terms his misbehaviour and lack of reverence, and this was eventually accepted. However, he steadfastly refused to admit any actual wrong-doing. 'For the untrewthe therof' he would never subscribe to a submission he was offered twice, by which he would have admitted 'his mysdemeanor appearing in the matter before your Honours', i.e. that he was at fault in the case at issue.

Release from the Fleet was not the same as escape from Sir Anthony Cooke's toils. The full course of events is in places obscure, particularly as it is recorded exclusively in complaints, answers, replications and rejoinders in the law suits, together with answers to *ex parte* interrogatories;[49] it is always difficult to distinguish truth from invention in these sources. According to Peter Temple, Cooke took advantage of his being in prison by having his bailiff refuse to accept the rent from Peter's agents. He was then able to enter on the pasture to recover in kind the rent due.[50] However, the methods he used were intended mainly to destroy Peter's own profit. Naturally, they were endured by the latter with exemplary patience.

Cooke's first move was to put 160 bullocks into the pasture, 'which by the nature of the ground and the season ... being very wett and soft, was so trampled with treading, and so bare with eating, that he sought to famish Peter Temple's sheep'. Next, just at lambing time, he put in 1,400 Welsh wethers 'of a very hard sort of sheepe', to leave the lambs no fodder. The next moves involved the rams. First, Cooke's servants made gaps in the hedges, letting the

[47] The sources used in J. R. Dasent (ed.), *Acts of the Privy Council* (London: H.M.S.O.), 1558–70, are very defective at this period. They mention one petition from Temple, but give no other references.

[48] These survive as a complete roll of fair copies, together with copies of the warrant for his release, and the submission he refused to sign; N.R.O. Temple Stowe Box 7/5A. There are also a number of drafts elsewhere in the Stowe MSS.

[49] At least four cases were involved, and have records in the Stowe collection (Temple Law, cases 209–12). For only one, the Star Chamber case of 1568–9, has material also survived in the Public Record Office.

[50] P.R.O. STAC 5/C77/29, a file of answers and rejoinders in Cooke v. Peter, John and Anthony Temple and John Woodward. Although this dates from *c.* 1568, Peter and John's answer recites the course of events back to Peter's imprisonment. STAC 5/C55/17 and 5/C65/13 contain further documents relating to the same case.

rams in at the wrong time of year, so that the lambs would be born in the winter and die. He then put in three or four score Welsh rams 'of a very coarse kind of woole'. Peter Temple had to buy eight ells of canvas, 'to cover the hinder partes of the ewes'. Finally, Cooke ploughed up 10 acres of the pasture, ostensibly to conform to the requirements of the Inclosure Act of 4 Henry VII. In fact, he had received full pardon for any offences under this act, and Peter Temple claimed that as he had ploughed some of the best pasture, but sowed no seed, his intention was simply to damage the land.

Cooke, of course, had his own view of some of these events, and claimed that John Temple with 'a great crowd of butchers, plaiers at weapons and other ill-disposed persons' had met Cooke's servants and surrounded them in their house for six days. On another occasion, nine women, including John's wife Susan, attacked one of his servants who was driving cattle into the pasture, and struck him and the cattle with cudgels.[51]

These dealings and activities are perhaps most interesting not for the dispute itself, but for the techniques of the Tudor grazier revealed in them: the careful control of stock numbers, the selection of breeding stock, and the control of their fertility. Safeguarding the ewes with canvas would have been very useful in the mixed flocks grazing on an open field.[52]

The resolution of their differences at this point in the dispute is not clear, but in 1564 Cooke gave Peter Temple a covenant for peaceful occupation.[53] It may be that Cooke ceased his harassment because he had developed a new tactic. Thomas Wotton made a verbal agreement to sell his third of Dassett to Cooke, at the good price of thirty years' purchase. This would have put Cooke in a very strong position to deal with Peter. However, Peter persuaded Wotton to withdraw his offer, to Cooke's amazement at his befriending such a despicable creature. Sir Anthony then sought and received a decree in Chancery to enforce the sale. To block this, Temple and Wotton moved a writ of partition in 1567. In fact, according to Wotton, Cooke in a more friendly mood one day in London, had agreed to a partition to be drawn up by Giles Spencer (see Pedigree 3), as long as he could make his choice of the portions.[54] With the writ, and the

[51] From Cooke's answer to Temple's complaint to the Privy Council, in a copy by Peter Temple in ST Temple Law, case 212.

[52] This technique is used at the present day in Scottish hill flocks, but there appear to be no other historical records. I thank Dr. M. L. Ryder for advice on this matter.

[53] ST Deeds List 2, Box 36.

[54] ST T2587, a letter dated 23 December 1572. It may have been intended to enlist support for Temple and Wootton from the unnamed recipient 'your good Lordship'.

APPENDIX: THE MANUSCRIPT

1. *Description*

HUNTINGDON Library MS. ST 36 is a book now of eighty-four paper folios[1] bound in a parchment sheet. The outer cover carries on its top edge the words 'A Note of Reckoning by Peter and John Temple'; this is in the hand of Sir Thomas Temple, first baronet, and is one of very many similar annotations he made on the Stowe muniments. One outer corner has been much darkened by damp, and the edges have crumbled in places and been repaired by the library; fortunately very little text has been lost. The folios measure 12 in. by $8\frac{1}{4}$ in., and have a watermark of a handled pot with foot, probably Briquet 12835, indicating Rouen manufacture in about 1535.[2]

The structure is complex, though essentially it consists of gatherings of 4 bifolia to f. 56, and 3 bifolia thereafter. A number of single sheets and a few bifolia have been removed, probably as blank sheets in most cases. In detail the arrangement is as follows:

Quire	*Bifolia*	*Folios*	*Comments*
1	1	1-2	
2	2	3-6	One written bifolium certainly removed, between ff. 3-4 and ff. 5-6
3-5	4	7-14; 15-22 23-30	
6	1	31-32	
7	4	33-37	Three sheets cut out after f. 37
8	1 leaf	38	Blank
9	4	39-43	Blank, three sheets removed
10	4	44-50	One sheet removed after f. 50

[1] It has a modern pencil foliation from 1 to 83, but duplicating f. 56 (as 56b). There are also five loose sheets in the volume, foliated 31a, 31b, 43a, 56a, 61a; most of these have clearly been in place since the book was originally written.

[2] It is interesting that the only other volume written by Peter Temple at this period has the same watermark. It is now a series of dis-bound quires in ST L9 E1, Temple Land, Bucks., and contains transcripts of leases for Burton and other parts of the Belknap estates (together with later Buckinghamshire ones); it was probably compiled by Peter when he became bailiff. Even though there are no Heritage entries in it, it must also originally have belonged to Thomas Heritage.

Quire	*Bifolia*	*Folios*	*Comments*
11	4	51–56b	One sheet removed after f. 56
12	3	57–61	One written sheet removed after f. 61
13	3	62–66	One sheet removed before f. 62
14	2	67–69	One sheet removed after f. 68; perhaps also one bifolium lost
15	3	70–73	One sheet removed after f. 72, and one after f. 73
16	3	74–78	One sheet removed after f. 78
17	3	79–83	One sheet removed after f. 83

2. *The Hands*

Two principal hands appear in the manuscript, both identifiable by internal evidence.

The first (see Pl. IV) is that of Thomas Heritage (TH below). It is cursive and rather inconsistent, with words and letters often poorly formed, and there are usually wide gaps between items and between lines within items. His shillings sign has the form of a Greek sigma (σ); 'of' is usually spelt 'off'. Items often start 'Memorandum that I Thomas Heritage ... ', though in one opening identified in this way (**144–5**), the script is quite different, very formal and neatly set out; it is not clear if this is the work of another scribe copying Heritage's text. Most TH items have been struck through (not noted in the text).

Peter Temple (PT below) also wrote a cursive hand (Frontispiece, Pls. IV, V, VI), of very variable size and character, ranging from the fairly clear to the completely illegible; his terminal *n* often has the form η, and his shillings sign is similar to a Greek phi (φ). *John* is always 'Jhon', and *received* 'resceyved' (or 'resc.'). In 1553–4, his shillings sign changed to a more conventional Greek sigma (σ), seen in **45–6** and **149–50**. When writing jottings, his hand became considerably more formal, though the writing is often faint and confused with other text (Pl. IV).

A few other hands occur in the account book, particularly countersigning accounts, and also on the loose sheets. These are noted in the text.

3. *Editing*

The manuscript has needed little editing to produce the printed text, and as far as possible this follows the recommendations of Hunnisett.[3] The few abbreviations have been expanded (unless unclear), apart from *di.* (*dimidiam*) and a few units of measure. Sums of money have been put into standard form. *Thorn* (written as *y*) was frequently used by Peter Temple, and y^e, y^r, etc. have been converted to *the*, *there*, etc. Superscripts *xx*, *c*, *m* (for 20s, 100s, 1000s) are retained. Punctuation is almost absent in the original, and some has been inserted for clarity. Dots indicate illegible words, holes, etc., and square brackets are used for restored text (Roman type), and editorial comments and titles (italics). If only one calendar year is given for a regnal year, it is that to which the account apparently refers.

The only substantial departure from Hunnisett's recommendations concerns the numerous erasures. Because these are often immediately significant in their context, they are given in the body of the text as $(\ldots)^{er}$, rather than footnoted.

As noted in the Preface, the material has been rearranged by subject, and each item in the accounts is given a reference number (bold type). These are keyed to the pages of the manuscript in the following section of the Appendix. The arrangement within each item is retained where practical, though some sections in multi-column have been rearranged. Marginal notes are retained where they are continuous (e.g. the cattle accounts), but elsewhere they are brought into the text, noted [*Margin*], usually after the entry referenced.

4. *Concordance*

The following table gives the arrangement of the items on each page, with the hand, date and item reference; for minor hands see the text. A * indicates an item that is only included in the appendix. For each page, the items are listed in the order in which they were written, as far as this can be established.The loose sheets inserted in ST 36 follow the main sequence, their folio references starting L. Similarly, the supplementary documents are given an initial S.

[3] R. F. Hunnisett, *Editing Records for Publication* (London: British Records Association, 1977).

Folio	*Part*	*Hand*	*Date*	*Item*	*Position in MS. and Subject*
1	A	TH	[*c*. 1540]	**132**	main; harvesting costs
	B	PT	[1543]	**210**	across top and bottom; summary accounts
	C	PT		**48**	around A; summary accounts
	D	PT		**244**	jotting
1 v	A	PT	1544	**2**	main; cattle bought
	B	PT	[?1544]	**211**	base; money paid
2		PT	[1544]	**3**	cattle sold
2 v	A	PT	[?1544]	**4**	main; cattle bought
	B	PT	[?1548]	**190**	top corner; New Year gifts
	C	PT	1549	**175**	inverted; wood sales
3	A	TH	1533	**93**	main; wool purchases
	B	PT	[?1544]	**5**	base; cattle bought
	C	PT	[?1544]	**212**	top; money received
	D	PT		*	scribblings
3 v		PT		**239**	legal charges
(One folio probably missing between ff. 3 and 4.)					
4		TH	[1533]	**94**	payments for wool
4 v	A	TH	1534	**95**	main; payments for wool
	B	PT		**75**	base; field account
5	A	TH	1532	**112**	top; purchase of iron
	B	PT		**76**	base; field account
5 v		PT		**77**	field account
(One folio probably missing between ff. 5 and 6.)					
6	A	TH	[1532]	**113**	main; iron sales
	B	PT		**243**	transverse; draft of bond re Thomas Underhill
	C	PT		**244**	jottings
6 v		TH	[1532]	**114**	iron sales
7	A	TH	[1532]	**115**	main; iron sales
	B	PT		**244**	between heading and text of A; jotting
7 v	A	TH	[1532]	**116**	main; iron sales
	B	PT	[?1544]	**8**	base; cattle money
	C	PT		**244**	top margin; jotting
8		TH	[1532]	**117**	iron sales
8 v	A	TH	[1532]	**118**	main; iron sales
	B	PT		**244**	base and transverse; jotting
9		PT	[?1543–5]	**182**	household costs [*see Pl. V*]
9 v	A	TH	[?1534]	**96**	top; note of wool

Folio	Part	Hand	Date	Item	Position in MS. and Subject
9 v	B	PT	1543	**208**	base; summary financial account
10	A	TH	1533	**99**	main; wool purchase } [*see Plate IV*]
	B	PT	1543	**209**	several sections; draft of f. 9 v. B } [*see Plate IV*]
	C	PT		**244**	over much of page; jottings } [*see Plate IV*]
10 v		PT	1546	**214**	debts due
11	A	TH	1534	**101**	main; wool purchase
	B	PT	1544	**74**	left and right sides; field accounts
	C	PT	[?1544]	**6**	base; purchase of a cow
	D	PT	[1545]	**215**	top margin; debts
	E	PT		**244**	after l.A3; jotting
11 v	A	TH	[1534]	**102**	main; wool purchase
	B	PT	[?1544]	**7**	margin and in gaps; cattle sales
	C	PT		*	top corner; doodlings
12	A	TH	[1535]	**103**	main; goods delivered for wool
	B	PT	[?1544]	**9**	between l.A1–3, and base; cattle prices
12 v	A	TH		**104**	main; wool sale
	B	PT		**201**	after l.A6; servants' wages
	C	PT	[1545]	**220**	base; payments made
	D	PT		**244**	top and bottom margin; jottings
13	A	TH		**105**	main; wool sale, continuing f. 12 v. A
	B	PT	[?1545]	**216**	top left; debts
	C	PT	[?1545]	**217**	lower right; debts
	D	PT	[1545]	**218**	lower centre; cash and debts
	E	PT	[1545]	**10**	right, transverse; cattle in pasture
	F	PT	[1545]	**11**	left, transverse; sale of these cattle
13 v		PT	1545	**12**	cattle bought
14	A	TH		**100**	top; payment for wool
	B	PT	[1545]	**12**	base; continues f. 13 v.
	C	PT		**244**	top margin and after A; jottings of sums
14 v	A	PT	[1545]	**12**	top; continues f. 14. B
	B	PT	[?1545]	**1**	base; perambulation of fields

Folio	*Part*	*Hand*	*Date*	*Item*	*Position in MS. and Subject*
15		PT	1545	13	cattle sold
15 v		PT	[1545]	13	continues f. 15
16	A	TH		**189**	top; valuation of plate
	B	PT	1545	50	base; sheep bought
	C	PT		244	jotting across B
16 v		PT	1545	51	sheep sold
17	A	PT	1545	52	main; sheep bought
	B	PT	[?1545]	140	top margin; memorandum relating to Hertfordshire (1538)
	C	PT		188	base; recipe for medicine
17 v		PT	1546	198	servants' wages
18	A	PT		143	top; receipt
	B	PT	1545	14	top; sale of cattle
	C	PT	?1546	15	base; cattle kept in pasture
	D	PT	[?1545]	16	top margin; money, probably for cattle purchase
	E	PT		244	top margin; jotting
18 v		PT	1546	17	cattle bought
19		PT	[1546]	17	continues f. 18 v.
19 v		PT	[1546]	17	continues f. 19
20	A	PT	[1546]	17	continues f. 19 v
	B	PT		244	top margin; jotting
20 v		PT	[1546]	17	continues f. 20. A
21		PT	1546	18	cattle sold
21v		PT	[1546]	18	continues f. 21
22		PT	[1546]	18	continues f. 21v
22 v		PT	1547–8	199	servants' wages
23		PT	1548–9	200	servants' wages
23 v					blank
24	A	PT	1546	53	top; English sheep bought
	B	PT	1546	54	centre; English sheep sold
	C	PT	1549	232	base; small debts
24 v	A	PT	1546	55	top; Welsh sheep bought
	B	PT	1549	231	centre; debts
	C	PT	[1549]	68	base; sheep sold
	D	PT		244	line 5; jotting
25		PT	1547	21	money for buying cattle
25 v		PT	[1547]	22	cattle bought and sold
26		PT	1547	23	cattle bought
26 v		PT	[1547]	23	continues f. 26

Folio	*Part*	*Hand*	*Date*	*Item*	*Position in MS. and Subject*
27		PT	[1547]	23	continues f. 26 v
27 v		PT	[1547]	23	continues f. 27
28		PT	[1547]	24	cattle sold
28 v		PT	[1547]	24	continues f. 28
29	A	PT	1548	25	cattle bought
	B	PT	1548	26	money for buying cattle
29 v		PT	1548	27	cattle bought
30		PT	[1548]	27	continues f. 29 v
30 v		PT	1548	28	cattle sold
31					blank
(L. 31a-b here)					
31 v	A	PT	1548	29	cattle sold
	B	PT	1549	32	cattle kept in winter
32	A	PT	1549	33	top; cattle bought
	B	PT	1549	34	base; money for buying cattle
32 v		PT	1549	35	cattle bought
33		PT	1549-50	37	cattle sold and kept in winter
33 v		PT	1550	38	money to buy cattle
34		PT	1550	39	cattle bought
34 v		PT	[1550]	39	continues f. 34
35		PT	1550	40	cattle sold
35 v		PT	1551	41	account of money to buy cattle
36	A	PT	1551	42	top; cattle bought
	B	PT	1551	43	centre; cattle bought
	C	PT	1552	44	lower; cattle bought
	D	PT	1553	45	base; money to buy cattle
36 v		PT	1554	46	cattle bought
37-43 v (includes L. 43a)					blank
44	A	PT	1542	141	upper; Hertfordshire rent
	B	PT	[?1548]	168	lower; Banbury rental
44 v	A	PT		72	main; cattle and sheep sales
	B	PT		244	top margin; jotting
45	A	TH	1536	123	top; sheep accounts
	B	PT		73	in gap in A; sheep sales
	C	PT		*	margins; pen trials
45 v		PT	[1541-2]	137	corn sales
46	A	PT	[?1541-2]	138	main (three sections); payments to servants
	B	PT		244	top margin; jotting
46 v		PT	[?1542]	142	Hertfordshire expenses

Folio	*Part*	*Hand*	*Date*	*Item*	*Position in MS. and Subject*
47	A	PT	1541	**134**	Main; arable costs
	B	PT		**244**	corner; jotting
47 v	A	PT	[1541]	**134**	top; continues f. 47
	B	PT	[1541]	**135**	left top margin; corn produced
	C	PT	[1554+]	**203**	centre; servants' wages
48					blank
48 v	A	PT	[1541-2]	**136**	main; corn delivered
	B	PT		**244**	top margin; jotting
49		PT	1549	**90**	wool bought
49 v		PT	1549	**91**	wool received
50		PT	1550	**92**	wool received
50 v-51					blank
[Ff. 51 v-59 form a single sequence, written inverted, and are therefore listed in reverse order.]					
59		PT	1548-9	**156**	bailiff's payments
58 v		PT	[1548-9]	**156**	continues f. 59
58		PT	1549-50	**158**	bailiff's payments
57 v		PT	[1549-50]	**158**	continues f. 58
57					blank
56b. v		PT	1549	**157**	bailiff's receipts
56b		PT	[1549]	**157**	continues f. 56b. v
(L. 56a included here.)					
56 v		PT	[1549]	**157**	continues f. 56b
56		PT	1550	**159**	bailiff's receipts
55 v		PT	[1550]	**159**	continues f. 56
55					blank
54 v		PT	1551	**161**	bailiff's receipts
54		PT	[1551]	**161**	continues f. 54 v
53 v		PT	[1551]	**161**	continues f. 54
53-52					blank
51v		PT	1551	**160**	bailiff's payments
59 v	A	TH		**106**	top; money delivered
	B	PT		**202**	inverted, over A, payments to servants
	C	PT		**244**	inverted, bottom margin; jotting
60	A	TH		**107**	top; continues f. 59 v
	B	PT	1544	**81**	base; account with Robert Temple
	C	PT		**49**	top margin and between l. 7-8 of A; cattle price

Folio	*Part*	*Hand*	*Date*	*Item*	*Position in MS. and Subject*
60 v		PT	1550	**176**	wood sold
61		PT	[1550]	**177**	wood sold, continues f. 60 v?
(L. 61a included here.)					
61 v		PT	1550	**180**	money received for wood sales
[One sheet written by PT torn out after 61, leaving only the tails of words.]					
62	A	PT	1551	**147**	Coventry rents
	B	PT	?1552–3	**148**	follows A; same
	C	PT	1554–5	**149**	follows B; same
	D	PT	1555	**150**	follows C; same
[The following sheets are in reverse date order, but were not written inverted.]					
62 v		PT	1551	**71**	sheep sold [*Frontispiece*]
63		PT	1550	**70**	sheep sold
63 v		PT	1549	**66**	sheep sold
64	A	TH	1534	**121**	main; sheep bought
	B	PT		**84**	between 1.6 and 7 of A; note about wool
	C	PT		**244**	top margin
64 v	A	TH	[1534]	**122**	main; agreement on sheep pasture
	B	PT	[1548]	**172**	interlined; bailiff's memoranda
	C	PT		**244**	continues B; jotting
65	A	PT	[1548]	**64**	top; sheep deliveries
	B	PT	[?1548]	**62**	lower; sheep bought
65 v	A	PT	1548	**61**	top; sheep sold
	B	PT	[?1548]	**63**	lower; money for sheep sales
	C	PT	[1549]	**36**	top corner; cattle bought
66	A	PT	1548	**65**	top; sheep in pasture
	B	PT	[?1549]	**67**	centre; sheep sold
	C	PT	1550	**69**	base; sheep sales
[For ff. 66 v–69, each opening was written right before left, starting from 69.]					
69		PT	[1548]	**86**	wool bought
68 v		PT	[1548]	**86**	continues f. 69
68		PT	[1548]	**86**	continues f. 68 v
67 v		PT	[1548]	**86**	continues f. 68
67		PT	[1548]	**88**	wool received
66 v		PT	[1548]	**88**	continues f. 67

Folio	*Part*	*Hand*	*Date*	*Item*	*Position in MS. and Subject*
69 v	A	PT	[1548]	**229**	top; money lent
	B	PT	1548	**205**	next; building costs, continuing f. 72 v
	C	PT	[?1548]	**183**	next; grocery costs
	D	PT	1548	**87**	top margin; wool total
70	A	TH	[?1539]	**127**	top; pasture letting
	B	PT	1547	**224**	lower; money due
	C	PT	[1548]	**226**	base; account with James Clarke
	D	PT		**244**	top margin; jotting
70 v	A	TH	[?1539]	**128**	l. 1–4, 11–12, 15–16; pasture letting
	B	PT		**240**	l. 5–10; money due
	C	PT		**85**	l. 13–14; wool bought
71		PT	1546–8	**221**	debts due
71 v		PT	1546–8	**221**	continues f. 71
72		PT	1548	**205**	building costs
72 v		PT	[1548]	**205**	continues f. 72
73	A	PT	1546–7	**58**	top; sheep in pastures
	B	PT	1548	**124**	base; hay sales
73 v	A	TH	1539	**129**	top half; pasture letting
	B	PT		**174**	base, inverted; letter draft
	C	PT	1549	**228**	extreme base; account with James Clarke
	D	PT		**244**	after A; jotting
74	A	PT	1546	**223**	top; account with Anthony Ashefeld
	B	PT	1547	**82**	lower; money received for wool
	C	PT	1548	**227**	base; corn received
	D	PT		**244**	base; jotting
74 v	A	TH		**108**	main; account with Thomas Heritage, clerk
	B	PT	[1545]	**219**	top margin, top left corner, bottom left; debts due
	C	PT		**244**	between title and text of A; jotting
75	A	TH	1537–8	**194**	top and centre; hire of servants
	B	PT	1546	**222**	in gap in A; debts due
	C	PT		**244**	above B; jotting

Folio	*Part*	*Hand*	*Date*	*Item*	*Position in MS. and Subject*
75 v		TH	[?1536]	**139**	rent of a mill
76		TH	1538	**195**	hire of two servants
76 v	A	TH	[1538–9]	**196**	top; hire of two servants
	B	PT	1549	**191**	base, transverse; New Year gifts
	C	PT	1550	**192**	continues B; New Year gifts
	D	PT		**244**	near top; jotting
77	A	TH	1540	**197**	top and centre; hire of two servants
	B	PT	[?1546]	**56**	in gap in A; memorandum on wool
	C	PT	1546	**57**	base; payment for sheep
	D	PT		**244**	after 1.3; jotting
77 v	A	PT	1547	**59**	top; sheep sold
	B	PT	1548	**230**	base; account with Cuthbert Temple
	C	PT		**244**	top margin; jotting
78	A	PT	1547	**60**	top; sheep delivered
	B	—	1548	**83**	base; receipts by Thomas Lee for wool
78 v	A	TH	1533	**144**	main; Stepney rents received
	B	PT		**244**	jotting
79		TH	1533	**145**	continues f. 78 v. A
79 v	A	TH	[?1539]	**130**	top; pasture letting
	B	PT	[?1548]	**167**	base, inverted; note of rent
	C	PT		**244**	top corner; jotting
80	A	TH	[?1539]	**131**	top; pasture letting, continuing f. 79 v. A
	B	PT	[1548]	**206**	lower; building costs
80 v		TH	1533	**119**	money and sheep in pasture
81	A	TH	[?1533]	**120**	top; sheep and cattle counts
	B	PT	[?1545]	**173**	base; payment for Burton beacon
81v	A	TH	1536–7	**193**	main; hire of a servant
	B	PT	[1540s]	**125**	base, transverse; pasture letting
82	A	TH	1533	**109**	centre; delivery of goods
	B	PT	1545	**213**	in gap in A, double column; money received and paid
	C	PT	[1548]	**171**	at end of A; bailiff's notes
	D	PT	[1540s]	**126**	base, transverse; pasture letting

Folio	*Part*	*Hand*	*Date*	*Item*	*Position in MS. and Subject*
	E	PT	[1547-8]	**225**	base; money due
	F	PT		**244**	top; jotting
	G	PT		**244**	base; jotting
82 v	A	TH		**110**	centre; delivery of goods
	B	TH		**98**	margin; delivery of goods
	C	PT	1548	**30**	in gap in A, inverted; cattle account
	D	PT	1548	**31**	beside C; cattle account
	E	PT		**151**	base; account with Mr. Sheldon
	F	PT		**181**	in gap in A, list of names (wood sales?)
	G	PT		**241**	in gap in A; financial note
83	A	TH	1533	**97**	centre; money and goods delivered
	B	PT		**152**	in gap in A; Coventry rent
	C	PT		**244**	beside B; jotting
83 v	A	TH		**204**	top centre (l. 8b–9, 13, 14, 16–19); cost of a window
	B	TH		**111**	l. 20–29; money due
	C	PT	[1547]	**19**	l. 10–12, 13a, 15; cattle left in pasture
	D	PT	[1546–7]	**20**	top (l. 1–7, 8a); valuation of cattle in pasture
84a (inner side of end cover)					
	A	TH		**133**	corn deliveries
	B	PT		**244**	centre; jotting
84b (outer flap of end cover)					
		PT		**244**	jotting

Loose Sheets Inserted into ST 36

L31a: bifolium, with one corner damp stained.

Part	Hand	Date	Item	Position in MS. and Subject
A	PT	[1549]	**207**	sides 1 and 3; building costs
B	PT	[?1548]	**170**	side 2, longitudinal; bailiff's memoranda
C	PT		*	side 2, transverse and repeated longitudinally; the figures *v^c^xvj li. iij s.*
D	PT		**184**	side 3, inverted; shopping list
E	PT	1549	**233**	side 4; summary debt list

Folio	*Part*	*Hand*	*Date*	*Item*	*Position in MS. and Subject*
	F	?PT		*	side 4 transverse; address: *Rychard Stodart at the Gylden Crosse in Tems Stret*
L31b: single sheet, damped stained					
	A	–		*	side 1, transverse; address: *To my loveyng Freynd Mr. Temple at Dorsot*, perhaps Wast's hand
	B	PT	[1548]	**155**	side 2, top; notes on bailiff's accounts
	C	PT	[1548]	**89**	side 2, base; wool not delivered
L43a: single sheet, not damp stained, only one side written					
		–		**242**	letter to Peter Temple
L56a: single sheet, not damp stained, relating to adjoining pages of the accounts					
		?Wast	[1548]	**169**	rental for Wappenbury and Hunningham
L61a: single sheet (though folded and then damp stained)					
		?Wast	[?1550]	**178**	receipts from wood at Wappenbury
		PT	[1550]	**179**	verso; receipts from Wappenbury

Supplementary Documents Transcribed

Piece	*Part*	*Hand*	*Date*	*Item*	*Position and Contents*
S1: ST L9 B7, Temple Accounts, Box 56 (unsorted); a single folded sheet					
S1	A	–		*	transverse, by centre fold; address *Too the ryght worshipfull and my verye freende Mr. Peter Tempell Esquyer*
	B	PT		**163**	left top; draft receiver's accounts
	C	PT		**164**	dorse; similar to B
	D	PT		**78**	right side centre, transverse; sheep summary
	E	PT		**79**	left side base, transverse; similar to D

Folio	*Part*	*Hand*	*Date*	*Item*	*Position in MS. and Subject*

S2: ST L9 A1, Temple Accounts, Box 1, piece 14; a single sheet

S2		PT	1550	**146**	Stepney rental

S3: ST L9 A1, Temple Accounts, Box 1, piece 6; two folded sheets, hand perhaps that of Thomas Burbery the accountant

S3	ff. 1–2	–	1537	**153**	parsonage accounts
	ff. 3–4	–	1538	**154**	same for next year

S4: ST L9 A1, Temple Accounts, Box 1, piece 46; two bifolia, hand of a formal scribe with two autograph additions by Peter Temple

S4	ff. 1–1v	–	1557	**162**	parsonage accounts
	ff. 2–2v	–	1557	**162**	Burton Dassett rent account
	ff. 2v–4v	–	1557	**162**	accounts and receipts for other estates

S5: ST L9 D1, Temple Business and Legal, Box 1; single sheet

S5		PT	1560	**165**	notes for receiver's account

S6: ST L8 A, Temple Law, Case 211; this contains a small group of accounts and notes on separate sheets, which has been given a modern foliation; most are taken up with notes for Peter Temple's defence at law.

Piece	*Sheet*	*Hand*	*Date*	*Item*	*Contents*
S6.A	2	–	1563	**80**	sheep counts
B	7–7v	–	1560	**166**	bailiff's account
C	19	–	1561	**187**	expenses of a journey
D	19	PT	[?1561]	**234**	base, transverse; money received
E	19 v	PT	?1561	**47**	cattle bought
F	19 v	PT	[?1561]	**235**	base, transverse; money received
G	20 v	PT	[*c.* 1560]	**186**	short household account
H	23–23 v				
		PT	1562	**236**	financial summary [*see Plate VI*]
	23 v	PT	1562	**237**	right side; money received
I	23 v	PT	[?1562]	**185**	left side; shopping list
J	24	PT	1564	**238**	debts due

INDEX OF PERSONS

This and the other indexes follow with some simplifications the recommendations of R. F. Hunnisett, *Indexing for Editors* (London: British Records Association, 1972). Christian names, but not surnames, are normalized. When there is no evidence that two mentions of the same name are to different individuals, a single index entry is used. Places are in Warwickshire, unless otherwise stated.

INDEX OF PLACES

The county (pre-1974) is Warwickshire, unless otherwise specified.

INDEX OF SUBJECTS

RECORDS OF THE SOCIAL AND ECONOMIC HISTORY OF ENGLAND AND WALES

VOLUMES I–IX

I. Survey of the Honour of Denbigh 1334. Edited by Sir P. VINOGRADOFF and F. MORGAN. 1914.
II. The Register of St. Augustine's Abbey, Canterbury, commonly called the Black Book. Edited by G. J. TURNER and H. E. SALTER. Part I. 1915.
III. The Black Book. Part 2. 1924.
IV. i. A Terrier of Fleet, Lincolnshire. Edited by N. NEILSON.
ii: An 11th Century Inquisition of St. Augustine's, Canterbury. Edited by A. BALLARD. 1920.
V. Documents illustrative of the Social and Economic History of the Danelaw. Edited by Sir F. M. STENTON. 1920.
VI. The Account Book of a Kentish Estate 1616–1704. Edited by E. C. LODGE. 1927.
VII. The Cartulary and Terrier of the Priory of Bilsington, Kent. Edited by N. NEILSON. 1928.
VIII. Feudal Documents from the Abbey of Bury St. Edmunds. Edited by D. C. DOUGLAS. 1932.
IX. Records of the Templars in England in the Twelfth Century: the Inquest of 1185 with Illustrative Charters and Documents. Edited by B. A. LEES. 1935.

A reprint edition of volumes I–IX is available from: Kraus-Thomson Organization Limited, FL-9491 Nendeln, Liechtenstein.

RECORDS OF SOCIAL AND ECONOMIC HISTORY

NEW SERIES

I. Charters of the Honour of Mowbray 1107-1191. Edited by D. E. GREENWAY. 1972.
II. The Lay Subsidy of 1334. Edited by R. E. GLASSCOCK. 1975.
III. The Diary of Ralph Josselin. 1616–1683. Edited by ALAN MACFARLANE. 1976.
IV. Warwickshire Grazier and London Skinner 1532–1555. By N. W. ALCOCK. 1981.